THE
UNITED STATES
IN THE
TWENTIETH CENTURY

MARKETS

Edited by Grahame
Thompson

SECOND EDITION

Hodder & Stoughton

in asscciation with

The Open
University

This text forms part of an Open University course D214 *The United States in the Twentieth Century*. The complete list of texts that make up the course can be found on the back cover. Details of this and other Open University courses can be obtained from the Course Reservations Centre, PO Box 724, The Open University, Milton Keynes MK7 6ZS, United Kingdom: tel. (00 44) 1908 653231. Alternatively, much useful information can be obtained from the Open University's website http://www.open.ac.uk

Published in Great Britain by Hodder & Stoughton Educational, a division of Hodder Headline Plc, 338 Euston Road, London NW1 3BH; written and produced by The Open University.

Orders: please contact Bookpoint Ltd, 39 Milton Park, Abingdon, Oxon OX14 4TD. Telephone: (44) 01235 400414, Fax: (44) 01235 400454. Lines are open from 9.00 – 6.00, Monday to Saturday, with a 24 hour message answering service. Email address: orders@bookpoint.co.uk

British Library Cataloguing in Publication Data

A catalogue record for this title is available from The British Library

ISBN 0 340 75825 2

First published 1994

Second edition published 2000

Impression number   10 9 8 7 6 5 4 3 2 1
Year   2004 2003 2002 2001 2000

Edited, designed and typeset by the Open University.

Printed in the United Kingdom by The Bath Press, Bath.

22833C/D214b2prelimsi2.1

CONTENTS

PREFACE

The five volumes in this series are part of an Open University, Faculty of Social Sciences course *The United States in the Twentieth Century*. In many respects the course has been a new venture — it is the first time that the Open University has entered the field of American Studies and it did so at a time when resources were not abundant. So the development of this course is due, in no small part, to the enthusiasm and support of many colleagues in the Faculty of Social Sciences. There are too many people to thank individually, but my appreciation must be recorded for some of them.

The United States in the Twentieth Century would not have been made without my academic colleagues, Anthony McGrew, Jeremy Mitchell and Grahame Thompson. Their role was central to the conception and planning of the course and their presence made the production of it an intellectually stimulating as well as an enjoyable experience. Mike Dawson, the Course Manager, took all the tension out of a process that is normally fraught and difficult. His calm efficiency, common sense and good humour got the rest of us through the production process with few anxieties. Jeremy Cooper of the BBC not only ensured that the course has an excellent audio-visual component, but made a very important contribution to its overall development. The Course Team owes a substantial debt to the editorial work of Stephen Clift and Tom Hunter who did all that was asked of them plus a great deal more. The designs for the covers, and indeed for the entire course, by Sarah Crompton were immediately and enthusiastically welcomed by everybody. David Wilson of the Book Trade Department was always available and his advice was both appreciated and heeded. Our colleagues in Project Control and in the Operations Division of the university were unfailingly supportive and helpful. However, none of these books would have seen the light of day without Anne Hunt who, along with her colleagues Mary Dicker and Carole Kershaw, typed successive drafts of the manuscripts of all five volumes without complaint and with remarkable accuracy and speed.

These books owe an enormous debt to our Americanist colleagues in institutions other than the Open University. This series has drawn on their scholarship and expertise, and above all on their generosity in being willing to participate in this project. The Course Team owes a particular debt to Professor David Adams, Director of the David Bruce Centre at the University of Keele, the external assessor of *The United States in the Twentieth Century*. His tough advice and wise counsel assisted us greatly. We incurred a similar obligation to Professor Ian Bell, also of the University of Keele, who helped us far beyond the call of duty. Doctor Ronald Clifton, who has done so much for American Studies in Britain, was enormously helpful and supportive in making sure this course came to fruition.

Finally there were moments when it might have been easier for Margaret Kiloh, the Dean of the Faculty of Social Sciences, to have been less than enthusiastic about *The United States in the Twentieth Century* but her support never wavered.

Richard Maidment, Course Chair
Milton Keynes, December 1993

I would like to thank the contributors to this volume who wrote quickly and efficiently under the pressure of very tight deadlines. Without their enthusiasm and co-operation the book could not have been completed. Tom Hunter performed his editorial duties with particular diligence and with his usual good humour. Jennifer Frances provided me with advice and encouragement in drafting the Introduction, for which I thank her. Finally, my colleagues on the Course Team of *The United States in the Twentieth Century* deserve a huge collective acknowledgement for the time and effort spent commenting upon various drafts of the chapters.

Grahame Thompson,
Milton Keynes, December 1993

PREFACE TO THE SECOND EDITION

I would like to thank the contributors to this volume who wrote quickly and efficiently under the pressure of very tight deadlines. Without their enthusiasm and co-operation the book could not have been completed. Kate Hunter executed editorial matters with particular diligence and her usual good humour. Jennifer Frances provided me with advice and encouragement in drafting the Introduction, for which I thank her. Finally, my colleagues on the course team of *The United States in the Twentieth Century* deserve a huge collective acknowledgement for the time and effort spent commenting upon various drafts of the chapters.

Grahame Thompson,
Milton Keynes, October 1999

MARKETS: AN INTRODUCTION

Grahame Thompson ★

This book examines the economic aspects of 'The United States in the Twentieth Century'. It is organized around the theme of 'the market' since this encompasses the quintessential American representation of the economic mechanism. The market is interpreted widely in this volume however. The chapters deal with the organization of consumption, with production process technologies and management styles, with productivity and growth, with gender aspects of the American economy, with regional and geographical issues of production, and with the way a number of particular markets work in the USA. The book thus offers a comprehensive overview of the American economic system in the twentieth century. The interdisciplinary character of the book is designed to appeal to as wide an audience as possible. It will interest those studying American politics, its public policy and business administration, and also its geography, as well as those concerned with the American economy and economics.

In this introductory chapter a number of themes that inform the book as a whole are highlighted. The authors of the main chapters are concerned to elaborate what is distinctive about the US economy. In addition they elaborate its more general and universal characteristics, and how these have been played out in their particular contexts during this century. As the individual chapters unfold it will become clear that there are some underlying features of the American economy that illustrate its particular character; its strengths, its weaknesses and its problems. Many of these features have been pervasive throughout the century. Others have arisen, become a problem and then declined in importance. Still others have a more recent origin and remain to illustrate the contemporary dilemmas of the economy. It is roughly this sequence that structures the discussion that follows, but such a three-fold division is not meant to imply total mutual exclusivity between the themes identified.

The book begins with a chapter on 'Consumption', which becomes a theme picked up in a number of the subsequent chapters (3, 4, 5, 6 and 10 in particular). Part of the American celebration of the market mechanism is the prominence given to its consumption possibilities. And this is not just a feature of the American public's own engagement with the economy. It has also structured the academic and theoretical understanding of the market

through the notions of 'consumer sovereignty' and the 'consumer preferences' that are thought to best dictate the outcomes for production and
output.

The American economy, then, has been the economy of consumption in this
century and the chapters here chart the progress of this endemic feature of
American society; they document the institutional structures and business
strategies built to encourage conspicuous mass consumption. But they also
point to its consequences; the under emphasis on personal saving and corporate and public investment for instance; the relative neglect of production
and particularly manufacturing at times. Indeed some would argue that this
commitment to consumption and relative neglect of the specifics of production, particularly in the post-Second World War period, led to a major
contradiction for the economy through to the end of the 1980s; namely that
deadly combination of low growth rates and high consumption expectations.
This presented an intractable problem for an economy that was in relative
decline; how to manage the consequences of these twin but contradictory
features. We return to this conundrum and more recent developments below.

Of course, the American economy has not always suffered from the contradiction pointed to immediately above, though it has since the 1920s at least
celebrated, emphasized and organized for mass consumption. But the
American economy has also been the economy of 'mass production' since
the 1920s, and it has demonstrated the outstanding success of this technological and managerial strategy. A second underlying theme of this book,
then, is the changing nature of American production processes and the way
that mass consumption has been linked into these processes. Here we enter
a controversial and current field of debate; exactly how to specify the nature
of the changes in American production process technologies, and their significance for the trajectory of the economy overall (Chapters 3, 5, 6, 9 and 10
in particular). Broadly speaking, this is a debate about the possible move
from a period dominated by 'mass production' to one increasingly informed
by 'flexible' and 'lean' production methods, and the possible systemic implications of such a change (if, indeed, it is going on in quite this stark form).
More recently this has connected to the whole issue of the importance of
information technology to the current state and future of the US economy.
This debate is set up in Chapter 3, the main one dealing with the organization of American production, and is returned to in a number of the subsequent chapters, particularly Chapter 6. Readers are left to judge for
themselves exactly where they stand on the issues involved in this debate.

However, what is not at issue is the remarkable success of American production systems throughout much of this century. It was the Great Exhibition in London in 1851 that marked the beginning of an interest in what
was subsequently characterized as the distinctively 'American system of
manufactures'. With the advent of Henry Ford's developments in producing
cars in the early part of this century, American success in organizing production to meet the mass demands of its consumption system was secured
and America became the home of 'mass production' in its various guises; a
model for the rest of the developed world to follow. But this did not last.

Alternative centres of manufacturing and productive excellence emerged in the post-Second World War period, notably in Europe, Japan and some other Asian countries. These served to challenge American manufacturing dominance, which in turn worked to raise fears associated with America's relative decline, something forming another theme of the chapters that follow.

In fact a number of additional closely interrelated themes arise here. The first of these is the cyclical nature of the US economy. Of course this is not a feature unique to the American case. But it is one that has a significance for us all because of the importance of the US economy in terms of world demand and growth. It is still the case, and has been for much of this century, that when the USA sneezes the rest of the world catches a cold. There are two aspects to this cyclical nature of economies, both of which have characterized the US example during this century. The first is the short-term business cycle, typically lasting for five or six years. The second is the longer-term and deeper cyclical downturn and upturn that moves from depression or prolonged recession to boom and dynamic growth over a 40 or 50 year period. The first instance of the downturn in this longer-term cycle was the Great Depression of the early-1930s, the origins and character of which are analysed in Chapter 4. The subsequent recovery from this depression in the USA was also crucial to the recovery in the rest of the world.

This raises a further issue, namely the importance of wars, and military spending more generally for the health of the economy. Here a difficulty is posed since military spending can be a boost to growth at some times while at others it can act as a constraint on growth. The US involvement in the First World War (Chapters 4 and 7) probably had only a marginal impact on the health of the domestic US economy because that involvement was brief and at this time it was not yet such a key player in the international arena, a position it was to fulfil with a vengeance during and after the Second World War. The First World War was not unimportant however, as is indicated in Chapter 4.

It was the Second World War and its aftermath, however, that propelled the US economy into a new prominence. To a large extent, this war, along with the domestically orientated New Deal initiatives, secured the end of the Great Depression. The 'long boom' that followed, itself initially aided by the pent up demands resulting from the Second World War and the expenditures associated with the Korean War in the early 1950s, provided for an expansionary phase in the USA and the world economy that was unprecedented and has not been repeated since. This was a period in which the US economy presided almost unchallenged over the liberal and multilateral trading system of the 'West' (Chapters 5 and 7).

But once again, the long-term cyclical nature of the economic mechanism manifested itself to devastating effect. The dynamic of the long-boom petered out from the early 1970s. The US economy, along with much of the rest of the developed world, plunged into a deep recession, one that raised comparisons with the earlier depression of the 1930s. In this case it was defence expenditure and war that was thought to be one of the main villains of the piece. The USA had financed its involvement in the Vietnam War through international borrowing, which produced domestic and international inflationary pressures, resulting in the worldwide increase in inflation in the 1970s. In addition the USA's long commitment to upholding the virtues of the liberal multilateral trading mechanism of the Bretton Woods period meant it had borne a disproportionate burden of military spending more generally (Chapters 5, 9 and 10). 'Military overstretch' and the 'imperial burden' had this time served to undermine the health of the economy and given competitor nations a chance to challenge the dominance of the USA.

In effect, then, the 'hegemony' of the USA in a range of dimensions was heavily undermined during this process of 'relative decline'. That hegemony had been established on the back of the productive success of the economy that appeared from the twenties onwards (with the exception of the disastrous years of the Great Depression, of course). But not only was this a period of hegemony for the US economy, it was also a period of hegemony for US economics. By the 1950s American economics, and particularly the American (in fact, perhaps more accurately, the 'Anglo-Saxon') version of what was understood by 'the market' and competition, had been almost universally established as the orthodoxy, at least in academic circles. And it was this ideology of *laissez-faire* that propelled the American-led neo-liberal policy programme that swept the globe in the 1980s and 1990s.

This century has thus seen the progressive insertion of the American economy into an evolving international environment, if hesitantly and reluctantly at times (Chapters 3, 4, 5, 6, 7, 9 and 10). Although the USA is home to strong nationalist tendencies, isolationism was swept aside in the post-Second World War period. Not only did the American-owned productive base expand abroad — via the direct investments of its multinational corporations — but its international financial and banking activity also expanded rapidly (Chapter 7). These twin features became the spearhead of American power and influence in the world, for good or ill. In addition, the internationalization and 'globalization' of economic relations have had the effect of drawing the American domestic market progressively into the international arena. This became a new and important feature of the post-1970s period. Before that many sections of the American domestic economy had remained surprisingly isolated from international influences (though this was not the case of its agricultural and financial sectors — see Chapters 3, 5 and 7). But the 'relative decline' period from 1970 to the end of the 1980s saw not only the opening of the US domestic market to imports of manufactured goods to an unprecedented degree, but also a flood of external investment into the economy, a situation to which neither the US public nor its policy makers have as yet quite fully adjusted.

All these themes and features of the American market economy should not blind us, however, to another enduring element in its organization, namely its continued regulated and managed nature (Chapters 4, 5, 6, 7 and 8). Well before this century began, American public policy towards the economy was experimenting with elaborate legally defined regulatory systems (Chapter 7). The advent of the twentieth century did nothing to suppress this tendency, indeed it enhanced and fostered it in various ways. One of the paradoxes of the American economy explored in the chapters that follow is the relationship between the commitment to an open, free and competitive market based economy on the one hand and successive systems and schemas designed to regulate and manage it on the other, of which protectionism of various kinds is just one example. Of course these systems and schemas have been subject to the vagaries of political, theoretical and policy fashion — they have succumbed to periods of weaker and then stronger deployment — but in no way can the American economy of the twentieth century be accurately described as a totally free and non-interventionist one. In addition, the USA led the way in regulating the international economy in the post-Second World War period via the Bretton Woods system and other management mechanisms.

In part this relates to the cyclical nature of the economy described above. The temptation has been to react to this with new programmes of intervention and then non-intervention. Thus the role of government with respect to the economy has been a profoundly ambiguous and uneasy one. This is largely because of the entrenched and enduring hostility to all things collectively organized by the government in American ideology, as at the same time it has embarked upon just such collective initiatives to regulate and manage the economy. More recently, however, there has been a move away from the sentiments of intervention as the cycle of regulatory scrutiny has waned.

But the role of public intervention in the economy first arose in the immediate post-Second World War period because of another feature that forms a theme in the chapters that follow. Despite an emphasis on the beneficial and optimal outcomes thought to arise from the unfettered operation of the market system, in fact the USA has never been a particularly egalitarian society. Very significant racial and gender differences in the consumption, employment and life chances of the American people speak to the continued inequalities in the outcomes emerging from that market system (Chapters 2, 5 6 and 8). Regional and local patterns of economic activity add another dimension to this structure of production and distributional inequalities (Chapter 9). All these have at times, with different emphases and effects, led to calls for action on the part of various public authorities to attempt the amelioration or reversal of the unequal trends so identified. This has opened up another arena for the regulation and management of the economy.

Finally, these characteristic themes and features are nowhere more acutely focused than around the contemporary debate about the future for the American economy (Chapters 3, 5, 6, 7, 9 and 10). This is itself intimately related to the theme of 'relative decline' explored in Chapters 5 and 10 in particular, which was a pervasive feature of economic debates in the 1980s. Where was the American economy heading? Could it restructure itself sufficiently to regain a renewed competitive dynamic? Where was the international system itself going, of which the US economy was such an integral and important part? It was in respect of both domestic and international initiatives that the answers to these kinds of questions were found. The election of a new President in 1992 with a new agenda to tackle the problems of the US economy injected some new optimism into the domestic body politic. The economy also at last began to show signs of a sustained recovery with better economic fundamentals in place. On the international front, the attempted construction of a North American Free Trade Area (NAFTA) — involving the USA, Canada and Mexico in the first instance — seemed to have revived that old American confidence in the international arena after a strong showing from protectionist measures and potential isolationism.

In many ways the debate about the economy was refocused during the 1990s as a consequence of the emergence of an economic boom that was stronger and longer-lasting than almost anyone had originally thought possible. No longer was an 'American decline' on the agenda, rather the focus now was on the 'new economy'. Perhaps at last the economy had escaped from the perennial short-term business cycle to embark upon a new, long and sustainable boom. This issue occupies the bulk of the discussion of Chapter 6. Without wishing to pre-empt anything, however, it would perhaps be optimistic and premature to suggest that a fundamentally new era was upon the USA in respect to its economy. As the new century loomed closer, the realistic expectation had to be for a downturn some time soon. A more worthwhile assessment would be of whether the downturn, when it eventually arrives, will be sudden and acute or gradual and gentle. If nothing else the analyses contained in this book would lead us to expect that the ideas of the 'market' as explored in the chapters that follow will play a key role in the way these issues are understood and managed in the future.

THE ORGANIZATION OF AMERICAN CONSUMPTION

Margaret Walsh ★

1 INTRODUCTION

Americans have the reputation for being the world's major consumers. They enjoy purchasing goods and services and regard consumption as a way of life, if not — like the pursuit of happiness — a basic right. Their expectations of consumption rest on the basis of a century and more of economic abundance, mass production and competitive retailing.

1.1 THE CONTEXT

> The American citizen's first importance to his country is no longer that of a citizen but that of a consumer. Consumption is a new necessity.
>
> (Lynd and Lynd, 1929, p.88)

So concluded Robert and Helen Lynd after asking the residents of the typical small city of Middletown why they worked so hard. The Lynds were not alone in noting the rise in the purchase of goods and services by many American families. The 1933 *Report of the President's Research Committee on Social Trends* also commented that the buying of household goods in the increasingly urbanized culture of the United States of America had become so commonplace that a study of consumption habits was essential to any understanding of American life (*Recent Social Trends in the United States*, 1934, p.857).

The prosperity decade of the 1920s has frequently been highlighted as the key period in which Americans took to buying like a duck takes to water. The much vaunted consumer durables revolution seen in the shape of automobiles, household appliances and synthetics heralded the shift of American industries from production to marketing. Higher standards of living enabled Americans to buy new commodities while greater leisure encouraged the growth of services such as entertainment and vacationing. Yet the 1920s were neither the start nor the apogee of the American love affair with spending.

Consumer culture and the American preoccupation with buying had its roots in the late nineteenth century when entrepreneurs realized that standardized consumption was necessary to absorb the outputs of large-scale mass production. Though at that time the word 'consumption' still had the destructive connotations of burning, squandering, or using up rather than meaning a useful or enjoyable experience, selling large quantities would soon become a business objective (Lampard, 1991, p.19). When packaged and presented attractively this economic necessity would become a social habit involving pleasure, comfort and entertainment. It would not, however, become either a mass experience or a democratized pastime until the affluence of the post-Second World War years enabled more groups throughout the nation to partake in the real or imaginary world of purchasing products. Encouraged by the mass media and helped by easier access to finance, many more citizens then rushed to consume goods and services. By the 1960s consumption had become a way of life which Americans increasingly exported to the rest of the western world. Coke and Pepsi became everyday names, McDonald's meant a hamburger and audiences on either side of the Atlantic recognized the characters of television soap operas. Indeed, consumption was becoming globalized.

1.2 THE APPROACH: THE ANALYTICAL FRAMEWORK

Marketing was the critical agency in making consumption into an everyday desirable phenomenon. The development of marketing techniques and facilities over the course of a century was closely related to three influences: technology, demography and information flow.

1 *Technology* encompassed specific industrial and commercial inventions such as refrigeration, the internal combustion engine or electronic data processing; it included forms of transport such as motor vehicles and aircraft and forms of motive power such as electricity.

2 *Demography* not only meant a larger population and its propensity to geographical mobility, but also embraced rising living standards, longer lifespans and the decline of patriarchy. The process of urbanization is also involved here.

3 *Information* flow directed by manufacturers and agencies through the voice of the media identified and moulded consumers' needs and popularized their desires. In addition, a crucial element in such information flow for consumption has been the progressive extension and refinement of credit lines to consumers.

The marketing mix was in a state of constant flux as opportunities to create and expand sales were seized and exploited, but the process of change is best understood by examining new forms of retailing. Traditional country stores and city corner shops were replaced by department stores, chain stores and mail-order houses. These in turn were joined by supermarkets, discount stores and franchises, increasingly located in suburban shopping malls. In consumer services amusement parks offered wider satisfaction than traditional theatres and concert halls, while movies, television, sports arenas and vacation resorts extended entertainment facilities to millions.

The changing face of Coca-Cola advertising

The popcorn-eating teenager who can be transported from the joys of the home video movie to the neighbourhood swimming pool by stepping into the family car is a product of incremental marketing changes ongoing since the late-nineteenth century. These changes can, however, usefully be discussed at three chronological timepoints which can be regarded as stages of consumer development.

1   The early manifestation of popular consumption developed in the 1890s when big business entrepreneurs sought markets to absorb the increasing output of their factories. By the 1920s these producers and their agents offered commodities which gave satisfaction rather than which merely sold.

2   The packaging and branding of goods together with persuasive advertising and better access to finance laid the foundations of the 'American Way' in which the new American became the Lynds' consumer.

3   Yet consumer culture did not spread throughout the nation until the affluent society emerged in the third quarter of the century. Then the mixed economy of government spending and economic growth enabled a consensus to flourish while the instant cash revolution and mass media penetration encouraged the consumer ideal. By the 1970s Americans had built their consumer society.

Ironically, having achieved this status, they then started to differentiate between purchasers and to create specialist segments. Niche marketing would sit side by side with mass retailing.

2   THE EARLY MANIFESTATION OF CONSUMPTION

2.1   BIG BUSINESS REQUIRES NEW DISTRIBUTION HABITS

Already in the mid-nineteenth century American entrepreneurs were producing a medium-quality article which appealed to a majority of the American population rather than merely to a wealthy elite. The new methods of transportation and communication — the railroads and the telegraph — opened up the possibilities of a national market, while the growth of cities created a large-scale and compact demand. Changes in industrial technology, such as continuous process machinery and refrigeration, and in the organization of production to facilitate speed and volume made it possible for manufacturers in a range of industries — from textiles and processed foods to metal making and metal working — to create huge throughput. Ready-made clothing, shoes, cigarettes, crackers and biscuits, canned foods, kerosene (paraffin) and chilled meats all became more readily available in the last third of the nineteenth century.

Yet the ingenuity of entrepreneurs in creating large-scale standardized goods in huge amounts called for a transformation in both the channels of distribution and in the art of persuading Americans to acquire commodities. Marketing had to be organized and consumption encouraged. By the 1890s manufacturers had invested huge amounts of capital in mechanization and needed both control and predictability if they were to gain dividends. Unless their products were sold as quickly and as effectively as they were made, costly stock piles would result. New aggressive selling was required. Traditionally producers were not involved in marketing, preferring to hand over output as unbranded commodities to an independent commission merchant or wholesaler who then disposed of the goods at their leisure (Lampard, 1991, pp.18–20). Such a system needed to be improved or replaced.

In the new world of consumer durables manufacturers wanted their marketing agents not only to demonstrate and install equipment, but also to offer after-sales service and repairs and to undertake consumer credit arrangements. When existing wholesalers could not cope some firms became directly involved in marketing. The Singer Sewing Machine Company built up its own network of retail stores to ensure sales, while McCormick Harvester franchised dealers whose activities they co-ordinated and supervised. In perishable products entrepreneurs soon realized that commission merchants did not have the facilities to undertake their distribution. Meat processors such as Gustavus Swift thus organized his sales networks which included refrigerated railroad cars, branch houses and local advertising. In brewing and distributing bananas, Pabst and United Fruit also developed national shipping and sales operations. These business firms which had benefited from technology thus pioneered their own retailing to ensure that sales matched outputs (Chandler, 1977, pp.391–411).

Other volume producers were content to leave the physical handling of their output to wholesalers provided that these increasingly specialized and could sell in a national market. Companies such as Libby, McNeil & Libby who used continuous process canning for their milk and meats, Proctor & Gamble who used a high-volume mechanical crusher in the production of Ivory soap and the American Tobacco Company which adopted machinery to manufacture cigarettes hesitated to assume the further financial burden of distribution to thousands of small retailers. They preferred the services of wholesalers whose branch offices and warehouses in major cities were likely to have or to develop extensive local and regional connections (Strasser, 1989, pp.79–80). To ensure that the travelling salesmen favoured their commodities rather than those of their competitors, such manufacturers promoted and packaged their products rather than selling in bulk. In flour milling James S. Bell and the Pillsbury family packed and advertised their brands, Gold Medal Flour and Pillsbury, nationally. In cereals Henry Parson Crowell used a carton which could be mass produced and filled and on which he could print his trademark — a figure of a man in Quaker clothing. Quaker Oats could thus be identified as a desirable purchase. Consumers were further encouraged to ask for this particular cereal by the recipes printed on the carton (Strasser, 1989, pp.32–57; Schudson, 1984, pp.164–6). Producers clearly recognized the potential of packaging as a means of targeting the consumer.

They also quickly recognized the importance of providing information about products in a market which was becoming larger and more impersonal. Without specific knowledge of new commodities consumers needed to be told, for example, why they should buy Quaker Oats in a box rather than have their oats scooped out of the grocer's bin, or why they should opt for the new cigarettes rather than pipe tobacco or snuff. Newspapers and magazines could tell the reading public about new products. Initially advertisements were printed in a small typeface like today's classifieds, but gradually larger spaces were used and advertisements were illustrated. Indeed, the print media came to depend financially on advertising. Billboards and streetcar advertising further reinforced promotional messages as producers and their agencies became involved in stimulating desire and building up consumer preference for new and newly-packaged commodities.

2.2 THE NEW RETAILING

Producers and wholesalers, however, were not the only parts of the marketing structure to change. New retail outlets became important in attracting the attention of consumers. Previously customers patronized small and often dingy stores where they asked the proprietor, whom they often knew, to go to his shelves or his back room for a specific item over whose price they would haggle. Such traditional outlets could neither cope with a large volume of goods and a quick turnover, nor deal with vast numbers of unknown clients. Department stores, chain stores and mail-order houses evolved gradually as large-scale retailers with purchasing organizations capable of buying directly from the manufacturer and with stock turnovers which would eventually outstrip the traditional wholesaler. They also introduced many people, both urban and rural, to the delights of shopping. Women in particular learned new social habits which included going out and getting together with friends and neighbours to shop and to compare purchases (Leach, 1984, pp.319–42; Benson, 1986, pp.76–8).

The early department stores emerged in large cities after the Civil War because of the size of the urban market. They developed either as adjuncts to a wholesaling establishment such as Marshall Field's in Chicago and A. T. Stewart's in New York, or as clothing or dry goods enterprises which added new lines in an attempt to capture more business, such as R.H. Macy's in New York and Wannamaker's in Philadelphia. From the commercial viewpoint all department stores aimed to profit from high turnover of goods by selling at low prices and low margins. All adopted the pre-set 'one-price system'. There could be no bartering in a shop where thousands of sales were made by hundreds of clerks. Slow-moving lines were discounted to maintain high volume sales and extensive local advertising was undertaken in the press. Other services such as charge accounts, home deliveries and liberal exchange policies were extra incentives to consume and these proved useful tools in the increasingly competitive world of mass retailing (Boorstin, 1974, pp.101–9; Chandler, 1977, pp.225–9; Benson, 1986, pp.12–30).

Department stores attracted large numbers of customers not only because they were efficient business units, but also because their downtown location was accessible via the relatively new form of urban transport, the street railway. They did not, however, serve most city shoppers because they were consumer palaces rather than consumer bazaars. Tall elegant buildings with beautiful fittings and ample space attracted the middle classes rather than the working classes, who, though they were free to look, did not have the money to buy (Strasser, 1989, pp.207–10; Boorstin, 1974, pp.101–9; Benson,

1986, pp.31–67). The middle classes were the main patrons of another retailing innovation which emerged in the late-nineteenth century — the chain store.

Chain stores with centralized buying and administration appeared in trades such as groceries, drugs and furniture, where the existing retailing system had not yet developed mass outlets. The Great American Tea Company, later known as A & P Grocery, is often considered to be the prototype of the chain store. By buying tea in bulk the company developed a chain of stores selling below the prevailing price. Starting in New York City in 1859 it spread initially in the north-east of the United States and then across the Appalachians, reaching a total of some 100 units in 1881. By the turn of the century A & P had 200 stores located across the country, selling a broader range of groceries. Customers with cash were willing to forgo some of the traditional sales services such as delivery and credit for the benefit of cheaper prices (Lebhar, 1963, pp.25–6; Tedlow, 1990, pp.188–91). Embryonic chains also started in drugs, shoes, jewellery, furniture and cigars, though these were fewer in number (Chandler, 1977, pp.233–5).

F.W. Woolworth made the chain concept more popular when he developed the variety store, or the poor person's palace. He aimed to entice a broader range of people into his shops by selling goods at the low, fixed price of either five or ten cents. He was able to keep his prices low not only as a result of volume buying and price lining, or the production of commodities to sell at a planned price, but also because he adopted a type of self service. With sales assistants only stocking shelves, wrapping purchases and taking money, fewer were needed than in other retail outlets and wages thus cost less. Furthermore, Woolworth did not spend money on advertising because his goods were cheap enough to be their own advertisement. Indeed, such was Woolworth's appeal that his seven stores of 1886 had become twenty-five by 1895 and fifty-seven by the turn of the century, when his sales turnover was valued at $5 million (Lebhar, 1963, pp.35–8; Boorstin, 1974, pp.113–5).

The seeds of an extensive urban consumption were well established by the end of the nineteenth century. But what about the rural population? More Americans lived on farms, in villages and in small towns than in cities and these Americans were unlikely to visit downtown department stores or suburban chain stores. In 1880, 72 per cent of the country's 50.2 million people, or 36 million persons, were country dwellers; twenty years later the percentage had declined to 60, but there were still 45.8 million country dwellers (*Statistical History of the United States from Colonial Times to the Present*, 1976, pp.8, 11, 12). The needs of some of these millions were met by mail-order outlets which offered direct access to the commodities pouring off the production lines by using the new technologies of printed and illustrated catalogues and rail transport in conjunction with the post office.

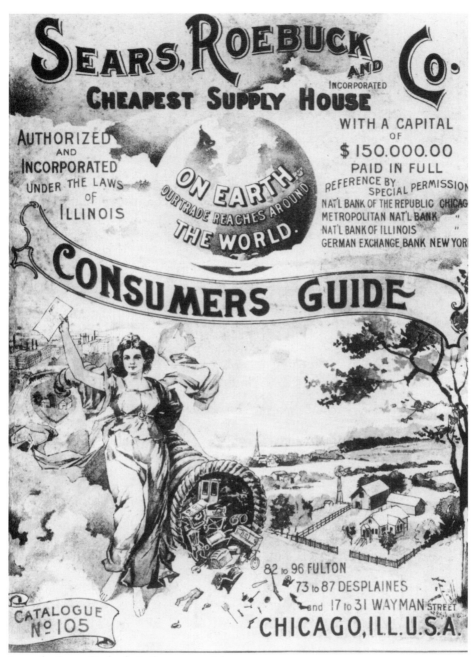

An early Sears, Roebuck & Company catalogue cover

Early attempts to retail goods by mail order had been limited to small quantities of single commodities, but Montgomery Ward and then Sears, Roebuck & Company offered both a wide variety of goods and a warranty of service. Ward bought in bulk directly from manufacturers. He then used the Grange, the largest farmers' association in the United States in the 1870s, to make cash sales to farmers, thereby eliminating both middlemen and credit risks. Basing his activities in Chicago, the nation's rail hub, and taking advantage of the increase in post offices — from 30,000 in 1871 to 76,945 by 1901 — Ward expanded his range of merchandize. He gained more customers' confidence by allowing them to inspect the goods before payment. By the 1880s, when most of the 10,000 items of merchandize listed in the catalogue were illustrated by a woodcut, his market was nationwide. A decade later Ward was offering over 24,000 items for sale, but by this time he was facing the competition of Sears, Roebuck & Company. Starting off selling watches by mail, and relying heavily on advertising in newspapers and then periodicals, this firm soon retailed a wide variety of goods. Sales grew even during the depression years of the mid 1890s (Emmet and Jeuck, 1950, pp.13, 19–26; Chandler, 1977, pp.230–3; Boorstin, 1974, pp.118–29). Improvements in the postal service, first in rural free delivery and then in parcel post in the early twentieth century, promised an even greater extension of business to catalogue companies (Fuller, 1964, pp.36–58, 199–227). By 1910, 50 million people, or 54 per cent of the total of 92 million Americans, were still rural (*Statistical History*, 1976, pp.8, 11, 12).

2.3   NEW CULTURAL FORMS

Americans were not only interested in consuming a growing range of mass-produced goods; as their living standards and leisure time increased they also wanted to buy services. Entertainment, amusement and recreation previously limited to the genteel classes were set to be turned into popular culture. Commercial interests happily exploited opportunities to create enjoyable and profitable diversions from the toils and tribulations of urban industrial life. For example, they expanded the forms of show business to include popular drama, musical comedy and vaudeville and they formalized sports into big business in the shape of professional baseball (Norton *et al.*, 1998, pp.555–9).

In the literary world advances in printing techniques and changes in the financing of publications brought an explosion of large-circulation newspapers and magazines in the 1890s. Mass-production methods like timed scheduling, conveyor systems and assembly lines, and technological advances like the rotary press, allowed entrepreneurs to turn out cheap, attractive journalism. An increase in the volume of advertising both by local stores and of branded products provided not only new revenue but also popular reading. In metropolitan cities newspapers such as Joseph Pulitzer's *New York World* extended their circulation by dramatizing news stories, by including sports coverage and women's items and by adding comics (Norton, *et al.*, 1998, pp.560–1). Magazines such as the *Ladies Home Journal*, which became an outlet keyed to the taste and needs of middle-class women, achieved a circulation of 850,000 in 1900 (Peterson, 1958, pp.1–17). Indeed, between 1890 and 1905 the aggregate circulation of monthly magazines and periodicals expanded by 256 per cent to reach 64 million

(Lampard, 1991, pp.27–8). The new reading millions might not yet constitute a mass reading audience, but their emergence did signal new levels of cultural consumption.

Increased incomes and leisure again combined with technology to produce another popular cultural form in the late-nineteenth century, namely amusement parks. To improve traffic on their omnibuses during slow weekends and evenings, owners of street railways helped promote pleasure parks at the end of their lines. Starting as wooded picnic areas, often near a body of water, these parks grew rapidly in popularity with the addition of regular entertainments such as boat rides, dance halls, sports fields, restaurants and mechanical amusements. Coney Island, with its beach location, became a working-class playground for the urban masses of New York City. There, enclosures such as Steeplechase Park and Luna Park brought low-cost mechanical amusements within the reach of millions within a few years of opening at the turn of the century. The meshing of engineering technology and retailing had opened the doors to a popular entertainment of escape and illusion (Adams, 1991, pp.41–56; Peiss, 1986, pp.115–38). Commercial culture was on the horizon.

Luna Park, Coney Island around 1905

SUMMARY

In the late-nineteenth century the growth of mass production in the United States, together with the economic requirements of 'running full', stimulated new patterns of selling. Wholesaling techniques were altered and retailing innovations emerged to distribute goods and services more widely and quickly. The early commercialization of consumption, however, was also dependent on the spread and stimulation of values and attitudes in which pleasure rather than work satisfaction was the goal. Such consumerism was more visible among the upper and middle classes who had higher incomes and more time to spare.

3   THE 'AMERICAN WAY'

3.1   BUY NOW AND ENJOY WHILE YOU PAY

What commodities were available to would-be consumers seeking happiness in the 1920s? Packaged perishable and semi-perishable goods continued to pour off conveyor belts. Improvements in continuous flow technology and the introduction and spread of the moving assembly line resulted in increases in productivity. The systematic organization of labour through scientific management and the general adoption of electric power in manufacturing industries created even higher outputs, while science stimulated a range of new products. Branded foods such as Heinz or Campbell soups, Kelloggs' Toasted Corn Flakes or Carnation Milk supplied Americans' increasing demands for convenient foods processed to a standard quality. Packaged household items such as Ivory Soap, Royal Baking Powder or Listerine antiseptic, healthcare products such as Colgate dental cream and Sal Hepatica laxative, grooming products such as Coty powders and perfumes and Gillette Safety razors, and pleasure goods such as Wrigley's chewing gum, Coca Cola or Lucky Strike cigarettes were just a few of the commodities with a national identity. These small items were increasingly joined by a range of durable goods produced by science-based and engineering industries. Of these, the automobile was by far the most attractive and the most expensive. But many Americans also bought electrical household gadgets such as irons, vacuum cleaners, cookers, washing machines and refrigerators, and synthetics like rayon, plastics and paints. Delightful products were available for purchase (Marchand, 1985).

The pleasurable aspect of acquiring these commodities was communicated through a massive expansion of advertising. Between 1913 and 1927 total advertising expenditure in 30 leading weekly or monthly magazines alone grew from $25 million to $148 million, or by about 500 per cent (Presbrey, 1929, p.593). In the 1920s the term 'Madison Avenue' came to signify a major block of advertising agencies which were an industry in their own right.

Moving well beyond explaining the nature and function of a product, advertising agencies wrote copy and designed graphics to appeal to the psychic needs and emotions of consumers. Concentrating on endowing the newspaper and magazine reader, the radio listener or the moviegoer with happiness, newer advertisements for soap, for example, implied days of leisure as cleaning tasks were accomplished more quickly. Those for vacuum cleaners promised gleaming floors which were the envy of any woman's next door neighbour. Many commodities were still described without frills, but many others offered the 'good life' to which Americans were encouraged to aspire (Pease, 1958, pp.20–43; Marchand, 1985). Progress and paradise were being marketed as a matter of owning more and better material possessions.

It was one thing to persuade Americans that what they wanted was consumer goods which would proclaim their status in society, it was another thing to turn desire into ownership. How could a larger proportion of the population be persuaded to buy these 'desirable' goods and services? Although the 1920s have been labelled 'prosperity decade', prosperity was limited to specific groups. Industrial wages had increased in the late nineteenth and early twentieth centuries, but during the 1920s the rise was relatively modest and did not match general productivity gains. Families with higher incomes, whether from the male earnings alone or from two wages, could buy some new goods outright if they saved. Others needed to use the credit purchase route, not only for major items such as automobiles, but also for intermediate items such as household furniture and the more expensive electrical appliances.

Instalment buying was not a new concept in the United States. As we have seen, rural storekeepers, urban corner shops and the newer department stores had a tradition of offering short- and longer-term payment schemes (Strasser, 1989, pp.67–70). It was in their interests to accept deferred payments and, increasingly, financial institutions such as sale finance companies, small loan offices, credit unions and industrial and mercantile banks became involved in the credit business. The automobile, however, set important precedents in stimulating an expansion of credit and in making it respectable (Mandell, 1990, pp.14–7). In the years from 1922 to 1929, 75 per cent of car purchases were made as credit sales. Between 75 and 80 per cent of phonographs, mechanical refrigerators, other appliances and radios and almost as high a percentage of pianos and home furniture were also 'bought on time'. Such purchases, however, were made by the middle classes. Workers still preferred to pay cash and avoid the possibility of losing their new acquisition by default. This meant that at the start of the 1930s only 40 per cent of families owned a radio, 30 per cent a vacuum cleaner, 24 per cent a washing machine and 8 per cent a mechanical refrigerator. Only one in 5.5 Americans owned either a new or a second-hand car (Lampard, 1991, p.34; Cohen, 1990, pp.101–4; *Statistical History*, 1976, pp.8 and 716). Credit had opened the door to a new level of consumption for some Americans, but it was not yet ubiquitous.

3.2 SELLING AND DISTRIBUTING PRODUCTS

Whether paying cash or using credit, Americans who wanted to consume a growing range of commodities usually bought these in the retail institutions established in the late-nineteenth century. These outlets were now expanding and adapting to cater to an increasingly mobile and wealthier population. Chain stores became the spearhead of retail growth: from an estimated 500 stores in 1900 they had increased to 8,000 by 1914 and then to between 27,000 and 50,000 by 1920. Growth continued in the 1920s. Major chains such as A & P, Kroger and Safeway in groceries, F.W. Woolworth in variety and J.C. Penney in apparel quickly added hundreds of stores, while hundreds of smaller chains added a few branches. If a chain is defined as an operation with a minimum of four stores, these multi-units reached 148,037 in 1929, while those with two or three stores reached 212,620 in the same year. Chains with four stores then accounted for 20 per cent of the total retail sales, while those with two or three branches accounted for 29.7 per cent. Chain stores would continue to hold a similar proportion of retail sales for the next 30 years (Lebhar, 1963, pp.52–64, 69).

Chain stores became popular because of their economy, their variety and their approach to selling. Bulk purchasing together with fewer sales assistants meant cheaper prices for the customer. The multi-unit operation also facilitated a wider range of merchandize and, in food, fresher produce. Then as new branches tended to be built in the more prosperous suburbs of large cities the shops themselves were inviting in style and appearance (Tedlow, 1990, pp.191–6; Lebhar, 1963, pp.81–104). Middle- and upper-income Americans enjoyed shopping in chain stores and thought they were getting convenience and bargains. Ironically, working-class families who needed bargains could not afford to shop in chains because the strictly cash policy was too inflexible for their limited budgets. They still patronized the local 'mom and pop stores' where they could pay at the end of the week if they ran out of cash. Moreover, they tended to shop daily rather than weekly because they did not have ample storage or refrigerator space. Chain stores were popular among moneyed Americans (Cohen, 1990, pp.106–14).

The rapid expansion of chain stores in the early twentieth century affected the operation of other retail outlets. Department stores also depended on the custom of the middle and upper classes. They had attracted this custom both by the convenience of offering a broad range of goods under one roof and by the quality of their service, which included a pleasant environment, courteous and helpful assistance, delivery and credit. Though clients were still prepared to pay more for the niceties of life, department store managers, whether in the larger operations such as Macy's, Wannamaker's or Marshall Field's, or in the smaller units located in small cities and towns, found that they needed to increase efficiency. By cutting out the wholesaler and buying directly from manufacturers and by adopting scientific management practices they could offer attractive bargains or cheaper prices while still retaining their gentility. Macy's was not competing directly with Penney's in clothing sales or Kinney's in shoe sales. They might both be patronized by middle-class women, but the former continued to appeal to those women who liked to spend time shopping in nice surroundings and who wanted attention and the assurance of follow-through service. There were enough of these customers to sustain over 4,000 department stores in the 1920s (Strasser, 1989, pp.210–1; Benson, 1986, pp.31–67; Lebhar, 1963, p.75).

Chain and department stores were urban institutions. Prior to the First World War most rural consumers shopped in the local village store or ordered goods from a mail-order catalogue. In the 1920s automobile technology increasingly offered them the possibility of going to town to get their purchases. Whether they acquired a utilitarian Model T from a Ford dealer, or a more stylish vehicle from a General Motors dealer, or could afford only a second-hand motor, and whether they paid fully in cash or used an instalment plan, country dwellers were taking to wheels. Greater car reliability and improvements in road surfaces made it easier, for women in particular, to drive to nearby towns (Tedlow, 1990, pp.120–46, 165–7; Morain, 1988, pp.126, 131). But did rural consumers make many changes to their shopping habits as a result of their increased mobility?

They were still likely to buy small items, especially food and household commodities, from a nearby family-run general store. Though chain stores in county seats or larger towns offered discounts for cash and carry, it was often easier and not significantly cheaper, once transport costs had been added in, to buy locally. While a greater variety of items and more packaged goods were available in urban shops, rural residents found that many country storekeepers, anxious to retain their livelihood, modernized their businesses. They extended their range by offering meat and dairy produce and became almost a one-stop shop; they improved the quality of their stock and became more price competitive and brand conscious. Aided by the growth of motorized transport, including trucking, they were able to obtain more supplies and offer a wider choice. Provided they adopted more efficient accounting and management techniques they were able to hold their own in the 1920s. Only the traditional country store faced insolvency, more often as a result of rural than urban competition (Morain, 1988, pp.132–4).

It was more tempting to drive to town to shop for consumer durables and the more expensive or 'big ticket' items. Previously these mass-produced, serviceable and rather unstylish goods had often been ordered from the mail-order catalogue and delivered by parcel post or to the nearest rail depot to be picked up. Now more male as well as female country dwellers began to go and see what was available in town and to choose from a fashionable stock. They were prepared to make periodic trips to look at household appliances, furniture, tools and clothing even though they would have the bulky items delivered. This new consumer mobility was recognized early by the major mail-order company, Sears, Roebuck, which decided to move into retail sales in the mid 1920s. There should be counters as well as catalogues to give mobile Americans more choice. The new Sears stores were to be built near highways in the suburbs where not only the country people, but also the suburbanites could drive and park. Located on cheap land and with huge parking lots, these stores testified to the arrival of the

The interior of one of Sears, Roebuck's new stores

auto-industrial age (Tedlow, 1990, pp.284–300; Emmet and Jeuck, 1950, pp.131–23). An increasing number of motorized Americans were about to influence consumer behaviour.

3.3   THE AGE OF PLAY

Already in 1927 the consumption of new types of leisure was an important phenomenon for the 56 per cent of American families with cars. Initially using the car for local trips to visit beauty spots or to visit relatives, some drivers became more confident as roads improved and started making longer pleasure journeys. With annual vacations becoming a job benefit for white collar workers, and with discretionary income also rising for this group, cars opened the way to motor tourism and camping. Following the example of upper-class tourists who had sought to escape crowded resorts, thousands of middle-class families now drove to the nation's beauty spots. Often finding hotels too formal and expensive, they took to camping by the roadside in municipal and private camps. Seeing a golden opportunity to entice more consumers, entrepreneurs started to provide cabin camps for non-campers. Expenditures on tourism soared (Belasco, 1979, pp.41–103, 129–73).

The automobile also allowed rural dwellers access to another leisure commodity, the motion picture. Most communities of any size had at least one movie theatre, which meant that increasing numbers of Americans could relax and enjoy escaping into other worlds. Whether comedies, sex tales, adventures, historical romances or mass spectacles, films were very popular (Braden, 1988, pp.185–8). By the end of the decade the 40 million movie-goers of 1922 had doubled (*Statistical History*, 1976, p.400). Many of these consumers did more than escape. They learned about material possessions and new habits. Films offered insights into upper- and middle-class patterns of behaviour and increasingly they set standards and shaped social values. With the arrival of the talkies there was less room for active audience participation and films more clearly offered a package which was based on the 'good life' (Cohen, 1990, pp.125–9).

The movies were not the only form of leisure to provide information about consumer goods and services. The technological innovation of the radio combined commercialism with relaxed entertainment for small family groups across the nation. Though many radio stations in the early 1920s were local in orientation and were virtually public services, the need to find

An outdoor part of the assembly line at Ford's Highland Park plant

financial support soon allowed producers and distributors of brand name products to sponsor programmes, while the emergence of network radio later in the decade gave advertisers a national audience. The intimate intrusion of voices mentioning brand names in the living rooms of 40 per cent of American families by early 1930 opened another door to a popular culture which was linked to new wants and aspirations (Braden, 1988, pp.118–9; *Recent Social Trends*, 1934, p.905; Cohen, 1990, pp.129–43; Marchand, 1985, pp.88–108).

Moving further than spectator sports, magazines, tabloid newspapers or amusement parks, the new leisure pursuits of the early twentieth century were not only enjoyable but themselves became advertisements for more consumerism. As yet their audiences were still fragmented by income, status, ethnicity and race. There was no general consumer consensus. National standards were still in the minds of their creators, the manufacturers and their advertising agents. Popular culture was not yet mass culture because social diversity and lack of economic purchasing power was still widespread.

SUMMARY

In the early twentieth century technological innovations in road transport and in science-based industries, the continuing spread of urbanization, changes in methods of communication and the modernization of financial credit enabled consumer culture to spread. During the 1920s moderate-income families were converted to the joys of buying as a means of obtaining happiness and growth of the American economy soared, at least temporarily.

4   THE FLOWERING OF CONSUMER CULTURE

4.1   INTRODUCTION

Both the Great Depression of the 1930s with its high levels of unemployment and America's intervention in the Second World War with its priority on military demands interrupted the growth of consumerism. Reconversion of the economy back to peacetime production, however, paved the way for its return. Pushed in new directions by productivity gains, technological innovations, demographic changes, media saturation and greater financial accessibility, the consumerism of post-war society became more of a national way of life enjoyed by the majority of white Americans. Indeed, with the mass-communication revolution of the big and small screens the 'good life' and the 'American Way' became a model of aspiration for many Western and developing nations in the late twentieth century.

Affluence underwrote the return of consumerism. Stimulated in part by government spending, the long boom ran without serious interruption from

1948 to 1973. With increasing outputs, the average annual growth rate of real Gross National Product was 3.8 per cent (Gordon *et al.*, 1980, p.165). In this prosperous society Americans earned and spent more. Between 1947 and 1979, even with the value of the dollar adjusted to take into account inflation, the average family income doubled. Real purchasing power rose by 15 per cent in the 1950s and by 32 per cent in the 1960s (Norton *et al.*, 1998, p.829; French, 1997, p.183). With improved living standards — and nearly 60 per cent of the population had achieved a middle-class standard of living in the mid 1950s in contrast to 31 per cent in the last year of prosperity before the Great Depression (Chafe, 1991, p.112) — more Americans could afford more goods and services than either their grandparents could have dreamed about or their European counterparts could entertain. By the 1960s some 5 per cent of the world's population produced and consumed over a third of the world's goods and services (Norton *et al.*, 1998, p.832).

The age of electrical appliances dawned in the 1920s. Here the sales force of an appliance store in Louisville, Kentucky, pose with some of the goods designed to make the housewife's life easier

4.2 BUY MORE AND CHARGE IT

The great American engine of production roared onwards and upwards creating an even greater abundance of commodities. Fueled by improvements in mechanization, by the introduction of automation and by the growth of research and development, more manufacturers could produce enormous quantities of identikit goods. In the perishable lines, canned, packaged and now frozen foods continued to offer convenience together with improved and more sophisticated diets. Branded household commodities and health and beauty-care products became available in much greater volume and variety. Semi-perishable, often 'fashion' items like clothes, footwear, toys and jewellery from the light manufacturing sector were increasingly marketed as annual purchases. Leisure goods for sporting activities, holidays or home amusements became big business. Consumer durables moved onto new planes with automatic washing machines, televisions, home freezers, air conditioners and clothes dryers, all run by electricity and increasingly restyled to encourage obsolesence. American business clearly had the capacity to provide consumers with whatever goods they wanted or might be encouraged to want (French, 1997, pp.188–93).

And increasingly in post-war society American appetites to consume were whetted by advertising. Now big business itself, 'Madison Avenue', adopted systematic methods of consumer research and analysis and used technology and artistic skills to create enticing images which were dispersed through the mass media (Schudson, 1984, pp.44–89). In addition to newspapers, magazines, radio and the movies, advertisers now had a new and powerful tool of penetration, television. The small screen was able to combine the impact of sound and moving pictures to intrude into the domestic intimacy of people's lives. Already in the early 1950s over 60 per cent of American families watched television. By the mid 1960s 94 per cent of households owned at least one set and in subsequent years the quality of communication was improved by the spread of colour sets (*Statistical History*, 1976, p.796). Television rapidly attracted advertising dollars ranking second only to the print media and it soon became regarded as the most impressive medium of persuasion (Schudson, 1984, pp.66–73). Daily doses of advertising in the form of 'commercials' or sponsored programmes directly stimulated the urge to buy while entertaining dramas, comedies, shows and even news coverage indirectly encouraged the materialism of the 'good life' through suggesting standards of behaviour. Economic hardship and the values of thrift were banished in favour of carefree consumption.

But could Americans afford such consumption? Their economic ability to consume a variety of goods and services was initially fed by wartime savings and then by full employment and higher wages. It was further stimulated by new techniques and devices in the commercial finance sector which allowed easy and at times almost instant credit. Charge cards issued by retailers to bind customers to their stores became a convenient extension of the traditional store credit. Oil company courtesy cards issued initially to frequent clients started to be mass distributed. Travel and entertainment cards such as American Express and Diners Club then pointed the way towards universal cards and bank cards such as BankAmericard and Master-Charge. Financed by charging both the seller and the buyer user fees, 'plastic' became a way of allowing consumers to purchase without having to pay the full amount immediately. They could pay the entire sum when billed by the credit company or they could spread the payment over several months, paying interest on the amount owed. Credit cards became so popular that by the 1970s they were carried by nearly half of all American consumers and soon they would become a preferred method of payment. Consumer debt grew, but so too did business (Mandell, 1990, pp.17–51; Boorstin, 1974, pp.427–8).

4.3 THE GOVERNMENT BECOMES INVOLVED

Financial intermediaries were not alone in facilitating post-war consumerism. The federal government, anxious to avoid general instability and unemployment, was willing to underwrite capital-intensive projects in housing and in transport, thereby promoting new levels of family-centred spending (May, 1988, pp.165–6; French, 1997, p.41). Housing shortages during the Second World War had resulted in high rents and unacceptable levels of shared accommodation. Families were raring to move and the government was willing to assist them to do so. The Servicemen's Readjustment Act of 1944 (known as the GI Bill of Rights) guaranteed veterans access to $2,000. When added to the mortgage facility offered by the Federal Housing Authority this sum provided the opportunity of home ownership at low interest rates and with no downpayment (Issel, 1985, pp.88–90; May, 1988, pp.168–9; Chafe, 1991, pp.112–3). In the 1950s some 18 million white Americans moved to the suburbs to inhabit 11 million new mass-produced, box-like houses (Chafe, 1991, p.117). This upwardly mobile section of the population then wanted to fill their homes with appliances.

Housing subsidies encouraged the white working classes to join the spending middle classes; transport subsidies encouraged them to keep spending. Life in the suburbs was isolated and miserable without access to facilities. New roads were required to allow easy mobility. These initially came onstream with the Federal Aid Highway Act of 1944, which authorized expenditure on highways and provided help for both rural and urban roads. Then the Interstate Highway Act of 1956 provided up to 90 per cent federal funding for 41,000 miles of toll-free expressway. Together, the combined road expenditures of local, state and federal governments encouraged suburbanites to run increasing numbers of automobiles (Issel, 1985, pp.91–3). Registrations increased from 25.8 million in 1945 to 61.7 million in 1960, when 75 per cent of American families owned cars (*Statistical History*, 1976, p.716; Lebergott, 1993, p.130). But one car was no longer sufficient for each household. Aspiring families aimed for two cars — one for the father to commute to work and the other for the mother to 'gofer' children and shopping. The modern American lifestyle was to be based on mass personal automobility.

4.4 THE MALLING OF AMERICA

This increased mobility was tied into changes in the distribution system which encouraged Americans to shop by car. A more rational retailing strategy for food, introduced in the depressed 1930s, offered cheaper prices and more choice. The supermarket was a large, no-frills, one-stop store with free parking. By building in low-rental districts on the outskirts of towns and by operating on a self-service, cash and carry basis, the first Big Bears, King Kullens, Great Tigers and Handy Andys were able to sell large volumes of branded goods cheaply to motorized shoppers. Such grocery sales returned very low profits, but they were meant to be traffic builders if not loss leaders because concessions which handled meat, produce, dairy, deli and household items brought in high dividends. Other grocery stores such as A & P soon adopted supermarket methods and by the late 1930s both the national chains and the pioneer supermarket entrepreneurs were building bigger and more attractive stores. Construction and improvements were halted during the Second World War, but were resumed quickly thereafter. By the early 1950s supermarkets were opening almost faster than they could be counted (McAusland, 1980, p.59).

Indeed the supermarket came of age in the post-war affluence. In 1950 it accounted for 35 per cent of American food sales; a decade later this percentage had doubled (McAusland, 1980, p.59). Not only did the low prices appeal to consumers' sense of value, but the supermarket fitted the middle-class way of life. Motorized suburban residents wanted to take the weekly supply of food home in one haul, store it in the refrigerator and kitchen cupboards and use the time saved from daily shopping for other activities. Supermarkets responded to their growing popularity by becoming bigger and better. They stocked their shelves with new branded products and more sizes of prepackaged foods. The choice of items increased from some 3,000 in 1946 to nearly 6,000 by 1960 (McAusland, 1980, p.83). Recognizing that impulse buying was as important as the shopping list in food purchasing, supermarkets enticed customers to buy more by attractive display, special offers, use of colour and heavy advertising. They also tempted consumers with the convenience of non-food items such as housewares, stationery, magazines, drugs and soft goods. Though price had been the initial attraction of the supermarket, the ability to offer a greater variety of items along with a convenient shopping environment kept consumers coming in droves in their cars.

The success of the supermarket encouraged some retailers to adopt economy-like strategies, while others looked to attract motorized custom. Many stores increasingly saw the retailing sense of self service, cash savings, check-outs and one-store shopping — tactics which were formerly thought suitable only for low-income Americans. Drugstores such as Walgreens, threatened by sales of pharmaceutical products in supermarkets, became super drugstores with numerous cheap items, price bargains and check-out counters. Department stores adopted partial self service by giving customers easy access to goods while still retaining clerical assistance. Mail-order firms and retail stores with catalogue sales capitalized on the notion of low-priced, home-based self selection. They sought both orders by telephone and by post from suburban and rural Americans by improving catalogues and advertising more widely. Discount stores emerged as a genre. Operating on low profit margins they became popular, not only in hard lines such as electrical appliances and furniture, but also in soft lines such as clothing, linen, bedding and gifts (Cundiff *et al.*, 1985, pp.220–1). All retailers were aiming to increase consumption by making it cheaper.

They also aimed to make it easier by having abundant parking facilities and a fast recognizable service of a consistent quality. Shopping centres or malls and franchising became central pivots of post-war distribution. Designed to facilitate car access and to offer a variety of services in a one-stop journey, malls increased from eight in 1945 to 3,840 by 1960. A decade later there were over 10,000 (Harris, 1990, p.279). Frequently anchored by department stores which seized the opportunity to abandon building branches in suburbs, malls accommodated a number of different shops and services, thereby drawing in consumers from either the neighbourhood or the region. Once there, consumers were tempted to keep spending in an artificial environment where controlled temperature and lighting, easy walkways, piped-in music, glass and colour, all screened them from outside distractions (Harris, 1990, p.282). Soon the mall concept was adopted to fit the downtown central business district and was expanded to include leisure facilities like movie theatres, bowling lanes, beauty parlours and eating places. Then malls became social gathering places for Americans of different ages and interests, and soon commentators were talking about the 'malling' of America (Kowinski, 1985).

Another component of rationalized consumer society was the emergence of fast, reliable goods and services sold by speciality franchises such as Midas Mufflers, Dunkin' Donuts, Kentucky Fried Chicken and One Hour Martinizing. Franchising was not a new phenomenon. As a right granted by the owner to a retailer to sell goods or services under a brand name, it started in the early twentieth century when automobile manufacturers allowed dealers to sell cars and gasoline companies franchised filling stations to distribute their brand of petrol. Franchising not only facilitated the sale of a product in numerous and widespread outlets; it also helped dealers set up in business by giving them a reliable product, a market area and national advertising (Boorstin, 1974, pp.429–34; Cundiff *et al.*, 1985, pp.224–5).

Franchising, however, accounted for a relatively small proportion of sales until it was adopted by some of the new tertiary industries in the post-war years. Motorized Americans persuaded by the mass media to want fast, standardized services looked for national chains with drive-up or drive-in facilities. McDonald's hamburger business is often regarded as the epitome of modern rational franchising, offering efficiency, calculability or quantity control, predictability and control (Ritzer, 1996, pp.9–11, 31–2). Started in 1954, it had eighty-two outlets making sales worth $218 million in 1966. Six years later it ranked second of all the food service operations in the United States with over 1,000 franchises. The rapid delivery of a uniform quality mix of prepared foods in a clean, orderly and cheerful environment underwrote the success of the 'Golden Arch' operation. McDonald's was not alone. Other franchises such as Western Auto in car parts and accessories, Howard Johnson in restaurants, Holiday Inns in accommodation, Dairy Queen in ice cream and International House of Pancakes helped standardize the American landscape by providing a uniform, fast-production model of life (Boorstin, 1974, pp.431–3; Cundiff *et al.*, 1985, pp.224–5; Ritzer, 1996).

4.5 MASS ENTERTAINMENT

Entertainment also became more uniform and sanitized. As relaxing at home became part of daily life, the consumption of amusement gadgetry grew. Television became the dominant form of domestic entertainment, leaving the

Television became the dominant form of domestic entertainment

movies, creative games and the radio far behind (Baughman, 1997, pp.57–8, 91). When not glued to the television, aspiring home-based Americans took to DIY and also enjoyed the social life of the barbeque or, occasionally, the swimming pool. More venturesome consumers travelled as vacations became popular in the 1950s. Aeroplanes increasingly carried many people long distances, bringing foreign as well as domestic resorts within relatively easy reach. Millions more drove their cars along improved highways, using motels, franchised food outlets and camping grounds. Tourism became a nationwide phenomenon as Americans visited national parks, drove to the beach, took trips to see relatives, visited historic sites and went to sanitized theme parks such as Disneyland (Rae, 1971, pp.139–44; Adams, 1991, pp.93–104). Soon the weekend became a mini-vacation through offering standardized sporting events or encouraging participatory sports. Affluent America eagerly participated in mass leisure activities.

SUMMARY

For white Americans consumption approached a mass experience in the affluent post-Second World War years. Promoted partly by federal government spending and encouraged by greater productivity, continuing technological innovations, and easier financial access, they bought advertised, branded goods in uniform retail outlets and enjoyed more leisure services at home and in purpose-built centres. Americans had become the world's all-time 'big spenders'.

5 WHITHER MODERN AMERICA?

In more recent years Americans' desires and capacity to consume have deepened and widened as marketing entrepreneurs have targeted specific groups of customers and Civil Rights protests have challenged the exclusion of people of colour from the benefits of materialism. Niche marketing and limited sales sit side by side with the mass retailing of standardized goods and services (Walsh, 1992). Consumers are segmented by age, sex, race and income. The retired pension-possessing grandparent generation has time and income to travel and enjoy leisure activities and it also requires more health care and retirement housing. Modern working women want to consume more ready-prepared meals, better household gadgets and convenient household services in order to reduce the time and energy spent in homemaking (Lebergott, 1993, p.51). Males have been targeted for impulse buying in the softer lines of food, clothing and giftware as well as the more conventional hard lines of cars and high-tech gadgetry. With lower birth rates, fewer children receive more attention and thus can acquire quality possessions. In the entertainment world, cable television and videocassette recorders (VCR) have significantly downsized the impact of networked television channels (Baughman, 1997, pp.212–6). The growing segmentation of markets, or subgroup retailing, does not deny the existence of national markets for highly advertised, branded products. These remain popular. Indeed, for black Americans and racial minorities who have until recently been the victims of discrimination, and who have been cornered into separatist consumer groups, encouragement to join the mainstream patterns of consumption is seen as a welcome reversal of historic trends. But recent trends towards accepting cultural diversity are paralleled by market variety.

Over the course of a century Americans, living in an industrializing and a mature industrial society founded on economic abundance and personal access, have enjoyed high levels of consumption. Entrepreneurs using mass-production techniques aimed to sell as many commodities as possible. Initially they and their agents persuaded the middle classes to purchase goods and services. This group quickly learned to enjoy the pleasures and conveniences of better living and were joined by the white working classes and eventually by many of the nation's racial minorities as production continued to expand. By the third quarter of the twentieth century Americans were renowned for their commitment to standardized commodities and to high standards of living (French, 1997, pp.45–52).

Consumer demands and expectations have continued to grow as Americans pursue happiness (Lebergott, 1993). In recent years, however, environmental concerns, perhaps signalling a new ideology of thrift, have sounded warning bells about shortages and wastage and international competition in the marketplace from both industrialized and developing economies has suggested that Americans may have to rethink the basis of their plentiful society. Whether entrepreneurs will use their traditional measures of technology and information flow to overcome these problems and whether consumers themselves will prefer to opt for fewer and higher quality commodities remain matters for conjecture.

Meanwhile, commentators continue to debate the standardized forms of American consumption or what they sometimes call 'the McDonaldization of society'. McDonaldization of a society refers to 'the process by which the principles of the fast food restaurant are coming to dominate more and more sectors of American society as well as the rest of the world' (Ritzer, 1996, p.1). It involves increasing the 'efficiency' of consumption by finely packaging and quantifying products; controlling customers by regulating their desires; making the product flow predictable, standardized and yet heterogeneous. The quintessential arena for such a consumption pattern is the shopping mall, though it can also involve home delivery or electronic shopping. Indeed, the logic of a McDonaldized consumption culture is to regulate all forms of economic interaction through the full use of information technology. The McDonaldization thesis sees this form of American business organization being adopted globally as more and more societies succumb to the Americanization of a consumption-orientated culture.

REFERENCES

Adams, J.A. (1991) *The American Amusement Park Industry*, Boston, Twayne.

Baughman, J.L. (1997) *The Republic of Mass Culture, Journalism, Filmmaking and Broadcasting in America since 1941*, (2nd edition), Baltimore, Johns Hopkins University Press.

Belasco, W.P. (1979) *Americans on the Road: From Autocamp to Motel, 1910–1945*, Cambridge, Mass., MIT Press.

Benson, S.P. (1986) *Counter Cultures. Saleswomen, Managers and Customers in American Department Stores, 1890–1940*, Urbana, University of Illinois Press.

Boorstin, D. (1974) *The Americans. The Democratic Experience*, New York, Random House, Vintage Edition.

Braden, D.R. (1988) *Leisure and Entertainment in America*, Dearborn, Michigan, Henry Ford Museum and Greenfield Village.

Chafe, W.H. (1991) *The Unfinished Journey. America Since World War II*, (2nd edition), New York, Oxford University Press.

Chandler, A.D. Jr. (1977) *The Visible Hand. The Managerial Revolution in American Business*, Cambridge, Mass., Harvard University Press.

Cohen, L. (1990) *Making a New Deal. Industrial Workers in Chicago, 1919–1939*, New York, Cambridge University Press.

Cundiff, E.W., Still, B.R. and Govini, N.A.P. (1985) *Fundamentals of Modern Marketing*, (4th edition), Englewood Cliffs, New Jersey, Prentice Hall.

Emmet, B. and Jeuck, E.B. (1950) *Catalogs and Counters. A History of Sears, Roebuck and Company*, Chicago, University of Chicago Press.

French, M. (1997) *US Economic History Since 1945*, Manchester, Manchester University Press.

Fuller, W.E. (1964) *R.F.D. The Changing Face of Rural America*, Bloomington, Indiana, Indiana University Press.

Gordon, R.J., Okum, A.M. and Stein, H. (1980) 'Postwar macroeconomics: the evolution of events and ideas' in Feldstein, M. (ed.) *The American Economy in Transition*, Chicago, University of Chicago Press, pp.101–82.

Harris, N. (1990) 'The changing landscape. Spaced out at the shopping center' in Harris, N. (ed.) *Cultural Excursions. Marketing Appetites and Cultural Tastes in Modern America*, Chicago, University of Chicago Press, pp.278–88.

Issel, W. (1985) *Social Change in the United States, 1945–1983*, London, Macmillan.

Kowinski, W.S. (1985) *The Malling of America. An Inside Look at the Great Consumer Paradise*, New York, William Morrow and Company Inc.

Lampard, E.E. (1991) 'Introductory essay' in Taylor, W.R. (ed.) *Inventing Times Square: Commerce and Culture at the Crossroads of the World*, New York, Russell Sage Foundation Inc., pp.16–35.

Leach, W.R. (1984) 'Transformations in a culture of consumption: women and department stores, 1890–1925', *Journal of American History*, vol. 71, no. 2, pp.319–42.

Lebergott, S. (1993) *Pursuing Happiness. American Consumers in the Twentieth Century*, Princeton, Princeton University Press.

Lebhar, G.M. (1963) *Chain Stores in America, 1859–1962*, New York, Chain Store Publishing Corporation.

Lynd, R.S. and Lynd, H.M. (1929) *Middletown. A Study in American Culture*, New York, Harcourt, Brace and Company.

McAusland, R. (1980) *The History of a Remarkable American Institution. Supermarkets, 50 Years of Progress*, Washington, D.C., Food Marketing Institute.

Mandell, L. (1990) *The Credit Card Industry. A History*, Boston, Twayne.

Marchand, R. (1985) *Advertising the American Dream. Making Way for Modernity, 1920–1940*, Berkeley, University of California Press.

May, E.T. (1988) *Homeward Bound. American Families in the Cold War Era*, New York, Basic Books.

Morain, T.J. (1988) *Prairie Grass Roots. An Iowa Small Town in the Early Twentieth Century*, Ames, Iowa, Iowa State University Press.

Norton, M.B., Katzman, D.M., Escott, P.D., Chudacoff, H.P., Petterson, T.G. and Tuttle, W.M.Jr. (1998) *A People and A Nation. A History of the United States*, Vol.II, *Since 1865*, (5th edition), Boston, Houghton Mifflin Company.

Pease, O. (1958) *The Responsibilities of American Advertising. Private Control and Public Influence, 1920–1940*, New Haven, Yale University Press.

Peiss, K. (1986) *Cheap Amusements. Working Women and Leisure in Turn of the Century New York*, Philadelphia, Temple University Press.

Peterson, T. (1958) *Magazines in the Twentieth Century*, (revised edition), Urbana, University of Illinois Press.

Presbrey, F. (1929) *The History and Development of Advertising*, Garden City, New Jersey, Doubleday, Doran & Co. Inc.

Rae, J.B. (1971) *The Road and the Car in American Life*, Cambridge, Mass., MIT Press.

Recent Social Trends in the United States (1934) *being the Report of the President's Research Committee on Social Trends*, New York, McGraw Hill Book Company Inc.

Ritzer, G. (1996) *The McDonaldization of Society. An Investigation into the Changing Character of Contemporary Social Life*, (revised edition), Thousand Oaks, California, Pine Forge Press.

Schudson, M. (1984) *Advertising. The Uneasy Persuasion*, New York, Basic Books.

Statistical History of the United States from Colonial Times to the Present (1976) New York, Basic Books.

Strasser, S. (1989) *Satisfaction Guaranteed. The Making of the American Mass Market*, New York, Pantheon Books.

Tedlow, R.S. (1990) *New and Improved. The Story of Mass Marketing in America*, New York, Basic Books.

Walsh, M. (1992) 'Plush endeavors: an analysis of the modern American soft-toy industry', *Business History Review*, vol. 66, (Winter), pp.637–70.

FURTHER READING

Boorstin, D. (1974) *The Americans. The Democratic Experience*, New York, Random House, Vintage Edition.

Lampard, E.E. (1991) 'Introductory essay' in Taylor, W.R. (ed.) *Inventing Times Square: Commerce and Culture at the Crossroads of the World*, New York, Russell Sage Foundation Inc., pp.16–35.

Schudson, M. (1984) *Advertising. The Uneasy Persuasion*, New York, Basic Books.

Strasser, S. (1989) *Satisfaction Guaranteed. The Making of the American Mass Market*, New York, Pantheon Books.

Tedlow, R.S. (1990) *New and Improved. The Story of Mass Marketing in America*, New York, Basic Books.

THE ORGANIZATION OF AMERICAN PRODUCTION

John Williams, Karel Williams and Colin Haslam ★ ★ ★ ★ ★ ★ ★ ★ ★ ★ ★ ★ ★ ★ ★ ★ ★ ★

1 WHAT IS MEANT BY THE ORGANIZATION OF PRODUCTION?

The prime purpose of the Great Exhibition of the Works of Industry of All Nations which was held in Hyde Park in 1851 was to demonstrate and celebrate Britain's industrial dominance. It succeeded in this, but it also offered a showcase for the productive achievements of other countries. Of these, it was the exhibits from the USA which made the greatest impact, registering in the public mind for the first time the difference and possible superiority of aspects of American manufacturing and production processes.

American participation began badly since many of the exhibits failed to arrive for the opening (Rosenberg, 1969, p.8), but once the problems of transatlantic delivery dates had been overcome, it was the McCormick reaper, the Hobbs locks and Colt revolvers which attracted most attention amongst the exhibits. *The Times* loftily enthused that 'the reaping machine from the USA is the most valuable contribution from abroad, to the stock of our previous knowledge, that we have yet discovered' (*The Times*, 27 September 1851, quoted in Rosenberg, 1969, p.8).

The novelty and showmanship of that presentation drew the crowds to these contributions: British engineers and manufacturers were more impressed by qualities relating to the methods and organization of the production of these goods. Discussions at the Exhibition itself were followed by reports on visits to the USA by leading engineers (1854) and a parliamentary committee (1855: both reprinted in Rosenberg, 1969). The observers were particularly struck by the much greater extent to which the objective of production in America was to make cheaply large amounts of uniform products, the attainment of which depended on a more general use of machinery. Samuel Colt, for example, told the Institute of Civil Engineers that he used machinery:

> ... to the extent of about eight-tenths of the whole cost of construction ... [because] with hand labour it was not possible to obtain that amount of uniformity, or accuracy in the several parts, which is so desirable, and also because he could not otherwise get the number of arms made, at anything like the same cost, as by machinery.

(Rosenberg, 1969, p.16)

Three-quarters of a century later, in the mid-1920s, a similar point was made with equal force in an article on mass production in the *Encyclopaedia Britannica* attributed to, although not actually written by, Henry Ford. It asserted that the term:

> As commonly employed ... is made to refer to the quantity produced, but its primary reference is to method ... Mass production is the focussing upon a manufacturing project of the principles of power, accuracy, economy, system, continuity and speed ... Three principles underlie it: (a) the planned orderly progression of the commodity through the shop; (b) the delivery of work instead of leaving it to the workman's initiative to find it; (c) an analysis of operations into their constituent parts ... [it] involves shop planning on a large scale and the manufacture and delivery of material, tools and parts at various points along the line ...
>
> (*Encyclopaedia Britannica*, 1926, pp.821–2)

Even so brief a quotation should convey that the article, drawing directly on the practices and attitudes at the Ford factories, continued the emphasis of the 1850s of being primarily directed towards the actual methods of production. It is this concentration on the activity of production which is to be the subject matter of the present chapter. It is thus different from the more frequently encountered studies of 'industrial organization' which are concerned with the, mostly legal, forms taken by enterprises and the relationships between themselves, consumers and the State. 'Industrial organization' is thus interested in whether the enterprise is owned by a single individual or family, or is a partnership, a joint stock limited liability company, a multinational enterprise, a nationalized concern, and so on. It is also interested in whether any particular industry is operating under conditions approaching 'perfect' competition (a large number of relatively small firms), oligopoly (a few large firms) or monopoly (a single firm controlling all the supply in a particular market).

In contrast the prime objective of the present chapter is to consider the productive process. The central concern is thus with manufacturing, or more precisely with the way in which the activity of manufacturing has been organized and developed in the USA over the last century. The essence of the activity of manufacturing can be encapsulated by asserting that: all manufacturing involves the *physical* conversion of raw materials and components into different products; and, in a market economy, this physical conversion aims at the *financial* activity of adding extra value.

An obvious deduction is that, for a firm, success in the organization of production may not itself be sufficient. Firms must also satisfy the financial requirements which means not only paying attention to issues of cost on the supply side, but also meeting the needs of the market on the demand side. Given its subject, this chapter will necessarily be concentrating on the productive process, but it recognizes that the needs of the firm are more complex. As a rough rule of thumb it could be said that overall and sustained success for an enterprise requires the maintenance of a viable balance between the triad of production, marketing and finance. The story of the organization of production in the USA is in part the story of the shift in the place of production in that balance. For most of the twentieth century American manufacturers and managers gave serious weight and attention to the productive processes, but there were mounting signs over the last quarter of the century that such considerations were increasingly being eclipsed by the dominance given to finance. This shift in balance, combined with a decline in America's relative industrial importance, led to many doubts being expressed around the late 1970s about whether the industrial leadership of the USA, previously unquestioned, would be sustained. Chapters 5, 6 and 10 of this book return to these issues. From the 1990s onward, however, a renewed confidence in the ability of American manufacturers to re-engage with the international competition was manifest, which is commented upon in the later part of this chapter (see also Chapter 6).

2 PRODUCTIVE ORGANIZATION IN THE USA, CIRCA 1900

Mid-nineteenth century observers were not deluding themselves: there were some strong differences between European and American productive practices. In particular the Americans did make a greater use of machinery, especially special purpose machines, to produce more standardized goods. Explanations of this and of why — despite the enthusiasm of engineers and official commissions — American practice was only very partially implemented in Europe have taken two broad forms. One (Sawyer, 1954) stresses social and institutional characteristics such as American openness, lack of class barriers, and mobility; the other (Habakkuk, 1962) stresses economic considerations such as relative differences in the endowment of the factors of production since, in contrast to Europe, labour was relatively scarce in America whilst land was relatively abundant.

The premise of this debate is that there was, for much of the nineteenth century, a distinctive 'American system' of manufacturing defined by standardization, machinery and the interchangeability of parts. But more recent scholarship (Hounshell, 1984) has demonstrated that the *extent* of these transatlantic differences was rather less than the immediate post-1851 excitements had led contemporaries and historians to suggest. Two of the firms most frequently cited as exemplars of the American system were Singer and McCormick, where the processes of production of the sewing machines and mechanical reapers were assumed to embody the new methods. Hounshell (1984, Chapters 2 and 4) subjected the manufacturing practices of these two firms to detailed examination. The basic findings are that, until well into the 1880s, neither firm paid close attention to improving production methods; that McCormick's attachment to standardization was also sharply modified by the belief that annual model changes were necessary; that the huge commercial success of both firms was founded on marketing rather than seeking reductions in production costs; and that neither firm placed much stress on the interchangeability of parts.

The archive material does not exist for these firms for the late nineteenth century but Hounshell suggests (1984, pp.120, 180–2) that they were then moving to (re-) instate production as a central concern of management and, in particular, to seek to secure greater interchangeability of component parts. In the case of Singer, for example, the very rapid rise in annual output at this time, from 100,000 machines in 1870 to 500,000 a decade later, forced such a re-balancing of objectives. This process was then powerfully reinforced by the brief bicycle boom from the late 1880s to 1897. Again the scale of output was a critical factor; at its peak in the mid-nineties the industry had an annual production of 1.2 million machines (Hounshell, 1984, p.201). Under this pressure manufacturers struggled (Hounshell, 1984, Chapter 5) to improve the uniformity of components by more accurate drop forging (in Eastern manufactures) and by steel stamping or pressing (in Midwestern works). A contemporary claimed early in the twentieth century that the bicycle boom 'led to the installation of the interchangeable system of manufacture in a thousand and one shops where it was formerly thought to be "impractical"' (Woodworth, 1907 quoted in Hounshell, 1984, p.189).

Hounshell's revisions act as a powerful antidote to the impression, easily gained from many of the general texts, that a distinctive and well-defined American productive system emerged more or less full-fledged around the time of the 1851 Exhibition. But if Hounshell convincingly demonstrates that any general applicability of, in particular, interchangeability was still new in 1900, he offers little guidance about the equally vital issue of factory and workshop organization of production. A series of engravings (reproduced in Hounshell, 1984, pp.100–4) shows that the Singer factory at Elizabethport, New Jersey, in 1880 had a totally separate department for each major process and that each department had its own banks of special purpose machines which seemed to be spaciously arranged. A couple of engravings in the chapter on bicycles suggests a similar organization (*ibid.*, pp.93–5), but whilst the text is informative on such technological developments as the use of electrical welding by Singer and the bicycle firms at the turn of the century, it says surprisingly little about layout, cycle time and other crucial production issues. Yet in any multi-process manufacture involving the fabrication and assembly of numerous parts, the layout of the work within and between processes, as well as the cycle and lead times, are of crucial concern. There is a similar paucity of information on the management of labour, as opposed to industrial relations. It is thus not possible to assess how far American manufacturers at the beginning of the twentieth century were exercised about reducing labour input, or altering the composition of labour between craft and unskilled, or direct and indirect workers.

These absences, together with other reasons (Williams *et al.*, 1993), make it difficult to accept Hounshell's broad argument that by around 1900 all that was required to move to the system which became known as 'mass production' was the innovation of the moving assembly line. More recently (Williams *et al.*, 1992), it has been shown that Henry Ford achieved his productivity gains and remarkable cost reductions by a wide variety of methods: including novel ideas of factory layout; the use of a wide range of mechanisms (the moving assembly line was just one) for transferring work within and between processes; methods for quick change-over and machine set-ups: and a more or less total managerial prerogative over labour. Such aspects constitute the core of productive organization. An analysis of Ford's practices will show both the contribution they made to his ability to reduce prices, and will also serve to undermine the myth of the centrality of the moving assembly line. It will further contribute to an understanding of the essentials of the productive side of large-scale, repetitive manufacturing.

SUMMARY

This section has shown that the previous acceptance of a distinctively nineteenth century 'American system' of manufacturing has recently been called into question. Its assumed characteristics, especially the interchangeability of parts, were only beginning to become widespread around 1900.

3   POST-1910 HENRY FORD AND MASS PRODUCTION

As the nineteenth century progressed, US manufacturing naturally saw numerous changes: these were, however, more evident in 'industrial organization' than in the organization of the productive process itself. This is epitomized by the fact that most texts on American economic development have a chapter or, more usually, a whole section covering the years from around 1860 to circa 1914 with some such title as 'The rise of big business'. What is there recounted are two main themes: first, how the giant corporations emerged through various institutional arrangements — pools, trusts, mergers, holding companies — which generally kept them at least one jump ahead of the ambiguous legal curbs on monopoly power; and second, the leap between 1898 and 1904 into finance capitalism where bankers like J. Pierpoint Morgan put together such vast new corporations as United States Steel in 1901. But at the same time the general productive principles remained intact: the quantity manufacture of standardized products increasingly characterized by interchangeable parts and the use of a growing array of machine tools and specialized jigs and fixtures. These methods were becoming more typical of American manufacturing as they gradually spread into additional industrial sectors and to the larger firms.

There is, however, a general acceptance that from somewhere around the second decade of the twentieth century a change of a different order took place. It was, moreover, seen to be essentially a change in the way production was organized. In consequence people, both at the time and since, ceased to speak of the 'American system' and referred instead to 'mass production'. Equally, then and now, the shift is inextricably associated with

Henry Ford. Nonetheless these terms and this association is surrounded by much confusion: the next section will use the case study of Henry Ford's operations first at the Highland Park plant and then at River Rouge to clarify the nature of mass production and its connection with Ford.

These form the subject matter of one part (Chapters 6 and 7) of Hounshell's (1984) book, which both aims to describe the essential ingredients of mass production and to show the central role played by Ford in putting the last necessary piece into place. Hounshell's method of doing this is to demonstrate that the 'American system' had met most of the necessary prerequisites: interchangeable parts which could be randomly chosen yet fitted together with little or no filing or adjustment; standardization of products; the use of machinery and machine tools, with production mostly taking place in a factory environment. But he argues that full mass production could not be said to exist without continuous assembly. This needs to be set out with some precision: it would certainly not be sufficient to say it was just assembly which was missing. Assembly was, indeed, a logical conclusion to production of interchangeable parts and the novelty of it was registered by the fact that the 1855 *Report of the Ordnance Committee* always placed the word between inverted commas (Rosenberg, 1969). But the process of assembly was typically managed by bringing supplies of all the parts in appropriate bins for one stationary man, or a small team, to complete the task of assembling the final product.

SUMMARY

The late nineteenth century changes in American manufacturing were mostly concerned with 'industrial organization' and especially the rise of giant corporations. But in the early twentieth century a major productive shift into what became called mass production took place, associated with Henry Ford and thought to be mainly about the use of the moving assembly line. A close examination will show this to be an over-simplified view which understates Ford's achievements.

4   THE ORGANIZATION OF PRODUCTION AT HIGHLAND PARK

The breakthrough to mass production which Hounshell identifies was the introduction by Henry Ford at Highland Park in 1913 of the moving assembly line. It is recognized, of course, that there were antecedents: there usually are. It could be said that continuous processing goes back to the 'automatic' flour mill using moving conveyers built by Oliver Evans of Philadelphia in the 1790s (Williamson, 1964, p.162). And from the 1880s onwards, when the use of refrigerated cars allowed the establishment of giant meat-packing plants near the stockyards in Chicago, Gustavus Swift and Philip Armour used conveyor methods to transport the carcasses from station to station: clearly what was embodied was the principle of the moving production line even if the object in this case was dis-assembly. Nonetheless it is right and reasonable for Hounshell to attach a special significance to the use of such methods by Henry Ford to produce automobiles. Ford's nineteenth century predecessors had processed liquid or sheet products like oil, flour and textiles or lightweight products which involved few or simple processes. No one had attempted to use these methods to manufacture a heavy, complex mechanical product like Ford's Model T. The weight was significant: although one of Ford's achievements was to produce a relatively robust, light car it still weighed 1200 lbs which meant that when he was producing a thousand cars a day in 1914, 625 tons of metal were being shipped out each day and that weight had to be handled many times over between production stages (Williams *et al.*, 1992, p.525). In addition around 10,000 separate numbered parts went into each Model T and around half of these were manufactured at Highland Park in hundreds of thousands of separate process operations.

If there is no doubting that Ford made a substantial breakthrough in the organization of production at Highland Park, it is less certain that so much of the stress should be placed on the one aspect of the moving assembly line. Hounshell's method of looking for just one characteristic to complete the long march of American manufacturing towards mass production leads him to privilege the part played by the moving assembly line and to attribute too much to it both as an innovation and as the main agent of Ford's cost reductions. This obscures the range of productive methods brought together at Highland Park, as do later attempts (see for example Piore and Sabel, 1984) to fit it into a stereotype of mass production, defined as the use of dedicated special purpose machinery with unskilled or semi-skilled labour to produce long runs of standardized products. The following account of the organization of production at Highland Park puts into perspective the claims made for the moving assembly line, and questions the attempt to capture Highland Park as the prototype of later manufacturing development in the United States. The details in the rest of this section are drawn from Williams *et al.* (1992) where specific references are given.

The essence of Henry Ford's achievement can be summarised by noting that when it was introduced in 1908 a fully-equipped touring Model T cost $950, and that just seven years later, in 1916, the comparable Model T cost only $360. Remarkably, despite the huge fall in price the profit per unit sold remained much the same at around $100 per car. Still more remarkably the costs were reduced despite the fact that Ford chose to build more of the parts and components himself. In itself building more of the car in-house necessarily increases the complexity of production which, unless offset, would raise costs. Nonetheless, if the difficulties could be overcome there were large potential gains: in 1909, $590 of the cost of the Model T consisted of bought-in materials and components. Ford was from the outset confident he could capture these gains by building more for himself, more cheaply. This represented a double change in the organization of production. Up to 1910 American car firms typically assembled parts they bought from others: Ford reversed this process and also organized production so that, in most cases, the costs of a component were halved when brought in-house. Change in the organization of production was clearly at the heart of the dramatic cost reductions attained at Highland Park. How was it done?

Table 3.1 Ford cars per man and labour hours per car, 1909–1916

Date	Cars shipped	Number of employees	Cars per man year	Labour hours per car
1909	13,941	1,655	8.4	357
1910	20,738	2,773	7.5	400
1911	53,800	3,976	13.5	222
1912	82,500	6,867	12.0	250
1913	199,100	14,366	13.9	216
1914	249,700	12,880	18.8	127
1915	368,599	18,892	19.5	123
1916	585,400	32,702	17.9	134

Source: Ford Archives; Nevins and Hill (1954) p.648.

Again, we can start with a simple, summarizing statement: the costs were cut by reducing the amount of labour needed. From 1910 to 1916 (Table 3.1) labour hours per car fell from over 400 hours to 130 hours. Such extraordinary savings could not be made simply by cutting the direct labour which engaged in tightening wheel nuts and operating crankshaft grinders, etc. Most of the labour saving came from reducing indirect labour which was involved in moving materials around the factory, storing stocks, providing maintenance and supervision, etc. This was unavoidable. Then, as now, cars like most manufactures only embodied a modest amount of direct labour: 61 hours in a Model T in December 1913, and only 37 in February 1916. Ford at Highland Park kept the ratio of indirect workers to direct workers down to 2.5 : 1. To give this a point of reference, in the late 1980s the comparable ratio for American manufacturing in general was eight indirects for every direct worker, and for Japanese manufacturing it was four to one.

The labour was taken out by reorganizing production in a variety of ways. The use of the moving assembly line was merely one of these and it was by no means the dominating influence. This is implied by what has already been said about the minority role of direct labour; final assembly labour was just one part of the total direct labour input. It is also demonstrable from the fact that two-thirds of the saving in labour hours had already been effected before the moving assembly line was first applied to fly wheel magneto production in the spring of 1913 (see Williams et al., 1993, for details). Another significant source of saving was through making changes in the layout within the factory. The parts and components of a complex, heavy product had to be moved and handled many times between production stages: whenever work was not immediately to hand for the direct workers, extra indirect labour was required to handle stocks that accumulated between processes. Improved layout could thus increase the flow of work between processes and cut the labour time wasted by walking or waiting at each work process.

The fly wheel magneto production line at Highland Park, April 1913

In re-designing layouts to ensure that work in progress travelled shorter, more direct routes Ford used two basic principles: putting the machines close together, and arranging them according to their order of use. Visitors to the shops commented that the machines and workers were jammed together much more closely than in other American factories of the time: in 1913 the 5,500 machine tools in the machine-shop each had an average floor area of 55 square feet, including access aisles and inter-process storage space. In addition, in place of large banks or a whole shop filled with the same machines, the machines were arranged in sequence so the work went from one process immediately to the machine to be used for the next process. Thus annealing furnaces and enamelling tanks were to be found in the machine shops placed in their proper order of use.

Such productive re-organization could produce dramatic results. For example, the distance travelled between finishing operations for an engine block casting fell from 4,000 to 334 feet. As a further consequence the stocks of engine blocks that had to be held were reduced to just one-twelfth of their previous level. And as a final bonus the short-travel layout saved the handling, when production was at a thousand blocks a day, of 480 tons of work in progress each day. The last factor illustrates how, and how important, the organization of production could be in taking out indirect labour: moving the 480 tons would have needed the full time services of 24 hand truckers.

If layout was constantly being adjusted to reduce the distance travelled by work in progress, close attention was also given to the means by which the travelling was to be effected. The moving assembly, even after its introduction, was just one of a variety of transfer methods. By the spring of 1915, moving, chain-driven lines had been applied extensively in final assembly, body and trim. At this stage the factory had one and a half miles of moving line, roughly half of which was conveyor directly used for manufacturing and half for transferring materials between processes. However, in the machine shop, the main transfer device was a one and a quarter mile long overhead monorail which, in early 1914, was moving 1400 tons of work in progress each day. For the delivery of bought-in materials and components to the shops, strategically-sited craneways played an increasingly important role. Besides these formal methods of transferring materials between departments at Highland Park there was also a series of much simpler transfer mechanisms used between processes. These were no less important and were widely commented upon by the stream of expert engineers who were given open access to the plant (see for example Arnold and Faurote, 1915, p.105). Gravity slides were used everywhere for inter-process transfer along with roller beds and racks of pipe and angle iron. The simple inter- and intra-process transfer devices both removed indirect labour and raised direct labour productivity by ensuring that workers had the necessary materials to hand when needed without walking or waiting.

An overhead conveyor at the Ford plant

SUMMARY

Henry Ford at Highland Park drastically reduced costs and prices but maintained the amount of profit per car. This was managed through close attention to the way production was organized — involving many innovations in layout, change-over, transfer mechanisms in the factory, etc. To concentrate only, or mainly, on the moving assembly line is to misrepresent these productive achievements. In particular, the object was to reduce the number of hours of labour, especially indirect labour, required to make a car.

5   DID FORD AT HIGHLAND PARK REPRESENT MASS PRODUCTION?

In one sense this question is irrelevant for our present purposes: what mattered was the way production was organized, not the label subsequently attached to any particular method. Nonetheless the question needs to be addressed both because of the power attached to the concept of mass production in twentieth century historiography and sociology, and also because tackling it provides an effective way of indicating the principles of productive organization behind the factory practice at Highland Park.

Mass production is commonly taken as entailing the following basic features: dedicated single-purpose equipment; semi-skilled workers subjected to the methods of Taylorized scientific management; and a standardized product. The efficiency of mass production at high volume is then associated with a strong degree of rigidity and inflexibility. How faithfully do these features characterize the way in which the Model T car was produced at Highland Park? With regard to machinery, some use was made of purpose-built dedicated equipment in jobs like automatically painting rear axles. But most of the metal cutting for engine and gearbox was done on bought-in, series-built lathes, drills, millers and presses. Manufacturers like Cincinnati or Ingersoll delivered a stripped-down tool to which Ford engineers added special jigs and fixtures that — *temporarily* — adapted a machine for a single task. The jig or fixture guaranteed the essential interchangeability of parts because it automatically set the same depth and angle of cut for each successive workpiece. But Ford engineers could then cheaply and easily re-use the equipment for a different purpose by changing the jigs and the drive sprockets which set operating speed.

As for the workforce, it is true that Ford was obsessed with the utilization of labour time. The pre-occupation was (and is, as the Japanese have recently demonstrated) quite rational since Ford's labour cost (payroll) was on average about twenty times greater than the depreciation cost of capital at Highland Park between 1910 and 1916. It is, however, not legitimate to leap from Ford's preoccupation with taking labour out, to the presumption that this was primarily achieved through the use of Frederick Taylor's scientific management. The stopwatch and motion study were used and tasks, especially hand-tasks, were sub-divided to produce productivity gains. But the presence of these elements of Taylorism disguise a fundamental difference of approach. The essence of the Taylor system was to dissect and time a particular labour function with the object of then setting a 'scientific' *standard* for it which would be semi-permanent: the essence of the Ford approach was continuously to raise the output norm.

It was not simply that Ford used 'working foremen' and loyal company 'pace setters' to show that a job could be done faster: more important was the requirement that workers had to be infinitely flexible about the definition of the task to be performed and, at the same time, had to acquiesce in progressive de-manning of operations. Endless changes in the labour process were a crucial pre-requisite for productive reorganization, and the use of labour varied with the needs as perceived by the company. At the one level assembly tasks were increasingly subdivided to give workers small detailed repetitive functions, whilst on the machine line tasks could be combined to create multi-tasked workers who sometimes tended more than one machine.

Much of the machinery could be easily re-used for different purposes

Building Model Ts on the assembly line

Finally the notion that the plant was inflexible in that it could only produce the one standardized product of the Model T, needs two major qualifications. In the first place the T was not an unchanging product. When it initially went into volume production in 1909, American cars were open, gas-lit, crank-started and artillery wheeled: when its production ceased in 1927 they were closed, electrically lit, self-started and balloon tyred on demountable rims. Ford could not ignore all this, but met it by incorporating changes rather than developing new models. Customers were always offered, amongst other things, a choice of body types, but the essential point can be more simply conveyed by the fact that by 1913 the company was making more than 100 T part specification changes every month. The brief (18 months) involvement of the United States in the First World War constitutes a further dramatic disproof of the notion that the Highland Park plant was inflexible. During this period Model T production dropped by one-third and spare capacity was used to build a marvellous assortment of military equipment (Bryan, 1990): 825,000 steel helmets; 5,000 Liberty V12 aero engines; 25 sets of 2,500 h.p. marine boilers, steam turbines and reduction gear; a two and half ton tank powered by two Model T engines; the prototype for the 600 foot Eagle submarine chaser (which was also fully designed in-house). Ford finally capped all this with an offer to build 150,000 fighter aircraft for 25 cents per pound weight.

For all these reasons it would be a more accurate characterization of productive organization at Highland Park to say that it was in a state of constant flux. Far from establishing the stereotype for American manufacturing for the next 60 to 70 years, many of Ford's early practices were — independently — reinvented by the Japanese and, in the 1970s burst into American deliberations on productive activity as total novelties. Pull-through production, low stocks, multi-tasked workers, the cheap modification of general purpose equipment, machines close together and in order of use, layout changes and de-manning could all be said to be partial rediscoveries. It would be imprudent to press comparisons very far, but Henry Ford around 1915 would have been very comfortable with the Japanese notion of *kaizen*, of continuous improvement.

SUMMARY

Mass production is commonly characterized as using dedicated, single-purpose equipment and semi-skilled workers to produce a standardized product by inflexible production methods. This section has shown that contrary to traditional views, the productive practices at Ford's Highland Park factory did not match these characteristics. More precisely, Ford applied principles of repetitive flow manufacturing to a heavy, complex mechanical engineering product. The achievement was signficant because similar principles could then be applied to other manufacturing goods, provided the market could absorb the volume.

6 FORD AT RIVER ROUGE AND GENERAL MOTORS

'Re-discovery' and re-invention, plus the discrepancy between Highland Park practices and the concept of mass production, all suggest that this was not the model for American manufacturing firms (including Ford) from the 1920s onwards. Ford had put the stress on production, but few American firms faced the overwhelming demand pressure which generated and legitimized Ford's hard-driving productionism of the 1910s. Marketing was de-emphasized because Ford had faced an insatiable demand for the Model T which was fed by productive reorganization that cut costs and allowed profit per unit to be maintained even as prices fell. In this context financial considerations became secondary: the money more or less automatically piled up. Moreover, although there were many specification changes, the production problem was eased by the concentration on developing the Model T. The company's engineers were able to work for nearly twenty years at the task of improving the methods of multi-process manufacture without being diverted by changeovers requiring the production of engines and chassis of different dimensions.

The nature of the productive regime at Highland Park was thus made possible by exceptional external and internal conditions which had largely gone by the mid-1920s. There was not an ever-expanding number of customers knocking on the door for Model Ts. Improving production was thus no longer a sufficient response, but it was the Ford response. The new plant which was opened at River Rouge in the 1920s was, in important respects, the logical development of the productive triumphs of Highland Park. It aimed to bring more or less everything in-house, so the company had its own coal and iron mines, as well as making its own components. And the moving line, which had been one of many transfer devices at Highland Park, became almost the sole method at Rouge where there were 27 miles of conveyors. It was a hugely ambitious attempt to create a continuous productive flow over an enormous span of operations from coal mining to final assembly. But the price was to build in inflexibility at just the wrong time: an essential pre-requisite for the initial Rouge method was that there was a waiting market for the product, and that had gone.

In other words, the problems with Henry Ford's River Rouge concept stemmed from issues of production as well as market considerations. It is true that by the mid-1920s the rate of growth of the American market had fallen from the heady rates initiated earlier by the market-extending cost reductions of the Model T (see for example Epstein, 1928, especially Chapter X on 'Market stabilization and industrial maturity'). It is also true that there was a demand for a wider range of products. These placed much greater constraints on Rouge, but in addition there is no clear evidence that the organization of the plant produced significant gains in efficiency. Ford recognized that continuous flow was the ideal form of manufacturing activity, and he aimed directly at that. It was to be achieved by totally mechanizing all material handling from raw material to finished product. This would reduce the indirect labour involved in transferring materials between processes: direct labour was then, at all stages, performed at fixed work stations as the materials went by. The process was activated by the almost exclusive use of electrically driven conveyors. But there was a wide variety of *types* of conveyors (screw, chain, belt, etc.) and some of these could only deal with parts of particular shape and size. These rigidities ruled out the endless variation of layout and cycle time that had been at the heart of the Highland Park approach. Since the ability of the Rouge system to reduce labour costs and improve profitability was unproven, and the possibility of such total integration was beyond almost all other firms, Rouge never became the productive model for manufacturing in America.

As Ford faltered through neglecting the market and finance, General Motors (GM) rose. Alfred Sloan, the rising star at GM, had a strategy of building a car for every pocket (Sloan, 1967). But the effects of this should not be exaggerated. GM's sales and revenues in the 1920s were dominated by the Chevrolet, the low-cost direct rival to the Model T. Sloan's strategy nonetheless reflected a major reality: the American car market had become more fragmented and would become still more so. GM's success in the market, and its financial success, also owed much to an early and positive acceptance of hire purchase selling when GM had set up its own instalment financing company, GMAC, in 1919.

If GM prospered, it was unable to reproduce Ford's earlier methods of reducing unproductive time. One indicator of this was the fact that GM operated throughout the 1920s with stock levels equal to fifteen weeks of sales: more than double the level of Highland Park in the early twenties. Since GM recruited a number of Ford's senior engineers (in particular, Knudsen to head the Chevrolet division) it is clear that it was technically difficult to transfer Ford's productive methods. Instead, GM concentrated a great deal of attention on organizational issues. Chandler (1962) reasonably identifies this as a major concern for the main American corporations operating over a range of markets and products. The solution — pioneered at such companies as Du Pont, Standard Oil and General Motors — was the so-called M-form organization of management. Essentially this involved a small central senior management team exercising control over executives in the separate de-centralized producing divisions. Whether or not this brought the benefits claimed by Chandler, it did necessarily increase the emphasis on strategy and financial control rather than productive considerations since the way of controlling the volume of information fed to the centre was to reduce much of it to a financial form.

According to Hounshell (1984) the greater attention given to financial control and the increased emphasis on a variety of products defines and constitutes a new stage of development called *flexible mass production*. The new management controls and organization were seen as the basis of enterprise success. Although other firms were involved, General Motors was seen as the exemplar because of the strategic place held by the car industry in twentieth century US manufacturing, and also because GM's relative success contrasted sharply with the struggles of the Ford company in both the depression of the 1930s and the revival of the 1940s. Nonetheless, there is nothing to suggest that GM added anything new and substantial to the organization of the productive process at this time: it sought and found advantage in other ways.

Gravity slide for transporting pre-assembled bodies to another part of the Ford plant

SUMMARY

In the 1920s Ford at the River Rouge plant attempted to carry flow production to its logical limits. The resultant productive inflexibility was exacerbated by the change from an insatiable market demand for a single model. General Motors more successfully adapted to the market and financial needs of the time but was unable to reproduce Ford's earlier productive successes.

7   DEPRESSION AND WAR: THE DIFFUSION OF REPETITIVE MANUFACTURING

The spread of flow manufacturing was already evident in the USA before 1914. There are good reasons why this development should have gone further and faster in America than elsewhere. Already by 1900 the total national income of the USA was double that of the United Kingdom, and four times that of France or Germany: income per head had passed that of Britain and was well above the levels of the European continent. The USA thus offered an exceptionally large and growing domestic market which was, moreover, substantially protected for domestic manufacturers right up to the Second World War. Until 1914, however, the organization of production along anything like continuous flow was mostly restricted to relatively simple processes usually associated with such final consumer goods as meat, beer, cigarettes and canned goods.

Once Ford had shown — literally, since he ran an open house system for industrial visitors — that the production of heavy and complex goods could be organized along similar lines, the affluence and size of the American market ensured emulation. In particular the 1920s and still more the 1930s saw the growth of large-scale markets for a whole range of consumer durable goods — radios, vacuum cleaners, refrigerators, washing machines. These lent themselves to high-volume repetitive manufacturing and demand was hugely stimulated by the extended use of electricity. In 1939 some 96 per cent of American households were said to have electric lighting (Lebergott, 1976). At the same time electricity established itself as the dominant source of power in factories. In 1910 about one-quarter of factories in the USA used electricity; by 1930 the proportion had leapt to three-quarters (Devine, 1983). This was significant for productive organization as Ford had already shown at Rouge, releasing factories from dependence on long belt-driven transmission from a central steam engine greatly widened the opportunities for flexibility in the layout of machinery on the shop floor.

The inter-war years also witnessed the dramatic progression of two forms of standardization which impinged upon the organization of production. The first was the extensive use of time and motion studies for labour management. Few firms adopted the full apparatus of Frederick Taylor's 'scientific management' — where control of the labour process was, strictly, the last link in a long, painstaking chain of factory reorganization — but time and motion studies combined naturally with large-scale repetitive manufacturing which rapidly and regularly put the work before the workers and required it to be performed within the given, limited, time. Equally, the standardization of parts within companies was, in the inter-war years, complemented by the standardization of sizes for many parts and products between companies. A campaign for inter-company technical standards in cars was launched in 1910 by Harold E. Coffin, the president of the Society of Automotive Engineers; twenty years later such standardization was the norm in the motor vehicle industry (Thompson, 1954). A more general, but similarly successful, campaign was fought in the 1920s by Herbert Hoover during his seven years as Secretary of Commerce, which immediately preceded his briefer, more ambiguous, period as President (Cochran, 1972, p.19). If reducing nuts, bolts, gears, screws and so forth from scores of different sizes to just a few lacked glamour, it contributed mightily to extending the possibilities and benefits of flow manufacture.

If, in these ways, the inter-war years saw a considerable consolidation of the newer methods of productive organization, the Second World War saw their triumphant vindication. The war experience of US manufacturing also vindicates the stress which we have placed on productive developments in the car industry. That emphasis already rested on the firm foundation of the relative importance, and extensive linkages, of the industry: by the mid-1930s the industry 'comprised some thousand factories owned by over eight hundred companies, as well as thousands of smaller subcontractors and dealers' whilst it used half the country's malleable iron, 20 per cent of steel and nearly three-quarters of all glass and rubber (*ibid.*, p.168). The war firmly underlined this dominance in two crucial respects: by the amounts produced within the industry, and by the way this demonstrated the adaptability of its methods of flow production.

General Motors alone was granted $14 billion worth of war contracts and over half the prime contracts went to the top three car makers (Sobel, 1972, p.163). Ford demonstrated that, whatever the company's travails in the 1930s, it had not lost its productive ability by turning out:

> 8,685 Liberator bombers, 57,851 aircraft engines, 277,896 jeeps, 93,217 military trucks, 26,954 tank engines, 4,291 gliders, 2,718 tanks and tank destroyers, 13,000 amphibians, 12,500 armoured cars, 113,893 universal carriers, 2,400 jet bomber engines, 87,000 aircraft generators, 53,000 superchargers, 1,202 anti-aircraft directors, magnesium and aluminum castings and gun mounts … and supplied engines of its own design for the medium tanks made by Chrysler and General Motors.
>
> (Nevins and Hill, 1963, pp.226–7).

Moreover it was the production methods most closely associated with the car industry which were seen as central. In particular 'the production line … has proved to be a highly flexible device. As [the car industry] and many others converted to defense, production and assembly of new and highly complex products was broken down into minute parts and fed through such a line' (Adams, 1954).

Even in industries, like aircraft and shipbuilding, where the nature of output created obstacles to the direct adoption of the assembly form of production, the attitudes behind it were applied to transform the rate of output. In the inter-war years, changes in the organization of production in the aircraft industry were inhibited and delayed by the small scale of output: in the mid-1930s only about 3,000 aircraft, civil and military, were being produced each year in the USA, which ranked forty-fourth in the world by value of product in 1939 (Simonson, 1960, pp.366–7). In May 1940 Roosevelt made his apparently absurdly inflated request that the industry should be able to produce 50,000 planes a year: in 1942 (almost) 48,000 were produced, in 1943 (almost) 86,000, and in 1944 (over) 96,000 (*ibid.*, pp.370, 374). An important factor was that 'as the scale of production increased, assembly line methods were used more extensively and greater specialization of labor was afforded' (*ibid.*, p.372). Similarly, the output of shipbuilding in the USA during the war totalled five million dead-weight tons (equivalent to the entire pre-war steam fleet of the British Empire), and the Kaiser yard reduced the time to build a Liberty ship — the standard slow freighter — from 200 to 17 days. Central to this achievement was the total reorganization of production, and especially the sub-assembly of large sections of the ships at secondary plants, and a high degree of standardization (Cochran, 1972, p.154).

SUMMARY

Through an affluent, protected market America in the first half of the twentieth century offered favourable conditions for large-scale repetitive manufacturing to spread through a wide range of industries. Those producing the new consumer durables (radios, vacuum cleaners, refrigerators etc.) grew even through the depressed 1930s. The needs of war then released the full output potential of the new productive methods, and underlined the leading role played by major car firms.

8 THE HIGH TIDE OF AMERICAN PRODUCTIVE DOMINANCE

In the immediate post-war years American industrial dominance was unchallenged: around 1950 the USA alone was responsible for over 40 per cent of total world manufacturing output. One consequence was that the rest of the world came to see how it was done. One such initiative was the establishment in October, 1948 of the Anglo American Council on Productivity (AACP). Under its auspices a tidal wave of 66 teams was sent to tease out the alchemy of American industrial success. Their reports may not have greatly changed British manufacturing (Tomlinson, 1991), but their reports do illuminate American productive methods in the mid-twentieth century. Their credibility as evidence is increased by the fact that the same message came back from such other pilgrims to the industrial mecca as those sent by the Organization for European Economic Cooperation (OEEC).

A major theme which ran through many of these reports was the important part played in American manufacturing by management accounting. A generation later, in the 1980s, what was seen as the USA's inability to compete with the Japanese was partly attributed to the stultifying effect of rigid financial formulae imposed on production by management accounting. It would, however, be a mistake to project this view back to 1950. At that stage what impressed the visitors from Europe was the way in which the information from management accounting was consistently linked to the needs of production. The use made of cost accounting was particularly commented upon. The OEEC report remarked that in Europe the main object was for pricing purposes and the function was left to accountants whose main concern was the 'accuracy necessary for financial accounting'. But in the USA the main aim was 'to assist management to control costs' (OEEC, pp.30–2). This was echoed in various AACP reports asserting that '… the emphasis is on costing as a tool of management and it is thought useful in so far as it results in control that is effective' (*AACP Industrial Engineering*, p.20).

There were many other ways in which the function of management accounting was seen as being, if not the hand-maiden of production, at least its facilitating partner. Before introducing a new or substantially changed product the costing information, it was said, necessarily brought together the sales manager, the production manager and the controller (cost accountant) all of whom had to be satisfied (*ibid.*, p.22). And a sharp contrast was drawn between the Chief Accountant of a British firm whose concern was simply with 'The production of the annual share-holders' report' and the 'distinctively American feature' of the Controller whose 'one aim is to serve management' by record-keeping related to the 'checking on performance' (*AACP, Management Accounting*, p.37); 'The Controller's department is looked upon as an essential service to production' (*ibid.*, p.10).

In all of this there is remarkably little direct mention of profit. The driving force for American management is seen as 'higher output at less cost' since 'low cost is the main object of American industry' (*ibid.*, pp.6, 7). The implication was that efficiency (and profit) would follow from the pursuit of increased output and reduced costs. American management is then credited with a series of behavioural aims, each of which is essentially production-directed. Central to these was the pursuit of continuous cost reduction: 'American management has, as the mainspring of its action, the well-founded belief that unit costs must be reduced each day and every day, week in and week out, year in and year out' (*ibid.*, p.7). The preoccupation with the mechanics of the organization of production pervades these reports. The visitors were impressed by the attention given to factory layout and to materials handling, the transfer of work in progress between processes.

What is still impressive is the weight uniformly given to issues of productive organization over a wide range of very variable industries. The *Final Report*, for example, provides quotes from a sample of such industries. In steel founding the Americans gave 'close attention to methods of serving moulders, to handling, layout, and getting a flow of work' (p.32), while the drop forging team commented on 'the attention paid to layout and handling', words which were almost precisely echoed in sectors as various as men's clothing and grey ironfounding (pp.32, 34, 35). The same themes were taken up by one of the few reverse teams of American industrialists visiting British establishments where they found good use of overhead cranes and monorails, but wanted more use of such transfer devices as chutes, roller conveyors, belt and chain conveyors and elevators, and thought 'it would be desirable to group the machines closer together to facilitate the movement of materials from one machine to another' (AACP, *British Pressed Metal Industry*, pp.5, 9).

Readiness to change was a further perceived characteristic of productive organization in American manufacturing: 'Several of the companies we visited had in the post-war years uprooted whole machine shops and relaid them in order to get a better flow of production' (AACP, *Management Accounting*, p.7). The flavour of the American scene at this period can, however, perhaps best be conveyed by the comment from a report on an industry, diesel locomotive production, which was more akin to small job-shop production than large-scale assembly:

> United States layout represented the best in text book principles, giving elaborate flow control of all production from raw material to the finished product ... This is constantly under review and there is no hesitation in re-grouping machines, equipment, or work stations in order to achieve the minimum of movement and the greatest concentration of effort. It was generally observed that machine tools and equipment are rarely made permanent either by securing to the floor or coupling to power supply.
>
> (AACP, Diesel Locos, p.39).

SUMMARY

The period immediately after the Second World War saw the USA totally dominant in terms of world industrial output. A series of investigators from Britain and Europe demonstrated that this was soundly based on great attention being given to the organization of production, and great flexibility over its methods of application.

9   LOSS OF BALANCE?

Even allowing for the possibility that some of the visitors viewed the scene with rose-tinted spectacles, it is difficult to avoid the conclusion that at mid-century the organization of production was a central concern of American management and contributed directly to the industrial superiority of the USA. Yet, by the end of the 1980s the superiority of Japanese manufacturing, especially in motor vehicles and electronics, had become axiomatic for many American commentators. (See for example *Fortune* 24 September and 19 November 1990.) Any full explanation of this reversal is beyond the scope of this chapter, but there are some strands which are relevant to our purpose.

Some seeds could be seen in the AACP reports. 'A note of concern struck by one forward-looking corporation was that the industry is likely to suffer because its present recruiting policy is not providing sufficient future replacement of administrative staff with practical training' (*AACP, Design for Production Report*, p.23). It was also noted that around half the firms already used standard costing and its use was spreading. In itself this was simply a method of controlling efficiency by comparing a calculated 'efficient' standard cost with actual cost. But both the standard and the formulae by which they were calculated tended to become fossilized, encouraging management to be satisfied as long as negative variances were avoided and these semi-permanent norms were reached. At the same time, financial accounting functions were 'strongly represented at the top executive level' (*AACP, Management Accounting*, p.8). Similarly, the attention paid to methods of material handling of central stocks was already characterized as 'Keeping stocks at the right level' (*ibid.*, p.9). The danger was to slide from an approach based on continuous cost cutting, to one of reaching more or less static targets, legitimized by their embodiment in financial formulae. It is thus indicative that by the 1980s, texts on management accounting routinely gave formulae for calculating standard costs and determining the 'right' level of stocks (see for example Ricketts and Gray, 1988). The centrality of labour costs also tended to be obscured by the convention of management accounting to include indirect labour under overheads (see for example Williams *et al.*, 1989).

A parallel trend was singled out for criticism once it was realized that something had gone wrong (Hayes and Abernathy, 1980); this was the development of formulae on which to base investment decisions. These formulae were generally introduced after the late 1940s. Apart from the consideration of whether techniques like discounted cash flow (DCF), which had been developed for managing share portfolios, were appropriate for industrial investment decisions, they tended to obscure the extent of the uncertainties involved. More seriously, outcomes could be manipulated by managers committed to a particular project or anxious for a particular decision (Williams *et al.*, 1987). In addition American critics like Hayes and Abernathy charged that such techniques as DCF had a systematic bias in favour of strategic competitive thinking and aggressive investment, a criticism which was also echoed by Magaziner and Reich (1982). Whereas the AACP had generally represented finance as the effective servant of American management, critics now blamed narrow and short-sighted financial calculation for American manufacturing decline.

Such possibilities were probably increased as, after 1950, M-form management organization spread rapidly in America, creating a small elite of top managers who made decisions based largely on financial information provided from below. All these changes increased the propensity for top management to be drawn from those with financial and accounting expertise. The broad institutional context of the stock exchange requiring short-run financial returns to avoid threats of take-over, reinforced top management's concern with financial considerations. A symptom, rather than a cause, was the tendency of the university business schools to concentrate on finance and accounting at the expense of production and engineering, and for the best students to see finance as the quickest route to the top. Interestingly, the counterweight was seen to be not so much productive expertise but business policy and competitor analysis.

SUMMARY

Increasingly from around 1960 American leadership in manufacturing excellence was challenged by, especially, Japan and Germany. American critics of the 1980s blamed the growing dominance in large US companies of financial considerations over those of production, and the application of accounting formulae in place of productive flexibility. Top management was recruited for financial expertise and often lacked knowledge of production.

10   POST-1970. LIVING WITH THE JAPANESE

If such factors were gradually relegating the importance of productive organization in American manufacturing, it is not surprising that the realization of this, and of its consequences, was slow to develop. This can be graphically illustrated by glancing at a report on German management (Booz, Allen and Hamilton, 1973, pp.18, 20) prepared for the West German government by a firm of American management consultants. The whole report is predicated on the presumption that the proper yardstick was current American management which represented 'best practice'. In making these comparisons the report incidentally illustrates what, in the judgement of a leading American consulting firm, had become the central concerns of top managers in US manufacturing. The basis on which top management should set company goals (its 'most important task') is firmly delineated as financial: '...returns on investment and the availability of financial means, represent the decision-making criteria of management at the top of the combine'. And German managers were chided because DCF techniques were little used in financial planning (ibid., p.21) and for failing to seek growth by takeovers when 'In the United States, it is precisely acquisitions and mergers which have been given priority in recent years' (ibid., p.24). The failure of German universities to offer courses comparable to American Business Administration was also commented on with the laconic conclusion that 'The German University wants to educate — not to train ... [which] ... does not lend itself to closing the management gap' (ibid., pp.78, 80).

In 1970, when this report was presented, it was still plausible to base recommendations on a presumption that American business practices were best. However, as the evidence mounted of the ability of Germany and Japan to compete successfully in the Americans' own market, notions of effortless American productive superiority melted away. In consumer electronics, for example, the Americans were evicted from the production of colour televisions and imported all their VCRs from Japan. Even more symbolically, imports of Japanese cars to the USA increased rapidly from the early 1970s, reaching 2.4 million in 1985 (Williams *et al.*, 1994, p.84), an invasion which the American big three car producers were unable to stem by producing smaller cars as they had done with the 1950s threat from Europe. The result was a characteristically open American analysis of causes, and search for cures. One avenue of enquiry was based essentially on the notion that it was the nature of production which had changed. The USA still dominated in what was labelled mass production but technical change now permitted the economic production of small runs, whilst consumers simultaneously demanded more individualized ('designer') products. So, in place of mass production (MP) based on semi-skilled workers using dedicated machinery to produce standardized goods, it was possible to have flexible specialization (FS) based on skilled workers producing a variety of customized goods. This concept was most fully developed in an influential book by Piore and Sabel (1984) where a whole new industrial world was predicated on the consequences of the opposition between MP and FS. Somewhat similar notions pervaded the first Massachusetts Institute of Technology (MIT) study on the world car industry (Altshuler *et al.*, 1984) with its suggestion that small car producers need not suffer acute disadvantages of scale. The wide-raging debate and criticism (see for example Williams *et al.*, 1987) need not concern us, but as Japanese (and German) production methods were exposed to greater scrutiny it became clear that they could not be made to fit within the orthodox definitions of FS.

The second MIT study (Womack *et al.*, 1990) followed essentially the same path. But the proposition popularized in the hugely successful book on *The Machine that Changed the World* was that the Japanese had invented an entirely new system known as lean production. Like FS, this system is founded on a direct opposition to MP and large claims are made for it: '… it uses less of everything compared with mass production — half the human effort in the factory, half the manufacturing space, half the investment in tools, half the engineering hours to develop a new product in half the time' (*ibid.*, p.13). Apart from any scepticism arising from the — less than fully substantiated — extravagance of these claims, the presumption of an entirely novel form of the organization of production needs to be approached with care. This is even more necessary if note is taken of comments made in one of the AACP reports forty years earlier when it was stated that: 'Machines are not always laid out in lines, but were sometimes grouped round an operator … If the cycle time of a machine permits the operator to undertake a further task, the appropriate machine is placed near him', and 'One assembly line was seen to have "stop" buttons within reach of every workman' (*AACP, International Combustion Engines*, pp.18, 27). The 1960s Japanese 'discoveries' of cellular layout, multiple machines per man, and worker control lines had not been entirely unknown in America.

The appreciation of these elements of recurrence became more general in the 1990s. There were still strong exceptions. The influential concept of lean production was generalized into lean thinking (stressing the significance of the removal of waste and the introduction of flow) to be applied to services as well as manufacturing, to small as well as large enterprises (Womack and Jones, 1996). The large claims also continued: 'Lean thinking can dramatically boost productivity — doubling to quadrupling it — while dramatically reducing errors, inventories, on-the-job accidents, space requirements, time-to-market for new products, production lead times, the cost of extra product variety, and costs in general …' (*ibid.*, p.295). But the more characteristic shift has been towards challenging the notion of clear chronological progression in the development of productive systems. Thus Sabel, who had in an earlier influential book presented FS (flexible specialization) as the way forward (Piore and Sabel, 1984), has more recently produced a more nuanced account which concludes that '… each period of economic history anticipates many of the strategies of its successors and ultimately comes to pursue them with means it has inherited from its predecessors. Hence the very idea of distinguishing radically different epochs of development according to their dominant economic strategy becomes … debatable' (Sabel and Zeitlin, 1997, p.5).

As the difference between productive systems becomes perceived as being increasingly blurred, the recognition of continuity and recurrence reflects the essential fact that the fundamental nature of the activity of manufacturing has not changed: it is physically about the conversion of materials and financially about adding value. Another reason is that the nature of the problem posed in using multi-process techniques to manufacture complex products also has a high degree of permanency: it is to maintain continuous productive flow. If that sounds straightforward, even a very stylized account of what is involved can suggest the complications and difficulties. Thus manufacturing a final consumer product normally involves:

- a large number of component parts, usually measured at least in tens, commonly in hundreds and, in the case of cars, many thousands;

- securing the flow of materials and components, from supplier factories and between processes within each plant and final assembly;

- ensuring that this brings the right parts together in the right quantities and at the right time;

- the whole process (lead time) from materials to final products normally spreads over weeks during which imbalances appear;

- remembering that the only productive time is when conversion is actually taking place, and that any waiting time (in warehouses or queues) is unproductive but involves costs (in storage, handling etc);

- keeping firm hold on the notion that the central object is thus to add value continuously.

It should not, therefore, be surprising to find that in the history of the organization of production few firms, and usually under exceptional circumstances, have even come close to solving the basic problem of attaining continuous productive flow.

Which suggests the third reason for caution before accepting that the Japanese had invented an entirely novel system. Such a claim denies the strong parallels and elements of recurrence between the achievements of late twentieth century Japan (or, more strictly, Toyota) and those made much earlier by Ford at Highland Park. In each case the basis of success rested on the ability dramatically to reduce the labour hours needed to build their cars. Moreover methods of obtaining these overall results were strikingly similar. Both companies followed a practice of putting machines close together and in order of use, and both recognized that the (payroll) costs of labour were greater than the (depreciation) costs of capital, thus justifying the Ohno principle that 'machines rather than men must wait'. There was also a mutual recognition of the importance of running with a low level of stocks and work in progress, especially, to cut down on indirect labour which was seen as the main source of labour costs: Toyota's system of *kanban* and 'just-in-time' was more structured than Ford's 'stock-chasers', but the object was the same. At Takaoka and at Highland Park layout was frequently changed and continuous improvement *(kaizen)* was a rule of life. One pre-requisite was total managerial prerogative over the workforce where each firm ran a largely coercive regime.

There were two main points of departure and novelty in the Japanese approach. The first was over the degree of vertical integration. Ford increasingly brought more and more in-house; Toyota buys-in something like 80 per cent of the value of the final product. Again the object was much the same: Ford thought (and demonstrated) that he could produce components more cheaply himself; Toyota aimed to cut costs by exerting pressure and giving assistance to suppliers and by taking advantage of the much lower wages paid by smaller manufacturers in Japan. The other contrast can be summarized by saying that Ford ran a linear system whilst Toyota adopted, in part at least, a cellular system. In the former system the work is moved to a stationary worker, cutting out any walking time but (depending on the cycle time) leaving the work with gaps between operations. In the cellular system the mobility of the worker is exploited: by getting workers to walk between several machines (often arranged in a U-shape) the employer more nearly realizes the object of productively using each worker's time for 60 seconds in a minute.

Two relevant comments flow from these comparisons and contrasts. The first is that in considering the fundamental aspects of productive organization it is probably best not to be too distracted by attempts to categorize different forms. Concepts like mass production, flexible specialization, Fordism, post-Fordism and lean production might — if sufficiently specified — be useful for some purposes, but in looking at the long-run development of American manufacturing it might be more fruitful to concentrate on changing approaches to basically common problems, defined by the relative weight given to the productive, the financial and the market. The 'new' Japanese production methods which so absorbed American producers, academics and politicians in the seventies and eighties were not inherently 'un-American' but were largely lost American discoveries. Lost because, institutional features like the stock exchange produced unfavourable economic attitudes (like short-termism), and because society had moved on: it is not possible — or desirable — in a modern, Western democracy for management to exercise a total prerogative over labour. What is underlined is that a successful resurgence of American manufacturing requires more attention to production and less weight to finance.

SUMMARY

In the 1980s and early 1990s commentators tended to stress the presumed deficiencies of American manufacturing and to exaggerate the superiority and difference of Japanese manufacturing. Japanese methods, so far from representing an entirely new form of productive organization (so-called lean production), largely represent the rediscovery of methods long known in America and practised much earlier by Henry Ford. The recurrence reflects the fact that many of the most formidable problems posed by large-scale repetitive manufacturing have not substantially changed. The section attempts to specify the similarities and differences in productive organization between best practice in Japan and America.

11   NON-MANUFACTURING PRODUCTION

The methods of manufacturing have so conditioned American life in the twentieth century that it would have been surprising if attempts had not been made to emulate them in other sectors of the economy. It was, however, rarely possible to transpose industrial practices direct onto the farm or into shops and offices.

11.1   AGRICULTURE

The interactions with agriculture are particularly complicated. Throughout the nineteenth century agricultural processing was one of the sectors which led in productive organization and innovation. The reason was obvious: these were products which naturally lent themselves to being processed on a flow basis. Flour mills at the beginning of the century, and the stockyards at the end, would be good examples. But in agriculture itself the main sources of output growth before circa 1900 came from other sources: the geographical spread of farming as the moving frontiers and populations gradually settled the sub-continent; and the process of regional specialization as, for example, the north-eastern States ceded wheat production to more suitable mid-western areas and shifted instead to truck farming.

Mechanization did play a part: the McCormick reaper had, after all, been one of the sensations of the 1851 Great Exhibition. After the Civil War, the American system of Land Colleges was one of several factors which made the diffusion of new methods and new knowledge faster than in Europe. Nonetheless the generalized use of farm machinery driven by something more than human or horse power has essentially been a phenomenon of the twentieth century. Steam-driven machines, including combine harvesters, were available but for farm and field steam-power was generally too cumbersome and static: it was impractical to have, as in a factory, an elaborate system of belt-drives distributing power from a central engine. For much the same reasons the early twentieth century tendency of industry to make greater use of electrical power was not allowed in the fields. Only the internal combustion engine, symbolized by the ubiquitous farm tractor, made machines in agriculture more or less universal.

As a result attention, previously largely confined to food processing, has been given to the organization of agricultural processes, especially at sowing and harvesting. Since the 1960s there have been nearly five million tractors on US farms (United States Bureau of Commerce, 1962; 1992), and many other farm tasks — such as spreading fertilizer and pesticides — are now performed from aircraft. Huge machines carrying packing and boxing crews and followed by trucks can be seen in some Californian fields packing 600 and more boxes of lettuces per hour, which, within hours, are being transported across the country (Highbee, 1968, p.504). No industry has been more visibly successful in achieving the basic Ford and Ohno objective of taking labour out of the productive process: in 1910 there were 13.6 million workers in US agriculture; by 1996 the number had fallen to 2.3 million (*Historical Statistics of the US* and *Statistical Abstract of US*, 1997, see also Table 3.2). Productivity, as most usually measured in terms of output per man, has in recent decades increased much faster in agriculture than in manufacturing: an annual rate of growth between 1948 and 1969 of 5.8 per cent in agriculture, against 2.7 per cent in manufacturing (Kendrick, 1977, p.41). Obviously advances in technology and genetics have been major driving forces in this but changes in the organization of agricultural production — often in response to, or made possible by, technical and genetic developments — have also contributed.

But we should not be carried away. Agriculture was far from following the same trajectory as manufacturing in respect to the organization of production. For a start the whole structure of the industry was different with the typical American farm having a relatively small, but rising, average size of 147 acres in 1900 and 469 acres in 1996, and employing little labour outside the family: in 1910, 75 per cent of the labour force was family and it

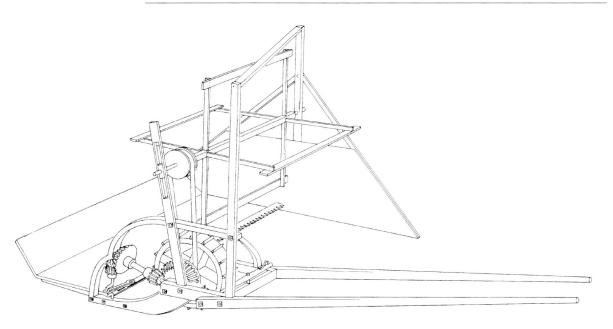

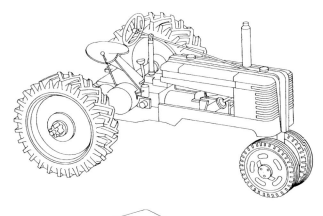

Farming mechanization: (Top) McCormick mechanical reaper; (middle) tractor of the 1930s; (bottom) modern tractor.

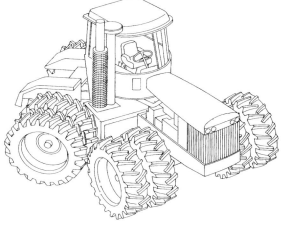

Table 3.2 Indicators of activity in US agriculture, 1900–1996[a]

Date	No. of farms 000s	Farm employment 000s	Average size of farm (acres)	Total acreage 000s
1900	5,740	13,555[b]	147	841,202
1950	5,388	9,926	216	1,161,420
1970	2,954	4,523	373	1,102,769
1990	2,140	2,891	461	987,000
1996	2,063	2,262	469	968,000

Sources: United States Bureau of Commerce, various years

Notes.

[a] The figures are not always strictly comparable over such a long period, but are sufficiently so to indicate the broad trends.

[b] Figure relates to 1910.

was still 70 per cent in 1990 (see Table 3.2). There were aspects of large-scale, high-volume activity, by semi-skilled workers using dedicated machinery — such as the mid-west mobile grain harvesting operation as it moved northwards from Texas — and a relatively high degree of standardization of the product had always been a feature of agriculture. But thus far much of mainstream farming activity has in its nature, as well as its more direct connection to nature, been resistant to many of the most characteristic aspects of productive organization in manufacturing. It is not commonplace in the field to find a Fordist stationary worker having his or her task continuously delivered by some form of moving line. There are exceptions but they mostly feature animals rather than crops, stock rather than men: dairy parlours or battery hen systems would most nearly fit such methods. The critical production changes have been more in the application of science, particularly modern genetics, to make crops and stock more controlled and predictable.

11.2 SERVICES

It is again more instructive to note some of the interactions of modes of production between services and manufacturing than to pursue some chimerical notion that the provision of services has been largely conditioned by practices in manufacturing. Of course, there has been much technical change and mechanization which has, for example, transformed offices or made supermarkets very different from country stores. It does not necesarily follow that these institutions have simply become more like modern factories. If some of the basic function is necessarily similar — adding value at every process stage — there are also sharp differences. One of these is that what is added is often intangible: knowledge, education, health, security, courtesy, mobility.

Naturally, developments in the service sector often have close parallels with those in manufacturing. It could, for example, be said that the mechanization of the office by the introduction of the typewriter brought methods of work (typing pools) and shifts in the labour force (substitution of cheaper, female workers), which were very similar to the changes introduced by early textile mills. Even before 1914 there are reports of office managers timing the work of stenographers (shorthand typists) and determining wages by the speed, accuracy and volume of work, whilst the National Cash Register Company had completely standardized the pitch of their salesmen (Shaw, 1911 in Chandler *et al.*, 1968, pp.280, 281). Equally it is even more obvious in services than in manufacturing that in organizing production the basic aim is to cut labour costs. Thus in a wide variety of service operations — in hospitals and schools as well as banks and shops — much attention has been given to layout and stock control. But it is, because of the nature of many service functions, often more difficult to take labour out. This has in many cases led — in a further interaction — to the development and use of manufactured products as substitutes for services: washing machines in place of laundries; television and video-cassette recorders in place of cinema; private cars in place of public transport.

The service sector is so diverse that generalizations are risky. Nonetheless it does seem that, over the twentieth century, the changes in organization have been especially marked in retailing. The great growth in department stores had already taken place before 1914 and they were relatively static from the 1920s, especially as the mail-order firms (Sears, Roebuck; Montgomery Ward) began to supplement their business by opening stores. Chains of variety stores also developed relatively early (Woolworth's already had over 1,500 stores in the USA by 1927) closely followed by more specialist chains selling, for example, drugs. Food chains were the most obvious and prolific: A and P had 14,700 stores in 1936 when it opened its first supermarket (Sobel, 1972, pp.60–4, 148). The supermarket structure — where walking, pushing, carrying and waiting by the customer is an integral part of the productive process — has spread well beyond food shops, and the 'out-of-town' shopping mall is now central to the organization of retail production. For these reasons productivity in retail trades in the years after 1945 tended to be higher than in other service sectors: 2.8 per cent per annum between 1948 and 1963 for food stores, against 0.3 per cent for barber shops, 1.7 per cent for dry cleaning and minus 0.5 per cent for hotels and motels (Kendrick, 1977, p.49).

SUMMARY

This section looks at the extent to which the methods of production developed in manufacturing have been taken up in the other major sectors of agriculture and services. Although labour has been removed from agriculture on a spectacular scale, the reasons for this are to be found more in technical progress and genetic developments than in productive organization. Nature imposes constraints on the application of many of the methods used in manufacturing. There are similarly large differences which prevent manufacturing practices being emulated in the service sector.

12 AMERICAN RESURGENCE

Most American commentators of the 1980s had focused on the physical superiority of Japanese manufacturing, a superiority which was often over-stated as in the claim that the Japanese could build a car in half the hours needed in the USA (Womack *et al.*, 1990, p.13). The reality was that a substantial part of the perceived Japanese superiority was financially based on wages which in the 1970s were, in dollar terms, half or less than those of the Americans. This became clearer from the late 1980s as the appreciation of the yen neutralized this Japanese advantage, and the message was reinforced by the extent to which, especially in cars and electronics, the Japanese supremacy was threatened by the rapid rise of Korea and Taiwan, the next generation of Asian low wage competitors. These developments, which preceded the general Asian economic crisis later in the late 1990s, indicated that by earlier over-stating Japanese productive innovations commentators lost sight of the fact that international trade in manufactures was also crucially dependent on such other factors as exchange rates influencing relative wage levels.

Well before these messages had reached most commentators and business schools some American firms had realized the importance of wage relativities and exchange rates. Thus the world's leading producer of heavy equipment, Caterpillar, had lobbied for currency realignment and not for trade protection against its thrusting Japanese competitor Komatsu. Caterpillar also had an ambitious programme of productive change which, among other aspects, involved the rediscovery of the sequential layouts (machines in order of use) which Henry Ford had pioneered and also the use of cellular organization as developed by Toyota. If the results were relatively disappointing, this illustrated another constraint on what it is possible to achieve through productive change: the conditions of the market. In the case of Caterpillar, as in many other sectors in the mature stage of industrial development, the problem was market saturation. Thus in the case of one of Caterpillar's major activities, earth moving equipment, the 1973 sales peak of 85,000 was not decisively surpassed for more that two decades. These conditions, together with the normal cyclical nature of demand, make it more difficult for firms, even world market leaders like Caterpillar, to recover their costs (Froud *et al.*, 1998).

More generally, the 1990s brought some re-evaluation of American manufacturing capabilities, reinforced by the crisis of the Asian 'tiger' economies. In part this was because of an appreciation that much of the higher productivity of such competitors as Japan and Germany in recent decades represented a process of catching up (Baumol *et al.*, 1992; Krugman, 1994; Lester, 1994; Spulber, 1995). In addition there was a dynamism stimulated more by new developments in productive organization than by changes in plant lay out. Particularly noted was the successful US involvement in what were seen in the 1990s as the two main trends in production methods: the spread of flexible labour practices (more short contracts, part-time working and out-sourcing of peripheral functions); and the adoption of new technical advances, especially in the use of computers and robots. 'American companies are more competitive than ever because they are creators and leaders of the information technology revolution … (accounting for) more than 40 per cent of the world's investment in computing' and thus leading to an above-trend growth in productivity in manufacturing of 3.9 per cent per year (*Fortune*, 9 June, 1997). The evidence is that American manufacturing is leading, rather than lagging, in the adoption of flexible labour practices and the use of information technology (but see Chapter 6).

The upward shift in American confidence about their productive abilities enabled economists like Krugman (1994) to describe fears about competitiveness as an illusion and dangerous obsession. This may have been an over-reaction, but there was little doubt that American manufacturing approached the millennium in a much stronger relative position than had seemed likely even a decade earlier. Table 3.3 shows that although American manufacturing, as in all other high income countries, declined as a proportion of GDP, the absolute number employed in this sector held up remarkably well. Whereas British manufacturing employment was halved from 8.3 million in 1970 to 3.9 million in 1996, employment in the comparable sector of the US only fell from 19.4 million to 18.2 million over the same years. The other significant trend identified in Table 3.3 is the growth of employment in the other two categories, which broadly represent the service sector of the economy. It is these kinds of figures that have given rise to the idea that the US economy is the first of the 'post-industrial' economies (see also Chapters 5 and 6).

Table 3.3   **USA: employment by sector 1970 to 1996**

	Selected sectoral share of GDP 1970–96 %				Number employed: selected sectors 1970–96 '000s			
	1970	1980	1990	1996	1970	1980	1990	1996
Manufacturing	25.51	22.22	18.48	17.70	19,410	20,354	18,615	18,164
Finance, real estate and business services	18.17	20.07	26.19	27.82	6,204	9,892	14,543	17,409
Community, social and personal services	7.59	8.49	10.48	11.16	10,306	13,664	16,250	19,889

Source: OECD National Accounts. Detailed Tables. Volume II, Paris.

Note: the three sectors shown (cut of ten) were those showing the greatest change during these years.

Against the productive achievements have to be set the financial constraints. Attention became increasingly focused on the paradox of an exceptional period of sustained economic activity being accompanied by inadequate financial rates of return. Across a wide swathe of American industry there is a problem of cost recovery, partly arising out of the combination of market saturation with cyclicity. Most public comment and analysis is thus directed at financial considerations such as raising the return on capital employed and similar financial indicators. Executive incentive schemes linked to financial performance targets have been presented as one remedy, but a more general approach has been the growing use of corporate restructuring (mostly through mergers, acquisitions or management buy-outs) to raise rates of return. Table 3.4 dramatically indicates the scale of this round of corporate consolidation when in most years from about 1980 onwards the sums spent on mergers and acquisitions in America have become large relative to the amounts invested in plant and equipment.

Table 3.4 USA: business enterprise expenditure on mergers and acquisitions (M&A) versus spend on plant and equipment, 1970–94

	Spend on M&A in US$ bn	Expenditures on new plant and equipment US$ bn	Spend on M&A as a percentage of expenditures on new plant and equipment
1970	5.9	79.7	7.40
1975	5.0	142.4	3.51
1980	44.3	282.8	15.66
1985	149.6	410.1	36.48
1990	205.6	532.6	38.60
1994	358.7	549.9	65.23

Source: United States Bureau of Commerce, *Statistical Abstract of the United States*, 'The National Data book', various years.

Note: from 1970 to 1979 data collected when assets of $10 million or more was spent on acquiring; from 1980 to 1984 data collected for transactions valued at more than $1 million.

It is not possible to say whether this trend will continue, nor is there agreement over its interpretation. Some welcome it as a means of securing a more efficient allocation of resources (Jensen, 1998). Others claim that 'in the American context corporate restructuring has been associated with widespread layoffs and worker terminations as a prevailing strategy' (Usui and Colignon, 1996, p.551) and that 'restructuring always results in fewer employees' (Hamel and Prahaled, 1994, p.124). What is clear is that the driving force is to sustain and increase 'shareholder value' which has become the mantra of the new age. One consequence is that American corporations in general, and manufacturing corporations in particular, approached the new millennium with yet another (and probably temporary) realignment of the relative importance of productive, market and financial consideration which redefines the American way as financial. (The potential consequences of this trend are also examined in Chapters 5 and 6.)

13   CONCLUSION

In the long run successful enterprises need to maintain a reasonable balance between the effective management of finance, the market and production. In this chapter attention has been concentrated on the twentieth century developments in the last of these while at the same time signalling the significance of markets and financial factors.

Recent research has shown that insofar as there was an earlier 'American system' of manufactures — based on greater output, more use of machinery and substantial interchangeability of parts — it was only just becoming widespread around 1900. It is then demonstrated that Henry Ford at Highland Park from around 1909 to circa 1920 did much more than add the moving assembly line. He attempted to approach a system of flow manufacture by concentrating on the organization of production. He constantly experimented with improved factory layout — especially through putting machines close together and in order of use; reduced change-over times; shortened cycle times; and the use of a wide variety of methods for transferring materials and parts in and between processes. It was a regime of infinite flexibility aimed at reducing the amount of labour, especially indirect labour, required to produce each car.

In the 1920s Ford attempted to design a plant — at River Rouge — which would give total flow from the production of raw materials to the manufacture of the final product. It failed because it could only be done by accepting inflexibility in the organization of production, and it required a ready market for all the output. Nonetheless America in the 1920s and 1930s presented a unique market for large-scale, more-or-less standardized output over a wide range of products — especially the new household consumer durables (radios, refrigerators etc.). The production of these used many of Ford's earlier innovations, whilst demand pressure during the Second World War revealed the full productive potential of American manufacturing.

By 1950 the dominance of the United States in terms of productive organization was universally acknowledged and recorded in a series of reports by visitors from other countries. At the same time a long-run tendency to enhance financial factors was beginning to reduce the stress given to production and to divorce top management from knowledge about the organization of production. The increasing competition from Germany and Japan drove this home, but it is shown that many of the 'new' Japanese methods were 'rediscoveries' of earlier American practices. By the 1990s American manufacturing was strongly addressing the problem of redressing the balance between, especially, the financial and the productive, and was also leading in the adoption of such new methods of productive organization as flexible labour practices and information technology.

Over the last 150 years or so, changes in the ways in which production has been organized in manufacturing have strongly conditioned such basic features of American life as urbanization and increases in the average material standard of living. If this makes it unavoidable and natural to adopt the same techniques elsewhere, it is equally clear that fundamental differences in both the output and processes of such sectors as agriculture and services makes it impractical simply to emulate manufacturing. In the nature of things it would seem highly improbable that there can ever be one economy-wide system of production.

REFERENCES

Anglo-American Council on Productivity (AACP) (1949–52) *Reports.* There were altogether sixty-six reports: references to specific reports are cited in the text.

Adams, W. (1954) *The Structure of American Industry,* New York, Macmillan.

Altshuler, A., Anderson, M. and Jones, D. (1984) *The Future of the Automobile. The Report of MIT's Automobile Program,* London, Allen and Unwin.

Arnold, H. and Faurote, F. (1915) *Ford Methods and the Ford Shops,* New York, Engineering Magazine Company.

Baumol, W., Blackman, S. and Wolff, E. (1992) *Productivity and American Leadership: the Long View,* Cambridge, Mass., MIT Press.

Booz, Allen and Hamilton (West Germany) (1973) 'German management: challenges and responses — a pragmatic evaluation', *International Studies of Management and Organization,* Spring-Summer, vol. 3, nos. 1–2, pp.9–98.

Bryan, F. (1990) *Beyond the Model T,* Detroit, Wayne State University Press.

Chandler, A. (1962) *Strategy and Structure: Chapters in the History of Industrial Enterprise,* Cambridge Mass., MIT Press.

Chandler, A., Bruchey, S. and Galambos, L. (eds.) (1968) *The Changing Economic Order: Readings in American Business and Economic History,* New York, Harcourt, Brace.

Cochran, T. (1972) *American Business in the Twentieth Century,* Cambridge, Mass., Harvard University Press.

Devine, W. (1983) 'From shafts to wires: historical perspectives on electrification', *Journal of Economic History,* vol. 43, no. 2, pp.347–72.

Encyclopaedia Britannica (1926) *Supplementary Volume to the Thirteenth Edition,* Chicago, Encyclopaedia Britannica.

Epstein, R. (1928) *The Automobile Industry — Its Economic and Commercial Development,* Chicago, Shaw and Co.

Froud, J., Haslem, C., Johal, S., Williams, J. and Williams, K. (1998) 'Caterpillar: two stories and an argument', *Accounting, Organisation and Society,* vol. 23, no. 7, pp.685–708.

Habakkuk, H. (1962) *American and British Technology in the Nineteenth Century,* Cambridge, Cambridge University Press.

Hamel, G. and Prahaled, C. (1994) 'Competing for the future', *Harvard Business Review,* July–August, pp.122–8.

Hayes, R. and Abernathy, W. (1980) 'Managing our way to economic decline', *Harvard Business Review,* July–August, pp.67-77.

Highbee, E. (1968) 'The technological revolution' in Chandler *et al.* (1968) pp.502–13.

Hounshell, D. (1984) *From the American System to Mass Production, 1800–1932,* Baltimore, Johns Hopkins University Press.

Jensen, M. (1998) 'Takeover controversy: analysis and evidence' in Stern, J. and Chew, D. (eds) *The Revolution in Corporate Finance,* 3rd edition, Oxford, Blackwell.

Kendrick, J. (1977) *Understanding Productivity*, Baltimore, Johns Hopkins University Press.

Krugman, P. (1994) 'Competitiveness: a dangerous obsession', *Foreign Affairs*, vol. 73, no. 2, pp.19–34

Lebergott, S. (1976) *The American Economy: Income, Wealth and Want*, Princeton, Princeton University Press.

Lester, R. (1994) *The Productive Edge: How US Industries are Pointing the Way to a New Era of Economic Growth*, New York, W.W. Norton.

Magaziner, I. and Reich, R. (1982) *Minding America's Business: the Decline and Rise of the American Economy*, New York/London, Harcourt Brace Jovanovich.

Nevins, A. and Hill, F. (1954) *Ford: the Times, the Man and the Company*, New York, Scribner and Company.

Nevins, A. and Hill, F. (1963) *Ford: Decline and Rebirth, 1933–2*, New York, Scribner and Company.

OEEC (1952) *Cost Accounting and Productivity in the U.S.A.*, Paris, OEEC.

Piore, M. and Sabel, C. (1984) *The Second Industrial Divide: Possibilities for Prosperity*, New York, Basic Books.

Ricketts, D. and Gray, J. (1988) *Managerial Accounting*, Boston, Houghton Mifflin.

Rosenberg, N. (1969) *The American System of Manufactures, 1855*, Edinburgh, Edinburgh University Press.

Sabel, C. and Zeitlin, J. (eds) (1997) *World of Possibilities: Flexibility and Mass Production*, Cambridge, Cambridge University Press.

Sawyer, J. (1954) 'The social basis of the American system of manufactures', *Journal of Economic History*, vol. 14, no. 4, pp.361–79.

Shaw, A. (1911) '"Scientific management" in business' in Chandler *et al.* (1968) pp.279–85.

Simonson, G. (1960) 'The demand for aircraft and the aircraft industry, 1907–1958', *Journal of Economic History*, vol. 20, no. 3, pp.361–82.

Sloan, A. (1967) *My Years with General Motors*, New York, Pan Piper.

Sobel, R. (1972) *The Age of Giant Corporations*, Westport, Conn., Greenwood Press.

Spulber, N. (1995) *American Economy: the Struggle for Supremacy in the Twenty-first Century*, Cambridge, Cambridge University Press.

Thompson, G. (1954) 'Intercompany technical standardization: the early American automobile industry', *Journal of Economic History*, vol. 14, no. 1.

Tomlinson, J. (1991) 'The failure of the Anglo-American Council on Productivity', *Business History*, vol. 33, pp.82–91.

United States Bureau of Commerce (various years) *Historical Statistics of the United States* and *Statistical Abstract of the United States*, Washington, United States Bureau of Commerce.

Usui, C. and Colignon, R. (1996) 'Corporate restructuring', *Sociological Quarterly*, vol. 37. no. 4, pp.551–78.

Williams, K., Cutler, T., Williams, J. and Haslam, C. (1987) 'The end of mass production?', *Economy and Society,* vol. 6, no. 3, pp.305–39.

Williams, K., Haslam, C., and Williams, J. (1986) 'Accounting for failure in the nationalised industries', *Economy and Society,* vol. 15, no. 2, pp.167–219.

Williams, K., Haslam, C. and Williams, J. (1992) 'Ford versus Fordism: the beginning of mass production', *Work, Employment and Society,* vol. 6, no. 4, pp.517–55.

Williams, K., Haslam, C. and Williams, J. (1993) 'The myth of the line: Ford's production of the Model T at Highland Park, 1909-16', *Business History,* vol. 35 no. 3, pp.66–7.

Williams, K., Haslem, C., Johal, S. and Williams, J. (1994) *Cars: Analysis, History, Cases*, Providence, Berghahn Books.

Williams, K., Williams, J. and Haslam, C. (1989) 'Do labour costs really matter?', *Work, Employment and Society,* vol. 35, no. 3, pp.282–305.

Williamson, H. (ed.) (1964) *The Growth of the American Economy,* Englewood Cliffs, N.J., Prentice Hall.

Womack, J., Jones, D., and Roos, D. (1990) *The Machine that Changed the World,* New York, Rawson Associates.

Womack, J. and Jones, D. (1996) *Lean Thinking: Banish Waste and Create Wealth,* New York, Simon & Schuster.

NEW ERA, NEW DEAL AND VICTORY:
the American Economy 1920–1945

Peter Fearon ★

1 THE US ECONOMY: 1920–1945

An analysis of the United States economy in this volatile period can be conveniently divided into four chronological sub periods. The 'prosperous' twenties, the Depression of 1929–1933 which saw Hoover ousted from the White House and replaced by Roosevelt, the New Deal years of 1933–1941 and, finally, the vigorous response of the economy to the demands of war. By 1945 the economy had been transformed partly by the New Deal and partly by the impact of war. Economic regulation was extensive and considered essential to peacetime stability. The adoption of Keynesian economics gave the state a new responsibility in economic management. The USA, by far the world's most powerful economy, had a crucial role to play in the new international economic order.

1.1 AMERICA AND PROSPERITY 1919–1929

The 1920s were a period of rapid economic expansion interrupted by one serious slump in 1920–1921 and two minor recessions in 1924 and in 1927. In spite of its inauspicious beginning the decade has been identified with prosperity. Relatively full employment, impressive productivity growth, stable prices, high levels of profit, a consumer durable and a construction boom were features of what was believed to be a 'new era' of capitalism. Visiting Europeans were impressed by American management techniques and cast envious eyes upon the large domestic market which was open to industry. The American model was seen by many as the only route to prosperity for Europe still struggling to recover from the effects of the First World War.

1.2 INDUSTRY IN THE DECADE OF PROSPERITY

In fact the annual rate of increase of real gross national product (GNP) during the 1920s was not as great as that which occurred between 1890 and 1910. Nevertheless, there were many reasons why the economic performance of the US economy at this time can be considered more than merely satisfactory. The two points which must be emphasized in any analysis of this era are firstly, consumer spending and secondly, the impact of the construction boom. More than 80 per cent of the rise in GNP during the twenties was dependent upon the flow of consumer goods (Figure 4.1). Vacuum cleaners, radios, electric irons, refrigerators and washing machines were avidly purchased, but the consumer durable which had the most dramatic effect on the rise in GNP was the automobile. The motor car exemplified twenties America. It was a triumph of mass production and standardization. Moreover, in an age of big business, output was dominated by two giant corporations: Ford and General Motors. The workers in the industry were highly paid and as they used purpose-built machinery in carefully planned factories, they were extremely productive. Automobiles, which in Europe could only be purchased by the better off, were so cheap that they were bought by factory workers and farming families, often on hire purchase terms. Rural families particularly welcomed the motor car as a release from the dreary isolation to which they were subjected. By the late twenties the industry used 85 per cent of the petrol consumed in the US, 83 per cent of the rubber and 60 per cent of the plate glass. Motor car ownership led to the growth of motels and petrol stations, it influenced residential construction and was instrumental in the rapid growth of both California and Florida (Flink, 1990).

European visitors were greatly impressed, not only by the auto industry but also by the USA's general manufacturing prowess; scarcely surprising since by the end of the decade US manufacturers accounted for 40 per cent of the world total. During the twenties US manufacturing output rose by 60 per cent, a figure which is doubly impressive if we remember that the manufacturing labour force was exactly the same size in 1929 as it had been in 1919. In other words, output per worker had increased considerably and it is worth analysing the reasons for this sharp rise in productivity.

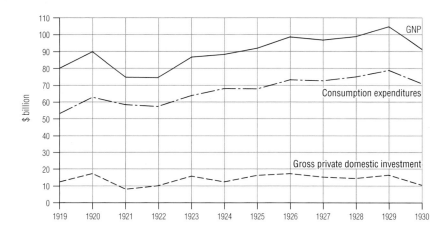

Figure 4.1 *Gross National Product and its components, 1919–1930 ($ billion – nominal figures)*

Source: J.A. Swanson and S.H. Williamson, 'Estimates of national product and income for the United States economy', *Explorations in Economic History*, 10 (1972–1973)

At the very core of our explanation is investment which provided workers with the most up-to-date equipment (Figure 4.1). But why was industry so enthusiastic to invest? In the first place incentives were strong since it was apparent that rewards, in the form of high profits, followed investment. Moreover, in an age of high profits, there were plenty of funds for investment. Where ploughed-back profits were insufficient, the banking sector and the stock market were more than willing to bridge the gap. This was an age of business optimism: expectations were high and confidence helps explain a willingness to invest.

Industry made use of the latest technology. Electricity for example was introduced into factories in order to power the newest tools. As old capital equipment was scrapped and replaced, there were massive efficiency gains. In addition, cost conscious management teams developed work study techniques which a largely compliant labour force accepted. Thus not only was high quality capital equipment purchased, but also a great deal of thought went into ensuring its most productive use (Fearon, 1987; Hawley, 1979).

We can, of course, link entrepreneurial optimism with buoyant consumer demand. This in turn was dependent upon full employment, and high wages, and was also influenced by advertising as potential consumers were made aware of the new products which were available. Much of the explanation for investment growth is circular: high profit leads to more confidence which leads to more investment which leads to higher profits. However, as we shall see in the thirties, an era of depression, it is by no means clear which of these variables can pull the others towards sustained growth.

It is important to note that the population as a whole benefited greatly from productivity growth. Price stability was one of the by-products of increasing efficiency and in spite of the vigorous boom there was no inflation. Many workers also gained through increased wages and by a reduction in the length of the working week. However, the improvements in productivity were great and the benefits passed on to consumers and to employees were relatively modest. It was the share holders and other owners who enjoyed the greatest advantage since the bulk of the productivity gains was distributed in the form of profits. In addition, the fact that a small proportion of the population were in receipt of such largesse helps to explain why the nation's income became more maldistributed (see for example Holt, 1977).

The second contributor to advancing prosperity was the construction industry which always exerts a powerful influence upon the economy. In 1926, at its peak, the value of new construction represented over 60 per cent of gross private domestic investment. The industry was also a major employer and absorber of raw materials. Until 1926 the driving force in the construction boom was residential building which then declined, but non-residential and public construction kept the aggregate level of activity high.

How can we explain the construction boom? The population was rising only modestly but the housing market was influenced by significant migration. This, however, merely tells us that there was a demand for housing and we need to know how that demand became effective. Stable costs, expanding incomes and public confidence interacted to convince potential home owners that they should take out mortgages. Smaller families led to a demand for more compact units; the wide-scale adoption of the automobile not only enabled substantial suburban development to take place, it also increased the demand for new roads. In addition, high profits enabled corporations to finance new offices and factories. The important link between consumer durable growth and the construction boom is the level of debt. People borrowed to buy motor cars and went further into debt to buy houses. This was not a problem when times were good but if economic circumstances worsened the high level of debt could become an intolerable burden.

It would be wrong to deduce from this account that all American industries were enjoying prosperity. Coal mining, for example, suffered severe contraction as alternative fuels became more attractive. Ship building, the railways and the cotton textile industry in New England all faced problems. We should also note that, in spite of our emphasis on manufacturing, public utilities and the service and financial sectors played a significant role in increasing the nation's wealth. Four million new entrants to the labour force found employment outside manufacturing in the 1920s. The fact that so many jobs were created as public service, domestic service and financial services expanded, ensured that there was no unemployment crisis. This was particularly important as there was no corresponding employment growth in agriculture, mining or manufacturing.

1.3 THE GOVERNMENT AND THE ECONOMY

This age of distinctive American capitalism owed little to Presidents Harding and Coolidge neither of whom, in terms of intellect or application, were out of the top drawer. The 'new era' was, however, exemplified by Herbert Hoover, who served as Secretary of Commerce until he assumed the Presidency in 1929. Hoover believed that the state should play an active role in eliminating the waste caused by economic fluctuations. An assiduous collector and disseminator of information, Hoover believed that full knowledge would enable businessmen to take policy decisions which would minimize the impact of recessions. The economy could be managed if more was known about it.

Hoover, and his acolytes, saw class and industrial conflict as a waste which the USA had eliminated but Europe could not. Social harmony in the USA was helped by high wages, which they recognized could prove to be a competitive handicap. In order to contain competition from cheap foreign labour, immigration controls were introduced and tariff protection increased. High wages which had previously been viewed as a cause of unemployment were now seen as essential to the 'new era'. European business leaders envied greatly the industrial peace and full employment which their American counterparts accepted as normal (Table 4.1). This was not, however, a time of governmental *laissez faire* at home or, as we shall see, abroad (Barber, 1985).

Table 4.1   The labour force and unemployment, 1920–1930 (in thousands, persons 14 years old and over)

Year	Civilian labour force	Unemployed		
		Total	% of civilian labour force	% of non-farm employees
1920	41,340	2,132	5.2	8.6
1921	41,979	4,918	11.7	19.5
1922	42,496	2,859	6.7	11.4
1923	43,444	1,049	2.4	4.1
1924	44,235	2,190	5.0	8.3
1925	45,196	1,453	3.2	5.4
1926	45,629	801	1.8	2.9
1927	46,375	1,519	3.3	5.4
1928	47,757	1,982	4.2	6.9
1929	47,757	1,550	3.2	5.3
1930	48,523	4,340	8.9	14.2

Source: *Historical Statistics cf US, Colonial Times to 1970*, 2 vols (Washington DC, 1975) Series D4, 8–10

The twenties was an era of budget surpluses and the principle aim of fiscal policy was to reduce the tax burden and to reduce the level of public debt. The substantial reduction in tax rates for the wealthy which were introduced became identified with national prosperity, with the benefits given to the rich supposedly trickling down to the less fortunate below. It seems far more likely, however, that the strength of the economy permitted Treasury Secretary, Andrew Mellon, to reduce taxes rather than vice-versa.

This decade saw a growing belief in monetary policy as a means of controlling booms and slumps. During the recessions of 1924 and 1927 liberal credit policies were employed and these downturns were brief. As a result, many economists drew the conclusion that the Federal Reserve, by manipulating interest rates and by varying the volume of credit, could be a powerful stabilizing force. (See Friedman and Schwartz, 1963; and Wicker, 1966 for two contrasting views.) The Federal Reserve's interests, however, were not merely domestic. Anxious to ensure that European countries stabilized their currencies and re-adopted the gold standard, American interest rates were kept low between 1924 and 1928. The differential between US interest rates and those overseas encouraged the growth of foreign investment and gave borrowers dollars which could be used to buy American goods.

1.4   AGRICULTURE

The large US farm population decreased both absolutely and relatively during the twenties. High non-agricultural incomes encouraged migration and rural America lost six million people who moved to urban areas defined in the census as any settlement of more than 2,500 people. Rural dwellers included not only virtually all farmers but also the residents of small towns and villages which provided services for the farming community. In 1920 the urban population, at 51 per cent of the total, was greater than the rural for the first time. By 1930 the farm dwellers were 25 per cent of the total population, a decline of 5 per cent during the decade.

American agriculture is very diverse with a wide variety of different soil types, weather systems and an enormous range of crops are grown. In the 1920s, many farms were so small, or poorly managed, that they could not support the family which occupied them. There was a big difference between the profitable, efficiently run, often highly mechanized market-oriented enterprises and the small tracts of infertile land which were cultivated by illiterate operators.

During the twenties many farmers complained bitterly about their lot and used the 'parity-ratio' to support their arguments. The 'parity-ratio' is an index of the relationship between two price indices: the prices which the farmers received for agricultural commodities and the average price of goods which farmers purchased (see Figure 4.2). The prices-received index is divided by the price paid index and the result multiplied by 100. This relationship, which was favourable to farmers before 1920, was adversely affected by the slump which began in that year. Farm prices fell more steeply than non-agricultural prices, but even when price stability was achieved, farmers found that a new and unfavourable relationship had been established. Moreover, the parity-ratio remained persistently below its base (1910–1914 = 100) which the farm community considered normality (Fearon, 1987). Farm pressure groups attached a great deal of importance to the parity-ratio mainly because it was a readily available calculation which they believed quantified their difficulties in a clear manner.

It would be unwise to rely solely upon the parity-ratio in an analysis of farm fortunes. Some operators, for example truck farmers, were able to capitalize upon the dietary changes which were evident amongst city dwellers during the twenties. Other statistical series show that the average farmer did not endure a life of unremitting misery in this decade. For example, the farm community as a whole saw their per capita income rise twice as fast as that of the non-farm population between 1921 and 1929 and farmers were avid purchasers of automobiles and expensive machinery. Yet farm pressure groups agitated constantly for governmental help to raise the price of basic crops.

The reason why so many of the nation's farmers were discontented has little to do with the prices of agricultural commodities in the twenties. The problem was that many farmers had gone into debt in the good years before 1920 and had even increased their debts when faced with the great hardship of collapsing prices. Mortgages had been taken out on the assumption that land prices would remain buoyant, but the value of farm property declined sharply between 1920–1922 and fell steadily for the rest of the decade. The expectations of dear land had not been realized, yet debts still had to be paid and living standards, consequently, declined. The discontented farmers were, therefore, victims of their own optimism (Johnson, 1973).

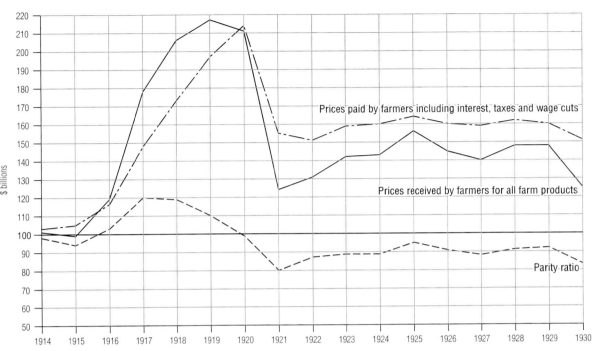

Figure 4.2 *Indices of prices received and paid by farmers and the parity ratio, 1914–1930 (1910–1914=100)*

Source: *Historical Statistics of US, Colonial Times to 1957*, (Washington DC, 1961)
Series K129, 137, 138

1.5   OVERSEAS TRADE AND CAPITAL FLOWS

During the 1920s the USA was, measured by value, the world's leading exporter and was second only to Britain as an importer. American purchases of imports, usually raw materials or semi-manufactures, were an important source of dollars for many countries. However, in spite of having a healthy balance of payments surplus and possessing a large gold stock, Congress passed the Fordney-McCumber Act in 1922 raising US tariffs. This was an act of particular insularity and illustrates a failure to recognize the difficulties which countries trying to discharge their debts to the USA, the world's major creditor nation, would face. It was, however, motivated by the fear that goods produced by cheap foreign labour might pose a threat to domestic economic stability.

Where the US government did not intervene, private citizens with state approval did. For example, the intervention of US bankers was instrumental in stabilizing the German mark after one of the most dramatic inflations of all time. The Dawes Plan (1924) seemed to put a stamp of approval on the German economy and soon American citizens were investing heavily in that country. Canada, Italy and several Latin American states also received a flood of US money (Costigliola, 1984).

The advantage for the recipient was that more goods and services could be purchased than would have been possible if countries had been forced to rely upon the earning powers of their own economies. The US investor was tempted by the possibility of a higher return than would have been possible if the money had been invested at home. Unfortunately both lenders and borrowers became less risk averse as the decade progressed. Many borrowers reached a position where servicing the debt would have been difficult if economic circumstances radically changed. The danger was that they had become dependent upon flows of US capital and would be unable to make a smooth adjustment if that flow dried up.

SUMMARY

To virtually all contemporary observers the US economy seemed exceptionally strong and vigorous during the twenties. With the benefit of hindsight, however, we can understand why those who saw this as a 'new era' should have been more cautious. The growth in manufacturing industry was heavily dependent upon producer and consumer durables both of which are prone to sharp cyclical fluctuations. Residential construction had peaked in 1926 and had fallen considerably by 1929. The distribution of income had become progressively less egalitarian thus thrusting upon a small number of very wealthy, the responsibility for continuing the consumer boom. Finally, the level of speculation was becoming disturbing as the Wall Street stock market and overseas lending both demonstrated a popular gambling spirit. There is no doubt that businessmen, investors and many members of the public were extremely optimistic about the future of the economy. However, the day of reckoning was not far away.

We can also note the emergence of a new economic philosophy. Hooverites were anxious to promote the role of the state which they saw as a guarantor of stability. Government would provide accurate information to industry so that more rational business decisions would be taken. Indeed the government at home had an active role as a regulator and as an organizer. It also had a role abroad as export growth was seen as vital for national prosperity and where interventions, such as the *Dawes Plan*, can be seen as part of a drive for international stability from which the US would benefit (Barber, 1985).

2 THE GREAT DEPRESSION: 1929–1933

In the middle of 1929 the economy seemed sound. Manufacturing activity was at a high level yet there was no pressure on either prices or wages. The optimism of investors was reflected in the booming stock market on Wall Street. There were no indications of the dramatic collapse which was soon to devastate the economy.

From the summer of 1929 to the spring of 1933, however, wholesale prices fell by 38 per cent, unemployment rose to 25 per cent and investment declined by over 90 per cent (see Tables 4.2 and 4.3; and Figures 4.3 and 4.4). Three waves of bank failures had such a devastating effect upon the financial sector that when Roosevelt took the oath of office in March 1933, the governors of the vast majority of the states had closed their banks. The fall in agricultural income was so acute that many farmers endured the hardship of foreclosure. America was engulfed in a depression which left few parts of the economy unscathed.

One of the characteristics of the Depression was a massive decline in manufacturing output and consumer durables was the sector most affected. The construction industry was also hit as the demand for new housing slumped dramatically. It is easy to see why consumers became hesitant. In order to purchase a motor car or housing, a purchaser had to go into debt. Few were willing to risk the burden of additional debt as the prospect of unemployment loomed. Moreover, the decision not to buy could be made easily. The existing stock of motor cars and other consumer durables was kept running longer than in the decade of prosperity. The prospect of taking out a new mortgage was so daunting that selling houses was a near impossibility especially as house prices were falling steeply.

Consumer durables and housing had been at the very core of the economic expansion of the 1920s. Now thousands of workers were laid off and purchases of raw materials kept to the minimum. The unemployed and those fearful of losing their jobs, minimized expenditure. Even workers who were classified as employed had their income reduced as wage cuts were imposed, as was short time working. In sharp contrast with the 1920s, company profits were slashed to such an extent that, in aggregate, profits were negative in both 1931 and 1932. Bankruptcies soared and the change in financial circumstances made some companies fearful of borrowing while others were deemed no longer credit worthy. Little wonder that investment fell to such a low point.

A further disturbing feature was the high failure rate of financial institutions. Particularly disturbing was the inability of the commercial banking sector to withstand the strains of the economic collapse. Depositors lost confidence in banks and withdrew their savings, not to deposit them in another institution because the fear of failure was widespread, but to hold their wealth in cash. The effect on the banking system was to force panic-stricken managers to recall most of their outstanding loans and to refuse requests for new borrowing. The failure of so many banks left small towns with no banking services and many depositors with savings trapped in a failed institution.

There was a massive fall in agricultural prices after 1929. Cotton which sold for 17 cents per pound in 1929 fetched less than 6 cents per pound in 1931; wheat fell from $1.00 per bushel in 1929 to 29 cents in 1932. These were not isolated examples. As the price of farm products fell more steeply than the prices of the goods which farmers bought, the parity-ratio also declined steeply (Table 4.2). As is usual in such depressions, the volume of manufacturing output declined but farm output remained virtually the same, leading to the growth of stocks which put an additional downward pressure on prices. Indeed, the natural reaction of farmers to low prices was to plant more which led, ultimately, to even lower prices as harvests were good.

Table 4.2   The parity ratio, 1928–1932 (1910–1914=100)

Year	Prices received by farmers	Prices paid by farmers	Parity ratio
1928	148	162	91
1929	148	160	92
1930	125	151	83
1931	87	130	67
1932	65	112	58
1933	70	109	64

Source: *Historical Statistics of US, Colonial Times to 1970*, 2 vols (Washington DC, 1975) Series K129, 137, 138

Farm families cut their consumption which contributed to the growth of urban unemployment. Farmers could not pay their debts and therefore made the downfall of small town banks which serviced rural communities inevitable. A depression of one year was tolerable, but as the slide continued an increasing number of farms were foreclosed by mortgage companies. Foreclosure sales were viewed with great bitterness by the farm community, and as they were often resisted by force a number of states introduced legislation to prohibit them. In spite of the distress in the countryside the number of farms actually increased during the worst years of the depression. This 'back to the land' movement gives us some indication of the plight of the urban poor. Subsistence on previously abandoned land was preferable to meagre relief in the cities (Fearon, 1987).

Table 4.3   Unemployment, 1929–1933 (in thousands)

Year	Total	Percentage of	
		Civilian labour force	Non-farm employees
1929	1,550	3.2	5.4
1930	4,340	8.9	14.2
1931	8,020	16.3	25.2
1932	12,060	24.1	36.3
1933	12,830	25.2	37.6

Source: *Historical Statistics of US, Colonial Times to 1970*, 2 vols (Washington DC, 1975) Series D8–10

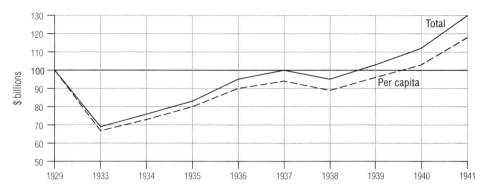

Figure 4.3   *Index of real Gross National Product (in constant $)*

Source: Calculated from *Historical Statistics of US, Colonial Times to 1970*, 2 vols (Washington DC, 1975)

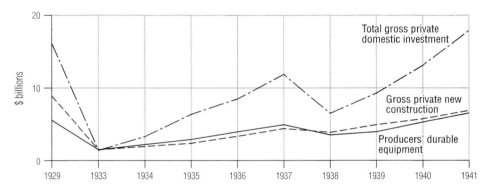

Figure 4.4   *Gross private domestic investment, 1929–1941 ($b.)*

Source: J.A. Swanson and J.H. Williamson, 'Estimates of national product and income for the United States economy', *Explorations in Economic History*, 10 (1972–3), Table A-2

2.1   AN EXPLANATION

Any analysis of the depression must address two questions. The first is: Why did things begin to go wrong in 1929? The second, and much more important, is: Why once begun was this crisis so deep and long lasting? What made 1929–1933 unique was the depth and the unremitting character of the downturn. Our analysis would be straightforward if there was widespread agreement amongst scholars but even after more than half a century of debate there is still a vigorous and continuing disagreement between monetarists and non-monetarists.

The monetarists, explain the onset of the depression by pointing to movements in the stock of money. Mounting speculation on the Stock Exchange worried the Federal Reserve (Fed). A stock market crash, it was believed, would destabilize the economy so, in 1928, the Fed introduced a tighter monetary policy in order to curb speculation. Their reasoning was that higher interest rates would make borrowing for speculation gradually more expensive and therefore less attractive. This new monetary stance had unfortunate and unexpected results. As speculators could borrow at high rates of interest and still make a profit, lenders now offered them even more money. Funds that previously had gone overseas went to the market as did the balances of profitable companies. There were international repercussions as nations dependent upon US capital had to raise their interest rates in a vain attempt to attract it. Monetary stringency became a world wide phenomenon and, inevitably, the demand for US exports declined.

The Fed's policies led to a slowing down in the rate of monetary growth which may well have restricted consumption, thus bringing to a halt the rapid expansion of the late twenties. Monetarists believe that misguided monetary policies were responsible for the decline in economic fortunes which began in the summer of 1929 (see for example Friedman and Schwartz, 1963).

Non-monetarists, however, believe other factors were the cause of the Depression. They note, for example, the importance of consumer durables and housing to the economic expansion of the 1920s. The demand for consumer durables, however, is notoriously volatile and their rapid expansion, on which economic buoyancy in the late 1920s was so dependent, could not possibly be sustained. A contraction could be expected because of an approaching saturation of the market. The same argument can be advanced for the housing sector which had, in fact, been in decline for several years. Thus two key sectors in the economy had reached their peak and were set for decline. A further strain came from the growing maldistribution of income which meant that the broadly-based demand on which the economy depended could not be maintained. Moreover, consumer confidence was badly affected by the collapse of the stock market in October 1929 then by rising unemployment and falling prices which made additional debt more expensive in real terms.

What we see is an economy which although seemingly strong had, by the end of the decade, become riddled with weaknesses. Automobiles and the housing sector were poised at a crucial point in their development and the restrictive monetary policy tilted the balance in favour of recession. When consumer confidence was replaced by uncertainty the decline became more pronounced (Kindleberger, 1973).

But why did the slide continue? Why did the economy not just experience a brief recession as had happened in 1924 and 1927? Once begun the economic decline was disturbing but in late 1931 the depression changed character. From that point the slide became alarming. It is easy to see that with mounting unemployment, short time working and pay cuts, demand was significantly reduced. Consumer confidence was severely shaken and most people could not be persuaded to go into debt to purchase motor cars or houses. There was a massive decline in investment; indeed business had little incentive to invest. The expectation of future profits was negative; this became an age of business retrenchment. Farm families also cut expenditure and kept their purchases of manufactured goods to a minimum. Thus communities in

Iowa burned surplus corn as fuel in the winter of 1931–1932 while in coal mining districts hunger was widespread as the demand for coal had sunk to such a low level that few miners were employed.

All this is quite straightforward and understandable. Another dimension is added by monetarists who claim that the most significant statistic of the Depression is that the stock of money declined by one-third between 1929 and 1933, a catastrophic reduction. The severity of the Depression, they claim, can be explained by an economy making a painful adjustment to the new, lower, money stock.

Why did the money stock decline? The culprit was the Federal Reserve which, by implementing a tight money policy, brought about a collapse in the banking system. Instead of pursuing liberal discounting and helping the distressed banks, policy moved in the opposite direction. But why should rational and experienced bankers have behaved in this manner?

The problem arose when the Fed reacted to speculative pressure against the dollar. After Britain left the gold standard and devalued sterling in September 1931 the dollar came under attack. In order to defend it, interest rates were raised. During the period between Roosevelt's election victory in November 1932 and his inauguration in March 1933, the dollar again became the target of speculators as rumours of devaluation persisted. Again the Fed moved to defend the currency, as the rules of the gold standard dictated, by raising interest rates. The problem was that while the actions of the Fed were a correct way to defend the dollar this action was extremely damaging to a commercial banking system which, by the middle of 1931, was under considerable strain. Distressed banks needed an easy money policy to help them weather the storm but Fed policy was, at crucial times, tight. As a result, bank failures increased and by the spring of 1933 the bank system had practically ceased to operate.

As banks failed, fearful depositors withdrew their savings from the other banks making them even more likely to fail. Such was the loss of faith that many people removed their savings from the banking system altogether. People felt that their money was safer at home than it was in a bank. Thus the banks which we normally associate with creating money were forced into contracting the money stock.

There is no doubt that the misguided actions of the Fed made the Depression worse but monetary factors do not explain all the reasons for the collapse. A combination of monetary and non-monetary forces confronted American citizens and policy makers with the most serious economic problems ever. Economists, businessmen and politicians were confused, alarmed and even fearful. Ideas were plentiful but solutions scarce (Chandler, 1970; Fearon, 1987; Temin, 1989).

2.2   HOOVER AND THE DEPRESSION

President Hoover was not inactive during these troubled years. He constantly urged the business sector not to cut wages and met frequently with bankers and industrialists in an attempt to boost their confidence. He signed into law the Hawley-Smoot Tariff Act which raised US tariffs but unfortunately this hindered recovery rather than helped it by the retaliation which it encouraged. For a while cotton and wheat prices were supported by federal agencies but there was insufficient funding to continue these operations for more than a short while. When support was withdrawn, prices collapsed sharply.

A new agency, the Reconstruction Finance Corporation, was created in 1932. It lent money to troubled banks, transport enterprises and to individual states but was cumbersome in its operations and, most significantly, was established too late to have the maximum impact. Unfortunately the President had little scope for direct action as the federal government was so small. Federal expenditure was only 2.5 per cent of GNP in 1929. Central government spending did increase but only by a minute sum in comparison to the collapse in private investment. Fearful of a large budget deficit, Hoover decided to raise taxes in late 1931. This was a sharply deflationary move and in contrast with the 1920s view that tax cuts were associated with economic advance. The reason for this damaging policy, however, was to give the correct orthodox message to speculators against the dollar. With a deflationary fiscal policy and a tight monetary policy operating together, it is little wonder that the economy collapsed so dramatically (Fearon, 1993; Stein, 1969).

SUMMARY

Hoover cannot be blamed for the Depression. Economic information and advice were poor; there was little that any president could do other than to rely upon exhortation. Even the damaging monetary and fiscal policies had a logic: support for a currency under attack. By 1932, however, the population was desperate. Increasing parallels were drawn between the Depression and the First World War. During the war the economy had not been left to its own devices but had been organized, even managed, by Washington. Government intervention seemed to have worked in the national crisis of war, so why, it was argued, should the same approach not be used in an economic crisis?

3 ROOSEVELT AND THE NEW DEAL, 1933–1941

In 1933 the American economy presented a sorry picture. Agriculture, industry and the financial sector had reeled under the force of heavy blows: morale was at an extraordinarily low level. The nation cried out for leadership; there was a desperate need for someone who could rapidly restore confidence so that the much needed sustained economic recovery could begin.

Business wanted an end to the debilitating deflation and a restoration of profits. Many industrialists identified excessive competition as a destabilizing evil and saw planning as a means of restoring order to markets. What sort of planning and who should implement it was, however, a matter of debate. Spokesmen for commercial farmers had also become converts to planning and they even advocated controls to curb output. It should be remembered that several business and farm organizations were very powerful pressure groups with a great deal of experience in dealing with government.

The new President presented himself to the electorate as a man who believed in sound finance and orthodox economics. He expressed a profound distaste for budget deficits but supported moderate inflation and some sort of planning. Roosevelt was vague in his election addresses for good reason: his policies were at a very early stage of formulation. The gap between his election victory in November 1932 and his inaugural address in March 1933 was a period of frantic activity as he and his advisers crafted the policy ideas which would be laid before Congress.

In the public mind, Franklin D. Roosevelt (FDR) is identified with the New Deal which began immediately on his assumption of the Presidency and was cut short by America's entry into the Second World War in 1941. The New Deal, however, was not a planned and coherent economic strategy. It was a complex mixture which can more properly be viewed as an exercise in politics rather than economics.[1] What was required, in the depths of depression, was a vigorous and expansionary macro-economic policy to boost aggregate demand. The high levels of public expenditure required to kick start the economy, however, would have necessitated large budget deficits which both business and the public would have found alarming and economists would have been unable to justify. Roosevelt did not believe that America could spend its way out of depression, a belief shared by practically all economists and political pundits. Unfortunately, no other strategy would attack the problem so directly and once measures to raise aggregate demand rapidly were discounted, the prospects of sustained recovery receded.

Partly because recovery was so elusive Roosevelt's policies changed to such an extent that some commentators see two or even three New Deals. The President periodically jettisoned initiatives which proved ineffective but also felt obliged to heed Supreme Court decisions, respond to powerful pressure groups, reflect the views of new advisers and to meet fresh challenges. Roosevelt's admirers see the New Deal as flexible and pragmatic; his foes criticize policies which they believe were motivated solely by opportunism.

The first New Deal placed an emphasis upon structural reform, brought about by central planning. Monopolistic agreements were encouraged and business saw these as necessary for halting deflation and restoring profitability. For a while the White House and the business community seemed united in their vision of how recovery could be accomplished. Within a few years, however, disillusionment set in and a new emphasis emerged to dominate Presidential thinking.

[1] There are a number of excellent monographs on the New Deal. Amongst the best are: Anthony J. Badger (1989) *The New Deal. The Depression Years 1933–1940*, Macmillan; and A. Romasco (1983) *The Politics of Recovery: Roosevelt's New Deal*, Oxford University Press.

In 1935 the New Deal stressed a more competitive, anti-monopolist economy in which the vulnerable would be protected through the promotion of trades unions and new welfare provision. Relations with business deteriorated and employers' organizations made frequent and bitter attacks on many aspects of Roosevelt's policies. The 1937–1938 recession was a great shock to the administration and Roosevelt's response was to embark upon a third initiative: a drive against monopoly capitalism and an acceptance that budget deficits would play a positive role in economic recovery. Keynes had provided the intellectual justification for deficit financing and his analysis had been absorbed by young American economists who found the President receptive to their new ideas. Roosevelt had no understanding of economics but Keynesian ideas offered him a life line. The financing of the New Deal could continue and the ensuing budget deficits be defended as contributing to recovery.

Roosevelt was a politician of consummate skill. His New Deal gyrations can be seen as a response to the complexities of political life. The electorate supported his policies. He was re-elected in 1936, in 1940 and again in 1944 by which time as he himself said, Dr New Deal had been replaced by Dr Win the War.

We will now analyse the complexities of the New Deal under the headings of agriculture, industry, and monetary and fiscal policy.

3.1   AGRICULTURE AND THE NEW DEAL

Farmers faced serious problems in 1933 which required immediate redress. The Roosevelt administration placed a great deal of emphasis upon the farm sector. Not only did the large rural population represent voting power, it was felt that agriculture had a significant role to play in the general economic recovery. As farm prices had fallen furthest it was felt they would revive rapidly and newly enriched consumers would pull the rest of the economy from its trough. This was a clear overestimate of the economic power of agriculture, but one which enjoyed much support amongst New Dealers.

The policy aim was to enable farmers to reach 100 per cent parity by persuading them to cut output and also by restoring order to rural credit markets. The Agricultural Adjustment Act (AAA, 1933) enticed farmers to reduce the acreage which they devoted to certain basic crops. Participants in this voluntary scheme were compensated by cash payments. Many had experienced such poverty over the preceding few years that the prospect of receiving cash was too tempting to resist. The attack on farm surpluses, therefore, involved no compulsion or production targets.

In addition, the Emergency Farm Mortgage Act made possible the refinancing of mortgages and the Farm Credit Act enabled the provision of cheap credit. The creation of the Commodity Credit Corporation (CCC) was another initiative to help farmers. It enabled producers to keep commodities off the market in anticipation of higher prices by loans to those who were prepared to store them on their farm. The farmer borrowed using his crop as collateral. If the price rose, the farmer could repay the loan and recover his crop. If it did not, he could refuse to pay and surrender his crop to the CCC. The loan rate constituted a minimum crop price and as a result farmers' risks were considerably reduced especially as those who defaulted were still eligible for loans during the next season. Although introduced as a temporary measure, the CCC remains even to this day a vital part of the price support given to American farmers.

In 1936 the Supreme Court invalidated the AAA (1933) and the Administration responded with new legislation: the Soil Conservation and Domestic Allotment Act (SCDAA, 1936). The atmosphere of crisis evident in 1933 had receded and was replaced by concern over serious drought and dust storms. The SCDAA sought to control both surpluses and soil erosion. During 1937, however, the rains returned and so did the problem of agricultural surpluses. A new attempt, therefore, was made to stabilize farm prices. The second Agricultural Adjustment Act (AAA, 1938) tried to ensure a managed surplus — or 'ever normal granary' — which would protect the farmer against low prices and the consumer from excessive price increases. The AAA (1938) was in operation for only a short while before the war in Europe began to exert an influence upon US farm prices.

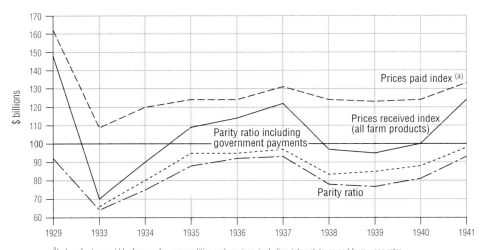

[a] Index of prices paid by farmers for commodities and services, including interest, taxes and farm wage rates.

Figure 4.5   *The parity ratio, 1933–1941 (1910–1914=100)*

Sources: *Historical Statistics of US, Colonial Times* to 1970, 2 vols (Washington DC, 1975); H.D. Guither, *Heritage of Plenty* (1972), p.174

How can we evaluate New Deal farm policy? We should not underestimate the difficulties faced by the New Dealers themselves. Millions of farms of different sizes growing a wide variety of crops had to be accommodated in any legislation. Moreover, any schemes had to have the support of farm pressure groups which represented the large commercial operators. Radical initiatives involving state direction were not an option, hence the voluntary nature of farm policy.

The stated aim was to achieve 100 per cent parity, but Figure 4.5 shows that this proved elusive. Two additional factors illustrated by this figure require comment. Firstly, if government payments are included in the parity ratio then the recovery to 1937 was impressive. However, the recession of 1937–1938 had a serious effect and the prospect of 100 per cent parity disappeared. Secondly, the prices received for all farm products rose steeply from a 1933 trough. To what extent did the acreage limitation schemes bring about price increases? Unfortunately, the acreage reduction schemes to control output were a failure. For those who participated there was a short term reduction but soon these farmers improved their efficiency and were able to grow more on their reduced acreage than they had originally. Those who did not participate could respond to improving prices by increasing both acreage and productivity. Indeed in 1937 aggregate farm output had exceeded 1933 levels, a position which remained unchanged until the decade ended.

Another encouragement to increased output was the CCC which set a floor on the price of several commodities. Where output was held in check, especially in 1934 and 1936, it was the severe droughts of those years which were responsible not New Deal policy. Farmers did, however, benefit from many New Deal initiatives but the benefits were heavily skewed towards owners rather than tenants and to large operators rather than small. What many of the desperately poor on the land required was the creation of large numbers of non-farm jobs to which they could migrate. It was the Second World War rather than the New Deal which provided this means of escape.

Roosevelt did manage to boost farm morale and to make significant moves towards an effective farm policy. Increasing farm fortunes helped general recovery as those on the land are producers as well as consumers. It is not possible, however, to envisage the farm sector leading the way to general recovery and the President and his advisers were wrong to believe that it was possible (Badger, 1989).

3.2   THE INDUSTRIAL STRATEGY

Planning was also seen as a means of attacking the American industrial malaise. Though there was widespread agreement that some sort of regulation was required to check the excesses of the free market, there were marked differences between industry and labour as to what form it should take. Inevitably these disagreements resulted in legislation which strove for compromise. The aim was clear: business confidence should be raised and so should wages. As sales and profits rose many new jobs would be created and the vicious circle of depression would be transformed into a virtuous upward spiral of hope.

The National Industrial Recovery Act (NIRA, 1933) was introduced to Congress in two parts. The first set up the National Recovery Administration

(NRA) which encouraged the creation of committees representing management, labour and consumers to draw up codes of fair competition for each industry. The watchword of the NRA was 'fair'. Competition was to be subject to regulation but not destroyed. Employees too were given a 'fair' charter which included minimum wages, maximum hours and the right to collective bargaining. The spirit of co-operation soon evaporated. The committees were seen as a bureaucratic nightmare, especially by small business. Big business, on the other hand, was well organized and able to exert a disproportionate influence when the committees met. Nevertheless, when recovery took place those companies, including large ones, who felt that they could benefit more from a relatively favourable economic climate were anxious to shed the restrictions of the NRA. The economic recovery, unlike that which immediately followed the depression of 1920–1921, was not vigorous; had it been, the NRA might have retained more supporters.

In May 1935 the Supreme Court struck down the NRA and in so doing the justices did what the President would soon have been forced to do. Few commentators have a good word to say on the economic impact of this legislation which was neither an exercise in planning nor a systematic attempt at recovery. Instead the NRA sponsored a large number of monopolistic agreements. Prices rose and so did wages but the rate of job creation was very disappointing. Indeed, in a low wage region such as the South, the imposition of minimum wages may well have priced a considerable number of workers out of jobs (Wright, 1986). For the employed the wage rises were a welcome bonus; the unemployed, however, did not gain from the NRA.

The second part of the NRA was the Public Works Administration (PWA) which attacked unemployment through the construction of public works such as dams and bridges. Though much was accomplished by the PWA up to the outbreak of the Second World War, it moved too slowly to make a rapid impact upon the unemployment figures. When urgency was needed the PWA gave America caution.

By 1935 the era of co-operation between business and the New Dealers was coming to an end. When the AAA was declared unconstitutional new legislation was quickly introduced but no attempt was made to replace the NRA. Business attacks on the New Deal became more hostile and the President rose to the challenge denouncing the corporations as 'economic royalists'. Legislation was introduced to make it easier for trade unions to win battles against well organized business. The President's attacks on big business and the evils of monopoly price fixing became even more pronounced after the 1937–1938 recession as he desperately tried to pin the blame in this sudden downturn on his enemies. Amongst the people who most looked to Roosevelt for help were the unemployed. Unfortunately the proportion of the labour force who failed to secure jobs remained high throughout the New Deal era.

Table 4.4 Employment and unemployment, 1929–1941

| Year | Civilian labour force | In employment | | | Unemployed |
		Total (millions)	Farm (millions)	Non-farm (millions)	(%)
1929	47.7	46.2	10.5	35.7	3.2
1933	50.9	38.0	10.0	28.0	25.2
1934	51.7	40.3	10.0	30.3	22.0
1935	52.3	41.7	10.1	31.6	20.3
1936	53.0	44.0	10.1	33.9	17.0
1937	53.8	46.1	10.0	36.1	14.3
1938	54.5	44.1	9.8	34.3	19.1
1939	55.2	45.7	9.7	36.0	17.2
1940	55.6	47.5	9.5	38.0	14.6
1941	55.9	50.4	9.1	41.3	9.9

Source: Cols 1–5: *Historical Statistics of US, Colonial Times to 1970*, 2 vols (Washington DC, 1975), Series D4, 6, 7, 9

As Table 4.4 shows, even in 1937 the unemployment rate was 14.3 per cent and not until 1941 did it fall below 10 per cent. These figures also show the savage impact of the 1937–1938 recession. In their defence, New Dealers could point out that one of the problems that they faced was a rise in the size of the labour force. Looking at the 1937 situation from a different viewpoint, there were as many Americans employed as there had been in 1929 when the unemployment rate had been a mere 3.2 per cent. The economy needed to create millions of additional jobs to reduce jobless totals to the levels which had been commonplace during the 1920s. Since this was not done an additional burden was thrust upon the relief services.

The key to the elimination of unemployment lay in the New Deal's failure to generate a vigorous revival in private investment (Figure 4.4). Construction remained a depressed sector but even if we consider producers' durables, the 1929 figure was not reached until 1941. Why was business so reluctant to undertake long-term investment? Industrialists would have been quick to accuse the New Deal of undermining confidence. Although the inconsistency of federal policy and the antagonism which was evident in exchanges between the White House and industry cannot have helped to create a stable atmosphere, this line of argument is much too simple.

In the first place the New Deal's anti monopoly stance was more noise than substance. It was recognition of the fact that the American public liked to support the 'little man' but also wanted cheap consumer goods which only the large corporations could provide (Hawley, 1966). The failure of investment to revive owes a lot to the shock of the depression, to the high levels of investment which had taken place in the twenties, and to the destabilizing effects of the 1937–1938 downturn (Figure 4.3).

To be industrially successful the New Deal should have introduced policies which increased aggregate demand to the point where full employment was achieved. Instead of using macro-economics they believed that the problems faced by the American economy were primarily structural and were best remedied by policies such as maximum hours, minimum wages and either monopoly or competition. A concentration upon micro-economic policy is, however, understandable given the state of economic theory throughout much of the 1930s. The use of a large budget deficit to generate a sharp increase in aggregate demand was not a course of action that could be defended until the late 1930s (Fearon, 1993, pp.138–43).[2]

3.3   MONETARY AND FISCAL POLICY

Roosevelt wanted to restore the price level to what it was before the depression began because he believed that rising prices would help recovery. A cautious man, however, he preferred to describe himself as a reflationist rather than an inflationist. Early in the New Deal the government embarked upon a misconceived strategy of gold and silver purchases which, it was believed, would raise prices. The experiment was a failure.

One of the most positive actions of FDR's Presidency was the restoration of stability in the banking system. Confidence in financial institutions returned and the number of failures dwindled. However, this was an era of passive monetary policy except for one crucial intervention by the Federal Reserve. Foreigners looked upon the USA as a safe haven for their gold and, as it poured in, bank reserves rose to higher levels than legally necessary for backing deposits. Fearing a credit boom, the Fed altered reserve requirements ushering in a period of tighter credit which coincided with fiscal stringency. The result was the disastrous collapse of 1937–1938, a serious self-inflicted wound. The fear of releasing the forces of uncontrolled inflation meant that even at the end of the decade prices had not returned to their 1929 levels.

Fiscal policy was dominated by Roosevelt's dislike of budget deficits. Although federal spending did increase after 1933 so did taxes. Spending was not directed towards general recovery, it was determined by what was necessary to finance the New Deal. Unfortunately, after the 1936 election the President, stung by criticisms of persistent budget deficits, cut expenditure. Federal spending recovered in 1938 and 1939 as the administration struggled to bring about recovery from the Depression which they had helped to bring about. However, at no time can we say that New Deal fiscal policy was Keynesian. The increase in public spending was better than none at all but its net effect was far too small to stimulate recovery. Expenditure on that scale was not far away. The Second World War blew away all inhibitions about deficits.

[2]For an alternative interpretation which stresses the role of monetary developments, see Christina D. Romer (1992) 'What ended the Great Depression?', *The Journal of Economic History*, vol. 52, No.4. pp.757–83.

SUMMARY

The New Deal was not revolutionary. Roosevelt was a firm supporter of the capitalist system and much of the experimentation or economic regulation of his Presidency was in line with American tradition. In 1933 the nation faced a frightening crisis and Roosevelt provided leadership and inspiration. The economic strategy pursued was, however, doomed to failure. But before Keynes provided a macro-economic framework, and economists accepted it, large-scale deficit financing was unacceptable. As a result, recovery policies were misconceived.

4 THE SECOND WORLD WAR AND ECONOMIC RECOVERY

The Second World War created the firm prosperity and the full employment which had eluded the New Deal. Once America was drawn into this conflict, very high levels of federal spending were acceptable as was direct governmental intervention in the economy. The expectation of high profits gave a boost to business confidence. Economic expansion raised problems but these new difficulties were the result of a rapidly growing economy not one locked in depression. Figure 4.6 shows the *real* gains as opposed to the *nominal* gains made at the time.

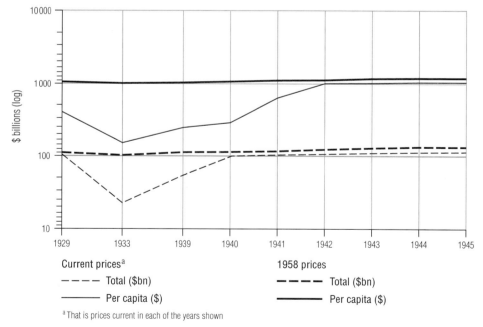

Current prices[a]

---- Total ($bn)

——— Per capita ($)

1958 prices

---- Total ($bn)

——— Per capita ($)

[a] That is prices current in each of the years shown

Figure 4.6 *Wartime GNP: total and per capita in current and 1958 prices*

Source: *Historical Statistics of US, Colonial Times to 1970*, 2 vols (Washington DC, 1975) Series F1–4.

By the late 1930s the New Deal had lost its early vigour. A solid conservative opposition, embracing politicians of both the main parties, ensured that radical measures would be blocked. Moreover, the President was forced to turn his attention away from the domestic political arena and became increasingly preoccupied with Europe. There was a strong isolationist movement in the USA which Roosevelt had to heed. Indeed he had promised during the 1940 campaign that he would keep America out of foreign wars. Roosevelt was, however, deeply apprehensive about the early Nazi successes; his personal sympathies were always with the Allied powers.

The American economy was able to respond rapidly to war demands from the old world. Agricultural surpluses which had been stored by the CCC could now be sold. New Deal conservation measures and the emphasis which had been placed upon the education of farmers now bore fruit. The farm sector was in an excellent position to raise output so long as the weather was favourable.

Industry, too, was anxious for customers having operated below full capacity for over a decade. Although business was handicapped because the capital stock had deteriorated during the Depression, as a result of low investment, and also because relations with the White House were poor, neither of these difficulties were insurmountable. Indeed, the prospect of profitable production was a powerful spur to activity as the dwindling numbers of unemployed testify.

Even before the Japanese attack on Pearl Harbor on 7 December 1941, the USA had taken positive steps to create a war economy. Conscription was introduced in 1940 and between 1939 and 1941 the federal deficit doubled. A number of regulatory agencies were established to rationalize priorities, to collect data and to institute controls of war profits. Many of those staffing these agencies had gained considerable experience serving on government bodies during both the First World War and the New Deal period.

5   THE FARM SECTOR AT WAR

For years the New Dealers had been urging farmers to restrict output but in war an increase was a priority. American farms had to provide food and raw materials not only for the domestic population but also for the US military and the Allies. At the same time there were checks on the incentives that could be used to raise output. High prices, for example, would persuade farmers to produce more but if prices were too high the effects on the non-farm economy would be adverse. In addition, the government, and those on the land, wanted to avoid the disastrous boom and bust of 1914–1920.

Initially farmers were very cautious in responding to the cry of greater production. They feared that the war would disrupt exports and in any case their problems were rooted in surpluses. Why should they add to them? Once the early fears were dispelled, the performance of the farm sector in the Second World War was far more satisfying than it had been in the First World War. The reasons for the rise in output were a mixture of good management and good fortune. A significant improvement in yields was a by-product of better farming techniques and better seeds. In addition, the use of flexible production targets in conjunction with price supports gave a guided stimulus to the farmer. Of crucial importance was the weather, which was particularly favourable during the war. If the droughts which had devastated animal husbandry and cultivation during the thirties had reappeared, the effect upon the war effort would have been serious.

Between 1939 and 1945 about five million people left farming for the armed forces or for non-agricultural jobs. In particular, the increasing opportunities presented by the burgeoning war economy enabled those who had been trapped on non-economic farms to leave. The poorest parts of rural America experienced mass out-migration, especially by tenants. There was a rapid change in the structure of agriculture as small farms were consolidated into larger and potentially more efficient units. Labour shortages provided an incentive to mechanize and there was a rapid increase in the purchase of farm equipment until 1943 when rationing was introduced. It was, however, the bigger farms which were able to make the most of the opportunities which the war presented.

One result of the mass exodus from the land was an increase in the wages of those who remained and from 1942 agricultural wage rates were controlled in an attempt to contain competitive bidding. The government was also quick to recognize the problems that would ensue if labour shortages became serious. Selective exception from military service was given to rural youth and foreign labour was recruited especially for harvesting. By increasing productivity, by working longer hours and by adding new workers to the labour force, the problems posed by a shrinking farm population were overcome.

An indication of the improvement in farm living conditions can be seen in the parity-ratio which reached 113 in 1943 (Table 4.5). Farmers and farm workers gained enormously from the war but the differentials between farm and non-farm income were still substantial in 1945. Rising land values accompanied increased prices, just as they had in the First World War, but the reaction of farmers in the 1940s was different. Instead of increasing as it did after 1914, mortgage indebtedness fell between 1939 and 1945. Farmers were, therefore, in an excellent position in 1945. Debts were relatively low but years of good prices had enabled them to build up an ample stock of savings. The commodity price supports introduced during the New Deal and used during the war were retained after 1945 as the government was determined to avoid the boom and bust which followed the First World War.

Table 4.5 Agricultural change during the Second World War

	1940	1941	1942	1943	1944	1945
Farm population (mn)	30.5	30.1	28.9	26.2	24.8	24.4
New change of farm population through migration (000)	−788	−1,587	−3,145	−1,740	−748	671
Per capita personal income of farm population from all sources ($)	249	335	487	629	671	705
Index of average value of farm real estate per acre (1967 = 100)	21	21	23	25	28	31
Total outstanding farm mortgage debt ($)	6.6	6.5	6.4	6.0	5.4	4.9
Parity ratio (1910 – 1914 = 100)	81	93	105	113	108	109
Index of total farm output (1967=100)	60	62	69	68	70	69

Source: *Historical Statistics of US, Colonial Times to 1970*, 2 vols (Washington DC, 1975) Series, K1, 3, 16, 361, 353, 414.

6 THE ECONOMY

After Pearl Harbor the USA strove to mobilize its resources to defeat Germany and Japan. Expenditure far in excess of what was possible under the New Deal was now undertaken calmly. Few thought that a government engaged in war should be cautious in its borrowing or its spending. Indeed, after a short time public opinion came to believe that public expenditure could bring about the sustained recovery in the economy which had eluded New Dealers.

A few figures give an indication of the rapid transformation in the economy. By 1943 the production of machinery had risen by over 300 per cent since 1939 and transport equipment by 600 per cent. Between 1941 and 1945, 300,000 aircraft were produced, 51 million tons of merchant shipping and 8.5 million tons of naval shipping. By 1944 war production was approximately twice as great as that of Germany, Italy and Japan combined. The USA was truly the arsenal of democracy.

This impressive expansion of output was achieved by a partnership between business and government; the ideological conflicts of the 1930s were laid on one side. Indeed, it was big business which gained most from the war. Thirty private companies received approximately half of all war contracts and most of the subcontracting was between large firms. Thus the foundation for the 'military industrial complex' was laid. Small businesses concentrated on civilian production where, since output had a lower priority, they encountered shortages in both labour and raw materials.

During the war years manufacturing industry spent $11.4 billion on new plant and equipment, a higher level of expenditure than for the 1930s. The government, however, spent more. Through the Defense Plant Corporation, $16 billion was channelled into private industry; a further $1.7 billion created additional industrial capacity for the government itself. Most of the increased capacity, therefore, was the result of public not private funding. War induced pressure led to the expansion of research activity in technological innovation from which sprang enormous benefits after 1945. Federal spending was crucial for industries under the greatest pressure in the war and it also had a dramatic effect on poor regions, such as the South, a happy recipient of new non-agricultural investment.

Not only was government spending far higher in war time than it had been during the Depression, it was directed to new ends. New Deal expenditure had been confined to projects such as roads or dams where no output resulted. During the war, however, the government invested directly in manufacturing and even managed some plants itself. The federal government was seen, even by businesses, as providing a vital role which, perhaps, should even be continued in peacetime.

Table 4.6 The labour force during the Second World War

| Year | Total labour force (000) | Armed forces (000) | Civilian labour force (000) | Employed | | Unemployed | |
				Farm (000)	Non-farm (000)	% of civilian labour force	% of non-farm
1940	56.180	540	55,640	9,540	37,980	14.6	21.3
1941	57,530	1,620	55,910	9,100	41,250	9.9	14.4
1942	60,380	3,970	56,410	9,250	44,500	4.7	6.8
1943	64,560	9,020	55,540	9,080	45,390	1.9	2.7
1944	66,040	11,410	54,630	8,950	45,010	1.2	1.7
1945	65,290	11,430	53,860	8,580	44,240	1.9	2.7

Source: *Historical Statistics of US, Colonial Times to 1970*, 2 vols (Washington DC, 1975), Series D1–10.

Although the size of the armed forces increased from 1.6 million in 1941 to 11.4 million at the end of the war, there was not a commensurate decline in the labour force. The employed non-farm workforce rose from 41.3 million in 1941 to a peak of 45.4 million in 1943 (Table 4.6). How was it possible to put so many people in uniform while at the same time see an increase in the non-farm labour force? Initially the unemployed flocked to fill the jobs which war expenditure created. They were joined by millions of rural people who were underemployed, by people who previously did not want to work or who would not have been employed because of age or disability. Women entered the labour force in large numbers, many leaving rural areas to find jobs in industry. Indeed, the majority of wartime migrants were women.

Employers were pleased to receive an eager workforce though, as many recruits had little or no industrial skills, careful thought had to be given to the way in which they could be used effectively. New capital equipment and an emphasis on training led not only to increased output but also to productivity gains of 25 per cent. High productivity ensured cheap production which was of great benefit during a time of inflation. The government's attempts to control inflation, a natural product of any war, were far more successful than during the First World War. Price controls moderated price increases, especially between 1942 and 1945. Unfortunately the controls were removed in 1946 and prices rose steeply.

Fiscal policy during these years was, on the other hand, disappointing. Higher personal taxation would have lessened the Treasury's dependence upon the banking system to finance the war and would, in turn, have led to lower inflation without destroying incentives. Congress, however, showed no inclination to introduce a disinflationary tax policy. The easy money policy introduced by the Treasury to increase the demand for government securities was inflationary and resulted in a large increase in the money supply. Price controls were therefore vital in restricting the advance of inflation.

SUMMARY

The war led to a dramatic transformation in the American economy, both internally and in relation to the rest of the industrialized world. Between 1939 and 1945 real GNP increased by over 70 per cent but the growth in manufacturing output far outstripped even this impressive performance. A massive investment drive by the private sector which was more than matched by government funding made possible a formidable growth in industrial capacity. Within a few years the manufacture of synthetic rubber, of aluminium, of electronic equipment and the atomic bomb were testimony not only to America's ability to produce but also to the power of her technology when under pressure. As labour migrated from low productivity farms to high productivity factories the industrial might of the USA reached new heights. The miseries of the Great Depression were eradicated by the exigencies of war.

7   CONCLUSION

International comparisons are notoriously difficult to quantify. Figure 4.7 attempts to trace the path of manufacturing output over the period 1920 to 1950 where the impact of three depressions — 1920–1921, 1929–1933 and 1937 — is evident in the line for the USA and, to varying degrees, in the others too. This figure shows clearly the enormous growth, absolutely and relatively, in US manufacturing activity between 1938 and 1948. As US industry was stimulated by the war European nations were smitten by it. In 1945 Germany, France and Italy were in ruins; even Britain faced serious problems. How was America to use her new position?

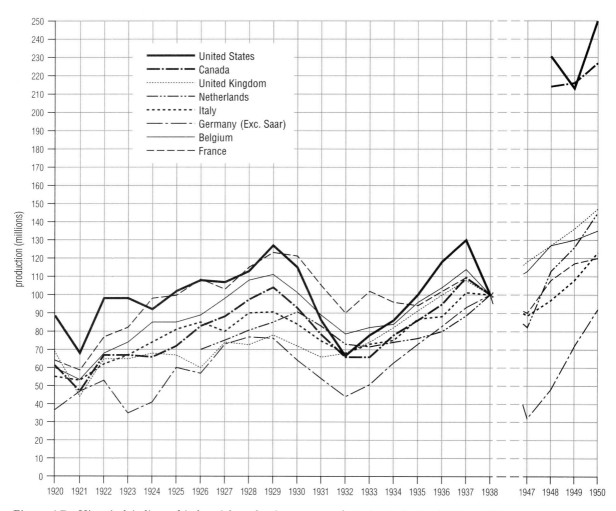

Figure 4.7 *Historical indices of industrial production — manufacturing industry (1938 = 100)*

Source: Industrial Statistics 1900–1957, (OEEC, Paris, 1958), Table 4,11.

In 1945 the USA was the most powerful nation-state in modern history. Its economy had been transformed over the preceding few years, though its commitment to capitalism, in spite of wartime planning, had not been shaken. America was the undisputed leader in creating a new world political and economic order. The United Nations, with its headquarters in New York and the World Bank and International Monetary Fund, both located in Washington DC, demonstrated a new international commitment on the part of the new world. A vibrant America faced the uncertainties of a post-war world with great confidence, sure in the knowledge that any economic threat to increasing prosperity could be defeated. Keynesian economics, which had been adopted during the war, gave the state a new responsibility for economic management which it was determined to grasp. Depressions with their attendant mass unemployment, could and would be avoided. It seemed that a golden age beckoned — could anything destroy this euphoria?

REFERENCES

Badger, A.J. (1989) *The New Deal, the Depression Years 1933–1940*, Basingstoke, Macmillan.

Barber, W.J. (1985) *From New Era to New Deal. Herbert Hoover, the Economists and American Economic Policy, 1921–1933*, Cambridge, Cambridge University Press, pp.7–41.

Chandler, L. V. (1970) *America's Greatest Depression 1929–1941*, New York, Harper and Row, pp.111–26.

Costigliola, F. (1984) *Awkward Dominion. American Political, Economic and Cultural Relations with Europe, 1919–1933*, Ithaca, NY, Cornell University Press, pp.111–26.

Fearon, P. (1987) *War, Prosperity and Depression. The US Economy 1917–1945*, Deddington, Oxford, Philip Allan, pp.51–9.

Fearon, P. (1993) 'Hoover, Roosevelt and American economic policy during the 1930s' in Garside, W.R. (ed.) *Capitalism in Crisis. International Responses to the Great Depression (1993)*, London, Pinter Publishers.

Flink, J.J. (1990) *The Automobile Age,* Boston, Mass, MIT Press, pp.112–28.

Friedman, M. and Schwartz, A.J. (1963) *A Monetary History of the United States 1867–1960*, Princeton, NJ., Princeton University Press, pp.296–98.

Hawley, E.W. (1966) *The New Deal and the Problem of Monopoly*, Princeton NJ, Princeton University Press, pp. 472–94.

Hawley, E.W. (1979) *The Great War and the Search for a Modern Order. A History of the American People and their Institutions, 1917–1933*, New York, St. Martins Press, pp.80–97.

Holt, C.F. (1977) 'Who benefited from the prosperity of the twenties?', *Explorations in Economic History*, Vol.14, No.3, pp.277–89.

Johnson, H.T. (1973) 'Postwar optimism and the rural financial crises of the 1920s'. *Explorations in Economic History*, vol. 11, no.2, pp.173–92.

Kindleberger, C.P. (1973) *The World in Depression 1929–39*, Harmondsworth, Allen Lane, pp.116-27.

Stein, H. (1969) *The Fiscal Revolution in America*, Chicago, University of Chicago Press.

Temin, P. (1989) *Lessons from the Great Depression*, Boston, MIT Press, pp.43–87.

Vatter, H.G. (1985) *The US Economy in World War II*, New York, Columbia University Press, pp.152–3.

Wicker, E. (1966) *Federal Reserve Monetary Policy 1917–1933*, New York, Random House.

Wright, G. (1986) *Old South, New South: Revolutions in the Southern Economy since the Civil War*, New York, Basic Books.

FURTHER READING

Badger, A.J. (1989) *The New Deal. The Depression Years 1933–1940*, London, Macmillan.

Barber, W.J. (1988) *From New Era to New Deal: Herbert-Hoover, the Economists and American Economic Policy, 1921–33*, Cambridge, Cambridge University Press.

Fearon, P. (1987) *War, Prosperity and Depression. The US Economy 1917–1945*, Deddington, Philip Allan.

McElvaine, R.S. (1984) *The Great Depression. America 1929–1941*, New York, Times Books.

Polenberg, R. (1972) *War and Society: The United States 1941–45*, New York, Lippincott.

Romasco, A.U. (1983) *The Politics of Recovery: Roosevelt's New Deal*, Oxford, Oxford University Press.

Wright, G. (1986) *Old South, New South: Revolutions in the Southern Economy since the Civil War*, New York, Basic Books.

FROM THE LONG-BOOM TO RECESSION AND STAGNATION? The post-war American economy to 1990

Grahame Thompson ★

1 INTRODUCTION

The international economy emerged from the Second World War battered and bruised but not totally destroyed. The economic turmoil of the inter-war years had been finally settled with the displacement of the UK as dominant economic power by the USA. The US economy became the undisputed power-house of world demand and growth. Immediately after the war the rest of the world was dependent on the USA for capital goods, financial assistance and markets. The USA eagerly adopted the mantle of provider for the world's pent-up demand released by the ending of hostilities. This position as engine of world demand and economic growth was central to the success of the post-war 'long-boom' which lasted until 1973. Even though the USA lost its lead position after the mid-1970s it still remained the largest economy and thus crucial to world demand and growth.

In this chapter we survey the trajectory for the economy over the post-Second World War period. The main focus is upon the years between 1950 and 1990. Although some comment is also made about the position in the early 1990s, Chapter 6 deals with this in greater detail. The overall aim is to give a series of snapshots of the way the economy was behaving, not to be totally comprehensive in all aspects of economic activity. Thus some of the data presented will be specific to particular periods and particular issues. There is also a difficulty in getting comparable pre-1960 data for some of the economic activity discussed, so trends from 1960 onwards will regretably have to suffice where this is the case.

In this chapter we are dealing essentially with the rise and decline of the US economy. Around the mid-1980s analysis emphasized the failings of the economy and wondered how it could regenerate itself. This became known as the 'declinist' argument, and much of this chapter concentrates upon this.

2 THE PICTURE OVERALL

The Second World War ushered in a period of unprecedented growth in the prosperity of Americans (although, as we shall see later, this prosperity was not shared equally by them all). While the population increased by some 60 per cent between 1940 and 1973, the output of the economy increased by a massive 255 per cent. Even after adjusting for inflation, average real incomes doubled between 1946 and 1973 (Rivlin, 1992, pp.43–4).

Around 1973 things began to go badly wrong, however, and the good years came to an end. International and domestic factors combined to push the US economy into a deep recession, a recession shared by much of the rest of the advanced industrial world. The reasons for this dramatic reversal of fortune are both varied and controversial. One of the most widely canvassed of the immediate factors was the 'supply-side shock' associated with the restrictions on the exports of oil from the Middle East followed by a fourfold increase in oil prices in late 1973 (with another increase in 1979). (The 'supply-side' refers to the inputs into any production system, and the conditions of their supply.) In addition there was a coincidental rise in world agricultural and other raw material prices, which added to the supply-side shock and inflationary trend. This was accompanied by a more general growth of international inflationary pressures, usually associated with the way in which the USA financed the Vietnam War. The war was paid for by international borrowing, which increased the liquidity of the international financial system and in turn led to inflation. Another, perhaps longer-term explanation invoked the importance of investment opportunities — in fact the lack of these — and a general decline in business profitability as the long-boom reached its maturity (Bowles *et al.*, 1989). Without a new round of clustered innovations opening up extensive investment opportunities aggregate economy-wide demand would not recover. As a response to all these developments the domestic authorities tightened the money supply and pushed up real interest rates, which exacerbated the recession.

Although there was some recovery after 1979, it did not last long enough to repeat the extraordinary success of the long-boom years. High unemployment, with continuing high inflation and the lack of a satisfactory growth record continued to haunt the American economy (and other economies), a situation that came to be known as 'stagflation'. Even as the 'mini-boom' years after 1983 unfolded, a deep sense of unease still hung over the American economy as growth once again faltered in the late 1980s. In general, however, the deep pessimism of the recessionary years seemed to have passed by the early 1990s as longer-term prospects and conditions for a sustained economic recovery appeared to be falling into place. Whether this is actually the case we shall return to below (and in later chapters of this book).

In the rest of this chapter we trace the trajectory for the US economy in greater detail. In the next section its overall configuration and changing structural features are highlighted. This is followed by a section dealing specifically with government involvement in the economy and with the position of the federal and state finances. Then we move into the international sphere for a look at the mounting problems of the economy in a comparative context. One of the most important explanatory devices for understanding the changing character of the US economy is the vexed question of its aggregate productivity, and the debate about this in the American context occupies the next section. This is followed by a review of the distributional outcomes of the economy — who has gained and who has lost relatively — as the trends outlined so far unfolded. Finally, we return to the 'ideological' nature of American economic policy making in the post-war period, and look again at the whole question of the role of the market and the government in recent American economic thinking.

SUMMARY

In this opening section we have traced the general trajectory of the US economy in the post-war years. It can be summed up as a period of a long-boom lasting until the early 1970s, followed by a period of increasing economic tensions and difficulties. The latter period is not a uniform one, however, since it has seen some short-term recovery, followed by another downturn. The introductory section has also served to highlight the main issues to be discussed in the rest of the chapter and their order of appearance.

3   CHANGING CONTOURS AND STRUCTURAL POSITION

The evolution of the main economic indicators for the economy is shown in Table 5.1 where they are compared to similar figures for OECD Europe and for Japan. An important element in any discussion of the American economy is raised in the context of these figures; that is the importance of its *relative* position. The post-war period has seen the emergence of a discussion that stresses the *comparability* of different national economies, charting their relative performance and assessing the reasons for this. As the international economy has become more integrated it is the changes in relative performative position of individual economies that has attracted attention and comment. While focusing on the USA, this is a trend we follow in the rest of this chapter.

But this relative focus for the analysis should not deflect us from a preliminary look at the changing absolute position of the US economy, something that anyway underpins the concern with its relative position. Between 1960 and 1990 US GDP expanded tenfold in nominal terms (from $507 billion to $5,400 billion), but the GDP of other economies expanded more rapidly. Japan, for instance, improved its position from 15 per cent of US GDP in 1960 to 55 per cent in 1990, it being the second absolute largest single economy in 1990 (US$ GDP 2,943 billion). The EC as a whole was even larger than the USA in 1990, at US$ GDP 6,014 billion.

The data in Table 5.2, however, reveal more clearly the real extent of the decline in the US economy relative to its main rivals. On a per capita basis, the 'standard of living' of Japan and (West) Germany (along with a range of other mainly European countries not shown here) was higher in 1990 than that of the USA, whereas it had been much lower in 1950. The extraordinary growth of Japanese per capita GDP is evident from the table.

Table 5.1 Comparative US economic indicators: 1960–1990

	1960–1967	1968–1973	1974–1979	1980–1990
Real GDP growth *(yearly % changes)*				
USA	**4.5**	**3.2**	**2.4**	**2.8**
OECD Europe	4.7	4.9	2.6	2.2
Japan	10.2	8.7	3.6	4.1
Gross capital formation *(as % of GDP)*				
USA	**18**	**18.4**	**18.7**	**17.6**
OECD Europe	22.9	23.5	22.4	20.5
Japan	31	34.6	31.8	29.4
Investment in machinery and equipment *(as % of GDP)*				
USA	**6.7**	**7.3**	**8.0**	**7.9**[a]
OECD Europe	9.2	9.0	8.9	8.8
Japan	n/a	14.4	31.8	11.2
Net savings *(as % of GDP)*				
USA	**9.8**	**9.2**	**7.7**	**3.4**
OECD Europe	15.3	15.9	11.9	9.1
Japan	21.2	25.1	20.2	18.3
Unemployment *(as % of total labour force)*				
USA	**5.0**	**4.6**	**6.9**	**7.0**
OECD Europe	2.8	3.4	5.1	9.0
Japan	1.3	1.2	1.9	2.5
Inflation *(% change per year)*				
USA	**2.0**	**5.0**	**8.5**	**5.5**
OECD Europe	3.7	6.3	12.2	8.3
Japan	5.7	7.1	9.1	2.6
Government sector balance *(as % of GDP)*				
USA	**-0.6**	**-0.6**	**-1.4**	**-3.4**[a]
OECD Europe	-0.2[b]	-0.3	-3.3	-4.2
Japan	1.0	-0.9	-3.4	-1.1
Trade balances *(as % of GDP)*				
USA	**0.7**	**0.1**	**-0.4**	**-2.0**
OECD Europe	-0.1	0.3	-0.5	0.5
Japan	0.2	1.5	0.4	2.0

Notes: Figures for EC rather than OECD Europe do not differ significantly except in the case of trade balances where the EC does marginally better.
[a] 1980–89 only
[b] EEC only

Source: Compiled from *OECD Historical Statistics 1960–1990*, 1992, OECD Paris,

Table 5.2 Per capita GDP for a range of countries relative to the USA: 1950 compared with 1990 (percentage of US total)

	1950	1960	1970	1990
USA	100	100	100	100
Japan	18[a]	28	57	111
Germany	52	84	94	110
France	55	69	83	98
UK	53	58	56	79
Italy	27[b]	38	48	88
Canada	80	84	91	100
EC	-	-	-	86
OECD Europe	-	-	56	78

Notes: [a] 1952
        [b] 1951

Sources: *Statistical Abstract of the United States 1980* (calculated from Table 1581, p.906); and *Statistical Abstract of the United States 1990* (calculated from a number of tables).

3.1 COMPARATIVE ECONOMIC POSITION

Some of the points made in the introductory remarks are clearly demonstrated by the data presented in Table 5.1. The growth record of the US economy has slowed since the 1960s, although as indicated earlier there was a slight improvement in the 1980s. But when compared with OECD Europe and Japan, the US record is consistently worse (apart for the final period in respect of Europe). When attention is directed to gross capital investment, whilst the US position looks relatively stable, again it is consistently worse than for either Europe or Japan. This position is confirmed if we turn to investment in just machinery and equipment, the basis for activity in the traded goods sector. The relative differences here are equally striking. An implication of lower proportions of GDP devoted to investment in the USA compared with either Europe or Japan is that there is a greater emphasis in the USA on consumption (compare Chapter 2). One of the consequences of the emphasis on consumption is that it reduces the resources available as savings and that in turn contributes to the lower investment levels. This is confirmed by the figures in the table, where the US savings ratio is shown as strikingly lower than that of the other countries.

If we now look at unemployment, the record here for the USA was also less favourable than for the other countries, that is until the 1980s when Europe in particular dramatically increased its unemployment record. The deteriorating position on this measure for all the countries after the mid-1970s is clear to see. On the issue of inflation the USA fared consistently better than either Europe or Japan right up until the 1980s. The increasing trend in inflation is evident for all three economies, but Japan managed to keep this well under control in the 1980s.

Similar comments can be made about the government sector balance; it went strongly into deficit for the USA, Europe and Japan after 1974. Finally, we can look at comparative trade balances. Here the variable position for OECD Europe is contrasted to the deteriorating position for the USA after the mid-1970s, and to the differences of both of these to the consistently positive position for Japan. We will have much to say about this measure later in the chapter. But it is these figures that lay behind the argument about the 'relative decline' of the US economy mentioned in the opening remarks to this chapter.

3.2 STRUCTURAL CHANGES

Another important point to make in this section relates to longer-term trends in the structure of the American economy. For instance, the decline in farm employment as a percentage of the total workforce continued apace throughout the post-war period. In 1920 it had been 28 per cent and was 17 per cent in 1940. After the war it continued to decline until 1970 when it levelled out at about 3 per cent. This is a considerably lower proportion than in most of the other advanced countries of Europe and Japan (the UK is the exception here; it also has a very low proportion of agricultural

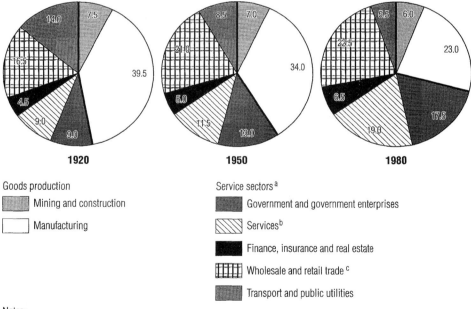

Notes:

a Service sector defined broadly to encompass non-goods production enterprises.
b Sub-category 'services' narrowly defined to designate those engaged in providing services directly to consumers.
c Excludes proprietors, self-employed, domestics and unpaid family workers (besides those employed in farm work).
d Includes full and part-time workers

Figure 5.1 *Non-agricultural employment in the USA 1920, 1950 and 1980 (percentage of total)[d]*

Source: compiled from 'The mechanization of design and manufacturing', T.G. Gunn, *Scientific American*, September 1982, p.42.

workers). But this does not mean that the *output* of the agricultural sector declined. Indeed it continued to rise, due to mechanization and productivity increases (see Chapters 3 and 4). An interesting feature of the American economy throughout the period from 1960 was the consistent and significant surplus in agricultural trade it returned on the balance of payments accounts. The USA has been a major exporter of agricultural produce. This positive net trade balance in agriculture peaked in 1981 however (at $26.6 billion) and by 1984 was down to $18.5 billion. It halved to only $9 billion the following year (by 1990 it was back to $16.5 billion). (The implications of this change are pursued later.)

The American economy is often thought to be the 'model' for the future of all advanced economies in its turning away from manufacturing towards services. In the post-war period this was summed up by describing the USA as a 'post-industrial' society. The data in Figure 5.1 confirms the continued increase in service-sector employment, particularly in the case of government employment and that providing direct services to consumers (again

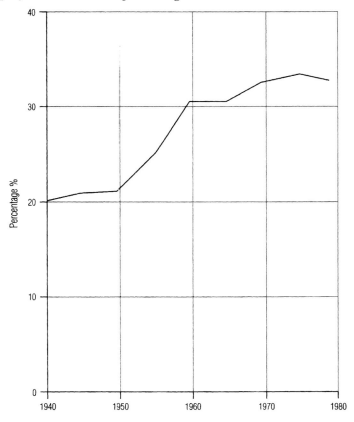

***Figure* 5.2** *Indirect labour[a] in manufacturing industries[b], 1940–1980 (percentage of total employment)*

Source: Gunn (1982), Table 2.

[a] For example; planners; expiditers; sales persons; managers, etc.

[b] Five industries included: fabricated metal products; machinery, electric and electronic equipment; transportation equipment; instruments and related products.

emphasizing consumption). By 1980 approximately two-thirds of US non-agricultural employment was in the service sector as opposed to one-third in the goods-producing industries.

But even this does not accurately represent the full situation, since even within the most highly mechanized manufacturing industries a growing proportion of employees were also engaged in service-type 'indirect' job categories, as is shown in Figure 5.2. Thus by 1980 about 33 per cent of the employees nominally in these manufacturing industries were actually employed in 'service-like' jobs, adding to the idea of a post-industrial society. As we shall see later, some of these trends have been identified as reasons for the relative decline in the American economy, and we return to them below.

SUMMARY

In this section I have provided some statistical background to the changing character of the American economy over the post-war period. In particular I have demonstrated the nature of the problems emerging after 1973, and the declining position of the American economy relative to its main competitors. The structural changes in the American economy have also been highlighted, particularly the basis for the argument that it was moving towards a 'post-industrial' economy.

4   THE GROWTH OF GOVERNMENT

The Depression in the 1930s brought the American economy close to collapse. In its wake it also radically altered attitudes towards the role of the government. From then on the highly unregulated and decentralized economy was gradually undermined by increasing government intervention in, and the management of, the affairs of private economic agents. It began the growth in importance of the federal government in particular and of government expenditure in general. After the war, this was aided by the commitment of successive American governments to a Keynesian demand management policy almost independently of their particular party political affiliations (but see below for a caveat on this point).

4.1   THE EVOLUTION OF PUBLIC EXPENDITURES

The evolution of US general government expenditures from 1960 to 1990 (as a percentage of GDP) in comparison with Europe and Japan, is shown in Figure 5.3. Whilst sharing in the general growth of government expenditure in all the OECD countries over this period, the USA began at a somewhat lower level (nearly 28 per cent in 1960) and ended up in an intermediate position (at nearly 37 per cent in 1990), but nevertheless still below the OECD average. On the one hand, compared with Sweden, say, which had a 59 per cent government expenditure to GDP ratio in 1990, the USA's position looks modest. On the other hand, compared with Japan, a country with a particularly low government expenditure, the USA was 7 percentage points higher at the time. Note that in all countries the period of rapid growth was in the early 1970s as the recession struck. The totals levelled off and even declined in the 1980s as the intellectual and policy tide turned against government involvement in the economy.

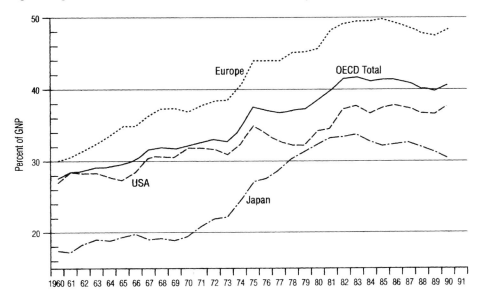

Figure 5.3 *General government expenditures USA, OECD Europe, and Japan 1960–1990 (as a percentage of GNP)*
Source: OECD, *Economic Studies,* No.17, Autumn 1991, Chart 5

The American system is a federal one, which means there are a number of tiers of government that have some autonomy in both raising revenues and in conducting expenditures. The relationship between the federal and local and state levels in terms of public expenditures is shown in Figure 5.4. There is a bulge in federal expenditure in the mid-1950s associated with the Korean War, but after that the steady rise in the total (with fluctuations associated with the business cycle) can be seen, at least up until the mid-1970s. The rise was mainly due to state and local government expenditure, which expanded more rapidly than federal level expenditure did. After 1975, the state and local level expenditure stabilized, while the federal level continued a fluctuating rise until the mid-1980s. It should be noted, however, that some of the federal expenditure is a transfer to lower levels of government, where the money is actually spent.

4.2   REASONS FOR THE GROWTH

There were a number of reasons for the growth of federal and state expenditures in the post-war US economy.

•   The *first,* was the legacy left by the Great Depression and the Second World War. The Depression posed the necessity of creating institutions, mainly federal ones, that would strengthen the economy by building a

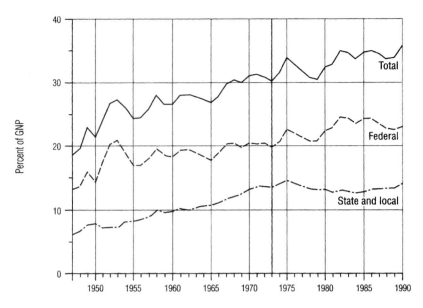

Figure 5.4 *US Government expenditures[a], by level of government 1947–1990*

[a] Federal grants-in-aid to state and local governments are reflected in federal expenditures. Total government expenditures have been adjusted to eliminate this duplication.

Source: A. Rivlin *Reviving the American Dream,* Brookings Institution, 1992, Figure 4–6, p.52.

regulatory and administrative apparatus to manage and supervise that economy. The war was partly fought and won in the context of a technicist ideology; it posed the possibility of organizing and managing the social order according to a set of programmes and technical projects. That set of administrative controls deployed to mobilize resources for the War effort, while quickly dismantled after the war, left a legacy that progressively invoked the public sphere in engineering solutions to social and economic problems.

- The *second,* related, reason was the realization that certain socially provided 'collective goods', like education, defence, and infrastructure investments, were central to the conduct of not only a successful economic policy but were also needed for strategic reasons.

- The *third* reason was the growing pressure to deal with the inequalities in American society, highlighted by the civil rights movement in the first instance, which involved the development and provision of a range of public services designed to redress the imbalances perceived to work against various 'minority' groups.

- In association with this, a *fourth* reason can be discerned which has to do with an explicit redistributive objective that arose acutely in the wake of the 1970s recession. Spending on welfare and housing, and particularly on Medicaid and Medicare, escalated. In addition, the crime wave and spreading drugs epidemic put added pressure on local and particularly city government. This led to a sharp deterioration in the states and local government fiscal position (as local taxes did not rise sufficiently to offset this increased burden of expenditure), which was met increasingly by grants-in-aid from Washington. It is largely these grants-in-aid items that accounted for the continued increase in federal level expenditures after 1973, as shown in Figure 5.4.

4.3 FEDERAL, STATE AND LOCAL RELATIONS

A good many of the initiatives associated with public expenditure arose in the context of tensions between the federal and the state and local levels. The states were seen as laggardly in meeting the new obligations incumbent upon a progressive and modernizing economy, and the federal government increasingly stepped in to try to right the situation as it saw it. One consequence has been something of a 'fiscal crisis' at both the federal and state and local level (Gramlich, 1992). The states have difficulty in raising revenue by increasing taxes because: (1) they have unequal resource bases on which to draw revenues (some states are much richer than others); (2) their tax base is more sensitive to economic fluctuations than is the federal tax base; and (3) they compete with one another, so there is a disincentive to increase taxes and an incentive to reduce them. At both the state and federal level there was a movement against tax increases as the 'New Right' policy agenda was strongly embraced in the 1980s, first by Ronald Reagan and then endorsed further by George Bush ('Read my lips … no new taxes'!). Through the 1970s and 1980s the state and local budgets were in rough balance, however. Partly to finance these the federal budget went into a sustained deficit from the mid-1970s. This escalated in the mid-1980s to produce one of the most intractable problems besetting the American economy: an overall, and seemingly 'structural', federal budget deficit (Table 5.1). The possible consequences of this, and how to manage it, became a central issue of political dispute in the 1980s and 1990s, which we return to below.

4.4 THE COMPOSITION OF GOVERNMENT EXPENDITURES

Differences in the composition of expenditures between countries are also important in understanding the American economy and its particular problems. Comparative statistics for 1970 and 1989 dealing with such differences are shown in Table 5.3. The significant differences relate to:

- Defence spending in particular, where the USA devoted considerably more to this area than the other countries shown (although the UK is also a big spender on defence).

- Expenditures on 'welfare state' items, where Germany and the UK lead and the USA was least involved in 1989 (although see the change in Japan's position on this item). Also note the particularly low proportion of expenditure on the direct purchase of goods and services within this category for the USA, while its income transfer share moved more into line with the other countries between 1970 and 1989 (compare this with the discussion in Section 4.3).

- The proportion devoted to the economic services item within the 'mixed economy' category, which includes capital investments and subsidies to industry. The USA was perhaps surprisingly high on this sub-category given its supposed well-known aversion to this type of 'intervention' (compare it with the UK for instance).

Table 5.3 Composition of general government expenditures, 1970 compared with 1989 (as a percentage of GNP/GDP)

	US		Japan		Germany[a]		UK	
	1970	1989	1970	1989	1970	1989	1970	1989
Total Expenditure	32.3	36.3	19.4	31.6	38.7	46.8	39.3	41.2
Traditional Domain	11.1	9.1	3.3	3.7	7.2	8.2	8.9	8.3
Defence	7.5	5.9	0.7	0.9	3.0	2.6	4.8	4.1
General public services and other functions	3.6	3.2	2.6	2.8	4.2	5.6	4.1	4.2
The Welfare State	15.0	17.8	10.4	18.1	22.6	31.2	20.1	25.7
Education, health and housing	8.7	6.1	8.0	10.9	10.0	12.7	12.8	12.8
Income transfers	6.3	11.7	2.4	7.2	12.6	18.5	7.3	12.9
The Mixed Economy								
Economic services	3.9	4.5	4.9	5.5	5.2	4.6	5.2	3.0
Public debt interest	2.3	5.0	0.6	4.0	1.0	2.8	4.0	3.6
Balancing item	0.0	-0.1	0.2	0.3	2.7	0.0	1.1	0.6
Net lending	-0.6	-3.1	1.8	2.5	0.2	-2.1	2.5	-0.1

Note: [a] 1988 for Germany

Source: Compiled from 'The role of the public sector: causes and consequences of the growth of government' by P. Saunders and F. Klau, *OECD Economic Studies No.4*, Spring 1985, Table 8; and 'Controlling government spending and deficits: trends in the 1980s and prospects for the 1990s' by H. Oxley and J.P. Martin, *OECD Economic Studies No.17*, Autumn 1991, Table 3.

Before we finish this section it will be useful to briefly highlight two particular trends with respect to US government expenditures. The first relates to the defence expenditure item mentioned immediately above. An important argument relating to the relative decline of the USA concerns the 'burdens of imperial power' and 'military overstretch'. Not only did the USA act as the guarantor of world demand for much of the post-war period, it also acted as guarantor of world security (at least for the highly industrialized western nations). Perhaps it did this at a cost, however. As indicated above, the USA consistently devoted a higher proportion of its GDP to defence expenditure than did most of the other advanced industrialized nations. It has been argued that this represented a burden of 'unproductive' expenditures on the part of the USA from which its main competitor countries gained in terms of their own security and order. While the USA was defending the liberal multilateral trading regime in a military sense, providing the much needed 'public good' of defence — for which American taxpayers footed the bill — Europe, Japan and the Far Eastern NICs were given the space and the resources to develop their own economies to eventually out-compete the USA. As a proportion of total government expenditure, defence expenditure still represented a staggering 49 per cent in 1960. It declined over the next twenty years to nearly 23 per cent in 1980, but then began to rise again in the period of the Reagan Republican Administrations to 27 per cent in 1985 (26 per cent in 1990) (*Statistical Abstract of the United States*, various years). An additional issue associated with this military spending debate is the skewed nature of US research and development (R&D) investment that it stimulated, something we will return to later.

The second particular trend worth noting in connection with government expenditure concerns the more general importance of investment in its overall composition. On a range of measures the USA shows both a relatively low level of capital formation undertaken by the government sector compared with other comparable economies, and a marked declining trend in this since the mid-1960s. The US public sector has not invested on a comparable scale to the OECD average. In addition, the USA has traditionally (that is, up until the 1980s) returned a small government budget deficit, and quite often a small surplus, each year. Only in the late 1970s and 1980s did the deficit become consistent and increase in size. Thus throughout the twenty-five years or so of the long-boom (1947–1974), the government sector was in rough balance (*Historical Tables: Budget of the United States Government 1992*, Table 15.6, p.183). The low levels of investment expenditure just about matched the levels of government budget deficits (*ibid*, Table 9.2, p.88).

The key point to note here is that this is not the behaviour of a full-blooded 'Keynesian' management of the economy. The public sector has been relatively unimportant in the USA and certainly not responsible for the long-boom. It did act to smooth out the business cycle over this period, but strictly speaking it was not solely, or even mainly, responsible for the sustained upward trend in demand over the long-boom period. This had more to do with the massive increase in private investment and the enormous growth in international trade, both of which were stimulated by, and sustained by, private sector household and commercial decisions. More on this theme in a moment.

SUMMARY

The role of the government has increased significantly in the US economy since 1945. The nature of that involvement, and the reasons for its growth, have been examined in this section. It has been shown that the USA was facing an acute 'fiscal crisis' on its budgetary accounts during the 1980s. The particular patterns of government expenditure in the USA have been highlighted, demonstrating the way defence expenditure seemed to dominate in overall expenditure, and the possible consequences of this were focused upon. Finally, it was argued that the experience of the US public sector during the period to the 1970s did not imply that 'Keynesian' regulation of the economy was very important to its overall success.

5   THE CHANGING INTERNATIONAL POSITION OF THE ECONOMY

Economies in sharp relative decline spend disproportionate amounts of money and energy on inquiries into why they are declining. This emphasis on studies concerning the reasons for American decline has been particularly prevalent in the case of productivity levels, which are examined in the next section. The number of studies dealing with this one subject are quite staggering. Though to a lesser extent, this is also true of studies and enquires into the short-comings of American international economic competitiveness overall which we concentrate upon in this section.

5.1   THE BALANCE OF PAYMENTS

It should be remembered, however, that the long-boom years were the good years before problems began to appear. An interesting feature of the US economy over the boom years, as revealed by the figures for the government budget position between 1960 and early 1970s shown in Table 5.1 and the analysis just completed above, is that the overall budget was only in slight deficit during that period. Indeed, solely on the current account it was in surplus for all of the post-1950 period to the mid-1970s. As indicated above, far from government *public* expenditure *stimulating* the domestic economy in a traditional Keynesian fashion, the fiscal position was tight and basically 'deflationary'. The role of the government was to dampen down the boom, itself stimulated by the enormous expansion of *privately* financed domestic and international investment, and by overseas trade expansion. The American economy not only became the financial centre of the world, providing unprecedented capital for domestic and foreign investment, but it also catered for the strong international demand for its traded goods.

Over the post-war period the USA had been in surplus on the current account of its balance of payments up until 1971, when it went temporarily into deficit for the first time. The position recovered somewhat in the mid-1970s and early 1980s, but virtually collapsed after 1983. In 1992 the USA still had a current account deficit of $56 billion (which was forecast to grow during the mid-1990s). But perhaps more indicative and important in terms of the underlying competitiveness of the economy is the merchandise trade account, consisting of the difference between imports and exports of traded goods (thereby excluding 'invisibles'). This had been in a continual surplus since as far back as 1893 — until 1971 that is, when it went into a precipitate deficit (except for 1975), some ten years earlier than the overall current account. In 1992 the merchandise account was still $89 billion in the red. It was the surplus on the agricultural trade account referred to earlier that allowed the economy to weather the threatening storm during these intermediate years; that is, to maintain its ability to consume by financing non-agricultural merchandise imports (Thompson, 1989, pp.13–23). But this room for manoeuvre was itself short lived as that agricultural surplus fell away during the 1980s. The overall result was a 'structural imbalance' on the international payments account to match that on the domestic budget account; the famous 'twin deficits' of the American economy, which many economists have seen as closely connected. I shall return to this topic again later in the chapter.

The price competitiveness of the American economy (measured in terms of relative unit labour costs) had been continually *improving* during the 1960s and over the entire 1970s, so it could not have been this that led to the demise of the American manufacturing competitiveness and the undermining of its merchandise account. After 1980, however, there was a rapid escalation in relative unit labour costs as the American economy became increasingly price uncompetitive with the rapid appreciation of the dollar against other currencies. This further threatened the current account, with the implications already outlined above.

It was, then, the consequences of the tumultuous years in the mid-1970s that so clearly marked the late 1980's view of America's economic problems. Average manufacturing import penetration into the USA began slowly, increasing by only 3 per cent between 1972 and 1982, but the USA continued to loose its value share of world exports (Thompson, 1989; Figures 2.4 and 2.5).

If this could not be directly attributed to a growing price uncompetitiveness what were the reasons for these changes? In the next section we will look at this in more detail.

Not quite everything was gloom and doom however. Reference to Figure 5.5 demonstrates that some US industrial sectors fared better than others. Commercial aircraft and chemicals maintained a strong positive balance. Indeed, other sectors including fuel oils and petroleum products, rubber products, agricultural fertilizers, ships and boats, and some metal products also improved their position when measured against import penetration ratios. However, as the figure shows, the other sectors went into a relative decline internationally, and that was mirrored by many other American traded good industries. The problem is that it was the more advanced and high-tech sectors that demonstrated the main failure to remain internationally competitive in this period. In 1989 the semiconductor industry alone was in the red by $2.7 billion (1990 estimate, $1.5 billion).

The recent position on bilateral balances (for a slightly different set of industries) between the USA and Japan on the one hand and the USA and the European Community on the other is shown in Figure 5.6.

This demonstrates that the main problem for the USA was in respect to Japan. The bilateral balances with the EC were much less marked, and the USA was in surplus for a wider range of industries. (The EC was itself also in a very adverse position in respect to Japan.)

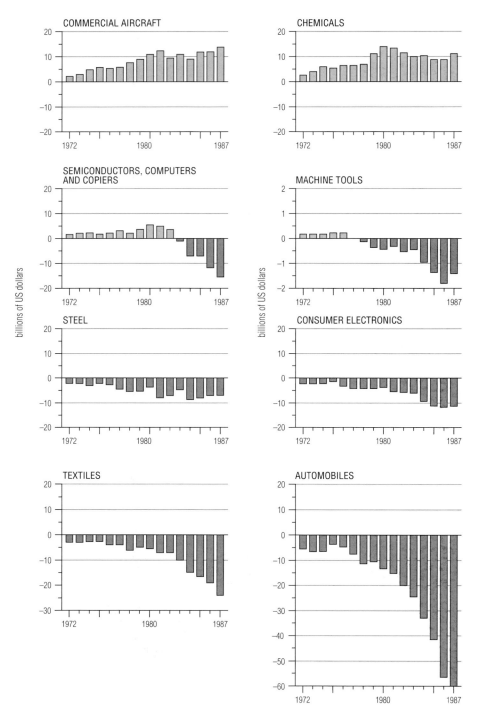

Figure 5.5: *Sectoral breakdown of balances of trade changes 1972–1987 (imports minus exports, US$ billions)*

Source: 'Towards a new industrial America', Suzanne Berger *et al., Scientific American*, vol.260, No.6, June 1989. Adapted from page 25.

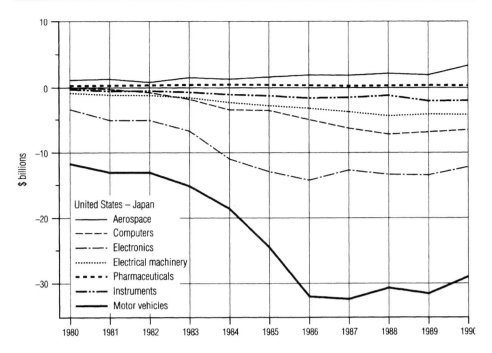

Figure 5.6a: *Bilateral trade balances: USA–Japan*

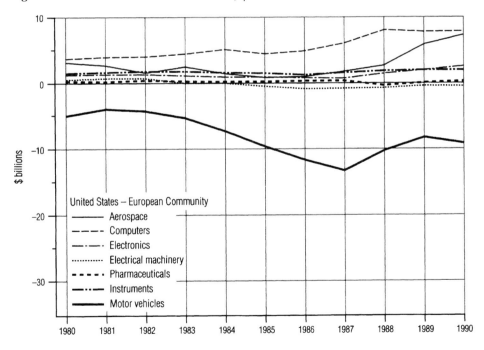

Figure 5.6b: *Bilateral trade balances: USA–EC.*

Source: *Industrial Policy in OECD Countries Annual Review 1992,* OECD, Paris, November 1992. Graph 16, p.147.

Furthermore, we should remember that the post-war slogan 'The dollar is as good as gold' also came to an abrupt end in 1971. The Nixon administration first suspended convertibility of the US dollar against gold in 1971, and floated it against other currencies in 1973. This broke the central plank of the Bretton Woods exchange rate system so carefully crafted by the Americans after the Second World War. It indicated the longer-term decline of American global power and an undermining of its hegemony (see Chapters 7 and 10). The inability of the USA to continue as the world's banker is no more clearly demonstrated than by the fact of it becoming a net debtor nation in 1985 for the first time since the First World War (Figure 5.7).

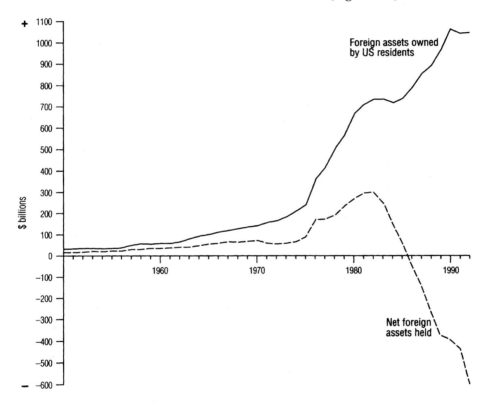

Figure 5.7 *Foreign assets: 1950–1992*

Source: *Balance Sheet For the US Economy, 1945–1992*, Federal Reserve, Washington DC, 1993.

Foreign debt was built up to meet the deficits on the current balance of its international accounts and the budget deficit emanating from Washington. It was the Japanese, and to a lesser extent the Europeans, who purchased this debt and who thus financed continued US domestic consumption by both government and private consumers (Thompson, 1990, Chapter 7).

5.2   THE FOREIGN ASSET POSITION

At this stage it is worth looking at the post-war history of the USA as banker to the world in a little more detail. In part this has two features; first the general growth of its foreign asset base and then the switch into a net-debtor nation, and second the role of US multinational corporations as the productive spearhead for US international capital flows.

In Figure 5.7 the money value of US net foreign assets is shown as a dashed line. There was a slow build up during the 1950s and 1960s, which quickened in pace during the 1970s and early 1980s. But the most dramatic feature is the precipitate decline into negative values after 1985. The other line in Figure 5.7 represents the foreign assets owned by US residents, which has remained in a strong positive position. This represents the total of US foreign investment abroad. (The reason the USA can be a positive investor abroad at the same time as it has net debtor status is that there is also foreign investment into the USA — the latter outweighing the former after 1982.) Such foreign investment can be of two basic types; portfolio investment and direct investment. The former represents the holding of financial assets while the latter represents the purchase of real productive assets. Much of this latter is the result of the operation of US multinational corporations, the activities of which we will now briefly explore further.

5.3   US MULTINATIONAL CAPITAL

The US multinational corporation (MNC) came to represent the quintessential image of international big business in the post-war era. In terms of sheer numbers, US multinationals continued to dominate the international scene. In the mid-1980s US MNCs comprised over 20 per cent of the world's total. Many of these vast companies deploy resources and have assets exceeding the GDP of even quite economically important countries. Thus they exercise considerable 'market power' — which they have often been accused of using to ill effect, either at the behest of their own private interests (exploitation, revenue maximizing and profit seeking), or at the behest of their real political masters, the US government (destabalizing and undermining legitimate though unfriendly regimes, or supporting illegitimate but friendly ones). These accusations have been particularly prevalent in respect to MNC activity in economically and politically weak less developed countries (LDCs).

It is interesting to note, however, that the main arena of activity for US MNCs was not the less developed countries but the more developed ones (MDCs). In 1990, 74 per cent of the cumulative stock of US outward direct investment was invested in the developed countries compared to 25 per cent in the less developed ones (OECD, 1992, Table 35, p.129). Thus for the most part they were dealing with advanced countries with strong governmental apparatuses. This does not mean US MNCs were all virtuous, of course, because they were probably more influential in the LDCs, and they can still exert considerable pressure within MDCs.

Table 5.4   Outward direct investment[a]: the US compared to other OECD countries: 1971–1980 and 1981–1990 ($ millions)

	Cumulative flows of direct investment	
	1971–1980	1981–1990
United States	134,354	143,027
Japan	18,052	185,826
Germany	23,130	86,287
UK	55,112	183,531
France	13,940	85,810
Total OECD	302,306	966,067

[a] Direct investment is investment in tangible assets where a controlling stake is sought.

Source: *International Direct Investment: Policies and Trends in the 1980s*, OECD, Paris, 1992. Derived from Table 1, p.13.

The 1980s saw important changes in the geographical patterns of foreign direct investment. Table 5.4 shows that, while the USA still remained an important player, its position has been eclipsed by both Japan and the UK. Just these three countries accounted for 60 per cent of all foreign direct investment (FDI) — about 20 per cent each – in 1990. The explosion of outward FDI from Japan during the 1980s is strikingly evident from the table. Of course, the importance of the USA as a destination for FDI escalated during the 1980s; it absorbed 46 per cent of this over the decade. In fact, inward investment was 2.5 times outward investment.

One consequence of the reversal of fortune of the USA in respect of FDI and other financial flows, and the enormous influx of foreign capital, was to raise domestic worries that the USA was being 'bought up by foreigners'. Just as US FDI in the 1950s and 1960s had raised fears in Canada and Europe that the USA was buying up their economies, the reverse mistrust surfaced again in the 1980s. But in 1988 the importance of FDI in the USA still remained small overall, and small relative to US holdings in other countries, as Table 5.5 demonstrates.

Table 5.5   Foreign direct investment as percentage of host country GDP, 1988

	Foreign holdings in the USA	US holdings abroad
UK	2.1	5.7
Japan	0.8	0.5[a]
Netherlands	1.0	6.8
Canada	0.6	12.2
West Germany	0.5	1.8
Switzerland	0.3	10.4
France	0.2	1.3

[a] Figure relates to 1987

Source: *Economic Report of the President 1990*, Table 4.3, US Government Printing Office, Washington, DC, February 1991.

5.4 THE PROBLEM OF THE TWIN DEFICITS

As suggested above discussion of the balance of payments deficit on current account has been closely linked to the discussion of the budget deficit. The possible relationship between these two has been the subject of much dispute (Thompson, 1990, Chapter 4). The conventional explanation sees the emergence of the budget deficit as the one mainly responsible for the payments deficit. The increase in interest rates (tightening of monetary policy) needed to attract funds to finance the growing budget deficit in the late 1970s and early 1980s led to the rapid appreciation of the dollar as investors moved into holding the then more lucrative US currency. This in turn led to a decline in the price competitiveness of US goods on world markets, and the relative cheapening of imports, with the consequent balance of payments problem.

Once this explanation was in place the remedy was clear. The budget deficit must be reduced to restore equilibrium in the exchange rate and reverse the process just described to right the trade imbalance. Reining in domestic demand (cutting consumption) would make room for exports and help stimulate the conditions required to produce domestic substitutes for imports. But a further tightening of monetary policy, by raising interest rates for instance to help lower domestic demand, would only put added pressure on an already appreciating exchange rate. An alternative policy of increasing taxes was ruled out on ideological and political grounds. A third option — to reduce federal public spending — whilst attractive to the political leadership in the 1980s, just failed to materialize to an extent that made a significant impact on the deficit — for reasons to do with the collapse of private welfare provision generally and the pressures for increased spending on these and related areas as the recession hit. In addition, as analysed above, defence expenditures began to expand once again as the Regan administration embarked on its 'Star Wars' initiative.

In fact the remedy was to offer no remedy. The problem was largely ignored, not to go away but to be temporarily forgotten as the mini-boom of the mid-1980s got underway. In fact, this was aided by a growing academic and political scepticism about any close connection between the twin deficits. This helped uncouple them as a result. It also seemed that the international community had grown to live with the new US position. As long as the deficits could be financed why worry? The USA was no different in the relative extent of its deficits to GDP ratio than some other comparable countries, it was suggested. Growth would eventually remedy the situation anyway, so sit tight in the interim period and wait. Finally, the exchange rate began to depreciate, a sign that the international community — in fact the financial markets — were getting used to the situation.

However, once the growth rate slowed again in the late 1980s some of these rather complacent attitudes were challenged by the realities of events. The USA had not become fundamentally more competitive. The deficits, particularly the budget deficit, had not gone away. Indeed it threatened to begin increasing again. Even the forcing down of domestic interest rates to as low as 4 per cent in the very early 1990s did not immediately stimulate the economy (though the fact that the USA could do this without precipitating a dramatic depreciation of the dollar is a sign that, at the international level at least, the markets had readjusted to a continuing large, but broadly stabilized, balance of payments deficit). This still left the US economy poised on something of a knife edge, however, with the potential for greater instability if the underlying conditions were to deteriorate any further. In the next section we will review some of the underlying conditions associated with the real economy (and in Chapter 6 the evolution of the economy during the 1990s is explored fully).

SUMMARY

The basis for the arguments about the relative international decline in the strength of the American economy have been analysed in this section. We have seen that this was mainly a result of the growing uncompetitiveness of its leading manufacturing industries. The reversal of fortune of the USA in respect of international financial flows was reviewed in this context. The relationship between the twin deficits was raised, and the policy options this posed discussed. Finally the still precarious nature of the economy in the late 1980s was highlighted.

6   PRODUCTIVITY AND GROWTH

One certain comment that can be made about the post-war US economy is that it was the slow-down in its productivity growth record above all else that served to focus attention on its emerging overall economic problems. The rising prosperity of the long-boom years was predicated on the increasing productivity of American industry and commerce.

As Table 5.6 shows, between 1948 and 1973 productivity grew rapidly on all measures and in all sectors. From 1973 it faltered, however. What is more, even from the 1960s US productivity had been growing at a slower rate than it had been in other advanced industrial countries, and although the reduced rates were shared by all countries after 1973, the reduction in the USA was the largest (except for the UK — Table 5.7).

The sectoral breakdown in US productivity is shown in Figure 5.8. One of the major unsolved economic mysteries of the post-1970s period remains why there was such a generalized slow-down in productivity growth.

Table 5.6   Average annual aggregate productivity growth, 1948–1987, selected periods

Measure	1948–1973	1973–1979	1979–1987	1973–1987	Change 1948–1973 to 1973–1987
Output per hour					
Business	2.94	0.62	1.32	1.02	-1.92
Non-farm business	2.45	0.48	1.11	0.84	-1.61
Manufacturing	2.82	1.38	3.39	2.52	-0.30
Non-manufacturing	2.32	0.16	0.33	0.25	-2.07
Multifactor productivity					
Business	2.00	0.10	0.61	0.39	-1.61
Non-farm business	1.68	-0.08	0.45	0.22	-1.46
Manufacturing	2.03	0.52	2.56	1.68	-0.35
Non-manufacturing	1.55	-0.29	-0.28	-0.30	-1.85

Source: Baily and Gordon (1988) Table 1, p.355.

Table 5.7   Growth of labour productivity[a] in manufacturing, selected developed countries 1960–1980 (annual percentage change)

Measure period	US	Canada	France	Germany	Italy	Japan	UK	Eight European countries[b]	Eight European countries plus Canada and Japan
1960–80	2.7	3.8	5.6	5.4	5.9	9.4	3.6	5.4	5.9
1960–73	3.0	4.5	6.0	5.5	6.9	10.7	4.3	5.9	6.4
1973–80	1.7	2.2	4.9	4.8	3.6	6.8	1.9	4.2	4.7

Notes: [a] Output per hour.
         [b] France, Germany, Italy, UK, Belgium, Denmark, Netherlands, and Sweden
Source: Lawrence, R.Z. (1984) *Can America Compete?*, Brookings Institution, Washington, DC (adapted from Table 2–9, p.32).

6.1   UNRAVELLING THE PRODUCTIVITY MYSTERY

At the aggregate level the productivity of all businesses had not recovered its pre-1973 level by 1987. Indeed the non-farm non-manufacturing sector had shown near zero to negative productivity growth after 1973. Generally, the slow down in the growth after 1973 was only partially reversed by 1987. The major exception to this is growth in the manufacturing sector, which recovered after 1979 to outstrip its pre-1973 level.

Of particular importance to the aggregate slow down were the changes in the non-manufacturing sector. According to Figure 5.8 there were reductions in the growth rates for all the branches in this sector, including finance, insurance and real estate, retail trade and communications. These are the main service sector branches, so the idea of the viability of a 'post-industrial society' referred to above should be approached with added caution on the basis of these figures. In addition, these sectors, along with transport, were the ones most heavily deregulated in the period in the name of a supply-side programme aimed at dramatically *increasing* their productivity record.

A number of suggestions have been put forward to account for this slow down which we review now in their American context.

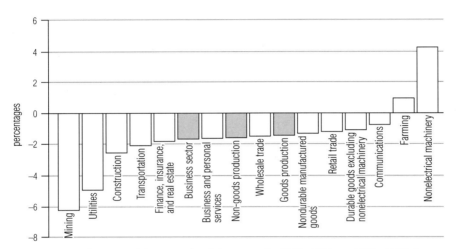

Figure 5.8 *Change in labour productivity growth, 1948–1973 to 1973–1987, by industry*

Source: Baily and Gordon (1988), Figure 1, p.362.

The first is to argue that perhaps there was no downturn after all. Maybe it was all just a measurement error; the 'real' changes in the productivity, produced by the increase in the use of computer technology for instance — the application of which had gone on apace post-1973, and which should have led to increases in productivity — were not being picked up by the figures. Although it was found that this might have been the case to some limited extent in the banking, securities, insurance and airline industries, Baily and Gordon (1988) stress it could not account for all the decline in these branches, and certainly not for the decline in the non-farm non-manufacturing sector as a whole.

Other reasons they suggested included a too rapid expansion of services in these sectors which simply duplicated one another without adding to over-all product quality and welfare. The expansion of low income and low value added jobs may also have been important (see the next section). High productivity requires high quality, high value added and skill remuneration. Above all else, however, the US example demonstrates that the simple application of computers to either the manufacturing or non-manufacturing sectors will not of itself suffice to lead to productivity increases. What is required is a thorough going overhaul of the entire production process. New

Right supply-side experiments involving deregulation and liberalization are simply not enough.

6.2   STRUCTURAL EXPLANATIONS

It is towards other types of deeper more structural explanations that we now turn. One of these involves questions of research and development expenditures (R&D) and innovative capacities. The USA is well known for the dominance of its defence-related R&D compared to the civilian equivalent, a feature connected to the more general emphasis given to defence expenditure in the US compared to other countries commented upon above. Defence accounted for only 3 per cent of Japanese government-funded R&D in 1985 while it accounted for a massive 70 per cent in the USA (Reich, 1989, p.22). This represented a third of the total US R&D effort. In addition, as Figure 5.9 shows, the USA had significantly lower industry-funded R&D expenditures as a proportion of GDP than other competitor countries (although the USA is better than France and particularly the UK in this respect).

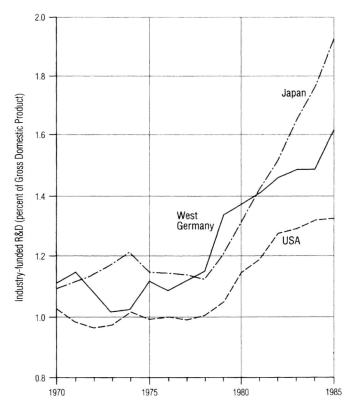

Figure 5.9: *Industry-funded R&D expenditure as a percentage of GDP 1975–1985*

Source: Adapted from 'Technology, employment and US competitiveness', R.M. Cyert and D.C. Mowery, *Scientific American*, vol.260, no.5, May 1989, p.34.

The argument is that while there may have been a causal relationship between applied research on military technologies and civilian applications in the past, the contribution of this kind of research to commercial applications in such technologies as microelectronics appears to have declined. Indeed, the direction of causality may have been reversed; military technologies now appearing to depend upon prior advances in civilian applications. For instance, while the USA increased R&D expenditure on military activities from about 50 per cent of federally-funded R&D in 1979 to 70 per cent in 1985, the trade balance on electronics moved from a surplus to a deficit. The lack of a strong US presence in the consumer electronics and other electronic based industries may be the result of this continuing emphasis on defence R&D expenditure.

In addition, the utilization of civilian R&D technologies has not been particularly efficient. It is generally recognized that American companies have not devoted enough attention to the manufacturing process. Only about a third of the R&D expenditures are devoted to improving process technologies, the key to efficient manufacturing. (In Japan the reverse is the case, with two-thirds devoted to this and only one-third to the development of new or improved products.) Many US companies also fail to co-ordinate their product design with their manufacturing processes, another key area for the effective utilization of R&D expenditure. Rapid commercialization of product and process innovations requires the tight integration of product design with product manufacturability, something only possible with the close physical and organizational integration of engineers involved in both aspects. The compartmentalization of tasks in the case of the USA, often with product designers centralized in technical facilities located well away from the plants producing the innovations, is inimical to productive success. Add to this the overall lower aggregate investment levels in the USA referred to earlier and the disappointing performance results. However, this story has not gone totally unchallenged. For instance, Griliches (1988) argues that these adverse R&D effects, though important, are not enough to account for all the slow down in productivity.

In this context we can revisit the problem identified earlier about the improvement in US international price competitiveness while its manufacturing base was being undermined. The point here is to emphasize the growing importance of *non-price* competitiveness in the determination of manufacturing success. The emphasis is shifting to the design, quality, reliability, marketing, and after-sales service aspects of products rather than to their purchase price as such, in accounting for successful selling. It is a relative under-performance on these aspects in the US case that, at least in part, contributes to its poor international showing.

But why should the USA be unable to reduplicate all these virtues of a successful manufacturing base? An important contribution remains the form of the financial system. The financial system acts to channel funds from savers to borrowers — it 'mediates' between these two parties (see Chapter 7). But exactly how effectively it does this remains the issue. Broadly speaking, successful manufacturing requires a long-term relationship between finance and real investment. If a company is to spend the necessary time to both develop or improve a product, set up a complex production process to manufacture it, and then wait until a reasonable return materializes, the relationship between the provider of finance for the investment and that organization producing the actual output must be a long-term one (even though, as suggested above, these time scales may be shortening for success-ful commercialization). The trouble is that the form of the American finan-cial system mitigates against such a secured long-term relationship, which can have perverse and pervasive effects on the ability to successfully manu-facture (see Figure 5.10).

The share form of raising finance and the operation of the stock exchange leads to a short-time horizon for financial investment. There is a prevalence of 'financial engineering' over 'production engineering'; the short-term enhancement of 'shareholder value' over longer-term returns for future viability. Numerous studies in the mid-1970s and 1980s also showed how US business was disadvantaged by the high cost of finance in the USA com-pared to its main economic rivals (Thompson, 1989, Table 2.2, p.38). In addition, company executive remuneration has become dependent upon the short-term value of the company's shares rather than upon whether they can deliver an enhanced long-term company net worth. The merger and take-over deal has displaced a careful internal organic growth strategy based upon successful nurturing of product developments. Companies are assessed on the basis of whether they can deliver cash resources now rather than solid returns later (so called 'cash-cow' management — milking the company cow now for liquidity and forgetting about its future viability and prospects). All these endemic features of the US financial system mitigate against the long-term success of its manufacturing base. In as much as they are embedded institutional features of the American system, they will prove very difficult to reform.

But perhaps all these explanations have missed the point and are exagger-ated. One response to the decline-of-American-business-dynamic argument is to suggest that in fact it is still very much alive and well, but increasingly located 'off-shore'. Thus Lipsey and Kravis (1985 and 1987) suggest that although there was a decline in the US territorially based manufacturing share in the 1950s and 1960s, if American *firms* are scrutinized then their share never fell at all but in fact increased a little. The exports of American owned and managed firms fared rather well, although much of this export-ing activity took place from abroad; it was undertaken by American mul-tinationals. The productivity and efficiency of these firms improved over the period. For these authors, the question to ask is why American firms found it necessary to locate off-shore to secure and maintain their competitive advantage. Lipsey and Kravis see the reasons as mainly to do with deteri-orating domestic macroeconomic conditions as described above, and with the increasing 'interference' of the government in shaping commercial decisions.

FIRST COMMERCIAL VIDEOTAPE RECORDER was made by the Ampex Corporation in Redwood City, Calif., but no U.S. firms were willing or able to devote the resources to bring unit costs down for sale to retail customers. Ampex concentrated on high-price, high-performance systems: other U.S. firms abandoned the field altogether. Japanese companies had the financial stamina to sustain low returns on investments while perfecting designs and manufacturing processes. The result is that the Japanese now dominate the consumer video-recording market. Moreover, by capitalizing on the profits, technology and economies of mass production built up in that market, they have begun to encroach on the upscale market as well.

Figure 5.10: *The failure of US video recorder manufacturing*

Source: 'Towards a new industrial America', Suzanne Berger *et al., Scientific American,* June 1989, p.23.

6.3   ADVERSE ROLE OF THE PUBLIC SECTOR?

Thus a further reason often offered for the long-term decline of American industrial capacity, and for the supposed sclerosis in its dynamic and innovativeness more generally, is the increasing role of the government sector. As we saw above, along with all other OECD countries, the role of the state expanded in the postwar period. It is the adverse consequences of this that are stressed by those opposed to government intervention on ideological grounds. This is thought to have undermined the traditional self reliance and fortitude of the American people, and of the American system, by making people reliant upon the welfare state to provide them with either jobs or benefits, and with unnecessarily increasing bureaucratic procedures which undermine inventiveness, the entrepreneurial spirit, imagination and enterprise, the work ethic, and so on. Costs are unnecessarily increased for businesses, taxes blunt the incentives to individual initiative, intervention and regulation stifle the rapid adaptation to changed circumstances and opportunities.

This catalogue of ills thought to emanate from 'the government' is well known. It certainly informed a change of mood in the 1980s, which, as we have seen, at least partly resulted in a stabilization of federal expenditure as a proportion of GDP during the latter-1980s (but did not lead to a reduction in its absolute level). This was accompanied by a rejection of 'Keynesian demand management' as the main theoretically sanctioned economic governance mechanism, and its replacement by an emphasis on 'supply-side management'. Whether this explicit rejection of Keynesianism made much difference in practice remains a mute point, however, since it was in fact accompanied by a massive *increase* in the budget deficit — just what such a Keynesian policy would have called for in a time of recession! In reality, then, the USA could be accused of conducting an old-fashioned, but surrogate, Keynesian policy during the ascendancy of the New Right. While such a Keynesian policy was not that important in stimulating and sustaining the long-boom, it might have been important in preventing an even more serious recession in the 1980s. This would place the 'public sector' in a benign role.

The trouble with the 'growth-of-government-as-undermining-productivity' argument is that any robust connections between the two have just not been made. This is reinforced by the observation that the growth in government has been a gradual and long-term one, encompassing the time of an unproblematical increase in productivity. The sudden drop in 1973 hardly coincided with any dramatic increase in such expenditures, though there was a temporary upsurge in 1975 (see Figure 5.3). What happened in 1973 was of course the (non-government inspired) supply-side shock of the oil price rises, and this looks the most likely immediate culprit for setting the decline in progress (Griliches, 1988). The problem here, however, is that even when the impact of this had passed, American productivity increases did not bounce back to their historic post-war levels as might have been expected.

6.4   INTEREST GROUPS AND SOCIAL SCLEROSIS?

This raises a further possible reason for the reductions. Perhaps the domestic response to such shocks, indeed to any shock, is somehow just not flexible enough to allow an adequate readjustment in the economic mechanism, or in society as a whole. This is an argument about the social embeddedness of interest groups in American society; they become so matured, powerful and moribund, that they fail the system when it is faced by a crisis. Mancur Olson makes this point in a number of publications (Olson, 1982 and 1988, for instance). He stresses the way collective action can generate coalitions of actors whose struggle over distributional issues establishes a set of institutional rigidities which inhibit anything other than a narrow defensive response to unexpected exogenous shocks. Once such coalitions become established they are very difficult to shift, and the whole of the society suffers as a result. For those countries with long traditions of plural government and continuity in social structure, cultural outlook, etc., this becomes ossified in a loss of dynamic energy for change. Such is the case of the USA, it is argued, with the resultant inability to respond effectively to a productivity slow down occasioned by the impact of the oil-price shocks. Long-term decline is the inevitable result, it is claimed.

While there may be some truth in this explanation, the problem is that it rather implies nothing can be done to improve the situation. Barring anything approaching a revolution the USA is stuck with a declining and increasingly inflexible economy. In addition, does the USA represent quite the plurally stable society so envisaged? It is certainly plural but is it so stable? An important aspect to the country is the enormous immigration that it still attracts, which adds to the already prodigious mobility of the population. It should be remembered, for instance, that despite the stubborn persistence of unemployment, between 1981 and 1987 alone the US economy managed to create some 12 million net new jobs. If nothing else this gives rise to a flexibility that to some extent must undermine existing distributional interest group coalitions in the longer run. These distributional issues are important so we will move on to discuss them in the next section.

SUMMARY

A seemingly intractable problem for the US economy is to explain its productivity profile and particularly the dramatic and persistent slow down in productivity growth after 1973. This is the main reason for the recent poor showing of the US economy in terms of its overall growth and international competitiveness. The possible reasons for these changes in the mid-1970s are numerous and wide ranging. None of them offers a single or full explanation. Thus the reasons for all this still remain a mystery, though the most likely candidate for immediately setting the whole process going was the price rises in oil in 1973 and 1979.

7   INEQUALITY AND INCOME DISTRIBUTION

US median family incomes rose on average by 2.7 per cent a year between 1947 and 1973. This was largely because the capital stock per worker rose steadily (after 1953 in particular) and output per hour rose along with it. In addition, the distribution of income between families narrowed a little (Rivlin, 1992, pp.44–7). During this period of prosperity average poverty rates also dropped as most shared in the general increase in the standard of living.

The continuing poverty of isolated rural dwellers and those in decaying urban areas was disguised during this period, particularly that of blacks. It was rediscovered in the 1960s. The Civil Rights movement highlighted the need for governmental action to at least ameliorate the plight of the black poor and others on very low incomes. The federal government launched the so called 'war on poverty' as a result. The effects of this were short lived however. The rapidly falling poverty rates from 1960 for blacks, the elderly and those under 18 years of age levelled out after 1973, but still with significant absolute disadvantage levels remaining (Table 5.8).

Table 5.8   Poverty levels by race, 1990 (thousands)

Race	Total persons	Number below poverty level	Per cent below poverty level
Total	248,644	33,585	13.5
African American	30,806	9,837	31.9
White	208,611	22,326	10.7
Other races	9,227	1,422	15.4

Source: *The State of Black America 1992*, National Urban League, Table 16, p.321.
Based on Bureau of the Census, *Current Population Survey*, March 1990.

The relative position of African Americans shown in Table 5.8 is worth particular note. In 1990 they were three times as likely to be below the poverty level as whites. This had mainly to do with differences in family income levels (Table 5.9).

Table 5.9   Median family income by race and family type, 1990

Type of family	African American	White	Ratio: African American/White
All families	$21,423	$36,915	58.0
Married-couple families	33,784	40,331	83.8
Male householder, no wife present	21,848	30,570	71.5
Female householder, no husband present	12,125	19,528	62.1

Source: *The State of Black America 1992*, National Urban League, Table 14, p.319.
Based on Bureau of the Census, *Current Population Survey*, March 1990.

In 1939 the average income of black people was just 39 per cent of that of white people. While there had been a significant improvement by 1990 the average income of black people was still only 58 per cent of that of white people. This continued disadvantaged position showed only a marginal improvement on the 1970 position, but it did indicate that incomes of black people have been increasing at a faster rate than those of white people since then. A lot of the underlying problem has to do with the differences in unemployment rates as shown in Table 5.10. Black people are systematically discriminated against in the American labour market, particularly black teenagers where a staggering 53 per cent had no real full-time job in 1990 if these figures are accurate.

General inequality increased from the early 1970s. By 1985 the income share of the bottom 40 per cent of Americans was lower than it had been at any time since the Second World War (just between 1979 and 1985 their income share fell from 16.8 per cent to 15.5 per cent). By contrast, the rich grew richer, aided by the 1986 tax reforms (which actually *increased* taxes on the very poor). After the 1986 reforms it would have been necessary to go back to the 1930s to find a tax rate as low as 28 per cent on a comparable level of real income (the then top rate), and as far back as the 1920s to find a lower maximum scheduled tax rate overall (Meltzer, 1988, p.535).

Table 5.10   Percentage unemployed by race, 1990

	Official	Hidden[a]
All Age Groups		
Total	5.5	11.3
White	4.8	9.9
African American	11.3	21.5
Teenagers		
Total	15.5	30.1
White	13.1	25.0
African American	31.1	53.1

[a] Hidden unemployment rate includes discouraged and involuntary part-time workers among the unemployed.

Source: Compiled and adapted from *The State of Black America 1992*, Tables 18 and 19, pp.322 and 323.

Not all disadvantaged groups suffered growing inequality however. The elderly, for instance, increased their income shares (particularly the elderly rich) through a combination of tax reductions and welfare transfers. It was families headed by younger women with children that fared the worst (refer back to Table 5.9 again). In addition, the majority of new jobs created during the 1980s were of the lower wage, unskilled, service employment type.

Thus it was a combination of demographic, cyclical, policy and deeper structural changes that led to the increases of inequality and poverty in this period. One consequence has been a decrease in welfare outputs. The rate of immunization against childhood diseases declined in the USA throughout the 1980s, and the rate of low-weight births, which had decreased steadily from the mid-1960s to 1980, levelled off and even began to increase for some groups (Rothschild, 1988, p.49).

SUMMARY

The USA has never been a particularly egalitarian society, despite its professed commitment to this sentiment. But there was a definite, though modest, improvement in the post-war years, aided by the prosperity of the long-boom. All this came to a sudden end in the mid-1970s, however, as the recession developed. Poverty and inequality increased. As a whole the disadvantaged black population rather held its own in this latter period. It was the vulnerable groups of black *and* white people who suffered disproportionately, particularly the young, single mother households, the disabled, unemployed women, and similar categories.

8   GOVERNMENT AND MARKET

'The land of the free; the land of the market'. This could easily serve as an epitaph for the American economy as we near the end of the twentieth century. The question is whether it makes for a truly viable economy in these latter years of the 1990s. The growing involvement of the government sector during the post-war period stimulated a reassessment of its position as soon as the long-boom collapsed in the mid-1970s. The free market and competition reappeared as the driving motif for the organization of the economy once again.

An interesting feature of this — one must add not particularly novel — reaction against the government was a counter argument that has gathered pace ever since. This was to argue that far from the problem being too much government intervention there had not been enough. Or more accurately, that the extent of government involvement had not been of the right type or form. The USA lacked a 'developmental state', one with the objective and capacity of a thorough-going reorganization and modernization of its economy. Such a developmental state was seen by many as being responsible for the 'economic miracles' elsewhere, particularly amongst the USA's newly emergent rivals around the Pacific Rim. Japan had its Ministry of International Trade and Industry (MITI); Korea a single minded leadership with rapid industrialization at the head of its agenda; Taiwan was moving down the road to technological excellence; a government-sponsored dynamic economy had emerged in Singapore; Hong Kong was acting as the power house for the still state-controlled Chinese economy; Malaysia would soon follow, also spearheaded by a determined state sponsorship. How should the USA react and how would it compete?

At an official level, at least, the USA seemed to ignore any lessons that might have been drawn from these examples. Rather, in typical almost rhetorical style, it effectively fell back on its tried and tested emphasis on the virtues of free competition and the supremacy of the market mechanism. If only the playing field were levelled, so that US manufacturers got a fair crack at the opposition, they would win through. The US government's still very considerable economic weight was thrown behind this strategy as a diplomatic effort ensued to open up markets to US goods where they were perceived to be closed before, and a new round of multilateral trade talks pressed into action (the Uruguay Round) to head off domestic protectionist sentiment and secure the compliance of friends and foe alike to US economic leadership once again. In the early 1990s the newly-elected President Bill Clinton pressed this approach with added vigour (see Chapter 6).

The outcome of this strategy remains to be seen (see also Chapters 9 and 10). Meanwhile, in the actual domestic arena it is private economic agents who are increasingly puzzling over the virtues of unrestrained competition and a totally free market. Of course there has always been a tension here, since the business world itself has historically led in the concentration and centralization of capital and the government and legal institutions have periodically attempted to limit and regulate (anti-)competitive activity.

But perhaps a new mood of 'co-operative-competition' is about to appear in American business circles. This is particularly so as the economy increasingly fragments along regional lines, making any renewed attempt at central direction or management by the federal government doubly difficult (see Chapter 9). Were this to properly mature it would not only stimulate collaborative initiatives between companies in the generation and development of new products and processes, but also stimulate collaboration between industry and elements of the government sector itself. New quasi-public/private liaisons and support mechanisms are developing, not so much involving additional large-scale strategic type investment on the part of the federal government to subsidize industry, but as a complement to the information and skills provided by the private market in various ways, and operating very much at a local or state level. This new mood of realism about the market — that there are a variety of different market systems — the key to the effective operation of which is to balance competition with co-operation and not to see these as necessarily opposed to one another, may yet win through to create a 'new American economic dream'.

The obstacles to this remain formidable, however, not least of which is that deep ideological aversion to anything thought to remotely undermine individual freedom in the name of collective action. This is a cleavage that continues to haunt the American economy as well as the American psyche more generally. In addition, whether desirable or not, it still remains central governments that have the power to determine exactly what lower tiers can do, and the legitimate limits to their powers. Thus without a real change of direction at the federal level, involving a political will, determination and the *ability* to overcome obstacles to radical change, things could just muddle along very much as before.

SUMMARY

The market *versus* the government is no longer a productive way to think about the relationship between competition and co-operation in respect to the economy. The characteristic American knee-jerk reaction to these terms may be on its way out. Although it may have served the American economy well through much of the twentieth century the idea of 'free market competition' and a minimally tolerated government sector is perhaps giving way to new innovative forms of collaboration between the public and the private domains, and between US companies themselves.

9   CONCLUSION

Can the American economy regain its dynamic, competitiveness and even leadership position once again? This is the question facing economic policy makers, business leaders, labour organizations and the American public at large. It is an issue explicitly taken up in Chapter 6. Some were already heralding the renewed vigour the economy displayed in the early 1990s as the possible beginnings of its manufacturing renaissance (Baily, 1993). Others, however, remain more cautious, stressing the need for a continued diminution of expectations in line with the realities of the 1980s (Krugman, 1992). In this chapter we have analysed the effects of the dramatic turn-around in the economy that began to appear in the mid-1970s. This opened the economy to international influence as it had never been experienced before. Since then Americans have had to become used to their position as one among a growing band of equals. The data in Table 5.1 indicated a seeming convergence of the three groups of economies onto a lower expectation horizon in the case of most of the economic indicators shown. But this has still not totally dislodged that American dream of regaining its number one position. A key to its present strategy is the construction of a new international trading block in alliance with Canada and Mexico — the North American Free Trade Area. Whether this becomes a successful strategy from the point of view of the USA remains something that only the events of the twenty-first century will properly tell. Perhaps fortunately, this will remain for others to judge. The next chapter explores these issues in the context of the trajectory of the US economy since 1990.

REFERENCES

Baily, M.M. (1993) 'Made in the USA', *The Brookings Review,* Winter, pp.36–9.

Baily, M.M. and Gordon, R.J. (1988) 'The productivity slowdown, measurement issues, and the explosion of computer power', *Brookings Papers on Economic Activity: 2*, pp.347-431.

Bowles, S., Gordon, D. and Weisskopf, T. (1989) 'Business ascendancy and the economic impasse: a structural retrospective on conservative economics, 1979-87', *Journal of Economic Perspectives*, Vol. 3, No. 1, Winter, pp.107–34.

Gunn, T.G. (1982) 'The mechanization of design and manufacturing', *Scientific American*, September pp.87–108.

Gramlich, E.M. (1992) 'The 1991 state and local fiscal crisis', *Brookings Papers on Economic Activity: 2*, pp.249–75.

Griliches, Z. (1988) 'Productivity puzzles and R&D: another non-explanation', *Journal of Economic Perspectives*, Vol. 2, No.4, pp.9–21.

Historical Tables, *Budget of the United States Government 1992,* Washington D.C.

Krugman, P. (1992) *The Age of Diminished Expectations: US Economic Policy in the 1990s*, Cambridge, Mass., MIT Press.

Lipsey, R.E. and Kravis, I.B. (1985) 'The competitive position of US manufacturing firms', *Banca Nazionale del Lavoro Quarterly Review*, Vol. XXXVIII, June, pp.127–54.

Lipsey, R.E. and Kravis, I.B. (1987) 'The competitiveness and comparative advantage of US multinationals 1957–1984', *Banca Nazionale del Lavoro Quarterly Review*, Vol. XL, June, pp.147–65.

Meltzer, A.H. (1988) 'Economic policies and actions in the Reagan Administrations', *Journal of Post-Keynesian Economics*, Vol. X, Summer, pp.528–40.

OECD (1992) *Industrial Policies in OECD Countries 1992*, OECD, Paris.

Olson, M. (1982) *The Rise and Decline of Nations*, Newhaven, Conn., Yale University Press.

Olson, M. (1988) 'The productivity slowdown, the oil shocks, and the real cycle', *Journal of Economic Perspectives*, Vol. 2, No. 4, pp.43–69.

Reich, R.B. (1989) 'The quiet path to technological pre-eminence', *Scientific American*, October, Vol. 261, No. 4, pp.19–25.

Rivlin, A.M. (1992) *Reviving the American Dream*, Washington DC, Brookings Institution.

Rothschild, E. (1988) 'The Reagan economic legacy', *New York Review of Books*, 21 July.

Statistical Abstract of the United States (various years).

Thompson, G.F. (ed.) (1989) *Industrial Policy: USA and UK Debates*, Routledge, London.

Thompson, G.F. (1990) *The Political Economy of the New Right*, London, Pinter.

FURTHER READING

Destler, I.M. (1992) *American Trade Politics*, Washington DC., Institute for International Economics.

Krugman, P. (1992) *The Age of Diminished Expectations: US Economic Policy in the 1990s*, Cambridge, Mass., MIT Press.

Reich, R. (1991) *The Work of Nations*, New York, Alfred A. Knopf.

Rivlin, A.M. (1992) *Reviving the American Dream*, Washington DC., Brookings Institution.

6

THE US ECONOMY: 1990–1999

Grahame Thompson ★

1   INTRODUCTION

This chapter traces the course of the US economy over the period from the early 1990s to 1998/99. This was a period that saw a sustained upward swing in the economic fortunes of the USA. Beginning in 1991 the average growth rate was 3 per cent a year, and this was accompanied by minimal inflation and historically low unemployment levels. These features led many commentators to predict that the traditional four stage business cycle of prosperity, transition, recession, and finally recovery — one that had typified the course of the post-Second World War US economy — was now over (Weber, 1997). It had entered a completely new era — the era of the 'new economics' — in which there is no business cycle, only sustained growth. What is more, it is argued that this new era will see the global resurgence of the USA with the emergence of another American economic miracle to parallel that at the beginning of the twentieth century, and one to rival that of the now exhausted German and Japanese economic miracles of the 1960s and 1980s respectively (Zuckerman, 1998). Indeed, it was the mercurial Chairman of the Federal Reserve Bank, Alan Greenspan, who raised the temperature on this 'new economics' debate by commenting on the possibilities of a new and sustained economic resurgence as he testified to the Senate banking committee in February 1997. It was Greenspan's handling of monetary policy during the mid-1990s that was widely credited as being mainly responsible for the 'good news' economy current at the end of that decade. But whilst Greenspan counselled caution on that occasion, a growth rate of nearly 4 per cent in both 1997 and 1998 (and forecasts of only a modest slowdown for 1999), fuelled the sentiment amongst business leaders and commentators that there really was a new paradigm governing economic activity in the USA. This was aided by the seemingly endless rise of the stock market, signalled by the graph and report contained in Figure 6.1. The good times were back again, and here to stay!

This chapter takes the issue of the 'new era' as the central point of reference and examines the arguments both for and against it. This provides an opportunity to assess the late 1990's state of the economy and what might have changed during the 1990s. The chapter thus chronologically carries on from where Chapter 5 left off (though not in terms of the exact analytical issues pursued there).

Dow Jones breaks 10,000 mark

US stock market reaches milestone as traders predict further share rises

By Richard Waters, John Labate and Andrew Edgecliffe-Johnson in New York

To muted cheering on the floor of the New York Exchange, the US stock market passed a historic milestone yesterday – and many traders and investors said the rise was set to continue.

The Dow Jones Industrial Average, the most widely-followed measure of US share prices, rose briefly above 10,000 during morning trading in New York, only 15 years after it first reached 1,000. It had taken 66 years to get from 100 to 1,000.

After the breathless media anticipation that had accompanied the Dow's rise towards the latest landmark, the breakthrough into five digits came as something of an anti-climax on the trading floor.

"It's just a number," said Theodore Weisberg, a white-haired trader who took a moment off to bask in the unseasonal sunshine bathing the pavement outside the NSYE's Manhattan home.

"When I started, I remember the Dow at 580. Breaking through 1,000 was a big deal."

Despite the subdued mood among traders, the event was generally expected to prompt further buying of US shares, particularly from the millions of ordinary Americans whose investments in mutual funds or directly in stocks have accounted for much of the market's rise in the 1990s.

"There is probably enough exuberance and cash to drive another spike [in share prices]," said Bill Meehan, chief market analyst at stockbrokers Cantor Fitzgerald.

Others warned that any euphoria following the Dow's latest milestone might fuel what many observers already fear are unsustainably high share prices. "If anything, it might create a false sense of security, like the tail wagging the dog," said Mr Weisberg.

The stock market's latest rise suggests that many investors have shaken off the concerns of the past 18 months that accompanied Asia's economic crisis, Russia's unexpected financial implosion and Brazil's currency collapse.

Ralph Acampora, chief technical analyst at Prudential Securities and one of the first to predict, in the mid-1990s, that the market could reach 10,000 before the end of the decade, said the US could be at the beginning of a 12-15 year "mega-market".

The jump in share prices has been aided by an easing of fears that the Federal Reserve would be forced to raise interest rates to prevent an overheating of the US economy. Long-term bond yields fell back below 5.5 per cent yesterday, after a bout of concern that a consumer boom was lifting the economic growth rate to an unsustainable level.

By the close in New York, the Dow had fallen back to 9,930.47, a drop of 28.3 on the day. The Standard & Poor's 500 closed down 0.90 at 1,306.36, while the Nasdaq composite, which has recorded the biggest gains during the bull market, was up 7.83 at 2,439.27, about 85 points from a record.

10,001: a stock odyssey, Page 16; Editorial Comment, Page 17; Lex, Page 18; Barry Riley, Page 19; Euro prices, Page 37; Bonds, Page 38; World stocks, Page 48

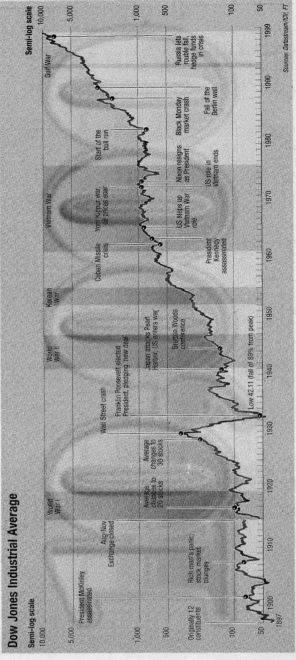

Figure 6.1 The rise of the stock market in the late 1990s

Source: *Financial Times*, 17 March 1999, p.1

2   CHANGING CONTOURS OF THE US MACROECONOMIC POSITION

We begin this assessment with the broad macroeconomic characteristics of the economy as compared to those of its two main economic rivals. Table 6.1 presents comparable economic indicators for the USA, the EU and Japan over the period 1990–98. Given there was a temporary slowdown in the US growth rate during 1995, this provides a convenient dividing point for the period considered as a whole.

Table 6.1   Comparative US economic indicators, 1990–98

	1990–95	1996–98
Real GDP growth		
(yearly % changes)		
USA	1.9	3.6
EU15	1.5	2.3
Japan	1.9	0.7
Gross capital formation		
(as % of GDP)		
USA	16.3	17.7
EU15	19.7	18.3
Japan	30.0	28.5
Investment in machinery and equipment		
(as % of GDP)		
USA	7.5	na
EU15	8.4	na
Japan	11.0	na
Net savings		
(as % of GDP)		
USA	4.1	na
EU15	7.4	na
Japan	17.4	na
Unemployment		
(as a % of total labour force)		
USA	6.4	5.0
EU15	9.6	10.6
Japan	2.5	3.4

Table 6.1 continued

	1990–95	1996–98
Inflation		
(% change per year)		
USA	3.5[1]	2.1
EU15	4.2[1]	2.0
Japan	1.6[1]	0.3
Government sector balance		
(as % of GDP)		
USA	–4.4[2]	–0.5
EU15	–5.4	–2.8[3]
Japan	–0.1	–3.8
Trade balances		
(as % of GDP)		
USA	–1.2	–2.4[4]
EU15	0.7	1.6[4]
Japan	1.7	2.4[4]

Notes
[1] 1989–95
[2] 1990–94
[3] Excludes Luxembourg
[4] 1996 and 1997 only

Sources: compiled from *OECD Historical Statistics 1960–1995*, OECD, Paris, 1997; *European Economy No. 65, Convergence Report, 1998*, EU, Luxembourg, 1998; *OECD Main Economic Indicators*, February 1999, OECD, Paris

Clearly, the growth rate (of GDP) after 1995 was more impressive than up to that point, and compared to its competitors the US position was even more impressive. In addition the USA had improved its position a little in terms of gross capital formation, while that of its rivals had fallen away slightly. But note how on these figures — and the more limited ones in respect to investment in only machinery and equipment — the EU and particularly Japan still demonstrated a superior position to that of the USA even as their relative advantage faded. This is confirmed in the case of net savings. The US savings rate plummeted, particularly between 1991 and 1994. Estimates put personal savings rates at almost zero in 1998 (0.2 per cent in the third quarter of 1998), so that it was corporate and particularly public savings that contributed the bulk of the 6 per cent overall ratio in 1998. For the time being at least the great personal savers in the international system still remain the Japanese (but the position here may change fast as the financial recession in Japan matures).

If we now move on to consider unemployment and inflation, the other two main performance indicators, again the US position is cast in a favourable light. Unemployment was back to its levels of the 1960s, while inflation seemed to have been almost completely driven out of the system. Not since the 1960s had there been a period of such strong economic growth combined with such low levels of unemployment and inflation. Clearly, in the case of the other economies, on the unemployment front both the EU and Japan turned in a deteriorating performance, with the EU's unemployment rate double that of the USA's between 1996 and 1998. A major element in the 'triumph of the US economy' story in the 1990s is made up of this difference to the European experience. The Europeans are accused of having neither created the jobs that the USA had done, nor solved their unemployment problem. In addition, it was also claimed that the Japanese would soon be heading for double-digit unemployment if their recession matured into a full-blown depression after 1999.

Turning now to the final two indicators given in Table 6.1, these show the position on the famous 'twin deficit' issue that confronted the USA throughout the 1980s. Clearly, the USA seemed to have almost solved its budget deficit problem by 1998, and the budget deficit in the EU also diminished considerably over the period. That of Japan rose, however, as a consequence of the essentially 'Keynesian' policies adopted by successive Japanese governments in response to the emerging recession in their own economy. They had tried to spend their way out of recession in the traditional manner by increasing government expenditures and reducing taxes (up until 1999 without much success, it might be added).

On the other hand, the USA had not solved the trade deficit problem. Indeed, this had burgeoned. The merchandise trade deficit was nearly $US 200 billion in 1997 (the current account deficit was over $US 150 billion), and rising. Despite the recession in Japan (perhaps even because of it), its trade surplus expanded. The formidable Japanese production machine rolls on, though again there may be a limit to this as the financial recession bites in Japan. The EU also shows a slightly improved position in the later part of the period.

SUMMARY

So much for the macroeconomic position. What these data signal is the reasons for the optimistic mood in the USA about the economy. US citizens had seen their economy growing, their personal wealth increasing (as the stock market boomed), and they had embarked upon a consumption boom as a result (hence the low personal savings rate). This in turn stimulated an improved aggregate investment record, but also a further serious deterioration in the balance of payments as imports were sucked in to feed the consumption boom. A lot of this good news is put down to the way the government (federal) deficit has been reduced (President Clinton's legacy) and the way inflation had been defeated (FED Chairman Greenspan's legacy). The relative contribution of consumption, fixed investment, government expenditure and net exports to the 1990s expansion, relative to their importance in two previous booms, are detailed in Figure 6.2. The contribution of consumption rose even further, and the investment record improved considerably.

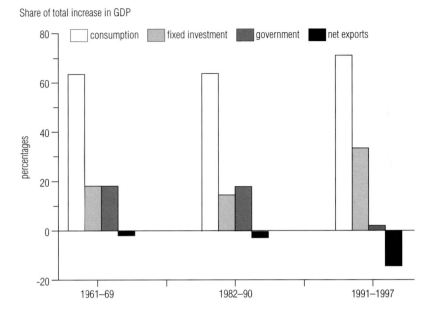

Share of total increase in GDP

Figure 6.2 *Contributions to economic growth in three long expansions*
Source: US Government Printing Office (1999) *Economic Report of the President 1999*, Washington DC, Chart 2.1, p.28

Now we need to examine this story in greater detail.

3   A BOOMING ECONOMY

What were the reasons put forward for the booming economy in the USA? Here two basic determinants have been identified: technological developments and 'globalization'. As we shall see, the story is considerably more complicated, involving much more than just these two elements, but for the moment we examine these in turn.

3.1   TECHNOLOGICAL DEVELOPMENTS

The argument about technological developments can be illustrated from the data plotted in Figure 6.3. The first part of the figure indicates the importance of investment in the 1990s boom, relative to that of previous post-war expansions. In particular it is producers' durable equipment that stands out as the significant major change from previous expansions (from a 10 per cent to a 25 per cent contribution to GDP change). The second part focuses on this crucial category of producers' durable equipment investment between 1990 and 1997, which is part of the 'equipment and machinery' category considered in aggregate terms in Table 6.1. Whilst the overall record in this respect was not particularly encouraging for the USA relative to other countries, its investment in 'information processing equipment' soared. In 1995–96 alone it grew by 21 per cent in real terms. (The rather lack-lustre relative international performance in the 'equipment and machinery' category overall is reflected in 'other producers' durable' investment shown in Figure 6.3b.)

a) Role of investment compared to other expansions (contribution to GDP change)

percentage of real GDP change

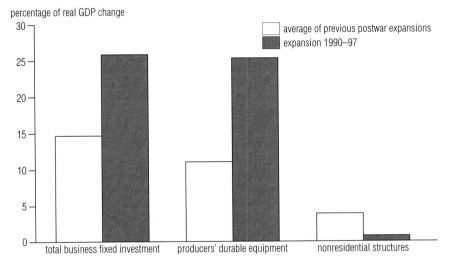

b) Role of producers' durable equipment in 1990–97 expansion (real changes in investment)

percentage change over 4 quarters

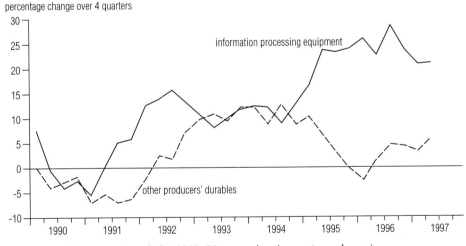

Figure 6.3 *Investment, and the 1990–98 expansion (percentage change)*

Sources: a) US Government Printing Office (1999) *Economic Report of the President 1999*, Washington DC, Chart 2–7, p.69; b) *OECD Economic Surveys: The United States*, 1997, derived from Figure 5, p.28

Thus the USA is in the middle of a profound 'technological revolution' it is argued, involving computers, semiconductors and other high-technology production, which is itself based upon advances in information technology.

The USA leads in many areas of information processing, which is driven by the re-equipment of its domestic economy. This is having profound implications for all economic activity, it is suggested. It means the reorganization of service and manufacturing production by American firms both at home and abroad, re-defining the nature of co-ordinated production and distribution between domestic and foreign operations for instance, so as to increase quality control and improve information systems to adjust supply, prices and output more quickly to market conditions. US firms now account for over 40 per cent of the world's investment in computing, spending twice as much on 'infotech' as do European firms, and eight times the global average. And this marks another step in a change in the whole direction of the economy towards service-type production (which consolidates an already firm trend in respect to the US economy — see Chapters 3 and 5).

The USA thus dominates the knowledge industries of the future, it is claimed, and its exporting successes reflect this advantage. Exports are growing in advanced semiconductors, computer network servers, personal computers, software and services, entertainment, finance, and telecommunications; as well as in the more traditional high-tech sectors like completed civilian aircraft. Basically, what the information technology revolution is producing, according to the optimistic advocates of a new economics, is a dramatic increase in productivity. This part of their story we return to in a moment.

3.2 'GLOBALIZATION'

The 'technological revolution' explanation for the unusually strong and sustained growth record is bolstered by an argument about the advent of 'globalization' and the way the American economy has both contributed to, and reacted to, this trend. There is a good deal of dispute about exactly what globalization means, and whether it genuinely represents a new structural stage in international capitalism. We avoid this discussion here and simply define 'globalization' as the increasing internationalization of economic relationships, involving a growth in integration and interdependence across national borders for all aspects of economic activity.

During most of the post-Second World War period, it is argued, the US economy remained relatively isolated from economic interdependencies and international integration. The USA was a very large 'continental' economy, trading and investing mainly within its own national boundaries. In 1970, for instance, the USA traded only 8 per cent of its GDP (sum of imports plus exports as per cent of GDP — see Figure 6.4), and despite the growth of its overseas multinational corporations, these still centred the vast bulk of their investment activity on the domestic territory (see Table 6.4 p.152). In addition, although the dollar operated as the main international currency, the internationalization of financial markets was also limited as countries maintained capital controls and heavily regulated their national economies and exchange rates.

All this changed during the 1970s and 1980s of course (see Chapters 3, 5, 7, and 10), so that it was in the 1990s that 'globalization' really took off. Liberalization, privatization and deregulation proceeded apace during the 1980s in particular, and became a world-wide phenomenon under an American-sponsored global neo-liberal policy agenda.

The statistics on US trade and multinational corporation (MNC) investments are illustrated in Figures 6.4 and 6.5, pointing to the accelerating growth on both measures during the 1990s' expansion.

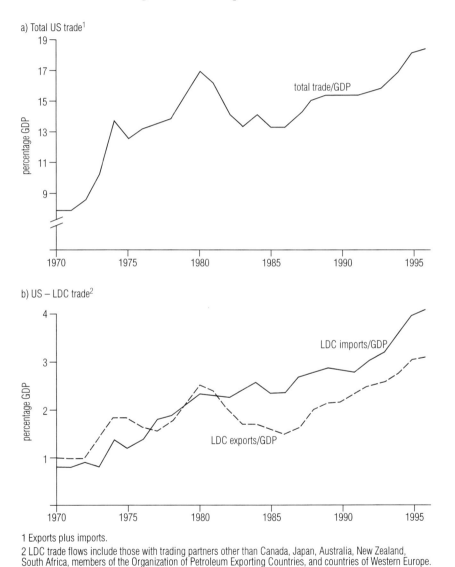

1 Exports plus imports.
2 LDC trade flows include those with trading partners other than Canada, Japan, Australia, New Zealand, South Africa, members of the Organization of Petroleum Exporting Countries, and countries of Western Europe.

Figure 6.4 *Trade openness of the US economy, 1970–1996*
Source: adapted from Borjas, Freeman and Katz, 1997, Figure 2, p.11

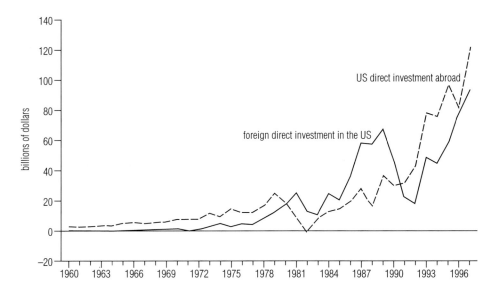

Figure 6.5 *US foreign direct investment flows*

Source: US Government Printing Office (1999) *Economic Report of the President 1999*, Washington DC, Chart 6–11, p.264

Thus, by 1998 the US economy was trading nearly 20 per cent of its GDP, a two and a half fold increase on the 1970 position. In addition, there was a surge in US direct investment abroad as well as foreign direct investment into the USA (clearly, there was a deficit overall here during the 1990s). So the USA too had now entered the global economy, and with a vengeance. From the perspective of the 'new economics', this full blown entry of the USA into the global economy is another reason why the economy had rapidly expanded. It capitalized on the opening up of other economies, inserting US business practices and financial acumen into the markets and organizations of what were previously sheltered and relatively isolated national economies. Here the globalization and technological revolution arguments fuse as US businessmen were shocked out of their own complacency by a newly invigorated international competition. Restructuring, re-engineering, down-sizing and vigorous cost-cutting were the response, it is suggested, so that now American companies have become vastly more efficient. The twin pressures of international competition and rapid technological change combined to announce a new era, to which American corporations were almost uniquely able to positively respond. And since the introduction of information technology and the process of globalization are only just beginning, there is a no obvious limit on the expansion of American capitalism either domestically or abroad.

Here it was a new version of the 'heroic entrepreneur' that served to fulfil the American dream once again. A culture of rugged individualism, entrepreneurialism, pragmatism and novelty — this time embodied in the small start-up company which rapidly rose to stock market flotation, personified by the likes of Bill Gates at Microsoft and Steve Jobs at Apple Computers — is invoked as the underlying microeconomic foundation of the positive macroeconomic results just described.

SUMMARY

For those making the argument that the American economy had entered a new phase of sustainable growth there were two sides to their position. One emphasized the importance of information technology in raising the efficiency and productivity of American firms. The other emphasized the significance of the process of gobalization in extending the range of US business influence across the globe and acting as a competitive stimulus to the domestic economic environment. These two aspects complement and reinforce one another. This was bolstered by the idea of a maverick entrepreneurial culture as a key support mechanism for that macroeconomic growth.

4   QUESTIONING THE 'NEW ECONOMICS'

4.1   A PRODUCTIVITY MIRACLE?

A central plank in the new economics approach relies upon the positive consequences of introducing information technology for productivity growth. Here we return to a long running issue in the modern history of the American economy, namely the 'riddle of productivity' (Chapter 5).

The recent record on US productivity is given in the first part of Table 6.2. This shows only one measure, but the results are similar if other measures of productivity are used. It is clear that for the economy as a whole the growth in output per hour worked was modest over the entire period 1990–97, with rates of over 1 per cent per year being recorded only in 1996 and 1997. The differences between the overall non-farm business sector and that for manufacturing as a part of this sector is also revealing. Clearly, productivity in manufacturing has been increasing at a much faster rate than that for the business sector as a whole (Chapter 3). On the surface this might seem odd, given the emphasis on the growth in investment in computing technology and informatics, and the decline of manufacturing as the key part of the US economy, as stressed by the 'new paradigm' story discussed above. With the growth of a post-industrial 'service economy' we might have expected productivity in the overall non-farm business sector to have led that in manufacturing. Clearly, however, what is still classified as manufacturing now involves a lot of service-type activities as well.

Table 6.2 US business sector productivity, 1990–97 (percentage change on previous year)

	1990	1993	1994	1995	1996	1997
Output per hour worked	0.7	0.2	0.4	0.1	2.0	1.9
Non-farm businesses	0.5	0.1	0.4	0.2	1.9	1.7
Manufacturing	1.8	2.2	2.5	3.2	3.7	4.4

Source: compiled from US Government Printing Office (1998) *Statistical Abstract of the United States*, US Bureau Census of Statistics, Washington DC, Table 689, p.433

In addition, given the emphasis on the USA's advantage in the new technology investment stakes, we might have expected its productivity growth to have outstripped that of its main economic rivals. Comparative productivity data are presented in Table 6.3. (All these figures are measured against the US levels, which is given a figure of 100 in each case). As can be seen, in terms of real GDP per person employed, Japan, France and Germany all improved their position on the USA between 1989 and 1996, if only modestly, and France and Germany still had a better productivity record than the USA in 1996. And in terms of real GDP per capita, both Japan and Germany improved on the USA, though France fell away a little. In terms of annual growth rates of productivity, between 1989 and 1998 both Germany and Japan had a better annual average growth rate than did the USA — 2.6 per cent and 4 per cent respectively compared to the US 0.9 per cent (*The Economist*, 1999, p.89).

Table 6.3 International comparisons of productivity and GDP: 1989 and 1996 (USA = 100)

Real GDP per employed person	1989	1996
Japan	73.9	76.4
France	90.2	90.6
Germany	84.9	91.4

Real GDP per hour worked	1996
Japan	70.9
France	100.4
Germany	106.8

Real per capita GDP	1989	1996
Japan	75.5	81.0
France	73.6	71.6
Germany	78.3	80.2

Source: adapted from Krugman, 1998, p.43

These data indicate that the USA's record in terms of productivity is not as outstanding as is implied by the 'new paradigm' thesis. Indeed, in many respects it demonstrated a productivity record over the 1990s no better than for much of the post-Second World War period prior to 1990 (see Tables 5.6 and 5.7 in Chapter 5). Improvements in the USA have been very modest — with the exception of the manufacturing sector in later years — and the USA has lagged somewhat in respect of its comparative international position as well. But the fact that, in part at least, the USA has held its own against its economic competitors is the result of the lack-lustre performance of those rivals over the same period. There is little evidence, however, that the USA itself has shown a breakthrough in productivity growth.

So why has this promised breakthrough failed to emerge? Here, many of the arguments that characterized the debate about the productivity slowdown in the 1970s and 1980s have resurfaced. The 'new economics' authors suggest that there are measurement errors which fail to record all the real productivity gains that have accrued in the service sector in particular. However, this is difficult to sustain since they make no quarrel with the GDP figures — which are celebrated — and productivity is simply these GDP figures divided by various measures of employment (Krugman, 1998). And any mismeasurement of output has been a perennial problem, not something just confined to the 1990s.

In fact there were a lot of methodological and cyclical changes that can account for much of the modest productivity growth over the 1990s. Underlying gains in 'multifactor productivity' (that productivity growth not accounted for solely by either increased capital input or the quality of labour use, but due to the way these two factors are better organized) were as low as 0.3 per cent a year between 1990 and 1996 (*Economic Report of the President 1999*, 1999, p.75).

One explanation for the limited impact of computer investment is that despite the torrid pace of such investment, and the USA's superior record internationally, it still represented a very small share of the overall capital employed in the economy: less than 5 per cent of the total net stock of equipment and less than 2 per cent of net non-residential fixed capital in 1998 (op. cit., p.75).

Probably the best explanation relates to the still early nature of computer technology investment. It may be that there is a long learning curve before the benefits of this become apparent, and only after a critical mass of such investment has been built up in the economy over time. This would mean that rising productivity follows major technical innovations with a considerable lag, so the promised benefits will only appear sometime in the future.

4.2   INCREASED GLOBALIZATION?

The other main reason for economic growth given by the new paradigm is that the USA is now a fully globalized economy, competing not only with the OECD countries of Western Europe and the Far East but also increasingly with the LDCs in the South. A complex set of issues arises here, not all of which can be dealt with in this chapter, so I concentrate upon a few main and illustrative ones only.

There can be little doubt that the USA has indeed increased its level of interdependence with the international economy over the 1990s period (see Figures 6.4 and 6.5, pp.147–8). But all economies have done this, and many to a much greater extent than the USA has done (Hirst and Thompson, 1999; Held *et al.*, 1999). Table 6.4 gathers together a range of measures of trade, foreign direct investment (FDI) and financial activity, which summarize the extent of the international integration of the US economy in the mid-1990s.

Table 6.4   Measures of US economic openness and internationalization

		percentage
1	Trade (imports + exports) as a % of GDP (1996)	19
2	Trade (imports + exports) with LDCs as a % of GDP (1996)	7
3	FDI flows as a % of GNP (1997):	
	in flows	1.2
	out flows	1.6
4	FDI stocks as a % of GNP (1997):	
	inward	9.3
	outward	11.8
5	Share of inward FDI as a % of gross fixed capital formation (1996)	7.0
6	Net capital flows (absolute value of current account as % of GDP — average 1990–96)	1.2
7	Foreign assets and liabilities of commercial banks as a % of their total assets (1996):	
	assets	2.6
	liabilities	8.2
8	Institutional investors' overseas assets holdings as a % of total security holdings (1993)	4–7
9	Percentage of financial assets finally held by households in overseas securities (end 1995)	11.0
10	Overseas holdings of US equities (end 1996)	5.0

Sources: all derived from statistics collected in Hirst and Thompson, 1999, Chapters 2, 3 and 4

The question is whether the levels of integration and internationalization indicated by these figures amount to a new era of global openness for the US economy. To some extent this is a matter of judgement. Clearly, the trade to GDP ratio at nearly 20 per cent is the highest percentage shown, but this still means that some 80 per cent of US GDP was not subject to the pressures of international trade in 1996 (Table 6.4, line 1). In addition, only 7 per cent of US GDP represented trade with the LDCs (line 2). Most commentators have argued that this is too small a percentage to be effective in putting much downward competitive pressures on either domestic US labour costs or on the prices of its manufacturing output (see, for example, Krugman and Lawrence, 1994).

If we now turn to the activities of MNCs, the absolute growth of the FDI flows shown in Figure 6.5 (p.148) can be misleading because when expressed as a percentage of GNP these amounted to only 1.2 per cent for inflows and 1.6 per cent for outflows in 1997 (line 3). The percentages for stocks of FDI (the accumulation of past inflows and outflows) were higher, but again only around 10–12 per cent in 1997 (line 4). And the share of FDI inflows in overall capital formation was just 7 per cent, so 93 per cent of domestic investment was generated from domestic sources in 1996 (line 5). Furthermore, the overall capital flows into the USA over the 1990s resulting from its current account deficit was no more than about 1.2 per cent of GDP per year on average (line 6).

The rest of the data in Table 6.4 refer to measures of the internationalization of US financial markets and institutions. Looking at the commercial banks first, their foreign assets and liabilities were still a small fraction of their overall assets in 1996 (line 7), and this was likewise the case for institutional investors (pension and mutual funds) (line 8). This relatively low foreign asset holding by financial institutions was reflected in the amount of financial assets households held in the form of overseas securities, 11 per cent at the end of 1995 (line 9). Finally, the reverse of this, the foreign holdings of US securities was just 5 per cent at the end of 1996 (line 10).

All in all, then, we might conclude from the brief review of the 'globalization' of the US economy that it had not proceeded that far by the mid-1990s. Although more integrated than in the 1970s, the level of increased integration is unlikely to have been sufficient to account for much of the GDP growth experienced in the 1990s. This is not to argue that the impact was nil, only that it does not represent a sufficiently large change to have the impact attributed to it. Of course the US economy may integrate much further and faster in the near future, but then, as in the case of technological benefits discussed above, the growth would also accrue sometime in the future.

SUMMARY

A key argument for the renaissance of the US economy over the 1990s concerned the supposed 'economic miracle' in productivity, brought about by the USA's exemplary record in computer and information technology investment. A close scrutiny of the out-turn productivity record, however, shows this not to have happened. The USA has demonstrated only a modest grow in productivity. The best explanation for this is that, despite feverish activity, computer-related capital remains a very small fraction of the overall capital stock — not enough to significantly affect average productivity growth — and that the full benefits will arise sometime in the future, if at all.

Similar points can be made about the globalization explanation. Although there was some undoubted increase in the international integration of the US economy during the 1990s, this was not as extensive nor deep enough to have accounted for the rapid expansionary phase. In many ways the US economy still remained surprisingly 'isolated' in the mid-1990s, continuing to display many of the features of the 'continental economy' of the 1960s and 1970s.

5 OTHER EXPLANATIONS FOR THE GROWTH RECORD

If we cannot explain the growth record of the US economy during the 1990s simply in terms of investment in new technologies and gobalization, what alternatives are available? Here we can re-visit some of the issues raised when we considered the macroeconomic performance of the economy in section 2. Whilst many of these have also been mentioned in the context of the 'new paradigm' discussion, they do not figure as centrally there as will be stressed here.

5.1 GOVERNMENT SPENDING

A key change in the trajectory of the US economy during the 1990s was the turnaround in the government finances. The way the federal government moved from a deficit to a surplus is shown in Figure 6.6. (Between 1969 and 1997 there had been a continual deficit.) Clearly, there is a close correlation between the degree of federal government savings and net domestic investment; it was this change in government savings that in effect financed the expansionary investment cycle (as well as borrowing overseas). Net private and state and local government savings, whilst positive over this period, declined slightly as a share of GDP, mainly as a result of the collapse in household savings commented upon above.

The reasons for this change-around are basically twofold. After 1990 there was a 'peace dividend' associated with the end of the Cold War. This enabled the rate of federal military expenditures to be cut back. For instance, calculated in real dollar terms, the 1999 defence budget called for a spending limit of $270 billion — down $50 billion from the Cold War average (and down $100 from the 1980s' average of the Reagan Presidency) (O'Hanlon, 1999, p.22). International affairs spending was also cut (involving items like official development assistance, military aid, spending on US diplomatic efforts and UN activity).

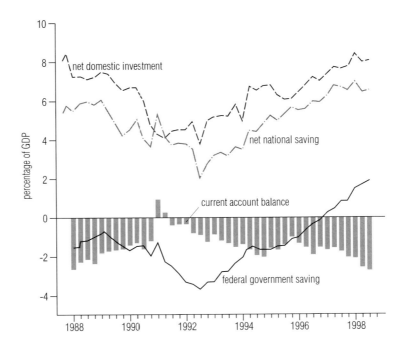

Figure 6.6   *Federal government finances and investment, 1988–1998*
Source: US Government Printing Office (1999) *Economic Report of the President 1999*, Washington DC, adapted from Chart 6–9, p.261

The other main area of expenditure savings has been in the social security budget. This did not strongly emerge until after 1994, as the welfare participation rate dropped dramatically — see Figure 6.7 (which shows the rate at which US citizens claim welfare benefits). The decline in the welfare rate seems closely correlated with the drop in the unemployment rate, but was probably aided as much by the passing of President Clinton's controversial Personal Responsibility and Work Opportunity Reconciliation Act (PRWORA) into law in 1996. This dramatically changed the welfare rules in the USA, making assistance work focused and time limited. It also shifted greater responsibility for welfare management to states and localities. The consequence has been a nation-wide reduction in welfare caseloads. Of course, this was aided by the generally buoyant nature of the economy and the job market (see below). The PRWORA has been judged as a success, however; it has meant less people on welfare, more in jobs and no seeming increase in deprivation — a virtuous trade-off (though see below). However, the real crunch will come if the economy experiences a contraction, particularly in respect to welfare benefit deprivation.

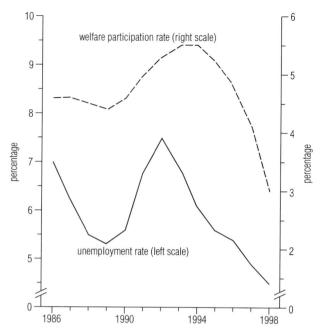

Figure 6.7 *Welfare participation and unemployment, 1986–1998*

Source: US Government Printing Office (1999) *Economic Report of the President 1999*, Washington DC, adapted from Chart 3–11, p.117

5.2 FINANCIAL DEVELOPMENTS AND THE COMPANY SECTOR

A second set of favourable developments during the 1990s involved financial conditions, broadly considered. Obviously the main manifestation of this was the booming stock market outlined above. This itself was fed by the rapid securitization of American private savings (the conversion of household surpluses into stocks and shares holdings, via the development of insurance companies, mutual funds, and other collectively-provided financial instruments like pension funds) which was itself partly the result of the liberalization of the domestic (and international) financial system. In addition, there had been another merger boom, with record numbers in 1996 and 1997 — see Figure 6.8 — which also fuelled the stock market.

Added to this was a robust growth in corporate profits between 1993 and 1997 (though these fell in 1998), a declining trend in interest rates and the plentiful availability of external financial capital (because of the decline in the federal government deficit). All these features helped stimulate the favourable corporate investment climate. These developments — the decline in interest rates, combined with low inflation and moderate monetary growth — enabled the FED to claim a good deal of the credit for carefully steering the economy along the path to growth. Insofar as there were

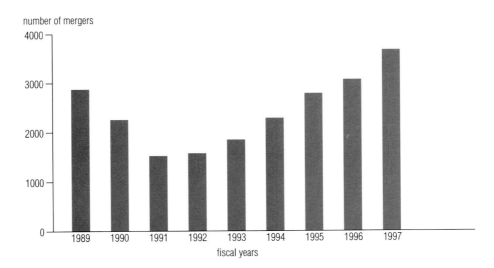

Figure 6.8   *Number of mergers, 1989–1997*
Source: US Government Printing Office (1998) *Economic Report of the President 1998,* Washington DC, Chart 6–11, p.197

exogenous shocks to the system, these were expertly handled by the Chairman of the FED, Alan Greenspan, who gained a reputation as an astute manager of the system, complementing President Clinton's own cautious and basically conservative approach to economic matters.

5.3   INTERNATIONAL CRISES AND REACTIONS

But this concentration on domestic matters should not divert attention from important developments at the international level. Here it is the US economy's sheer size and importance in the world on the one hand, yet its still relatively internationally isolated nature on the other (Table 6.4), that enabled it to ride out many potentially threatening events originating from overseas. For instance, during the 1990s there were a number of internationally-inspired financial crises: the ERM crisis of 1992–93 (when Italy and the UK were forced out of the exchange mechanism, devaluations took place amongst the remaining members, and exchange rate bands widened); the Mexican peso crisis in 1994–95, which was followed by 'tequila effects' as other Latin American currencies came under attack, and finally, the most serious of all, the East Asian crisis of 1997–98, which was followed by crises in Russia in August 1998 and Brazil in January 1999.

The Mexican and East Asian crises affected the USA the most, and it led important 'rescue packages' in response to each of them. It mobilized international support, put its weight behind the IMF initiated short-term 'stabilization policies' by granting extra funds to the IMF (US$18 billion in 1998), pressed for long-term 'policy reforms' in the emerging market economies to promote market-led recovery; adjusted its domestic interest rates to restore confidence and liquidity; and, finally, arranged support mechanisms for domestic financial institutions that got into difficulties as a consequence of the crises (e.g. in the case of the hedge fund, Long Term Capital Management, where the FED helped arrange a US$ 3.625 billion support loan in September 1998). All these measures undoubtedly helped stem the possibilities of wider disruption in the domestic economy and potential contagion effects throughout the international economy.

The size and importance of the economy and its underlying growth momentum also allowed the USA to take a policy of benign neglect with respect to its exchange rate. The dollar was depreciating against other main currencies up until 1995, but between mid-1995 and September 1998 it appreciated against both European and East Asian currencies in both nominal and real terms (a modest depreciation set in again in late 1998). The strong appreciation of the dollar since 1995 helped keep import prices down, especially for oil and other commodities, contributing to the drop in inflation and the improvement in the US terms of trade (a measure of the prices of exports relative to imports, so an increase in the terms of trade translates into an increased purchasing power of US goods in world markets and higher real US incomes). The strong dollar also supported the low interest rate policy pursued by the FED. But the strong dollar meant that exports were more difficult to sell abroad, so, combined with the increase in imports, the balance of payments continued to deteriorate. And the failure of domestic savings to meet the needs of investment meant the USA continued its borrowing abroad, so its net international investment position deteriorated further during the 1990s. The USA remains the worlds largest debtor country.

All in all, however, what is striking about these international developments is that, up until 1999 at least, they failed to seriously dent the shine of the US growth trajectory. The potentially quite adverse international crises were coped with and their affects shrugged off after only temporary interruptions to domestic economic activity.

5.4   DEVELOPMENTS IN THE LABOUR MARKET

Between January 1993 and the end of 1998 the US economy created a remarkable 17.7 million new jobs (*Economic Report of the President 1999*, 1999, p.1). In part this accounted for the reduction in unemployment as well as the ability of the USA to absorb a large net immigrant population. But how did the economy manage this feat? This is where the characteristics of the USA's legendary 'labour market flexibility' become important, and nowhere is this more clearly demonstrated than in the case of wages.

Table 6.5   US hourly compensation rates of change, 1990–1997 (% change on previous year)

	1990	1993	1994	1995	1996	1997
Real hourly compensation	0.3	-0.4	-0.9	-0.3	0.9	1.6
Non-farm businesses	0.1	-0.7	-0.8	-0.3	0.8	1.5
Manufacturing	-0.5	-0.1	0.0	0.1	0.2	1.2

Source: compiled from US Government Printing Office (1998) *Statistical Abstract of the United States, 1998,* US Bureau Census of Statistics, Washington DC, Table 689, p.433

The basic trends can be seen in Table 6.5. Between 1990 and 1995 real hourly wages in the USA fell almost every year. Only after 1996 did real wages begin to expand again, and then slowly. Thus the bulk of the US growth record over the first six years of the 1990s was built on the backs of a declining average real wage for those employed by businesses. This experience is almost unprecedented in modern advanced economies. In conventional economic theory reductions in real wages are thought to lead to an increased demand for labour, hence the growth in employment. Clearly, there has been an enormous downward pressure put on real wages, so that the hourly incomes of those in the wage-earning sector have declined. This has led to the emergence of longer working hours, second (even third) jobs, and larger numbers of multi-earner households in an attempt to maintain overall family incomes. In part this can also account for the drop in the personal saving rate, as these households used any surpluses they could generate in the face of declining incomes to maintain their consumption levels and patterns.

A further result of this process is the growth of income and especially wealth inequality over the 1990s. The OECD concluded that between 1975 and 1995 there was a general growth in income inequality within most OECD countries, but this was particularly marked in the case of the USA, which also displayed one of the highest inequality *levels* by the mid-1990s (OECD, 1997b, Table 19, p.51).

The OECD finding is confirmed for the 1990s by the data in Table 6.6, which shows the distribution of aggregate incomes for each fifth of US families, and that received by the top 5 per cent. Note how the lowest four-fifths all lost shares in the 1990s, whilst only the top fifth increased their share, and how there was a marked increase in the income share of the top 5 per cent of income earners. A remarkable 47 per cent of incomes went to just the top fifth of earners in 1996.

Table 6.6 Percentage distribution of aggregate income, 1988–1996

	Lowest 5th	Second 5th	Third 5th	Fourth 5th	Highest 5th	Top 5%
1988	4.6	10.7	16.7	24.0	44.0	17.2
1989	4.6	10.6	16.5	23.7	44.6	17.9
1990	4.6	10.8	16.6	23.8	44.3	17.4
1991	4.5	10.7	16.6	24.1	44.2	17.1
1992	4.3	10.5	16.5	24.0	44.7	17.6
1993	4.1	9.9	15.7	23.3	47.0	20.3
1994	4.2	10.0	15.7	23.3	46.9	20.1
1995	4.4	10.1	15.8	23.2	46.5	20.0
1996	4.2	10.0	15.8	23.1	46.8	20.3

Source: US Government Printing Office (1998) *Statistical Abstract of the United States, 1998*, US Bureau Census of Statistics, Washington DC, adapted from Table 747, p.473

Here we also need to focus on the actual business strategies of US corporations in their dealings with labour. The period after the 1980s saw an unprecedented attack on labour from business interests. Analysing this raises a set of more structural issues, including the role of bargaining power and collective action, not all of which can be accounted for simply by short-term changes in labour market conditions. A longer-term perspective is necessary.

The period from the New Deal to the mid-1970s in the USA was one of a strategic compromise between business and labour, marked by an acceptance of the legitimate interests of each in the conduct of business activity and in terms of a broad social accommodation in economic policy more generally (Roe, 1994, Part III; Korten, 1995, p.1–14). But this compromise was deliberately broken in the mid-1970s just at the time when the increases in inequality referred to above also began to emerge.

What is the possible connection between the loss of market power of manufacturing unskilled workers in particular and the decline in real hourly wages in general? The break in the historical compromise saw a renewed attack on the working conditions of American labour, and a release of the constraints on managerial prerogatives and managerial salaries. David Gordon has documented the consequences of this in detail (Gordon, 1996). His argument is that despite a rhetoric of 'downsizing' by American management, the actual facts go against this. There has been an increase in the numbers and levels of supervisory and management personnel. In addition, the wage bill for this managerial group has expanded at the expense of those very workers they are supervising and managing. In this context a corporate strategy of deliberately undermining the wages of production workers and shop floor employment cutbacks has emerged. This is demonstrated by the data in Figure 6.8. It shows the distribution of reasons for losing a job amongst those who actually lost a job between 1981 and 1995.

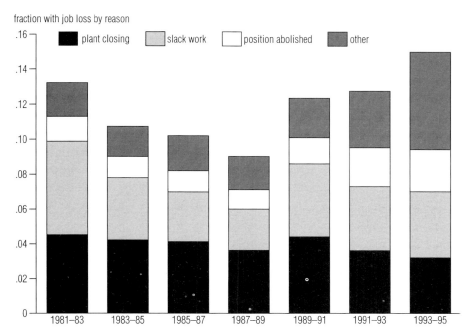

Figure 6.9   *Rate of job loss by reason, 1981–1995*
Source: Farber, 1997, Figure 1, p.68

What is striking about these data is that the job loss rate actually accelerated dramatically in the 1993–95 period despite the sustained economic expansion and decline in the unemployment rate. This result is consistent with the claims of a secular decline in job security and an increase in job 'churning'. Workers are experiencing a faster turnover in jobs, as they lose their job and find (perhaps) another one. What is more, this increased turnover was procyclical — it increased as the economic cycle took an upturn (rather than diminished, as in previous cycles). The growth of the category 'other reasons' for job loss shown in Figure 6.8 is intriguing, and not readily explainable. But Farber (1997) suggests that combined with the 'position abolished' category, it implies an increased trend for internal corporate restructuring in which labour bears the brunt of the uncertainty and restructuring costs. In addition, Farber's analysis demonstrates that it is those who lost their jobs who suffered the severest decline in wages as and when they found other work. The decline in real weekly earnings for displaced workers if they found another job was about 13 per cent for all re-employed displaced workers over the period 1989–95. Thus, not only did job security decline in America during the 1990s, it was this job loss mechanism that undermined real wages to the greatest extent.

At the same time this released the restraint on corporate management from rapidly increasing its own remuneration. The coincidental securitization of American savings and the stock market boom has additionally fed the incomes of stockholders and the well off. The outcome is the growth in inequality in the USA.

Here we have the seeds of an alternative explanation for much of the turn against the unskilled worker and the reduction of real wages in the USA. What is more, this is an explanation that is 'domestic' in origin. It provides an account for the surge in US growth rates, as wages were depressed and profits increased, that centres its account firmly in the domestic economic arena rather than in the more fashionable global one.

But this explanation itself is not without its problems. It probably underestimates the extent of downsizing that has actually occurred in the USA. Other accounts testify to a genuine cut in layers of management. It also ignores the increase in high skilled jobs being driven by the growth in technical grade workers in more sophisticated manufacturing processes, who tend to be classified in the supervisory and managerial grades. This might also account for the emphasis on the importance of so-called 'symbolic analysts' (those engaged in conceptual rather than manual tasks) to the American future, as stressed by the likes of Robert Reich (who was Labour Secretary for much of the first Clinton administration — see Reich, 1992).

SUMMARY

Four added elements to the picture of the reasons for the upturn in the American economy have been presented in this section. The reduction in the federal government's budget deficit, and indeed its move into the black in 1998, took pressure off interest rates and opened up financial resources for private investment. In part this stimulated a favourable 'monetary regime', encouraging a merger boom, higher corporate profits and, initially, the securitization of private savings which itself fuelled the demand for corporate securities on the stock exchange. The potentially destabilizing arrival of a set of international financial crises were shrugged off, while the strength and size of the economy allowed the USA to adopt a benign exchange rate policy that helped stimulate the rest of the world economy as imports were sucked into the USA. Finally, and perhaps most importantly, the admirable US job creation record was secured at the expense of lower real wages and increased job insecurity. This provided the crucial underpinning for the boom in corporate profits, the stock market and probably overall economic growth as well.

As a footnote to this last point, however, it should be noted that the job displacement rate analysed in respect to Figure 6.7 fell between 1995 and 1997 (from 15 per cent to 12 per cent) — though it was still a third higher than it had been in 1987–89, when the unemployment rate was at a similar level. In addition, the reduction in weekly earnings among those re-employed was only 5.7 per cent, much lower than for the previous periods in the 1990s (*Economic Report of the President 1999*, 1999, Chart 3–12, p.122).

6 CONTINUING PROBLEMS AND PROSPECTS FOR THE FUTURE

This section reviews a number of continuing and new problems that still characterize the US economy. Again, it is not a comprehensive survey but takes up a few of the main issues only.

6.1 CONTINUING ETHNIC INEQUALITY

One of the endemic features of US society is its entrenched inequalities. We have already seen this in respect to income inequality analysed above. But it is worth picking another dimension to this and looking at what has happened in respect to it over the 1990s. Table 6.7 presents data on the development of incomes amongst the different ethnic groups in the USA.

Table 6.7   Median income in constant (1996) dollars, 1989–96

	All families	White	Black	Asian/ Pacific Is.	Hispanics
1989	43,290	45,520	25,571	51,057	29,667
1990	42,440	44,315	25,717	50,715	28,128
1991	41,401	43,525	24,823	47,201	27,527
1992	40,900	43,245	23,600	47,255	26,342
1993	40,131	42,672	23,391	48,271	25,684
1994	41,059	43,284	26,148	48,830	25,746
1995	41,801	43,905	26,737	47,725	25,296
1996	42,300	44,756	26,522	49,105	26,179

Source: US Government Printing Office (1998) *Statistical Abstract of the United States, 1998*, US Bureau Census of Statistics, Washington DC, adapted from Table 746, p.472

Clearly, there are significant and entrenched inequalities in median family income for different ethnic groups. In terms of all families, the point made above about the reduction in average real incomes is shown in the first column. In 1996 real incomes were still lower than they were in 1989. This reduction characterized Whites, Asian and Pacific Islanders, and especially Hispanics. The only group to have been better off in 1996 than in 1989 were Blacks. This result is itself interesting and important, because it looks at last as though this particularly disadvantaged ethnic group may be beginning to show a relative gain in its economic position. However, the downside is that Hispanics may now be replacing Blacks as the most heavily disadvantaged group in America.

6.2   THE 'GREYING' OF AMERICA

The data in Table 6.7 shows that Whites and Asians had a median income twice that of Blacks and Hispanics. But these differences are much greater in the case of wealth, and particularly in the case of the elderly. Elderly Whites have five times the holdings of financial assets than do elderly Blacks and Hispanics, for instance, and over half the members of these later two groups have no financial assets at all, only their houses (if they own one) or other physical assets.

These inequalities amongst the elderly serve to raise a more general issue that is beginning to haunt America: the rapid movement to an ageing society — the 'greying of America'. The problem this poses is twofold: first how to sustain the elderly themselves, and secondly how to sustain the economy as a whole as relatively fewer and fewer people are actually of working age (indeed, the USA may soon have a shrinking population as its population ages and fertility rates continue to fall).

In Florida in 1998, 19 per cent of the population was 65 years of age or over (national average 12 per cent), and this is seen as the future for the country as a whole. It was estimated that 20 per cent of the population would be elderly in 2020. The most immediate problem here is to secure proper provision for old-age through viable retirement pension schemes. The current debate in the USA about how to do this is intense, and its consequences serious (Bosworth and Burtless, 1997; Gale, 1997). A key element in this debate revolves around whether to move away from 'pay-as-you-go' pension schemes towards 'funded' pension schemes.

The pay-as-you-go method — the current dominant one — broadly involves paying pensions and social security benefits out of current income, so it is the current working population who fund these benefits via taxation. However, as the population ages it is argued that this method no longer remains viable since the working population shrinks just as the need for more expenditure increases with an increase in the retired elderly. In addition, there has been an ideological move against the role of the state as mediating in this relationship via its taxation and expenditure programmes, even to aid the elderly.

By contrast, the funded method involves saving for retirement, so that pension provision can be paid out of the income earned from those saved funds, which are invested in stocks and shares. Clearly, this had a number of political advantages in the late 1990s. It met the ideological objection to state intervention by making people 'stand on their own two feet'. But perhaps more importantly in the short term, if it were introduced it would shore up the stock market boom even further by adding another layer of demand for stocks and shares. Thus, if this further bolster to share prices were to spread optimism into other aspects of the economy, the economic boom might continue longer than it would otherwise have done. Even the promise to move towards such a system could have the desired 'expectational' consequences of boosting share prices once again.

On the other hand, there is an ideological objection to the consequences of such a move, expressed most forcefully by the Chairman of the FED Alan Greenspan. In effect, if the federal government were to pursue such a policy, its long-term implication is the 'socialization' of share ownership as the state-controlled funded schemes bought up the stock market to fund the retirement provisions of the average citizen. Only if the funded schemes were beyond state control would this 'socialization of ownership by the back door' be avoided.

6.3   CONTROLLING GOVERNMENT EXPENDITURE

The final point to make in this section relates to the one just discussed. Can the US government really move all its welfare benefits, medical aid and pension provisions — or most of them — further into the private sphere, or take them out of its current expenditure by funding them? If this cannot be done quickly, then the prospects for further reductions in these types of government expenditures are slim. And the likelihood is that they will increase as, first, the economic boom begins to founder and, second, the ageing process gathers pace. The great challenge facing those in the government who are committed to further reductions in public expenditures — at whatever level of government — is to sustain the process begun in the 1990s in the light of these twin aspects to the American dilemma.

What is more, there is no guarantee that other areas where the government has been able to reduce expenditures will be sustainable either. The most noteworthy of these is in the realm of defence. Already in early 1999 there were calls for an increased defence budget (O'Halon, 1999). Cuts had gone too far for the USA to meet its planned defence needs. Pentagon sources were pressing for increased expenditures. Military spending on operation 'Desert Storm' in Iraq, in Bosnia and then in Kosovo, had reduced the levels of equipment and ammunition, and exposed the necessity to enhance the USA's capability in a number of areas. Peace-keeping operations were also proving to be costly. Thus an extra yearly US$13 billion foreign aid and defence expenditure was called for. Whether these increases could be resisted remains to be seen.

SUMMARY

There remained a number of areas in which economic problems persisted or which were quickly emerging onto the political agenda in mid-1999. The economic boom had not solved everything. Inequalities continued to be rife in the USA and had grown in the 1990s. The 'greying of America' threatened to pose a series of increasingly intractable problems for economic management. And, finally, there was no guarantee that the federal budget would continue its healthy positive balance.

7   CONCLUSION

The new economic paradigm with which we began this chapter painted a very rosy picture for the future of the US economy. But its twin candidates for the determinants of the booming 1990s' economy — a technological revolution in informatics leading to major productivity gains, and the rapid 'globalization' of the US economy — turned out not to be very convincing. Indeed the whole picture of a prosperous and booming economy for all looked increasingly shaky as the growing inequalities in income and wealth were uncovered. The consumption boom that led the economic growth trajectory must have been at best largely confined to the better-off sections of the population. The high import propensity of this section of the population also added to the balance of payments problems. Only in the very latter years of the decade was there any indication that prosperity might be becoming more widely spread.

But this widening of the benefits of the US growth decade was surely also threatened by the prospects of an economic downturn in the economy. In mid-1999 the World Bank's *Economic Outlook* predicted that some slowdown was inevitable, while Alan Greenspan commented that 'the spectacular rise in equity prices … has reached well beyond the justifiable' (*Financial Times*, 8 May, 1999, p.15). The only real debate was whether the deceleration would be gradual and orderly or abrupt and disruptive. Just a few maverick ultra-optimists remained convinced that a genuinely new paradigm was indeed still driving the economy.

However, perhaps it would be churlish to end this chapter on such a negative note. In many ways the sustained economic growth rate found in the economy as a whole was a significant achievement, one for which much of the rest of the world could be grateful. It helped the rest overcome their own crises and downturns, minimizing the damage to their own living standards.

REFERENCES

Borjas, G.J., Freeman, P.R. and Katz, L.F. (1997) 'How much do immigration and trade affect labor market outcomes?', *Brookings Papers on Economic Activity*, 1, pp.1–90.

Bosworth, B. and Burtless, G. (1997) 'Budget crunch: population ageing in rich countries', *The Brookings Review*, Summer, pp.10–15.

Economic Report of the President 1998 (1998) US Government Printing Office, Washington, DC.

Economic Report of the President 1999 (1999) US Government Printing Office, Washington, DC.

The Economist (1999) 'Desperately seeking a perfect model', 10 April, pp.89–93.

Farber, H.S. (1997) 'The changing face of job loss in the United States, 1981–1995', *Brookings Papers on Economic Activity: Microeconomics,* pp.55–142.

Gale, W.G. (1997) 'Will the baby boom be ready for retirement?', *The Brookings Review,* Summer, pp.5–9.

Gordon, D.M. (1996) *Fat and Mean: The Corporate Squeeze of Working America and the Myth of Managerial 'Downsizing',* New York, The Free Press.

Held, D., McGrew, A., Goldblatt, D. and Perraton, J. (1999) *Global Transformations: Politics, Economics and Culture,* Cambridge, Polity Press.

Hirst, P. and Thompson, G. (1999) *Globalization in Question,* 2nd edition, Cambridge, Polity Press.

Korten, D.C. (1995) *When Corporations Rule the World,* West Hartford, Con., Kumarian Press.

Krugman, P. (1998) 'America the boastful' *Foreign Affairs,* vol. 77, no. 3, pp.32–45.

Krugman, P. and Lawrence, R.Z. (1994) 'Trade, jobs and wages', *Scientific American,* April, pp.22–26.

OECD (1997a) *OECD Economic Surveys: The United States 1997,* OECD, Paris

OECD (1997b) *OECD Economic Outlook, No. 62,* December, 1997.

O'Halon, M.E. (1999) 'Defence and foreign policy: time to end the budget crisis' in Aavon, H.J. and Reischaver, R.D. (eds) *Setting National Priorities: The 2000 Election and Beyond,* Brookings Institution, Washington DC.

Reich, R.B. (1992) *The Work of Nations,* New York, Vintage Books.

Roe, M.J. (1994) *Strong Managers, Weak Owners: The Political Roots of American Corporate Finance,* Princeton, N.J., Princeton University Press.

Statistical Abstract of the United States 1998 (1998) US Bureau Census of Statistics, US Government Printing Office, Washington DC.

Weber, S. (1997) 'The end of the business cycle?', *Foreign Affairs,* vol. 76, no. 4, July/August, pp.65–82.

Zuckerman, M.B. (1998) 'A second American century', *Foreign Affairs,* vol. 77, no. 3, May/June, pp.18–31.

MONEY AND POWER:
the American financial system from free banking to global competition

Philip G. Cerny ★

> All financial markets rely on a legal order for their fundamental stability, and governments are the providers of that legal order. ... If we continue to ignore the public purposes of these markets, we will increasingly misallocate our real resources and eventually destroy the markets themselves.
>
> Martin Mayer, *Stealing the Market* (1992)

> 'Because that's where the money is.'
>
> Willie Sutton, nineteenth century American bank robber, when asked why he robbed banks.

1 INTRODUCTION: MONEY, THE STATE AND CAPITALISM

Money is at the heart of the paradox of capitalism. In order for people to behave as genuine 'economic' actors and to exchange the surpluses they produce (or own) in a systematic and efficient manner with a range of other specialized producers — producers too numerous to meet face-to-face — they need money. Throughout history, for money to be widely acceptable, usable and reliable, it has been provided and guaranteed by institutions and mechanisms which can stand *above* market processes as such — in the main by governments. And herein lies the paradox. For markets to be 'efficient', classical economic theory requires the greatest possible *decentralization* of decision making — the widest possible range of buyers and sellers exchanging price signals so that everything offered for sale is actually sold (the market 'clears'). But state provision of a functioning monetary system — and a system of financial regulation to support it — is normally the bottom line. This paradoxical relationship between a decentralized financial marketplace and the stabilizing and steering role of government can be seen in practice in the development of any monetary system. Each 'financial system' — made up of a monetary system, a system of financial markets and institutions, and a system of financial regulation — constitutes a powerful framework of rules, rewards and penalties shaping economic behaviour.

Different financial systems also interact with *each other* in the international financial and political arena. In examining the American financial system will attempt to weave together these three levels or subsystems by looking at three critical phases of development: (1) a long period from the late eighteenth century through the 1920s, during which early financial anarchy was gradually and unevenly overlaid by elements of centralization, both public and private; (2) a phase of domestic regulatory activism alongside the expansion of America's international financial role from the New Deal to the early 1960s, followed by the breakdown of that model at home and abroad in the 1960s and 1970s; and (3) the current era of 'deregulation' and 're-regulation', market restructuring and financial globalization since the 1970s. Several factors, some of which are specifically characteristic of the American financial system, make that system both highly problematic and vulnerable, and yet extremely flexible and resilient, in today's world. These factors include: (1) a particularly American tradition of financial pluralism, which weakens markets and institutions in critical ways (but strengthens them in others); (2) the divided system of financial regulation in the USA and the syndrome of 'entropy' or 'gridlock' found in American government in general, which block regulatory modernization at one level but adapt pragmatically and flexibly to global imperatives at another; and (3) the changing role of the USA in a world which looked a few years ago to be beating America at its own game but is today adapting painfully to the 'Washington Consensus'.

2 FROM FREE BANKING TO THE GREAT CRASH: THE ISSUE OF CENTRALIZATION

It is difficult to separate the history of the American financial system from the wider question of political and economic centralization. The ideology which lay behind the American Revolution was one of resistance to centralized political and economic power, and the American constitution was constructed around the principles of federalism and the separation of powers. Populist suspicion of centralized power has had many variants in the USA, from conservative to radical and from political to economic, cutting across class and region. Nowhere has this suspicion been more deeply rooted, however, than in attitudes towards the financial system. The legacy of these attitudes is still important today.

2.1 POPULISM AND FREE BANKING

In the period during and immediately following the Industrial Revolution, banking in both Britain and the USA was primarily carried on by small institutions located close to the users of capital — institutions which proliferated in the nineteenth century. Of course, in both countries, larger city banks and merchant banks emerged also, both to provide places where the country banks could turn to invest their reserves and/or use their assets as collateral for loans when they were short of funds, and to service the urban centres themselves as well as inter-regional and international trade.

The banking system became far more centralized in Britain than in the USA, however, with a key role being played by the Bank of England, established in 1694. In the USA, a number of factors stalled the process of centralization and even reversed it. The early USA was overwhelmingly rural, and internal development strengthened populist opposition to both political and economic centralization. On the one hand, there was a mushrooming of local banks through the first half of the nineteenth century. On the other hand, political opposition and the constitutional weakness of the national government combined to ensure that no real central bank was set up and that the individual states were in control of banking regulation. The First Bank of the United States (established 1791) was allowed to lapse in 1811 and the Second Bank (chartered in 1816) had its official status rescinded in 1836.

Opposition to banks in general was widespread. Populist leaders such as President Andrew Jackson were opposed to the issue of banknotes altogether. However, the main thrust of banking populism went in a quite different direction. This was the development of 'free banking'. Technically, free banking meant simply the passing by a state legislature of general regulations under which banks could be established without the need for a special act of incorporation to be sponsored. Providing a person could satisfy these regulations, he/she could set up a bank. However, the term has gained a wider usage, combining free banking in the narrow sense with: (1) the mushrooming of small banks in general; (2) the common practice of states in limiting or banning branch banking (banks were overwhelmingly 'unit banks' with only a main office, except in some large cities) and setting up barriers to interstate banking; and (3) the relative anarchy of the system of issuing banknotes.

Each bank issued its own notes at least until 1863; notes might be redeemed in specie (coin) at face value at the bank itself, but their value was increasingly discounted (reduced) the further away one got from the head office. There were therefore wide variations in the value of money.

Nevertheless, despite the seeming anarchy of the banking system, banks and other capital markets played an indispensable role in a rapidly growing economy. Although still predominantly rural, America was rich in natural resources, human capital and pioneering spirit. With the coming of the Civil War, the Federal Government took on a notably stronger role in the financial system, private financial institutions expanded at all levels, and the country embarked on a massive industrialization boom which propelled it to potential international leadership. But rather than leading to a high degree of centralization of the financial system, the characteristic financial pluralism of the system as a whole was reinforced. Until well into the twentieth century, the different levels of the system all expanded — especially, of course, during periods of economic boom. Not until the Great Crash of 1929 did a fully-fledged, system-wide shakeout occur.

2.2 A PLURAL BANKING SYSTEM

Some sectors did of course become highly centralized, reflecting the spectacular growth of the American economy and its increasing integration both across sectors and regions at home and in a rapidly industrializing capitalist world economy. The USA became the world's leading agricultural producer (and a powerful agricultural exporter) after the Civil War and in the 1880s became the world's largest industrial producer too. But other financial sectors remained highly decentralized, reflecting the geographical, demographic and economic diversity of the country. Political issues of a financial nature increasingly inflamed popular passions too, as calls for currency inflation, mainly from rural areas, conflicted with the increasingly constraining international Gold Standard. Booms and slumps — especially the Panic of 1907 and the Great Crash of 1929 — gradually changed the face of the system. The Federal Government took greater control of the currency, reshaped the system of financial markets and institutions, and established a more complex regulatory system too.

The American financial system developed during this period at five basic levels: the expansion of free banking at the national level; the development of the securities markets; the emergence of what has been called 'finance capital' (that is, the big investment banks); a reinforcing of the Federal Government's monetary and regulatory role, especially the establishment of a central bank; and growing interpenetration of the American economy and financial markets with international 'high finance', which, despite US isolationism, eventually drew the world's most powerful economy into an imperial role. The uneven relationship between these five trends was shaped by a series of booms and slumps, eventually coming unstuck in 1929.

These developments gave rise to a *dual regulatory system* at state and national levels which still exists today. The establishment of the national banking system following the passage of the National Bank Act in 1863 was not meant to lead to bank concentration; it was in fact based on 'free banking' principles. National banks were not allowed to set up branches; they remained unit banks until 1922. Under pressure from small banks, many states further restricted intrastate branching too. The number of commercial banks peaked at almost 30,000 in 1921 before steadily declining in the 1920s and dramatically shrinking after the Great Crash. Whereas European banking systems rapidly consolidated with industrialization and financial internationalization in the late nineteenth century, the combination of free banking, the dual regulatory system and the close links between commercial banks and a geographically and sectorally diversified economy ensured that financial services expanded on an increasingly pluralistic basis.

The Civil War was also a key period in the development of the securities markets, which complemented rather than competed with the commercial banking system. The New York Stock Exchange, although only one of several rival exchanges — there were more than two dozen below 14th Street during the frenzied speculation of the Civil War, as well as important exchanges in other cities — had already developed the closed corporate structure which was to epitomize the norm for a 'self-regulating' market: traders would trade only with one another; they would exclude outsiders; and they would charge agreed fixed rates for their services. However, even during the period of rapid industrial development in the later nineteenth century, the securities markets were mainly the exclusive sphere of the traders themselves and of the large investment banks and commercial banks which had grown up in the urban centres, especially around New York City's Wall Street. The investment banks, in addition to trading government securities (mainly for reserve purposes), were crucial middlemen in underwriting stocks and bonds for many of the huge new corporations dominating the American economic landscape, especially railroads and public utilities.

But these institutions not only dealt in stocks and bonds. They controlled the boards of key industries through direct representation and interlocking directorships; they channelled foreign investment both into the USA (British investment flowed in during the last third of the nineteenth century as British industry began to stagnate) and out (to Latin America and China in particular); and they played a key role in controlling the rest of the financial system. The largest and best known of these investment banks was J.P. Morgan, which became a legend in the financial world and a symbol of all that was worst in American capitalism for its radical critics. Morgan was not only the best connected American institution internationally — it was sometimes a channel for American foreign policy and frequently sought influence over that policy — but also the nearest thing the USA had domestically to what had come to be called 'finance capital' in Germany, Japan and other countries. (However, the use of the term 'finance capital' in Europe gave a greater role to state control of finance for industrial development.) Morgan also came to play a crucial role in stabilizing the wider banking system at times of crisis. While the mixed financial system described here was extremely flexible and effective in financing economic development, it was vulnerable to economic slumps and financial panics. There was little in the way of a control system when weaker institutions failed. Crashes on Wall Street, too, when major industrial firms failed or financial institutions became overextended, triggered wider panics downwards through the pyramid. Sound institutions were always at risk. In 1907, only the active intervention of Morgan in providing liquidity to institutions in trouble prevented the crash from spreading. This experience, along with political concern over financial stability and ever-present hostility to finance for monopoly practices and corruption, led the Federal Government to expand its control.

2.3   THE POLITICS OF BANKING

Political conflict over the monetary system had been a central feature of American politics throughout the late nineteenth century. This conflict pitted urban financial institutions, 'trusts' (the giant industrial and utilities firms which had come to dominate key sectors of the American economy) and the federal bureaucracy, on the one hand, against farmers, small business, small

banks, populist politicians and the new industrial working class organizations, on the other. Opponents of the Gold Standard argued that the scarcity
of commodity gold — the metal itself — created a general scarcity of liquidity which hurt farmers, small business and poor people by deflating the
economy and increasing the burden of debts. The Gold Standard became the
dominant issue of the 1896 presidential election. The Populist candidate,
William Jennings Bryan, won the Democratic Party nomination too with his
'Cross of Gold' speech, which has echoed through American history: 'You
shall not press down upon the brow of labour this crown of thorns, you
shall not crucify mankind upon a cross of gold'. Just as the gold issue was
reaching a crescendo following the financial panic of 1893 and the subsequent depression, however, new sources of gold were being discovered in
South Africa, Alaska and Colorado, and new mining techniques allowed
more of the metal to be taken out of the ground. This led to a reflation of
the economy, and allowed the Gold Standard candidate, Republican William
McKinley, to win the election. But the rapid economic expansion of the next
decade did not make the economy crisis proof. Indeed, a mild cyclical
downturn in the economy beginning in May 1907 was suddenly aggravated
in October by a banking panic; loans were called in, bank runs were spreading and the stock market was badly hit. Morgan's role in halting the panic
has been widely written about. He cajoled and bullied bankers, elicited
Treasury co-operation and injected cash directly and indirectly into banks
and financial markets. 'He had been, as it were, a one-man Federal Reserve
Bank' (Allen, quoted in Degen, 1987).

Monetary reform became a major issue both in Congress and in the 1912
presidential election, and was one of the first concerns of the new President,
Woodrow Wilson. In December 1913, Congress passed the Federal Reserve
Act, which was the result of a compromise between those who feared too
much Wall Street control and those who feared too much Federal Government control. The Federal Reserve System (the 'Fed') consisted of twelve
regional Federal Reserve Banks and a central Federal Reserve Board. The
Board was not a fully independent body, and until its reform in the 1930s
the Secretary of the Treasury and the Comptroller of the Currency sat on it
by right. The basic role of the 'Fed' was to guarantee the currency through
the provision of new Federal Reserve notes, to provide fiscal assistance to
the Treasury and, most importantly, to vary the money supply to adjust to
the cyclical needs of the economy. The latter was at first done mainly by
lending to banks when money was short (the 'discount window'). The system now had an official 'lender of last resort'. In the 1920s, the bank added
another key tool, open-market operations. By buying government securities
from banks, it could increase the money supply directly when Government
or Fed policy called for its expansion; by selling government securities to
the banks on the other hand, it could equally take money out of the system.
Thus the USA finally got itself a central bank, but one which had a semi-
decentralized structure and was intended to support, rather than to run
down, the plural financial system.

2.4 THE IMPACT OF INTERNATIONAL FACTORS

During the period from the Civil War to the 1930s, the American financial system also became more and more entangled with the international financial and economic system, even though large parts of the American economy remained relatively isolated for long periods. This paradox can be seen in the Gold Standard issue, discussed elsewhere in this book (Chapter 4). But it was not until the First World War that America's international financial role became central to the world economy. In that war, not only did the Allied Powers finance the war to a large extent by borrowing in the USA (Morgan, again, played a central role), but British firms and investors sold off a large proportion of their investments. Britain herself became a debtor nation. The USA became the world's leading creditor. However, this new situation put the USA in a problematic position. As well as having an economy centred in a huge, protected continental market — more isolated from external trade and payments than the developed European economies — the USA also attempted to return to *political* isolationism after the war. In other words, the international financial system now had a suspended Gold Standard, no international lender of last resort, a reserve currency (sterling) whose role was greatly reduced, and a potentially stronger currency (the dollar) whose international role was circumscribed by American isolationism.

In this context, the huge international financial flows of the 1920s, mainly revolving around the issue of war reparations, destabilized both the international economy and eventually the American economy too. All the factors discussed in this section fed into a process which came to a head in the domestic boom of the 1920s and the Great Crash of 1929. Huge cracks appeared in a financial system which was decentralized and potentially chaotic for most people, on the one hand, and yet where a few institutions such as Morgan, along with, at key times, the Fed and the Treasury, worked hard to re-establish the Gold Standard and to support its reintroduction at home and abroad (notably in Britain), on the other. The failure of reparations, huge loans to Germany, and the collapse of war debt repayments to the USA undermined rather than bolstered the dollar as an effective reserve currency. Wall Street, and Morgan in particular, supported a return to gold. The Fed was divided between those who wanted to use monetary policy for domestic stabilization and supporters of gold. The latter were dominant in the Federal Reserve Bank of New York, which because of its proximity to Wall Street has always been in charge of international operations and the stock markets.

Finally, of course, domestic US economic expansion not only overheated, but also fed into a financial bubble based on an unprecedented flood of stock market and real estate investment. This process drew savings from small rural investors as well as big urban ones, and lured banks and firms of all sizes into a dangerous credit pyramid. With the Great Crash on Black Thursday — 24 October 1929 — a cyclical downturn in the American economy turned into the most disastrous financial panic of all time. Historians will debate the precise role of the financial system in the crisis — whether the causes were fundamentally financial or whether the financial system merely magnified a wider problem, and whether the financial collapse was due mainly to domestic or to international weaknesses. In any case, the financial diagnosis led to the most comprehensive attempt ever to restructure the American financial system. Nevertheless, many of the embedded characteristics of the American financial system were not only retained, but elevated to legal and economic doctrine, reinforcing the legal status of systemic pluralism.

SUMMARY

The American financial system was highly decentralized from the beginning and early attempts at centralization were defeated, reflecting wider tensions between centralization and decentralization in the USA. Between the Civil War and the 1920s a plural banking system evolved in which thousands of small banks grew up alongside the kind of centralized 'finance capital' epitomized by J.P. Morgan and Wall Street. In times of prosperity, both components flourished and expanded; in economic downturns, however, the system was particularly vulnerable to panics and bank runs at both levels. In order to counteract such market failures, the Federal Reserve System was established in 1913. It was the first comprehensive attempt by the Federal Government to set up a national system for banking regulation, but it still had a decentralized structure, intended to support the existing pluralistic financial system. In the late nineteenth and early twentieth centuries, however, international factors increasingly affected the US economy, interacted with American expansion abroad and made the USA into a *de facto* financial superpower. Tensions grew between this international role and the domestic system. Developments in the 1920s exposed both sorts of tensions — not only within the pluralistic American financial system itself but also between domestic and international levels — leading to the Great Crash and to calls for a new regulatory system for American finance.

3   FROM THE NEW DEAL TO THE COLLAPSE OF BRETTON WOODS: MARKET COMPARTMENTALIZATION AND GLOBAL INTEGRATION

The American financial system developed as a highly pluralistic structure, with many thousands of small banks at the base of the pyramid but a concentrated set of powerful institutions and market players at the top. The strength of the system lay in its flexibility, while its weakness lay in the very openness that made it so flexible in the first place. It could service the demands of a wide variety of customers during boom periods but was extremely vulnerable to bubbles and panics — a vulnerability which was only partly countered by the establishment of the Federal Reserve System. A significant element in the flexibility of the system lay in the variety of tasks which could be undertaken by the institutions making up the system. Those institutions — commercial banks, investment banks, brokerage houses, etc. — on the whole performed different functions. Those functions, however, tended to evolve for pragmatic reasons. There was little to enforce their separation. At one end of the spectrum, small banks — some of the smallest of which were just separate counters in rural shops — could provide a range of financial services to the customer, from deposit taking to real estate brokerage to the buying and selling of securities. They were virtually mini-'financial supermarkets'. At the other end, the large investment banks like Morgan may not have taken deposits from the general public (although they did from their business clients), but they had their fingers in every pie from underwriting securities and manipulating markets to financing foreign governments and running huge industrial companies.

Whether selling bonds to rural customers or raising money for industrial undertakings, there was little regulatory control over what financial institutions could and could not do. They could frequently control the prices of financial instruments and manipulate both demand and supply. Indeed, such practices were generally neither illegal nor considered unethical if they provided liquidity to the markets. The willingness of a wide range of individual Americans, small banks and even other large institutions to purchase the bonds of Latin American governments, railroad consortia or mining companies, even where similar instruments had proven risky or even worthless in the past, was legendary. It was part of the mystique of adventurism which was seen to lie deep in the American spirit. Firms which made money from such risky business would plough that money back into the markets again or spend it in some manner so that others could supposedly benefit from its circulation. In the 1920s, they began to say that it would 'trickle down' to the worse off through economic growth, making everybody better off in the long run. But with the Great Crash, politicians, analysts and the public began to question more seriously the wisdom of allowing financial institutions such wide scope for their activities.

The history of the financial system from the Great Depression to the 1970s was that of a great experiment keeping different functions, and thereby different types of markets, legally and functionally separate from each other. This far-reaching attempt at *compartmentalization of the financial system*, enforced through a new system of regulation brought in by the New Deal, was intended to prevent the domino effect of market failure in one market or subsector of financial services from causing market failure in others, as was believed to have happened in the Great Crash. It also dovetailed with the new Keynesianism which argued that overdevelopment of the financial economy, driven by speculation, was harmful to the productive development of the 'real' economy of manufacturing and services, and which advocated the increasing intervention of government through macroeconomic demand management and the welfare state. That pattern of compartmentalization was to dominate the system until the 1970s, when a combination of economic stagnation, the breakdown of the post-Second World War international financial regime, and a political movement for 'deregulation' undermined the New Deal system.

3.1 COMPARTMENTALIZATION AND THE NEW DEAL SYSTEM OF FINANCIAL REGULATION

Although the Great Depression had a variety of causes and effects, among the most visible was the virtual collapse of large swathes of the financial system up to 1934. Close to 10,000 banks failed from the beginning of 1930 to the end of 1933 (4,000 in 1933 alone), a reduction from nearly 25,000 to around 15,000. The Federal Reserve System proved powerless to help. Every time that recovery seemed to be in sight, a new wave of bank runs and stock market falls would send the rest of the economy into a tailspin. Even before the 1932 presidential election and the coming of the New Deal, the Federal Government in effect got into the banking business by setting up the Reconstruction Finance Corporation, which provided $1.4 billion to financial institutions by the time President Franklin D. Roosevelt took office in March 1933. Also in 1932 the Fed was given additional powers to expand the money supply and the Federal Home Loan Bank System was set up to assist mortgage holders and providers, including small 'thrift' institutions ('savings-and-loan associations' or S&Ls), insurance companies, etc. But federal taxes were also raised in 1932, and both candidates promised balanced budgets! With Roosevelt's accession to the presidency, however, the Federal Government took on an even stronger role.

The 'New Deal system' included reforms of the Federal Reserve, begun in 1932 but extended in the Banking Act of 1935. The Fed had its Board of Governors strengthened and made more independent; it also received increased powers to control bank reserves, to lend to banks and to engage in systematic open-market operations. The USA followed the British lead and went off the Gold Standard, as did the other major industrial countries; in 1934, individuals were prohibited from holding gold and domestic currency was no longer redeemable in gold. However, the country also went onto a symbolic but significant 'Gold Exchange Standard'; this would later be used as the anchor for the post-Second World War Bretton Woods system of fixed exchange rates. The President was also given wide powers in 1933 to undertake a range of actions in the monetary field without reference to Congress. And in probably the key measure in halting the collapse of the banking system, the Federal Deposit Insurance Corporation (FDIC) was established, guaranteeing small deposits and undercutting the psychology of bank runs until the 1980s. The amount of capital required of national banks was raised, the regulatory role of the Fed expanded and Federal Deposit Insurance made available only to banks joining the national bank system.

Compartmentalizing the system

In terms of the overall institutional structure of the financial system, however, probably the most important reforms were contained in the Banking Act of

1933 and the Securities Exchange Act of 1934. The first contained (*inter alia*) provisions known as the Glass-Steagall Act. The Glass-Steagall Act prohibited commercial banks from engaging in the securities business — that is, they could not extend 'margin loans' for the purchase of stocks and bonds. Such margin loans were widely seen as a major cause of the 1920s financial bubble, when stocks could be bought for as little as a 10 per cent down payment — a payment which banks were happy to extend loans to cover while the markets were spiralling upward, but which caused havoc when they were called in after the crash. These provisions and others in the Act — provisions which were expanded and extended in the Banking Act of 1935 — were meant to separate commercial banking from the stock markets and from investment banking in a clear and fundamental way. Commercial banks could no longer have investment affiliates, nor could investment banks take deposits. Restrictions were placed on interlocking directorates. Probably the most visible consequence was that Morgan, unlike the majority of the big investment banks, decided to become a commercial bank, spinning off its investment banking activities in a separate company called Morgan Stanley.

In addition to the separation of institutions and markets *per se*, new regulatory controls were extended to both commercial banks and the securities industry. Commercial banks were prohibited from paying interest on ordinary 'demand' deposits (those which could be withdrawn at any time), and maximum interest rates could be set for 'time' (savings) deposits in order to prevent 'risky' interest rate competition. In the Securities Exchange Act of 1934, the stock and bond markets were put under a new body, the Securities and Exchange Commission (SEC), which would regulate and supervise the activities of brokers and dealers, attempt to control conflicts of interest and require extensive disclosure of information about securities issues. The Fed's powers were extended to control margin requirements, which were raised to 50 per cent. This compartmentalized system worked with little in the way of negative repercussions for about three decades. In the first place, the stock markets themselves remained relatively moribund until the 1950s. Even as economic growth resumed in the 1950s and the stock markets began to revive, financial caution prevailed and the structures were sufficiently strong to absorb new demand. A second reason for the durability of the New Deal system was the growing role of the Federal Government in economic management. Federal programmes affected the financing of the economy in many ways, both new and old. Not only did government spending — both state and federal — pump money into the economy which previously would have come from private sources, but the financing of government itself, whether through taxes or borrowing, soaked up private funds.

Protecting the domestic financial system

A final reason for the survival of the compartmentalized system was the relative isolation of the *financial* economy from international competitive and exchange rate pressures. After the Second World War, although a system of free trade and managed exchange rates (the Bretton Woods System) was set up, this went hand-in-hand with controls on international capital flows and

US support for various systems of domestic economic management — including the British Keynesian welfare state, the West German 'social market', French 'indicative planning' and the Japanese 'MITI' model of systematic promotion of export industries. There was, in effect, a trade-off after the war between this system of 'embedded liberalism' (Ruggie, 1983) in the international trading and production order, on the one hand, and increased scope for *domestic* economic management which would not be disrupted by external economic shocks, on the other.

However, to make this settlement viable, the compartmentalized financial system in the United States (and its counterparts abroad) had to be protected from foreign *financial* competition which might link financial market sectors across international borders and thereby put a strain on compartmental boundaries at home. This involved the official elevation at long last of the dollar, through the Gold Exchange Standard and a fixed exchange rate system, to the status of primary reserve currency for international transactions. It also involved the export of American capital — through the Marshall Plan, the Korean War boom and American multinational corporations investing abroad — to 'prime the pump' of international expansion. But the New Deal system was ultimately vulnerable to breakdown at several levels. As economic activity grew in the 1950s and 1960s, banks and financial markets looked increasingly for ways to get around compartmental barriers. The expansion of private sector economic activity also began to make the government's *domestic* economic policy instruments less effective at 'fine-tuning' the economy. In boom conditions, government borrowing and pump-priming lost their urgency too. Spending and reflation, rather than kick-starting economic activity, became 'sticky'. Finally, international financial interpenetration grew dramatically from the 1960s onwards (Strange, 1986; Khoury, 1990).

3.2 THE COLLAPSE OF THE NEW DEAL SETTLEMENT

The main structures of the American financial system were protected for about forty years by the New Deal settlement, bolstered by the post-war international financial regime. Pluralism was still the rule. In commercial banking, the system of small banks had been propped up not only by deposit insurance, guaranteed home loans and the separation of commercial banking from securities activities, but by federal restrictions on interstate operations by national banks too; the 1927 McFadden Act even went beyond existing state restrictions. The number of commercial banks dropped slightly from 15,000 at the end of 1933 to 14,000 in 1981; only about a fifth of this drop was caused by bank failures, with the rest due mainly to mergers and restructuring. Fundamental changes, however, were gathering momentum by the 1960s at the core of the financial system — the urban commercial banks, the investment banks, and the stock markets in particular — where the exclusive, club-like arrangements inherited from the nineteenth century came under serious threat from outside competition. These changes stemmed from the convergence and interaction of two crucial trends, one essentially domestic and the other international.

Pressures on the Keynesian welfare state

The first was a growing political and economic dissatisfaction with the wider Keynesian 'welfare state' settlement: with the increasing inefficiency of 'fine tuning' and demand management in an expanding economy in the 1960s; with the growth of government spending and regulation just as the reduction of poverty and the pursuit of social justice were attaining a higher political profile in President John F. Kennedy's 'New Frontier' and President Lyndon B. Johnson's 'Great Society'; and with an amalgam of stagnation and inflation (labelled 'stagflation') — once thought of as incompatible alternatives — which drew criticism from both Left and Right. New ways were sought to restart economic growth and to counteract what the Left called the 'fiscal crisis of the state'. Government was caught between the Scylla of stagnating tax revenues as the Long Boom waned and the Charybdis of increasing government expenditure — a syndrome found not just in the USA but all over the developed world.

Increased spending was caused not only by new social policies but also by older 'entitlement' programmes (for example, unemployment insurance rose as the economy contracted in the 1970s), by 'corporatist' wage settlements which fuelled 'cost-push' inflation, and by US spending on the Vietnam War. Each attempt to kick-start the economy through reflation had less impact on economic activity and worsened the fiscal crisis of the state at the same time. The Keynesian welfare state came under increasing pressure on the Right from monetarists and supply-side economists. These groups fundamentally disagreed on some issues, particularly over monetary policy. However, they both believed that government regulation and intervention inherently distorted the operation of the free market, that government taxes and borrowing were increasingly 'crowding out' sources of private investment, and that only by giving the financial markets their head could productive investment be rekindled and a virtuous circle of growth be restored. Keynesianism no longer seemed to work, and by the end of the 1970s finance had moved back to centre stage through both monetary policy and financial market deregulation.

The increasing internationalization of finance

These changes, however, were inextricably intertwined with a second set of trends at the international level. A profound transformation of world finance was taking place, one which could no longer be blunted by domestic economic policy. The political conditions which had made the New Deal system so durable — both the growth of state regulatory power in the 1930s and later the stability provided by the Bretton Woods System after the Second World War — began to break down. Financial globalization was only in its infancy at the end of the 1950s, but by the end of the 1960s it was an established fact. This process involved three overlapping structural trends: (1) the balance in the original Bretton Woods System between capital controls and trade liberalization was undermined; (2) the status of the USA itself changed as US policy makers reacted to growing tensions between America's national economic interests and the system which they had originally sponsored and guaranteed; and (3) the Bretton Woods System itself collapsed. American influence in the world financial system became more and more fragmented, until the USA opted out in 1971.

Lord Keynes, himself the main British negotiator at the Bretton Woods Conference in New Hampshire in July 1944, argued that if free trade were to lead to a virtuous circle of productive growth and lasting prosperity, there would have to be rules to *limit* the freedom of international financial flows. The rules would have to ensure that such flows were closely linked to trade flows and productive investment, and that speculative capital flows — that is what has been called 'hot money', seeking higher marginal rates of return from interest rate and exchange rate differentials, more liquid financial markets abroad, etc. — should be blocked. But the American negotiators were torn between intellectual agreement with the need for strong capital controls and the reviving influence of Wall Street. Apparently strong provisions for international capital controls to back up fixed exchange rates were built into Bretton Woods but were much vaguer than Keynes's original proposals. They would be progressively weakened as the world economy revived. The post-war economic system of 'embedded liberalism', therefore, was liberal with regard to free trade but in principle highly restrictive with regard to international finance (Helleiner, 1993).

This situation was gradually undermined, however. The powerful expansion of the world capitalist economy — given the stimulus of free trade, the Marshall Plan, US spending on arms and troops abroad, private American investment abroad (especially in the new European Economic Community after 1958), and a rise of new economic powers including Europe and Japan which could effectively compete with the USA in more open international markets — required ever-increasing quantities of free-flowing capital to service it. Wall Street expanded to meet the demand for international financial services. It also thereby increased its clout in American politics and with the Republican Party, which had returned to power with the election of President Dwight D. Eisenhower in 1952. In addition, the dollar shortage — the shortage of international liquidity in the aftermath of the war and the main target of the Marshall Plan — was replaced by a 'dollar glut'. This was in part the result of the general economic expansion discussed above. However, it also reflected the changing balance of economic power in the international system.

With Europe and Japan expanding more rapidly than the USA in the late 1950s and 1960s, the American balance of payments went into the red after 1958. Outflows of American capital continued — for investment, foreign aid and the US global military presence — leading to an increasingly 'structural' payments deficit. At the same time, the Kennedy and Johnson Administrations brought in social programmes requiring increased government spending. Expenditure on the escalating war in Vietnam fed not only into the American economy but into the world economy too. The dollar was the anchor currency of the Bretton Woods System, and its value was fixed in terms of gold; other currencies, however, were merely fixed in terms of their dollar value. In effect, the USA could continue to export dollars without having to reduce the value of the currency itself. Other countries, particularly France, accused America of 'exporting inflation'. The 'Euromarkets' — markets based in London where expatriate dollars were re-loaned without the sort of regulatory requirements applied to domestic currencies — rapidly developed to handle the new liquidity. European governments called for a devaluation of the dollar against gold, but the new Administration of President Richard M. Nixon, elected in 1968, argued that other currencies should themselves *revalue* against the dollar. American national economic interests no longer coincided with America's role as 'liberal hegemon' (Ruggie, 1983; Gilpin, 1987), guaranteeing the stability and soundness of the world capitalist economy.

Meanwhile, the strong dollar attracted more foreign imports and the balance of *payments* deficit turned into a chronic deficit on the balance of *trade* too. The Nixon Administration introduced import quotas and other protectionist measures. America was accused of becoming a 'predatory hegemon' — a country which used its pre-eminent economic power for its own short-term advantage rather than in the interests of the system itself. In August 1971, the USA broke the official link between the dollar and gold, and soon the world went on to a system of floating exchange rates. In effect, the attempt to control finance in order to privilege productive capital was abandoned. The bursting of the Bretton Woods dam resulted in the structure of the international economy being increasingly centred around rapidly globalizing financial markets and money flows. More and more money would be needed just to hedge against changes in exchange rates, interest rate differentials and divergent marginal returns between countries from different financial instruments. Futhermore, financial flows would penalize governments pursuing economic policies which reduced returns on financial instruments (for example, active fiscal policies, trade policies, social policies or industrial policies) and would undermine independent monetary policies too. Finally, globalization of financial markets made it more and more difficult for domestic financial markets to be effectively regulated and stabilized.

SUMMARY

The financial regulatory reforms of the New Deal were dominated by the compartmentalization of different types of financial markets, both in order to make the supervision of particular markets easier and to prevent market failure in one sector from spilling over into others. The cornerstone of this structure was the separation of commercial banking, on the one hand, from securities markets and investment banking, on the other. This system did not begin seriously to break down until the 1970s because it did not come under significant domestic or international pressure. However, demand for more flexible financial services developed during the Long Boom and grew rapidly in the crisis which followed. In the 1970s, both the difficulties of the Keynesian welfare state and the breakdown of Bretton Woods exposed the weaknesses of the New Deal system in a more open and interpenetrated world financial order.

4 FINANCIAL DEREGULATION AND GLOBALIZATION: DILEMMAS OF AMERICAN POLICY AND POLITICS

With the collapse of the New Deal and the Bretton Woods Systems, the financial stabilizers of the Long Boom were removed. After 1973 a new cycle of booms and slumps, inextricably intertwined with financial bubbles and panics, returned to the USA and the world economy. Not only external American financial power and hegemony thereby came under strain, but also the domestic American financial system came under severe pressure. Boundaries between financial institutions and markets were widely breached and severely eroded. This in turn set up pressures for regulatory change, usually referred to — imprecisely — as 'deregulation'. Volatility increased too, while far-reaching changes in communications and information technology revolutionized both global and domestic financial market structures. Walls between international and domestic levels became more and more permeable, producing complex knock-on effects and chain reactions.

In this rapidly evolving environment, centralization of the US financial system increased dramatically. Larger financial institutions, the 'money centre' banks, which pioneered the globalization process from the 1960s to the 1980s, pushed continuously against the boundaries of the regulatory system. However, they found international competition increasingly tough going in the 1980s. This in turn put pressure on the regulatory system in ways which the state could not efficiently handle. Futhermore, new powerful institutions — pension funds and mutual funds (the latter known in Britain as 'unit trusts') — came to dominate crucial aspects of the financial system. Meanwhile, the centre of gravity of international finance itself moved away from traditional banking to complex financial innovation and 'securitization'; the rapidly deregulating and integrating securities markets, led by Wall Street, set the pace for globalization. The world-wide stock market crash of October 1987, which started in the interaction of Wall Street and the new 'derivatives' markets in Chicago, demonstrated how far linkages between institutions and markets had gone. Finally, increasingly intense price competition cut a swathe through small institutions — the community banks and Savings and Loans. The number of banks fell from about 14,500 in 1984 (its post-war high point) to 12,000 in mid-1990, of which over 11,000 were small unit banks. It fell to around 7,000 in the late 1990s and is likely to fall considerably further as the current merger process, mainly amongst regional groupings of medium-to-large sized banks, continues to gather pace. Nevertheless, as the US Treasury has stated: 'If the United States had the same ratio of banks to population [as Canada], it would have about seventy five banks, of which about fifty six would operate nationwide' (United States, 1991, p.XVII–17).

Although key structural features of the American regulatory system are still protected by barriers to political change, many of these have been coming down. In particular, *regulatory pluralism* — a range of different agencies supervising assorted activities and sectors within the financial services industry — has resisted consolidation and streamlining. Agencies have defended their own 'turf', and pressure groups representing different industry sectors have put up fierce political resistance in Congress. Yet change has not been stopped. It has instead come through *ad hoc* 'regulatory arbitrage' — industry sectors whipsawing one agency against another to gain competitive advantages *vis-à-vis* other sectors. Agencies in turn have engaged in so-called 'competition in laxity' in order to favour their own client groups. An analogous process has been taking place *between countries*.

4.1 REGULATORY ARBITRAGE AND STRUCTURAL CHANGE AT HOME AND ABROAD

Change in the American financial system has not derived primarily from domestic causes *per se* but from attempts by American institutions and markets to adapt to the international changes described above. Erosion of the capital controls which maintained the Bretton Woods System increasingly involved larger American commercial and investment banks in international transactions — especially transactions in dollars — as the 'dollar shortage' turned into the 'dollar glut'. As the supply of dollars held abroad built up, American institutions became the main players in new unregulated markets for shifting these 'Eurodollars' to new uses. Furthermore, as American economic growth began to slow from its 1950s levels, big institutions looked to new investment opportunities, and those opportunities were abroad. The Euromarkets grew up in London, and this is where American houses began to establish larger branches and new activities. Profits from these transactions derived not from monopoly privileges — such as the prohibition of paying interest on demand deposits, fixed commissions on securities brokerage or the 'relationship banking' which previously dominated the American financial scene — but from the *volume* of transactions. Even given certain limits on profit margins — the narrower 'spreads' between bid and offer prices for currencies and securities in the more fiercely competitive Euromarkets — banks and brokers could bid for vastly increased business. That business often came from whole new sets of customers — borrowers and lenders — from outside the USA. Against this more open background, American regulations for nearly three decades proved increasingly counter-productive by pushing US customers abroad. Nevertheless, during the 1990s the dramatic recovery of the American economy has been fed by a more dynamic financial system, rapidly evolving to cope with the ultra-competitive global financial environment.

Adapting to the international marketplace

American interest rates were capped under the New Deal system by rules such as the Fed's Regulation Q to prevent excessive interest rate competition (thought to have played a destabilizing role in the 1920s), but these regulations did not have a notable impact until the 1950s. In the Euromarkets, however, interest rates were set by the market; in the 1960s, these rates grew much higher than in the USA. In addition to the new volume of business, then, interest rate differentials made profits higher abroad. Another disincentive to expanding domestic business was the Interest Equalization Tax, introduced in 1953. The IET taxed the higher rates of interest available on foreign bonds in an attempt to make them less attractive to American investors. However, with the growth of the Euromarkets, 'Eurobonds' (denominated in expatriate currencies, originally almost entirely in Eurodollars) could be *bought and held abroad* by American institutions without attracting the tax. American firms, both financial and non-financial, increasingly did so, often keeping their profits abroad too; this fed more liquidity into the Euromarkets, further increasing their attractiveness. Under pressure from US firms facing fiercer foreign competition — and also from other governments worried about inflation — the Johnson Administration introduced the Voluntary Foreign Credit Restraint Act (VFCR) in 1964 to restrict domestic bank loans for foreign purposes (with the aim of limiting capital outflows), making it mandatory in 1968. The VFCR actually made it more profitable for firms to take out loans abroad, boosting incentives for dealing on the Euromarkets. These factors — and more — reinforced the Euromarkets and internationalized the business of the securities markets and the larger US institutions too.

When Bretton Woods finally broke down, the need for firms to deal with floating exchange rates led to a rapid expansion of currency transactions; business flowed to the Euromarkets, which already had the infrastructure to handle it. Multinational corporations, both American and non-American, internationalized their *financial* operations as well as their productive operations. In the 1970s, two further factors dramatically expanded the pulling power of the Euromarkets: the increase in oil prices in 1973–1974 and again in 1979 led the oil-producing states to 'recycle' their new-found windfall profits (denominated in dollars) through these channels; and Eurodollar loans were vastly expanded to sovereign governments and public sector firms with government guarantees. Much went to the Third World to pay for oil and finance industrial development, leading to the Third World debt crisis of the 1980s. Thus new and volatile international circuits of capital reminiscent of the 1920s mushroomed, but through a much more complex system than that of the inter-war period. These circuits reached deep inside the US financial system itself.

It was American dollars, American banks and American multinational firms that were the major players. The possibilities for development — and for destabilization — were enormous. These internationalized markets were also the first to produce, out of competitive necessity, two more features which shaped structural change: (1) complex types of *financial innovation* which went far beyond the traditional instruments of bank loans and fixed-rate bonds, including a range of currency hedges, variable-rate bonds, perpetual notes, interest rate swaps, and 'off-balance-sheet' instruments such as revolving credit facilities; and (2) the introduction of *new technology* to process orders and trades. In this fiercely competitive environment, profits came increasingly from volume and volume-related fees and spreads rather than from safe, regulated returns. Commissions on transactions were fully negotiable, not fixed as in most domestic financial stock and bond markets at the time. There were no interest rate controls, but interest rate competition led to the convergence of market rates, and spreads between bid and offer prices narrowed.

As the American balance of payments worsened and domestic business stagnated in the mid-to-late 1970s — usually attributed to the 'oil shocks', the fiscal crisis of the corporatist welfare state and the failure of Keynesian demand management — pressures built up both within the political system and in sectors of the financial services industry for deregulation. Deregulation was not only fashionable in the financial sector, but was favoured by influential groups on both Left and Right for regenerating industries like telecommunications, the airlines and trucking. It was widely understood in the financial sector that pressures of international competition could no longer be blunted by financial protectionism or a return to fixed exchange rates and capital controls. The genie was out of the bottle. Although the larger institutions were the spearhead of the deregulation movement, it infected the smaller institutions too with the view that their only future was to be able to compete on price with the big boys for their specialized services.

Structural changes in the American system

Structural change within the American financial system took various forms. The major investment banks, which had followed the money centre banks into the Euromarkets, pushed for deregulation. Pressure was applied both in Congress and in the markets themselves. The key step was actually taken by the New York Stock Exchange on 1 May 1975 — 'May Day', the precursor of liberalization elsewhere, including Britain and France. May Day saw the end of the system of fixed commissions for securities trading. Negotiated commission rates ended the monopoly profits of securities brokers, and gave much more market power to the investment banks and to borrowers and lenders to shop around for cheaper prices for large transactions. For banks, the major changes came with the International Banking Act of 1978 (IBA) and, in particular, the Depository Institutions Deregulation and Monetary Control Act of 1980 (DIDMCA) — which legalized money market accounts and set a timetable for eliminating Regulation Q — although various decisions by federal regulatory bodies (especially the Fed) and by state governments were also significant (see Khoury, 1990, pp.81–2). Savings and Loans were deregulated in critical ways in the Garn-St. Germain Depository Institutions Act of 1982. The dynamic of change was further accelerated by the increasingly complex structure of *interaction between the domestic and international levels.*

How this worked can be seen clearly in the federal budget deficits that mushroomed under President Ronald Reagan. They led to a growing need to finance the deficit — a need significantly greater than the capacity of American institutions to meet from domestic funds. Domestic interest rates had to be raised to attract capital from abroad — mainly from Japan, to a lesser extent from Europe. There were also cuts in loans to the Third World after the debt crisis erupted in 1982. This had several effects. Other countries had to raise their own interest rates to compete for funds (and prevent capital outflows to the USA) — bringing about a convergence of interest rates around the world and thereby restricting those governments' economic policy autonomy. It also kept the dollar high despite a large trade deficit — worsening that deficit and undermining the international competitiveness of large sectors of American industry (the Rust Belt). This did, however, help to mitigate the impact of higher interest rates on *other* countries for a time, with the high dollar sucking imports into the USA. It also turned the USA from a creditor nation — a vital source of its economic and financial power under the *pax Americana* — into a net debtor by the mid-1980s.

Another example is the way that deregulation in the United States, still by far the world's largest economy, has forced other countries, big and small, to deregulate their own banks and securities markets. Britain's Big Bang in 1986 was probably the most comprehensive reform (Mayer, 1988), while the 'Little Big Bang' in France was mainly carried out not by a conservative government but by a socialist one (Cerny, 1989a). Indeed, the competitive deregulations of the 1980s have been compared to the competitive devaluations of the 1930s. An international 'ratchet effect' was at work. Each deregulation led in turn to increased internationalization, making a return to tighter national-level regulation less possible. The same process can be seen in the 'securitization' and 'disintermediation' of finance — that is the trend away from traditional bank loans (particular contracts between specific bankers and borrowers, based on the former's knowledge of the latter's creditworthiness) towards the selling of *negotiable* securities (which can be bought and sold by any 'bearer') — from certificates of deposit to complex mixes of debt and equity. The crucial feature is that these instruments can later be traded in a secondary market, and the most attractive and efficient of such markets — that is the most liquid — are international markets.

This process has also led to financial innovation — the design of new, complex and often specially tailored instruments. A notable example is the development of 'derivatives' markets — mainly futures and options — in which imaginary financial instruments are traded, ostensibly to hedge against loss in volatile markets. Derivatives markets developed mainly in Chicago out of the long-standing commodities futures markets. They first focused on currency options and futures to compete with the Euromarkets. From these beginnings, an American regulatory system for futures has developed that has provided a model of arms-length regulation widely copied in other countries. Indeed, futures and options markets, because they are the most 'abstract' markets (they do not require the actual buying and selling of the 'underlying' securities), are rapidly becoming one of the most globalized financial markets. However, the interaction of derivatives markets and markets in real financial instruments has also been seen as a source of volatility, especially in the way that stock market futures and options are 'arbitraged' against the basic stocks.

Many further examples could be cited. Government decisions — sometimes the strategic decisions of core political leaders and sometimes the micro-decisions of bureaucrats, regulatory agencies and other parts of the state — lead to irreversible structural changes, changes which in turn reduce the power of governments in general and thereby further increase the autonomy of financial markets. The essential mechanism of change is *regulatory arbitrage*. Once the dikes of domestic regulatory compartmentalization and international capital controls have been breached in key sectors and the centrality of money and financial markets reasserted — as in the breakdown of the New Deal system and Bretton Woods — other market sectors seek to reduce existing regulatory barriers in their own areas in order to compete for business. Governments and regulatory agencies desire to promote the health and profitability of their 'own' national financial systems (in the global context) and their 'own' sectors (in domestic terms). To this end they will seek to 'level the playing field' (to remove competitive disadvantages) and even to provide their own clients with *new* competitive advantages *vis-à-vis* rival nations or sectors. Globalization and deregulation are thus inextricably intertwined aspects of a virtuous — or vicious — circle.

4.2 MARKET CHANGE AND GOVERNMENTAL GRIDLOCK: THE AMERICAN POLITICAL PROCESS AND THE FAILURE OF REGULATORY REFORM

This process, however, is neither smooth nor uniform. There is what economists call a 'stochastic' element at work here — a situation where the random or unpredictable interaction of elements produces outcomes which are 'sticky'. The terms of the equation no longer hold with the same random distribution of probabilities in subsequent 'plays of the game'; future inputs and outcomes are constrained and shaped in structurally new and distinct ways. The development of the American financial system therefore should be seen as the outcome of an ongoing dialectic or set of games linking the American political system, on the one hand, and the pressures of market change, on the other. Specific conjunctural outcomes have become 'sticky' in both political and economic terms as they feed back into the process. Politicians and bureaucrats have lost much of their autonomy with (1) the erosion of domestic systems of protective financial market regulation (like the New Deal system in the United States) and (2) the collapse of international regimes which could sustain that capability, in other words, Bretton Woods. However, states acting unilaterally *do* still possess the capacity to take decisions which *open* financial markets. But as that opening process has, in turn, increased the complexity of those markets in transnational terms, states are finding it more and more difficult to take the kinds of decisions which *control* those markets — decisions which can effectively and systematically shape, stabilize and control not only the workings of the markets themselves but also the wider economic and political ramifications of their operation.

Gridlock and deregulation

This is a particularly acute problem for the USA. The American governmental system is profoundly shaped by its constitutional substructure, which has traditionally worked through a system of 'checks and balances' between different, competing and partially autonomous centres of power. The two main features of the system are (1) the separation of powers at the national level — based on the constitutional autonomy of the three branches of government, executive, legislative and judicial — and (2) the federal system, which reserves significant autonomous powers to the individual states. This structure is further complicated by the existence of a range of *a priori* rights over and against government in general granted to individuals by the constitution itself. This system may have worked effectively when the USA was relatively isolated from transnational forces, as in the nineteenth century, or when America was powerful enough on its own to control those forces, as in the post-Second World War period. However, it has become fragmented and unwieldy in an interdependent and interpenetrated international system. It tends towards 'political entropy' and 'gridlock', running around in ever decreasing political circles while control of the real issues slips away (Cerny, 1989b and 1994a).

This is nowhere more true than with regard to the American financial system. Despite the growing popularity of deregulation in the 1970s and 1980s, financial deregulation itself took place not through a strategic, proactive approach to a restructuring of the financial system, but rather through a series of reactive, sector-specific, pressure-group driven, and often *ad hoc* decisions by different and often competing 'power centres' within the American state. Susan Strange argues that 'non-decisions' were as important as, or even more important than, active decisions in the breakdown of Bretton Woods and the transnationalization of American financial institutions and markets (Strange, 1986). The move to floating exchange rates, perhaps the most momentous single event in the process, resulted from the Nixon Administration's refusal to consider devaluing the dollar within the Bretton Woods system or to negotiate a workable replacement for Bretton Woods. Deregulation of the banking system similarly involved a series of *ad hoc* reactions to a range of *faits accomplis* by the banks themselves, from their move into the Euromarkets to their experimentation with new financial instruments like negotiable certificates of deposits and other money market instruments.

The creation of new regulatory structures too — 'deregulation' being a misnomer which masks the creation of new regulations and agencies — has also occurred on an *ad hoc* basis. In the 1970s, the Commodities Futures Trading Commission was set up as an offshoot of the Department of Agriculture because such instruments as pork-belly futures were traded long before financial futures were invented (leading to an ongoing turf battle with the Securities and Exchange Commission). The Office of Thrift Supervision and the Resolution Trust Corporation were set up when the Savings and Loans crisis was already at its height at the end of the 1980s. A whole range of initiatives which changed the face of US financial regulation were improvised on the wing, from virtual nationalization of Chicago's collapsed Continental Illinois Bank in 1984 — the biggest money centre bank to fail — to a range of administrative and court decisions which have greatly widened the loopholes permitting banks — with Morgan at the forefront — to engage in an ever–increasing range of securities activities (since 1996, up to 25 per cent of their business) *despite* the fact that Glass-Steagall still remains on the statute books. At the beginning of the 1990s, a long-running campaign by the money centre banks, supported by the Administration of President George W. Bush (elected in 1989–93) to replace Glass-Steagall and to reform the banking regulatory system came to a head.

The American financial regulatory structure is unique among advanced industrial countries in being a multipolar, competitive system of regulatory bodies, each operating with a certain legal independence and discretion, competing over turf and developing clientelist relations with specific sectors of the financial services industry. At the level of the federal bureaucracy alone, the existence of distinct and competing regulatory authorities is testimony to the *ad hoc* and reactive nature of American institutions; these include the Office of the Comptroller of the Currency (part of the Treasury, with oversight over national banks), the Fed (with broad monetary and regulatory control over much of the banking system) and the Securities and Exchange Commission (which oversees the securities markets) — not to mention the Commodities and Futures Trading Commission, the Office of Thrift Supervision (which has absorbed the Federal Home Loan Bank Board), the Federal Deposit Insurance Corporation (which has absorbed the Federal Savings and Loan Insurance Corporation), and the Resolution Trust Corporation (liquidating failed S&Ls). There is also a parallel system of congressional oversight which shadows the regulatory agencies through the committees and subcommittees of both the Senate and the House of Representatives. Finally, a panoply of state-level regulatory institutions also act as competing centres of power.

In this context, forming the kind of broad coalitions needed to change the basic structure of the system generally requires both the *existence of a crisis* and the presence of *strong executive leadership*. As such conditions are normally absent in the USA, the system has by and large emerged one agency at a time. Futhermore, American public bureaucracies, especially the independent regulatory agencies, are highly susceptible to 'capture' by the very private interests which they are intended to regulate. Together, private interests and public agencies tend to form clientelist or corporatist networks or circuits of power. The more unified and centralized the *agency*, the more powerful the network. In this context, American economists argue that it is better to have several smaller 'captured' agencies than one big 'captured' agency. The danger of capture, therefore, is in theory circumscribed by setting a range of agencies to compete among themselves. The more European-centred, 'statist' view that independent, socially autonomous and centralized bureaucracies imbued with an ethos of the 'common good' are the *least* likely objects of successful capture and not the most, is rejected in favour of the neoclassical economist's analogy between the economic marketplace and the 'market' for regulation.

Gridlock and re-regulation

After the October 1987 crash, calls for re-regulation, which had been in the air for some time, were thrust into the limelight. However, these proposals tended merely to tinker around the edges of the problem of regulatory arbitrage. Broader proposals for regulatory reform had been examined several times in the mid-1980s, not least by the 'task group' headed by the then Vice-President, George Bush, in 1984. When the new President took office in 1989, the Treasury — still under the direction of Secretary Nicholas Brady, a long-time confidant of the President — dusted off its proposals and moved them up the 'President's agenda'. These formed the basis for a wide-ranging attempt to change the financial regulatory system itself. The Administration's proposals, along with independent initiatives by powerful members of the relevant congressional committees, included a wide range of key measures, especially: to set up a unified banking regulator, the Federal Banking Agency; to replace Glass-Steagall and the Bank Holding Company Act with a new structure permitting more integration of banking and securities and allowing ownership links between banks and commercial firms; to reform the FDIC, which was under increasing strain from the Savings and Loan crisis and commercial bank failures; to reduce barriers to interstate banking; and to give the Securities and Exchange Commission wider powers (United States, 1991).

The conflicts which this vista engendered stretched right into the White House and the Cabinet. They mobilized members of Congress, different regulators and industry pressure groups along different axes. The apparent consensus that 'something must be done' did not involve agreement on a common perspective on specific solutions. What was presented as 'far-reaching' legislation, even before it reached Congress, did not directly address the structure of the American financial services industry in the global context. Neither did it really address the major problem facing the US regulatory structure — its gridlock character — either in terms of the content of the proposals (despite the FBA proposal, I would argue) or in terms of what would be needed to successfully pass the legislation. For example, the existence of multiple networks linking different regulatory agencies with particular sectors of the financial services industry ensured that any specific proposal was certain to evoke objections from one or more networks, creating a potential situation of multiple veto. Finally, the proposals themselves, although far-reaching *in toto*, were a complex mixture of diverse specific recommendations. It was only to be expected that the package would be picked apart.

The Administration's approach was to present the proposals together as a strategic package. The omens were not entirely negative. Given the high profile of the S&L crisis, the growing problem of banking failures, increasing awareness that American money-centre banks were no longer the biggest and most successful in the world (there were none in the top twenty in 1991, most of which at the time were Japanese) and the debate over the role of the 'credit crunch' in the recession, there had emerged what seemed to be potential ingredients for a widening consensus that some sort of re-regulatory action was necessary. But putting the proposals forward together had several potential drawbacks too. It would require strong and cohesive executive leadership, as we have already mentioned. This was not a simple task. The executive bureaucracy and the regulatory agencies were deeply divided and fearful of losing turf. And then there was the problem of the legislative process itself. Following the deregulatory stampede of the late 1970s and early 1980s, Congress had proved increasingly stalemated on issues of re-regulation. Indeed, subsequent modifications to the system and substance of financial regulation tended to come out of the executive branch, the independent regulatory agencies, or the courts. In effect, the package had to be both negotiable enough to withstand the pressures of the legislative arena and far-reaching enough to ensure that the end result would involve significant and fundamental change whatever the alterations. In the event, this balance was not achieved.

The most obvious flop was the elimination, in committee, of proposals to set up a new Federal Banking Agency to centralize some of the functions of existing agencies. In contrast, however, the most *politically* credible of the Administration's proposals did eventually succeed. This was the refinancing or recapitalization of the Bank Insurance Fund (part of the post-S&L FDIC), which was precariously close to running dry as major banks ran into difficulties, and putting the BIF on a different — 'risk-based' — system of financing. These proposals were eventually passed as a separate bill, the Federal Deposit Insurance Corporation Improvement Act of 1991. Sandwiched between the failure of regulatory restructuring and the relative success of FDIC reform and the BIF recap, however, were the two most important proposals for reform of the American financial services industry: the lifting of federal restrictions on interstate banking; and the ending of key constraints on combining commercial banking and securities trading — the partial repeal of Glass-Steagall. The first of these proposals was expected to succeed even if the other failed, but effective lobbying by the small banks, which had strong constituency connections and a very active lobbying organization, managed to skilfully mobilize opposition. As for the attempt to repeal Glass-Steagall, the most controversial proposal in the original package, the key to the outcome was the process in the House of Representatives. Attempts by key committees and their chairmen to include strict 'firewall' provisions — *internal* barriers between banks and securities affiliates rather than the *external* barriers of Glass-Steagall — alienated both the pro-reform Bush Administration (and Republicans in Congress) and opponents of changing Glass-Steagall at all!

The *arena* of regulatory reform, especially on the issue of interstate banking, is already shifting away from the legislature and thus away from any comprehensive package. 'Reform' activity is again focused on the discretionary powers of regulatory agencies, the activities of state governments (some states, such as Delaware, seem to have the potential to play the role of the mini-'competition states'), and, of course, action in the courts. Restrictions on interstate banking are being sporadically and unevenly whittled away, while Glass-Steagall restrictions are being eroded too by decisions of the courts, of the Fed, of the Comptroller of the Currency and other agencies. Two further attempts to repeal the Glass-Steagall Act have failed to get out of Congress since 1991; at the time of writing, new bills have been revived in the relevant committees of both House and Senate, but crucial stumbling blocks remain even amongst players ostensibly committed to reform like Senator Phil Gramm (Republican, Texas), chairman of the Senate Banking Committee. The McFadden Act, however, was finally repealed in 1994, and the National Securities Markets Improvement Act of 1996 has brought many state and federal regulations into line. Financial market decompartmentalization, institutional concentration and regulatory arbitrage are still at work (Litan and Rauch, 1998). And in a world in which American economic recovery continues and international capital mobility are still expanding rapidly, American banks and securities markets have not only retained but expanded their leading international role.

SUMMARY

In the world of more open financial competition characteristic of the 1980s and 1990s, linkages between markets facilitate ever-expanding processes of regulatory arbitrage. Competition between states and between different branches and agencies within states interact with changes in international financial markets to promote processes of deregulation and re-regulation. American firms have been at the forefront of this process and have managed to overcome their apparent loss of competitive advantage of a decade ago. These developments are putting further pressure on the pluralistic character of the American financial system, primarily favouring larger market actors that can compete on an international scale. It has also put pressure on the gridlocked US governmental and regulatory system, promoting competitive deregulation but hindering systematic re-regulation.

5 CONCLUSION: THE FUTURE OF TRANSNATIONAL FINANCE AND THE AMERICAN FINANCIAL SYSTEM IN A MORE OPEN WORLD

The American financial system at the turn of the millennium is caught between powerful transnational market forces on the one hand, and less powerful but highly resistant domestic structures on the other. 'Free banking', however, is in free fall. Institutions and markets will continue to be drawn into more complex transnational structures of interaction. The distinction between the domestic and the international now makes little difference to the markets. This crucial feature of the markets also reflects the growing domination of money and finance over the 'real' economy — the productive and trading system. Without a much denser transnational regulatory order with the capacity to impose systematic controls on the financial markets — one which goes much further than recent proposals for a 'new architecture' of international financial regulation — narrow financial criteria will continue to play an ever-larger role in the allocation of capital across the world. Individual governments will be able to oil the wheels of market interpenetration, but will not be able to control its effects (Cerny, 1993). The stable door can only be shut once the horse has bolted, as demonstrated by the Asian financial meltdown of 1997–98 and its aftermath.

In terms of financial structures themselves, there has been a process of concentration of markets and institutions. Securitization is probably the most important single factor in reshaping different markets and institutions into a single system. The key advantage of securitization is that it provides geometrically increased prospects for flexibility. The capacity of institutions to avoid being burdened over long periods with specific assets and liabilities, that is their ability to *trade* those assets and liabilities in liquid secondary markets at a discount, has always played a role in the development of banking as well as being at the heart of stock and bond markets. But the possibility of selling literally anything — from huge 'block trades' of standardized securities to packages of small bank loans to specific customers — on to other institutions is growing vaster, and a whole range of new markets have grown up in and around traditional stock and bond markets to service this demand (Crawford and Sihler, 1991). Many of these new securities can only be sold on because they are attractive to buyers — and they are attractive to buyers because they can be sold on again, and again, if need be, in liquid secondary markets. It is therefore likely that international finance will become even more concentrated, because only the big institutions — often dealing with only the biggest non-financial firms — will have the economies of scale to be both flexible and profitable in a highly competitive environment where profit margins will be cut to the bone. Perhaps the most striking example of this tendency is the recent rapid growth of massive pension funds and mutual funds (unit trusts) — known as 'institutional investors' — which increasingly dominate the high end of the markets (O'Barr and Conley, 1992).

Secularization, in the broad sense in which we have been using it, is supposed to take some of the risk out of the markets by providing a wider range of hedging possibilities: however, this can in turn encourage speculation and further instability, a spectre raised by the failure of the hedge fund Long-Term Capital Management in 1998 (bailed out, as usual, by the Fed). Will, as Keynes argued, globalization and concentration merely crowd out long-term investment — especially 'productive' investment in the 'real economy'? Will it increase profitability at the expense of manufacturing production, real standards of living and jobs? Will it open the way to more booms and slumps, more financial bubbles and panics? And if government can no longer control this process in an effective, strategic way, will it not lead to what has been called a 'democratic deficit', in which the interests of the people do not seem to exist because there is no way to translate their expression through existing political systems into government action? The answers to these and other questions are as yet unclear. Despite the ongoing American boom, the Asian crisis and the Russian default on its international loans in 1998 have raised serious question marks.

Is globalization sufficiently comprehensive and inexorable to prevent governments from taking back some control? The relatively successful use of temporary capital controls by Malaysia in 1997–99 seems to have mitigated some aspects of the Asian crisis, on the one hand, while on the other international co-operation between finance ministers in the Group of Seven industrialized nations, along with the World Bank and the International Monetary Fund, seems to be getting more effective in dealing with certain aspects of such crises. At the same time, although governments are still sovereign, there seems little desire (and possibly little practical scope) for increased use of legal restrictions, as Martin Mayer (1992) recommended, to increase the 'friction' between different markets. Indeed, the predominant trend is in the other direction. Alternatives to the American approach — the so-called 'Washington Consensus' on liberalization of financial markets — seem to be eroding. For example, the big German 'universal' banks are rapidly moving into global markets and unwinding some of their support for industrial activities at home, while Japanese banks and securities firms have continued to lurch through ever more serious crises since the Japanese financial bubble burst in 1989.

Finally, what effect does size have in a global financial marketplace? The question of economies of scale is double-edged. Although big financial super-markets have some comparative advantages, so do small financial 'boutiques' — although how significant the advantages are in terms of capital allocation and price-setting in the overall system is still unclear. Can boutiques, by continuing to enter the market, make it more responsive, or will they simply be price-takers with a limited role? And will the kind of computerized networks required for effective global trade lead to oligopolies and cartels, as they seem to have done for airline reservations systems, or will the financial markets evolve towards the 'personal computer' model, where everyone can play? Thus far, all these trends seem to be evolving simultaneously, giving a comparative advantage to a flexible system like the American.

In any case, these questions will be increasingly determined by competitive forces in the *global* marketplace; governments will have either to adjust or see their options narrow even more.

In this context, the United States, despite the weaknesses of its processes of financial regulation, still holds some extremely good cards in its hand; it is rich in human capital in the financial services industry — especially in the supply of what Robert Reich (1991) has called the 'symbolic analysts' who are the source of 'value added' in the world economy and who play a key role in financial innovation and technological development. Furthermore, the USA is still the world's largest economy, and has been undergoing a steady non-inflationary recovery after the 'credit crunch' of 1991. Even its tradition of financial pluralism has important benefits in a global financial system. It is a very flexible system of financial institutions, and these have played a wide range of roles in the process of globalization *despite* entropy in the political and regulatory system. Not only have its larger institutions rebuilt their world position since 1991, but its *retail* banking system is also judged to be the most efficient in the world. Even its various regulators are more and more closely connected with their respective counterparts abroad. The Fed has more in common with other central banks, and the Securities and Exchange Commission with other securities regulators in other countries, than they do with each other, with any presidential administration, or with Congress.

In the last analysis, however, whatever the competitive advantages and disadvantages of the American financial system — its monetary system, its system of financial institutions and markets, and its system of financial regulation — its success or failure will be increasingly determined by transnational conditions, not by conditions in some imaginary, insulated domestic market. In this context, the debate over what to do in *global* terms to respond to what is now a global issue is only just beginning. It is bound to run and run.

REFERENCES

Allen, F.L. (1949) 'The great Pierpoint Morgan' in Degen, R.A. (1987).

Cerny, P.G. (1989a) 'The "Little Big Bang" in Paris: financial market deregulation in a *dirigiste* system', *European Journal of Political Research*, vol.17, pp.169–92.

Cerny, P.G. (1989b) 'Political entropy and American decline', *Millennium: Journal of International Studies*, vol.18, pp.47–63.

Cerny, P.G. (ed.) (1993) *Finance and World Politics: Markets, Regimes and States in the Post-Hegemonic Era*, Cheltenham, Glos. and Brookfield, Vermont, Edward Elgar.

Cerny, P.G. (1994a) 'Global finance and governmental gridlock: political entropy and the decline of American financial power' in Maidment, R. and Thurber, J.A. (eds.) *The Politics of Relative Decline: The United States at the End of the Twentieth Century*, Oxford and New York, Polity Press and Basil Blackwell.

Cerny, P.G. (1994b) 'The infrastructure of the infrastructure? Toward "embedded financial orthodoxy" in the international political economy' in Gills, B. and Palar, R. (eds.) *Transcending the State-Global Divide: The Neostructuralist Agenda in International Relations*, Boulder, Colorado, Lynne Reinner.

Crawford, R.D. and Sihler, W.W. (1991) *The Troubled Money Business: The Death of an Old Order and the Rise of a New Order*, New York, Harper Business.

Degen, R.A. (1987) *The American Monetary System: A Concise Survey of Its Evolution Since 1896*, Lexington, Lexington Books.

Gilpin, R. (1987) *The Political Economy of International Relations*, Princeton, New Jersey, Princeton University Press.

Helleiner, E.N. (1993) 'When finance was the servant: international capital movements in the Bretton Woods order' in Cerny, P.G. (ed.) (1993).

Khoury, S.J. (1990) *The Deregulation of the World Financial Markets: Myths, Realities and Impact*, London, Pinter Publishers.

Litan, R.E. and Rauch, J. (1998) *American Finance for the 21st Century*, Washington DC, Brookings Institution Press.

McKenzie, R.B. and Lee, D.R. (1991) *Quicksilver Capital: How the Rapid Movement of Wealth Has Changed the World*, New York, Free Press.

Mayer, M. (1988) *Markets: Who Plays, Who Risks, Who Gains, Who Loses*, London, Simon and Schuster.

Mayer, M. (1992) *Stealing the Market: How the Giant Brokerage Firms, with Help from the SEC, Stole the Stock Market from Investors ...*, New York, Basic Books.

O'Barr, W.M. and Conley, J.M., with Brancato, C.K. (1992) *Fortune and Folly: The Wealth and Power of Institutional Investing*, Homewood, Illinois, Business One Irwin.

Reich, R.B. (1991) *The Work of Nations: Preparing Ourselves for 21st-Century Capitalism*, New York, Alfred A. Knopf.

Ruggie, J.G. (1983) 'International regimes, transactions and change: embedded liberalism in the postwar economic order' in Krasner, S. (ed.) *International Regimes*, Ithaca, N.Y., Cornell University Press, pp.195–231.

Strange, S. (1986) *Casino Capitalism*, Oxford, Basil Blackwell.

United States (1991) Department of the Treasury, *Modernizing the Financial System: Recommendations for Safer, More Competitive Banks*, Washington, D.C., United States Government Printing Office.

FURTHER READING

Block, F.L. (1977) *The Origins of International Economic Disorder: A Study of United States International Monetary Policy from World War II to the Present*, Berkeley and Los Angeles, University of California Press.

Chernow, R. (1990) *The House of Morgan: An American Banking Dynasty and the Rise of Modern Finance*, New York, Simon and Schuster.

Gardner, R.N. (1980) *Sterling–Dollar Diplomacy in Current Perspective*, New York, Columbia University Press.

Grant, J. (1992) *Money of the Mind: Borrowing and Lending in America from the Civil War to Michael Milken*, New York, Farrar, Straus, Giroux.

Greider, W. (1987) *Secrets of the Temple: How the Federal Reserve Runs the Country*, New York, Simon and Schuster.

Helleiner, E.N. (1994) *The Reemergence of Global Finance*, Ithaca, N.Y., Cornell University Press.

Kindleberger, C.P. (1973) *The World in Depression, 1929–1939*, London, Allen Lane the Penguin Press.

Klebaner, B.J. (1990) *American Commercial Banking: A History*, Boston, Twayne Publishers.

Moran, M. (1991) *The Politics of the Financial Services Revolution: The USA, UK and Japan*, London, Macmillan.

Pizzo, S., Fricker, M. and Muolo, P. (1991) *Inside Job: The Looting of America's Savings and Loans*, New York, Harper Perennial, 2nd edition.

Sobel, R. (1977) *Inside Wall Street: Continuity and Change in the Financial District*, New York, Norton.

GLOSSARY

(Words in italics are cross-referenced elsewhere in the glossary.)

Capital/capital adequacy. Basic funds which are committed to a firm or *financial institution*. The activities of a bank can be financed by deposits or shareholders' capital; the gross assets of a bank must be equal to the sum of the two. Minimum capital adequacy requirements, in terms of minimum amounts of capital which have to be set aside to deal with problems, are set by law. In the 1988 Basle Accord, negotiated by the major financial countries through the Bank for International Settlements in Geneva, minimum capital adequacy standards for banks were set for all member countries. Basle imposes a minimum ratio for capital to other assets. Basle also recognizes that certain liabilities of a bank are intermediate between capital and deposits (bonds, etc.), and imposes a second minimum ratio for the sum of primary (equity) capital and these secondary obligations.

Casino capitalism. Keynes's term for the financial economy, which he charged with *short-termism* and a lack of *efficiency* in providing funds to fuel the *'real' economy*.

Clientelism. Clientelism is one side of the coin of what is called 'patron-and-client' politics. These are often seen as being characterized by ongoing interpersonal solidarities rather than 'contractual' relations — solidarities ranging from family- or friendship-based relationships, through traditional rural or tribal politics and feudal 'lord-and-vassal' relations, to institutional-ized favouritism and corruption. However, in contrast to 'patrimonial' or 'patronage' politics — which focus on the objectives of 'patrons' in dispens-ing favours — 'clientelism' implies that the clients themselves, directly or indirectly, are the main gainers from and even the dominant partners in the patron/client relationship. In contemporary political science, clientelism usually refers in particular to a type of bureaucratic and/or pressure group politics wherein the objectives and values of the 'clientele' of an agency or organization come to be 'internalized' by the agency itself, dominating its agenda and decisions. Such agencies are sometimes said to be 'captured' by the groups they are supposed to supervise or regulate (in a process seen by economists as a form of 'monopolistic behaviour').

Commercial banks. *Financial institutions* which obtain funds from depositors and lend these funds on to borrowers. The definition of a commercial bank is that it is primarily engaged in both of these activities in a systematically linked way (see *intermediation*). On both dimensions they are substantially different from *investment banks*.

Commissions. The basic payments made by buyers and/or sellers of securi-ties to *financial institutions* for their services. Traditionally, such institutions have operated through organized markets or stock exchanges which have had rules which have fixed commission rates, but probably the most signifi-cant form of deregulation has been the ending of fixed commissions and the move to *negotiable* commissions (see also *spreads* and *volume*).

Compartmentalization. The functional separation of different kinds of markets, such that particular *financial institutions* are limited to operating in specific markets (for example, dealing in particular kinds of *financial instruments*); compartmentalization is frequently an objective of regulatory policy and law, in order to prevent market failure in one market sector from causing failures in other sectors (that is the separation of banking and *securities* businesses). See also *firewalls*.

Derivatives. *Financial instruments*, also known as synthetic securities, which are essentially bets on the movement of market prices in other, 'real' or underlying instruments, especially futures and options which are linked to specific stock market indexes. An artificial price is derived from two or more actual prices. No underlying instruments actually change hands (unlike futures and options on agricultural or other commodities); payment is made by a combination of the buying and/or selling of more derivatives along with a cash payment for the difference.

Differential returns. Different rates of profit or loss which can be obtained in different regions or countries due to the disparities in interest rates, exchange rates, or marginal rates of return on *financial instruments* prevailing in those countries. A major reason why investors and borrowers shift funds around the world.

Disintermediation. The decline or reduction of *intermediated* loans as a means of providing finance to a firm or individual; such loans are usually replaced with *securities*.

Efficiency. Classical and neo-classical economic theory suggests that 'efficient' markets are those with the largest possible numbers of buyers and sellers. This condition makes it possible for every item offered for sale to actually be sold at the best possible price ('market-clearing'), and is believed to be at the heart of how market capitalism collects and uses the widest possible range of information in a dynamic process of adjusting supply and demand. In financial markets, this means that the most efficient allocation of capital is supposed to occur in the most *liquid* markets. *Monetarists* would agree. In contrast, Keynes and others have argued that financial markets which are 'efficient' in these terms are actually inefficient in providing funds to *the 'real' economy*, because of *short-termism* and the *casino capitalism* mentality.

Embedded liberalism. A characterization of the post-Second World War international political economy suggested by J.G. Ruggie. This refers to a system which has embedded within it certain 'liberal' 'rules of the game', especially the combination of: (1) a Free Trade order; and (2) a certain autonomy for national governments to intervene, in accepted but limited ways, in their own economies — so long as that intervention has the longer-term effect of promoting economic growth and greater international economic interdependence. Critical to the stabilization and expansion of such an order is the presence of a 'liberal *hegemon*', that is the USA.

Financial boutiques. Firms which restrict themselves to servicing limited 'niche' markets. See *financial supermarkets*.

Financial innovation. The devising of new *financial instruments*, especially in an attempt to fill gaps in the market or to find new market 'niches' in order to increase either profits or market share in competitive financial markets. Often linked in practice in recent years with *securitization,* although this is only one of a number of aspects of financial innovation.

Financial institutions. There are many sorts of financial institutions: some public, such as central banks (probably the most important financial institutions) or government agencies which redistribute or invest funds; some semi-public and semi-private; and, the most important after central banks, private sector institutions. The most important in this last category are *commercial banks, investment banks, securities firms, thrifts, non-banks,* and *financial supermarkets*.

Financial instruments. Contracts between lenders (firms and individuals with capital reserves who wish to profit by them) and borrowers (firms and individuals who need capital for whatever purpose). See *securities* and *financial innovation*.

Financial supermarkets. *Financial institutions* which seek to provide a wide variety of services overlapping with other categories of institution. A major focus in the debate over the future of the financial services industry is whether **all** *financial institutions* will have to become 'financial supermarkets' to survive in a competitive and globally integrated world. They are often contrasted with *financial boutiques*, which are limited to particular 'niche' markets.

Firewalls. Legal rules preventing specific branches of a firm from engaging in types of business which are legally reserved to other branches of the same firm, especially prohibiting different profit centres from: (1) mixing their business; (2) cross-subsidizing losses from one branch by using profits from another branch; (3) requiring customers of one branch to use another branch, etc. The British term for firewalls is 'Chinese walls'. Firewalls are therefore internal boundaries within firms, as distinct from the external type of *compartmentalization* characteristic of, for example, the Glass-Steagall Act.

Fiscal policy. Policy concerning the actual use of funds by governments — for example, budgetary policy, taxation, expenditure, borrowing, etc., especially when these are taken in the aggregate. Distinct from *monetary policy,* which concerns the manipulation of the currency, although governments usually attempt to use the two types of policy instrument in tandem, especially in Keynesian 'macroeconomic policy'.

Hedges. By definition, a hedge operation should reduce the overall riskiness of a portfolio. A market actor is 'hedging' (as in 'hedging his or her bets') when he or she seeks to find a *financial instrument* whose probable price movements are thought to be likely to go in the opposite direction from the ones which he or she already owns. In a context of flourishing *financial innovation,* the designing of more 'hedging instruments' is supposed to make it safer to take speculative risks in the opposite direction, thus significantly increasing the *liquidity* of the market without increasing overall risk unduly — an essential feature of *portfolio diversification*. Complex hedging strategies based on advanced econometric models have not always been successful, however, as demonstrated by the failure of Long-Term Capital Management in 1998.

Hegemony. Not merely the economic and/or political predominance of a particular country — a Great Power or 'Superpower' — in the international system (or major subsystem thereof, for example, the 'world capitalist system', the 'West' or the 'North'), but more significantly the capacity of such a pre-eminent state to set and enforce the basic 'rules of the game' of that system or subsystem. In neorealist international relations theory, which borrows from public choice theory, it is said that a hegemonic power will by definition possess both sufficient 'resource power' and sufficient 'political will' to provide on its own the 'public goods' (especially stability) required for the system to function efficiently — even if other countries 'defect' and become 'free riders'. Both Britain in the mid-to-late nineteenth century and the USA in the mid-twentieth century have been said to be 'liberal hegemons', providing not only stability but also certain prerequisites of 'efficient' economic exchange (capitalism), such as financial *liquidity* and stable exchange rates — that is, a stable world monetary system, whether based on the Gold Standard or the dollar-based Gold Exchange Standard — and also a Free Trade system. In other words, the economic power of the 'liberal hegemons' was more important than its political/military power for the stability and efficient working of the system itself. Finally, a 'predatory hegemon' is a country which has the capacity to be a true hegemon (or has been one in the past), but which uses that position to pursue its own interests to the detriment of the system as a whole.

Industrial policy. In contrast to Keynesian macroeconomic policies which involve the manipulation of *fiscal policy* and *monetary policy* in order to manipulate ('fine tune') the national economy as a whole, industrial policy involves the use of selective, targeted microeconomic policies (and sectoral or mesoeconomic policies) in order to promote the competitiveness of particular industries, sectors and firms. Old-style industrial policy often involved straight protectionism or subsidies, but contemporary approaches to industrial policy emphasize such things as: 'picking winners' in new fields like information technology by maximizing the 'competitive advantages' of particular industries in a more open world marketplace; restructuring industries which are declining; promoting 'precompetitive' activities such as research and development; providing new 'public goods' such as advisory services on exporting and global marketing; new forms of infrastructure such as 'high-tech highways' (using fibre-optic cables, etc.); the use of 'managed trade' rather than just multilateral rules to open new markets abroad; and the education and training of 'human capital' for the new 'high value-added' economic activities of the future.

Intermediation. The provision of finance to a firm through an intermediary, in this case a *bank* or other institution which obtains funds from a specific source and loans them on to specific firms (or individuals). In contrast to *securitization*, which is normally closely interrelated with *disintermediation* (the replacement of loans with *securities*).

Investment banks. *Financial institutions* which obtain funds from a variety of sources — from equity holdings, by borrowing from other institutions, or by dealing in *primary* and *secondary securities markets* (but not to any great extent from retail deposits) — and which then lend those funds to borrowers. Investment banks engage heavily in corporate finance and linked activities, including acting as *securities firms*, arrangers of mergers and acquisitions, and even managers of firms in which they have a stake. Unlike *commercial banks* they do not generally take deposits directly from the public, and may therefore have less reliable and *liquid* sources of funds. The boundaries between *investment banks* and *commercial banks* may vary considerably, depending upon the structure of financial markets in a particular country or region and — perhaps more importantly — upon the legal rules and regulations which apply (see *compartmentalization* and *firewalls*).

Issues. When *securities* are first offered for sale by a firm, they are said to be 'issued'; such an offer is referred to as an 'issue'. An issue is first sold in the *primary market*, and large issues are often *underwritten* to ensure that they do not flop and thereby undermine the issuer's market standing further.

Liquidity. The ease with which an asset can be converted into purchasing power — for example, ready funds available for buying and selling *financial instruments*. Markets where there are many potential buyers of such instruments are said to be 'liquid'; market liquidity is often taken, especially by monetarist and classical financial economists, to be one of the conditions (but not a necessary condition) which can lead to greater *efficiency* in a market.

Monetarism. An economic theory which starts from the premise that economic exchange is dependent above all on the provision of a stable and sound currency. In its strict and original form monetarism is the doctrine that money determines nominal income; it follows from this that the principal goal of macro-economic policy should be to control the quantity of money in an economy (see *monetary policy*). In this context, *fiscal policy* is likely to be ineffective. Most contemporary monetarists (such as Milton Friedman), but not all, would argue further that economic policies which depend upon other policy instruments are additionally flawed because they will actively tend to undermine the currency. They often also believe that the most *efficient* means of determining the real value of money — and the allocation of capital to its most *efficient* uses — is in the financial markets; in other words, if governments attempt to manipulate the value of money in a way which goes against the verdict of those markets, such attempts will prove counterproductive. Therefore there is a conundrum at the heart of contemporary monetarism: on the one hand, monetary policy is the only effective way that governments can intervene in the economy; but monetary policy itself can only be pursued within strict limits set by the markets if it is to be efficient. Monetary policy, done properly, is thus essentially non-interventionist. Finally, monetarists often believe not only that there is no conflict between the financial economy and the *'real' economy*, but further that the *'real' economy* will only grow if the financial markets are open and only minimally regulated; they reject charges of *short-termism* made by Keynesians and others against financial markets.

Monetary policy. The manipulation of the currency by government as a means of managing the economy (see also *fiscal policy*). Among the major variables which governments seek to control are: (1) the value of the currency itself (including exchange rate policy and a range of methods to attempt to control inflation); (2) the cost of money (interest rates paid by borrowers to lenders); and (3) the amount of money available overall (the money supply). *Monetarists* believe that the use of fiscal policy as a means to control the economy is flawed, and that the use of monetary policy is the only effective (although inherently limited) way that governments can influence the macroeconomy. One central and recurring problem of monetary policy in an open international economy is that the use of monetary policy instruments to manipulate the money supply is often counteracted by the resulting changes in the exchange rate, while the use of monetary policy to control the exchange rate often has counterproductive consequences for the money supply.

Negotiable. (1) Items, in this case *securities*, which are free of legal restrictions which would prevent their owners from selling them to virtually any buyer. (In contrast, certain limited types of non-negotiable securities, for example, can only be sold back to the firm which issued them or to buyers of whom the issuer formally approves.) (2) Variable by agreement according to market conditions, as distinct from fixed, as in *commissions* (see also *spreads*).

Non-banks. *Financial institutions* which provide a range of services either to individual customers (for example, money-market checking accounts) or to firms (loans, brokerage services) in competition with banks, but which are not legally regulated in the same category as *commercial bank*s because they do not take deposits. Non-banks, unlike *investment banks* (to which they are closest in the range of services which they potentially provide), tend to seek market 'niches'; however, the more ambitious may seek to operate as *financial supermarkets*.

Off-balance-sheet instruments. *Financial instruments* which do not fall into the legal categories of assets or risks which must be reported on the balance sheet, that is normally those which do not require new funds to be raised or capital or reserves to be set aside. They mainly involve commitments such as revolving underwriting facilities (lines of credit, like credit cards, where the balance is not necessarily drawn upon nor necessarily paid off), guarantees (such as standby letters of credit), and 'abstract' or 'market-related' transactions such as futures, options, *swaps,* etc., which do not involve the direct provision of funds or the direct trading of 'underlying' *securities*.

Perpetual notes. Basically bonds which have no maturity date, that is which do not require the issuing firm ever to pay back the principal so long as they keep paying the interest. Unlike traditional bonds, 'perpetuals' count as capital (like shares) because they are so long-term. However, they can be risky for the issuing firm, as they may become a greater drain on operating capital than shares would be, leaving the company with the dilemma of whether to pay them off or keep paying the interest year after year; today they are usually variable-rate (that is their interest rates vary with overall market rates) rather than fixed-rate.

Portfolio diversification. It is widely held by financial analysts that the *efficient* allocation of capital can be achieved with the minimum of risk by owning a relatively diverse set of financial instruments — this includes: (1) owning different sorts of instruments; (2) across different sectors of the economy; and (3) balancing *speculative* risks with *hedges* — rather than going for instruments which are thought to be inherently safe or conservative bets (such as 'blue chips', that is instruments issued by prestigious large firms).

Primary market. That group of market actors (individual or institutional buyers and sellers) who deal in new *issues* of *securities*. Sometimes they are formally organized into specific institutionalized and legally regulated markets or stock exchanges, sometimes their relationship is more informal.

'Real' economy, the. Manufacturing, agriculture and most non–financial services, in which 'real' tangible material goods are produced and change hands; as distinct from the '*financial economy*', which deals in 'abstract' or 'dematerialized' financial instruments. See *monetarism* and *short-termism*.

Secondary market. That group of market actors (individual or institutional buyers and sellers) who deal in *securities* which have already been *issued* and which their owners wish to re-sell.

Securities. Tradeable notes, bonds, shares, etc. Some securities are non-*negotiable*, but the most important are *negotiable* securities, because the ability to trade them in a 'market' means that they usually have a market price. This price is important because it reflects a number of factors about the firm, especially its reputation among existing and potential suppliers of new capital when the firm needs new finance to expand, modernize or restructure; thus more new capital can, at least in theory, be more easily raised the higher the price of its existing securities.

Securities firms. Firms which deal in securities. They may be simply brokers, which trade *financial instruments* on behalf of clients; they may be market–markers, 'trading for their own account' simply to profit the firm (formerly called 'jobbers' in the UK); they may be *investment banks*, which trade securities ultimately in order to provide investment capital to borrowers; or they may do a mixture of these plus a range of other things, depending upon the prevailing legal regulations (see *compartmentalization* and *firewalls*).

Securitization. Three interrelated trends in the development of financial systems in recent years: (1) the transformation by *financial institutions* (especially banks) of existing *intermediated* finance into securities by bundling, say, mortgages or car loans together into *negotiable securities* and selling them on to other institutions at a discount; (2) the trend for firms to raise more and more of their new capital through securities rather than traditional loans, leading to *financial innovation*; and (3) the restructing of banks themselves from concentrating on traditional loan business to expanding and diversifying into new types of *securities* business (including attempting to expand their presence on *securities* markets). The other side of the coin of *disintermediation*.

Short-termism. *Financial institutions* and markets are often charged with 'short-termism', that is putting short-term profits before long-term investment (which often requires periods of low profits or even loss before the investment pays off). The emphasis in contemporary markets on *volume* and turnover, along with the development of *off-balance-sheet instruments* and *financial innovation* in general, is sometimes said to drain funds away from *the 'real' economy* into an abstract financial economy dominated by the psychology of bubbles and panics; Keynes, a strong critic of *monetarism* and the dominance of finance over *the 'real' economy*, referred to financial capitalism as '*casino capitalism*' because of its short-termist, gambling character.

Speculation. See *hedges* and *portfolio diversification*.

Spreads. The difference between bid and offer prices (buy and sell prices) for a *security*, a currency, etc. When commissions on financial transactions are *negotiable*, there is a tendency for powerful market actors to force commission rates down, which means that traders are more and more dependent for their profits on the spread and on the *volume* of trades.

Swaps. The trading of like *financial instruments* but with key differences in the way that they are expected to perform. An important form of swap is the interest rate swap, where only the interest rate payments on particular types of bonds or other instruments are traded; if one lender thinks that fixed-rate repayments will be best for the firm (for whatever reason), he or she may seek to unload just the interest repayments on floating-rate bonds, swapping them with another lender who believes that floating-rate repayments on his or her equivalent set of bonds will be more profitable (or less unprofitable) in the future. Swaps are particularly important for the process of globalization because they may make more sense the greater the variation between market conditions in different places or different industries.

Thrifts. *Financial institutions*, especially Savings & Loan Associations (similar in principle to pre-1985 building societies in the UK) which benefit from special status and legal protection in return for limiting their business to providing specific long-term lending services to individual customers. Originally they were limited mainly to lending for housing mortgages. After they were deregulated in 1982, many thrifts began to engage in risky practices in order to compete for new deposits (especially 'brokered deposits' from other institutions) in order, in turn, to lend for newer and riskier purposes, especially real estate development. Caught in this double bind, and sometimes taken over by corrupt and/or incompetent new management, many thrifts failed in the late 1980s and had to be bailed out by the US government.

Underwriting. When securities are issued, the sale of part or all of the issue is frequently guaranteed by selling them first to one, or a group of, financial institutions, which contract to 'underwrite' the issue. These institutions then make their own arrangements for re-selling the securities either to other institutions or to individuals; if the entire issue is not re-sold because of a lack of buyers, the underwriters will hold on to them, often at a loss, either as a longer-term investment or in order to sell them later when the markets are more favourable.

Volatility. Rapid fluctuation in price, for example, of *securities*. Financial analysts are divided on whether deregulation and globalization lead to greater volatility in the financial markets, and as to whether any such volatility is a good thing (because it allows for more frequent correction of market prices and therefore improves the *efficiency* of the capital markets) or a bad thing (because it destabilizes currencies, national economies and the international economy).

Volume. The amount of securities traded, by total number or value; turnover. When *commissions* are fixed, the price of large-volume trades is proportionally higher than small-volume trades; when *commissions* are *negotiable*, however, the market power of large buyers and/or sellers can force *commission* rates down. As a consequence, *securities* dealers must sometimes operate at a loss in order to retain market share and/or maximize their profits from other volume-related fees and from *spread*s. In globalized financial markets, however, the rapid growth of large trades is by far the most important source of income.

GENDER ASPECTS OF THE AMERICAN ECONOMY

Joyce Jacobsen ★

1   INTRODUCTION

Although Americans overall enjoy a high standard of living and are the most productive workers in the world, women continue to occupy a secondary position in the economy, just as they do in the rest of the world. On average, American women earn less than men, have lower incomes and have a higher poverty rate. While there have been attempts to bring women into parity with men through changes in the law and social attitudes, these changes are not occurring sufficiently quickly to ensure parity within the foreseeable future.

Telephone exchange in Kansas City, Missouri in 1904

1.1   THE CONTEXT

Post-Second World War American society has undergone tumultuous economic and social changes, including the Korean and Vietnam Wars, the Civil Rights Movement, the rise of the Baby Boom generation, the great migrations from city to suburb and from east to west, the transition from an

For men, decreases in labour force participation have occurred predominantly among older and younger men. Many younger men have delayed entry into the labour market, investing instead in further schooling. Even more striking has been the decline in labour force participation among older men due to earlier retirement. The labour force participation rate for men aged 65 and over was 33 per cent in 1960, but only 17 per cent in 1997 (US Department of Labor, 1998, p. 164). The decline has also been notable among men aged 55 to 64.

For women, the most striking rise in labour force participation has occurred among married women with young children. Table 8.1 shows female labour force participation rates in 1960 and 1996 by marital status and age of youngest child. While all these groups of women have had an increase in labour force participation, the rise has been much greater among married women, with the rate more than tripling over this time period for women with pre-school children.

Table 8.1 Labour force participation rates for women by marital status and by age of youngest child for married women.

	1960	1996
Single, never married	58.6	67.1
Divorced, separated, or widowed	41.6	48.1
Married:	31.9	61.1
no children under 18 years	34.7	55.4
with children of 6–17 years	39.0	76.7
with children under 6 years	18.6	62.7

Source: US Department of Commerce, 1997, pp. 403–4. Data are for civilian women aged 16 and over.

Labour force participation rates give no indication of the hours worked, so they are imperfect measures of the relative amounts of time that men and women work. Women are much more likely than men to work part time (defined here as less than 35 hours per week on average): over a quarter of all employed women work part time; while only slightly more than 10 per cent of men work part time (US Department of Labor, 1998, p. 171). Part-time work is considered desirable by some workers and undesirable by others; when part-time workers were asked why they worked part time, some said it was by choice and others said it was because they could not find full-time employment. One factor to consider is that many part-time workers receive virtually no fringe benefits such as health insurance and paid vacation time. Therefore, even if the hourly wage rate is similar for two jobs, one involving part-time and the other full-time work, the full-time worker generally receives better average hourly compensation when fringe benefits are included.

Men also work more overtime than women: 40 per cent work more than forty hours a week, compared to 21 per cent of women (Jacobsen, 1998, p. 128). Interestingly, there is no significant gender difference in the percentage of workers who are multiple jobholders. In 1997, 6.1 per cent of men and 6.2 per cent of women held one full-time job and at least one additional part-time or full-time job, which in some cases involved self-employment or working as an unpaid family worker (US Department of Labor, 1998, p. 207).

All of these patterns are similar to those found in other developed countries, particularly in Western Europe. However, female labour force participation rates are somewhat higher than those found in the United Kingdom, particularly for women with young children, and part-time rates are lower.

2.2   WHY HAS FEMALE LABOUR FORCE PARTICIPATION RISEN?

The reasons behind the rise in female labour force participation can be divided into two general classes: arguments stressing an increased demand for female labour, which drove the wage up for women and attracted them into the labour market; and arguments stressing an increased supply of female labour, which would tend to have a depressing effect on wages.

There are three demand-side factors which are generally cited as of primary importance in explaining the rise in female labour force participation: (1) the general rise in the demand for labour; (2) the rise in labour demand in particular sectors; and (3) the rise in the level of education among women.

1   *The general rise in labour demand:* Demand for labour has been rising over most of this century, subject to business-cycle fluctuations around the long-term upward trend. Since labour demand is derived from the demand for goods and services, as the volume of traded goods, both domestic and international, has risen, so more labour has been needed to produce these goods and services. Technological innovations have led to increased demand for labour as production techniques have become more efficient, leading to increased per capita output.

2   *The sectoral rise in labour demand:* Over time, as the economy evolves, different forms of labour are required, reflecting the changing mix of goods and services. Additionally, technological change can influence the substitutability and complementarity relationships between labour and other input factors, and changes in the prices of other inputs influence the demand for labour as well. Demand for particular types of labour has fallen, in particular unskilled farm labour (where other inputs, in particular capital, have been substituted for labour) and both skilled and unskilled labour for use in manufacturing (where some capital substitution has occurred, and growth in demand for manufactured goods has been lower than growth in demand for services). Meanwhile, demand for other types of labour has been growing faster than average, in particular for clerical and service occupations. One analyst argues that the economy has shifted to requiring 'female occupations' that involve skill, but do not require either long-term commitment to work or specialized geographic location (Oppenheimer, 1976). These occu-

pations may be 'female' in the sense that they are compatible with women remaining in the role of primary provider of non-market output for their families over their lifetimes, and because married women in these occupations can accompany their husbands on moves for higher-paid work, without undue trouble in their own search for new employment.

3   *The rise in the level of education among women:* Education turns unskilled labour into skilled labour, and educated persons receive higher wages. As women have become more educated, the consequent rise in their wage relative to unskilled labour has made it more profitable for them to enter into market work. Additionally, shifts in demand for goods and services and the complementarity between capital and skilled labour — along with the substitutability of capital for unskilled labour, have led to increased demand for skilled workers relative to unskilled.

The increase in women's education is due to multiple causes, including a relaxation of social restrictions on appropriate levels and types of education for women, and greater resources on the part of families who might previously have had to ration higher education among their children. The increase may also be tied to the rise in life expectancy for women (and for men as well), which means that investment in education has a longer payback period and becomes more profitable to undertake.

All three of these demand-side factors lead to wage growth in real (inflation-adjusted) terms. Many analysts have argued that real wage growth can explain most of the increase in female labour force participation between 1950 and 1980 (Smith and Ward, 1985). The rising trend of female wages in the 1980s therefore leads to the prediction that female participation rates will continue to rise. However, there are three groups of supply-side factors influencing the increased rate of female labour force participation that must also be considered: (1) changing technology of non-market production; (2) changes in family composition; and (3) lower male earnings, translating into less unearned income available for married women.

1   *Changing technology of non-market production:* Changes in the technology of non-market production have had two outcomes: a greater availability of market-produced substitutes for non-market goods; and an increased efficiency of non-market production, in particular housework. As more market substitutes are now available for non-market goods at lower prices, this is having the effect of increasing labour supply because the efficiency of market production has increased, that is, the real purchasing power of money wages has increased. However, economic theory does not tell us whether increased efficiency will lead to more or less time spent in paid work. Households may instead decide to produce higher-quality non-market output.

During the twentieth century, technology has been widely adopted that has enabled families to produce non-market output at lower cost. In particular, we have seen the spread of market goods and services that serve as critical inputs into non-market production. In 1920, one-third of American homes had an electricity supply; by 1930, over two-thirds had an electricity supply (although only 10 per cent of farm homes); by 1960, practically all homes had an electricity supply. By 1940, 70 per cent of homes had a supply of running water (17 per cent of farm homes, 93 per cent of urban homes): by 1970, 90 per cent of rural homes had running water (Vanek, 1978, p. 363). However, it appears that many supposedly time-saving innovations have been widely adopted with no apparent significant saving of non-market time. No significant drop in time spent in meal preparation appears for families who own various so-called 'time-saving' household appliances; if anything, the time spent has risen. The implication would appear to be that families who own these appliances must be creating higher-quality meals than those who do not, for they invest both more capital and the same amount of (or more) time in meal preparation. Women still spend much more time on housework than do men, but the total amount of housework done by married-couple families appears to be dropping (Robinson, 1988).

2   *Family compositional changes:* Changing demographics can affect the labour supply decision through causing changes in tastes and changes in availability of unearned income. In particular, trends in marriage, family size, and divorce are critical determinants of labour supply. During the 1950s and 1960s, there were fewer young unmarried women available for work due to an increase in the proportion of married women and a drop in women's age at first marriage. Therefore, employers who had an increased demand for female labour had to turn to married women as a source of labour, recruiting them actively and offering them better wages (Oppenheimer, 1976). This compositional change in marital status can help explain the increase in the participation rates for married women during this time period.

This explanation for rising female participation appears less viable recently as the median age at first marriage began to rise in the 1970s and 1980s, and the proportion of single women increased. However, for single persons, unearned income in the form of spouse's earnings is unavailable, and the ability to increase non-market production through division of labour is absent. These factors can explain why the participation rate for single women is higher than for married women. Therefore, a shift in female labour force composition back towards more single women can help explain the continuing rise in overall female participation rates during the 1970s and 1980s.

Another trend concerns the effects of changing family size on labour force participation. People with dependents (children and/or elderly relatives) in their household may place a higher valuation on non-market time. For instance, complementarity of production processes can mean that their efficiency in producing non-market output increases (for example, being able to simultaneously watch over napping children, and prepare dinner). Therefore, we expect to see lower female labour force participation rates among women with more children. However, as family size is decreasing, this factor should be decreasing in importance as well. The decline in family size in the 1970s and 1980s can help explain rising participation rates during this period. However, family size rose in the 1950s and 1960s, but participation rates rose as well.

The rise in the divorce rate since 1960 provides another explanation for why female labour force participation has increased. A switch from marriage to divorce tends to reduce lifetime unearned income for women, which has the income effect of increasing their market work. Therefore, not only will divorced women have a higher rate of labour force participation than do married women, but married women may increase their labour force participation in response to the increased probability of becoming divorced. One study has found a positive lagged relationship between increases in the divorce rate and increases in the labour force participation rate of married women with young children since the Second World War (Michael, 1985). Another study found that women who subsequently divorce increase their labour supply in the three years prior to separation (Johnson and Skinner, 1986). These researchers calculated that the rise in the divorce rate can account for about 2.6 percentage points out of the 15 percentage point rise in female labour force participation from 1960 to 1980. Finally, several researchers have attempted to determine if the introduction in the 1970s of no-fault divorce has contributed to the increase in the labour supply of married women since 1970. Two studies using 1979 data both conclude that residence in a no-fault divorce state has a statistically significant positive influence on whether a married woman is in the labour force (Peters, 1986; Parkman, 1992).

3   *Falling male wages:* In the period after 1970, the female labour supply growth rate rose while the real wage growth rate fell. Several researchers have cited the high levels of uncertainty associated with future income streams in the 1970s as an important factor in married women's increased labour force participation (Blau and Grossberg, 1991; O'Neill, 1981). In particular, an increasing degree of uncertainty associated with future wages and therefore with future household income contributed by husbands appears to have contributed to the growth in married women's participation in that decade.

2.3   WHY HAS MALE LABOUR FORCE PARTICIPATION FALLEN?

There are two demand-side factors which are generally cited as of primary importance in explaining the decline of male participation: (1) the sectoral decline in labour demand in branches where men are predominantly employed, in particular the manufacturing sector; (2) the increased substitution of female for male labour. The possibility of greater substitution of female for male labour increases with changes in technology which allow for this substitution to occur, and with relatively high wages for male labour, which can be caused by unionization in male-dominated occupations, which increases the incentive for substitution. However, several studies have found that women predominantly have been substituted in production for young men, in particular for young black men, while prime-age white males have not been replaced by women (Hamermesh, 1986, p. 463). So reduced demand for men does not appear to be a primary cause of the overall downward trend in male participation rates, although it can explain lower participation rates for particular subgroups.

Instead, there are two supply-side factors that appear to be of primary importance in explaining the drop in male labour force participation: (1) rising real wages, through their effect in increasing lifetime potential income; (2) the rise in available unearned income for men, through pensions, disability insurance, and female earned income. The specific pattern of decline in male labour force participation, in particular the fact that the largest drop has occurred among men over 50, implies that reduced labour supply for men takes the form of earlier retirement. In particular, the growth in old-age benefits under the Old Age and Survivors Insurance programme and in the form of private pension programmes appears to be a key factor in the greatly reduced labour force participation of older men (Parsons, 1991).

2.4   UNEMPLOYMENT

A comparison of unemployment patterns allows us to determine whether the sexes share the burden of adjustments to labour market fluctuations. Figure 8.2 shows yearly rates of unemployment by sex, where the unemployment rate is defined as the percentage of the labour force currently either actively seeking work (having made some effort to find a job recently) or awaiting recall from a lay-off. Women had a higher unemployment rate than men before the 1980s, after which point the rates have become quite similar; the male rates have actually exceeded the female rates in recent years, starting with the recession of the early 1980s. In general, during recessions, the male rate rises faster than the female rate, reducing the gender gap, while in economic upturns, the male rate drops faster than the female rate, increasing the gap. However, divergence in unemployment rates by sex was greater during both upturns and downturns in the 1960s and 1970s than either

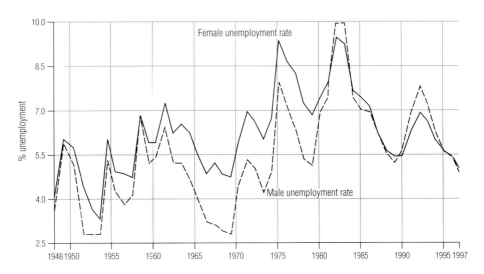

Figure 8.2   *Unemployment rates by sex, 1948–1997*

Source: *Economic Report of the President*, 1998, p. 330. Data are for civilian persons aged 16 and over.

before or after, indicating a relatively greater demand for both skilled and unskilled labour in male-dominated jobs, particularly in manufacturing, during these decades.

Unemployment is a measure of lost output, of idle resources in the form of people who want to work but are unable to find employment. On a human level, unemployment is hard on people who are unemployed. While most unemployed persons are eligible for unemployment benefits, these benefits are less than they would receive in pay. Additionally, the process of looking for work is usually unpleasant and at the very least time-consuming, so unemployed persons are not enjoying their time spent not working. It appears from the aggregate rates shown in Figure 8.2 that until recently women have borne more of the costs of unemployment than men.

However, looking in more detail at the composition of the unemployed population allows us to take the variables, reasons for unemployment and duration of unemployment, into account. After all, unemployment has different distribution effects if many people experience short spells of unemployment than if a few people experience long spells of unemployment; the same annual average unemployment rate can be generated by either of these patterns. It turns out that men are much more likely than women to be unemployed due to having lost their job; women are more likely to have voluntarily left their job or to be a re-entrant to the labour market who has not yet found employment. Also, women are more likely to have short periods of unemployment, with about 39 per cent of women being unemployed for less than five weeks as compared to about 37 per cent of men. While men and women are almost equally likely to have unemployment of medium duration (5 to 14 weeks), men are somewhat more likely to experience longer periods of unemployment, with about 32 per cent of them being unemployed 15 weeks or more, while about 29 per cent of the women have such long spells (US Department of Labor, 1998, pp. 202).

These differences imply that the causes and effects of unemployment for men and women are likely to be quite different, even if their unemployment rates turn out to be quite similar. One study found that for women, a rise in the probability that a labour force re-entrant was unable to quickly find employment accounted for more than three-quarters of the total rise in female unemployment in the 1970s. For men, the rise in the probability that an employed man would become unemployed accounted for over 40 per cent of the rise in male unemployment in the 1970s and almost three-quarters of the rise in male unemployment in the 1980s (Howe, 1990).

The trend towards greater similarity between the female and male unemployment rates appears to be related to the industrial distribution of women and men. Aside from the business cycle effect that men are hurt more by downturns and helped more by upturns, the long-term trend is that the high growth-rate industries have an over-representation of women, so the changing industrial job mix also favours lower unemployment rates for women. Of course this assumes that men continue to be over-represented in the low-growth and declining industries — men may switch their industry distribution in response to these changing conditions. However, the current structural reconfiguration process of the US economy appears to be causing higher unemployment rates for men.

SUMMARY

While male and female labour force participation rates have been converging, they are still quite far apart, with men still much more likely to be engaging in paid work than are women. Many analysts have emphasized growth in real wages for women as the main force behind the increase in female rates up until 1970 (Oppenheimer, 1976). Since 1970, the combination of rising divorce rates; continued growth of female wages, although at a slower pace; and falling male real incomes appears to explain the majority of the rise (O'Neill, 1981). Male labour force participation rates have declined, particularly for older men, mainly due to the rise in pensions and the availability of disability insurance. Male and female unemployment rates have converged in recent years, with various economic forces leading to the prediction that female rates will actually fall below male rates.

3 WHERE DO WOMEN AND MEN WORK?

3.1 OCCUPATIONAL AND INDUSTRIAL DISTRIBUTION

It is useful to know whether women are concentrated in particular areas of the economy, or whether their representation has risen across a wide range of jobs. The relative integration or segregation of women in the economy tells us whether strategies advocating greater integration or strategies advocating increasing the pay in female-dominated jobs are more likely to be effective in raising overall earnings for women.

Two ways of dividing up the economy that are commonly used for calculating female representation rates are occupations and industries. Tables 8.2 and 8.3 present data on female representation by occupation and industry from 1950 through 1990 at ten-year intervals. For these fairly broad categories of occupation and industry, it is clear that women have increased their representation in practically all occupations and industries, since 1950, although their rates continue to vary from sector to sector.

While women have increased their representation in all the white-collar occupational groups, they are concentrated particularly in clerical occupations, a feature which is true in all the sampled years. However, they have made their biggest percentage rise in representation in the managerial occupations. Blue-collar occupations remain predominantly male. In services, the proportion of women increased through 1980, but has more recently

Women clerks at work

Table 8.2   Percentage number of females by occupational group 1950–1990

	1950	1960	1970	1980	1990	% change 1950–1990
All workers	28	33	38	44	45	61
White-collar	40	43	48	55	56	40
Professional	40	38	40	46	51	28
Managerial	14	14	17	28	40	186
Clerical	62	68	74	81	80	29
Sales	34	37	39	49	49	44
Blue-collar	24	26	30	34	32	33
Crafts	3	3	5	6	9	200
Operatives	27	28	32	34	26[a]	26[c]
Labourers	4	4	8	11	–[a]	175[c]
Private household	95	96	96	97	–[b]	2[c]
Other services	45	52	55	61	60[b]	36[c]
Farm workers	9	10	10	17	16	78

[a]   Figure refers to operatives and labourers combined.
[b]   Figure refers to private household and other services combined.
[c]   Percentage change from 1950 to 1980.

Source: 1950–1980: Bianchi and Spain, 1983, p. 20; 1990: US Department of Labor, 1991, p. 42.

stabilized or even started to decline slightly, as men have started shifting out of manufacturing into the service sector.

Table 8.3 shows a rise from 1950 to 1990 in female representation across all industry groups except general merchandise and restaurant/bar retail trade (agricultural workers are excluded from this table). Female representation has levelled in services during the 1980s and has actually declined in the food service since 1960. The 1960s and 1970s appear to have been the time of most growth in female representation, although female representation in construction, transportation, and utilities continues to grow at the same absolute pace, while declining in percentage growth terms. The continuing variation in female representation across industries is notable.

Table 8.3   Percentage number of females by industry 1950–1990

	1950	1960	1970	1980	1990	% change 1950–1990
All private sector workers	32	35	39	43	46	44
Mining	2	5	8	12	13	550
Construction	3	4	6	8	11	267
Manufacturing	26	25	29	32	33	27
Durable goods	16	18	21	26	27	69
Nondurable goods	36	35	39	41	42	17
Transportation and public utilities	16	18	22	25	29	81
Wholesale trade	21	22	24	27	31	48
Retail trade	41	44	47	51	53	29
General merchandise stores	68	68	69	70	69	1
Apparel and accessory stores	65	72	66	75	76	17
Eating and accessory stores	65	72	66	75	76	17
Finance, insurance, and real estate	44	49	52	58	63	43
Services	58	62	63	61	61	5
Health services	74	77	79	76	82	11
All public sector workers	41	44	47	N/A	53	29

Sources: 1950–1970: Waldman and McEaddy, 1974, p. 4; 1980: US Department of Commerce, 1983, Table 4; 1990: US Department of Labor, 1991, p. 43. Data are for civilian workers on non-farm payrolls.

In the public sector, women continue to increase their representation at all levels: women in the federal sector rose from 27 per cent of the workforce in 1950 to 41 per cent in 1990; at the state level from 38 to 50 per cent, and at the local level from 50 to 58 per cent. As the public sector has also increased over time, so government employees now comprise one-sixth of the total

An early textile mill

workforce; government employment (much of which is clerical work or teaching) has been an important source of jobs for women, particularly minority women (who are over represented in government employment relative to their overall representation in the workforce).

While these tables give some idea of how women and men differ in their daily work experience, female and male work patterns vary in many respects within occupations and industries as well, with respect to such factors as working conditions, use of technology, and work schedule. For instance, a 1993 survey found that 52 per cent of women were using computers at work, but only 40 per cent of men (US Dept. of Commerce, 1996, p. 423). Many of these differences are not so easily quantifiable, even though they can be important in terms of determining remuneration, promotion possibilities, and other important economic factors which differ by sex.

3.2   SEGREGATION MEASURES

One summary way of evaluating the level of segregation for the American economy is to calculate an occupational sex segregation index. The most widely used index, the Duncan index, sums up the absolute value of the differences between the proportions of each sex (measured relative to each sex's total employment) for each occupation. The index ranges from 0 (complete integration) to 100 (complete segregation). Integration is defined as the situation where the proportional representation of each sex is the same in all occupations as for the national workforce. For instance, if 30 per cent of the national workforce is female, then the index would equal 0, or complete integration, only if each occupation were 30 per cent female. An interpretation of the index is that it shows what percentage of either group would have to switch occupations in order to achieve complete integration. If the index equals 40, either 40 per cent of men would have to switch into relatively female-dominated occupations, or 40 per cent of women would have to switch into male-dominated occupations.

Using this measure, there has been a clear downward trend in occupational sex segregation since 1960. At the fairly disaggregated level of 503 occupational categories in 1990, in 1960, 64 per cent of either men or women would have had to change jobs to drive the overall index down to 0; by 1990 only 55 per cent would have had to switch. However, this still indicates a high degree of sex segregation, especially when compared with the change in occupational race segregation indexes, which have dropped for men from 45 in 1960 to 24 by 1990, and for women from 50 in 1960 to 22 by 1990.

There are various explanations for the high degree of sex segregation, including: (1) sex differences in tastes for work activities; (2) sex differences in abilities for work activities; (3) the efficiency of separating the sexes so as to reduce work disruptions related to sexual tensions; (4) the need for women to balance market with non-market labour and other familial concerns; (5) imperfect information about relative abilities between the sexes on the part of employers; (6) exploitation of most women by men or by another subset of society, such as privileged men. All of these explanations provide partial guidance to interpreting what is actually occurring in the workplace. The last two explanations imply that labour markets do not currently function so as to eradicate discriminatory behaviour on the part of employers, while the fourth explanation implies that women's continuing double burden leads them to make compromises between career and family that men are still not generally forced to make.

Research on both other industrialized nations and preindustrial cultures provides an interesting balance to the discussion of sex segregation. In general, sex segregation is quite high across all cultures at all times. Countries that have been studied extensively include the larger Western European nations — in particular Sweden — Japan, Israel, and Russia (Jonung, 1988; Lapidus, 1976; Roos, 1985). In looking at data from these societies, which can be considered roughly comparable to the United States in terms of the distribution of occupations and the level of female labour force participation, it is clear that despite substantial variability in age patterns of labour-force participation and in the extent to which women engage in market work, there is substantial similarity across cultures in the high level of sex segregation. Moreover, the same occupations tend to be dominated by men or women in all these countries.

It appears that without drastic social change, no more than a slow downward trend in sex segregation is likely for the foreseeable future. Factors which could maintain the currently-observed high levels of sex segregation include the growth of jobs in occupations which are presently quite segregated, such as clerical jobs; and the possible slowdown of further rises in female participation in occupations, such as the professions, which have experienced an influx of women in the recent past. On the other hand, one should not look only at new positions as providing the possibility of reallocation of women and men across occupations. Mobility between occupations and jobs is quite high, and desegregation could be brought about primarily by job changers rather than by new entrants and exits from the labour market. However it appears that there is little possibility in the near future of achieving levels of occupational sex segregation as low as those currently found for race segregation.

SUMMARY

Male and female occupational and industrial distributions have converged over time, with women increasing their representation in almost all economic sectors, but women and men are still concentrated in different areas, women in clerical work and men in blue-collar work. Sex segregation indexes have moved slowly downward over time and appear unlikely to drop greatly in the near future.

4 EXAMINATION OF THE GENDER EARNINGS GAP

4.1 SIZE OF THE EARNINGS GAP

Probably the most widely-known and carefully-followed gender difference is that in earnings. Measured in either annual earnings terms or hourly earnings terms, this gender earnings gap is wide. Figure 8.3 plots year-by-year female/male median annual income ratios for all workers, all year-round full-time workers, and year-round full-time workers aged 25–34. While income for all persons shows a larger gender gap than income for full-time year-round workers due to fewer average hours worked by women, all three series display the same pattern of a downturn in the years following the Second World War, followed by a long period of only incremental rises, followed by a period of more rapid rise in the 1980s. The level in 1990 of 71 cents on the dollar for year-round full-time workers was duly noted in the popular press — the first time American women broke through the 70-cent barrier. The level as of 1996 stands at 74 cents on the dollar; somewhat higher than the United Kingdom, concurrently at 71 cents on the dollar.

Table 8.4 contains additional information on the trends in the gender earnings gap for different age groups. The most noticeable gains by women have occurred in the younger age groups in the sense of closing the gap, although the largest percentage gain from 1970 to 1996 occurred among women aged 35 to 44 years. Women aged 55 to 64 actually lost ground from 1970 to 1980, before managing a net gain by 1990, and the oldest group of women, those 65 and older, have actually lost ground since 1970.

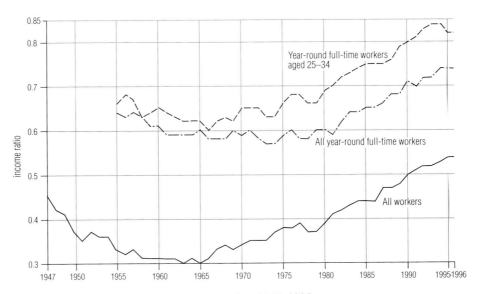

Figure 8.3   *Female/male median income ratios, 1947–1996*

Source: US Department of Commerce, *Current Population Reports* Series P-60 Nos. 132, 137, 142, 146, 156, 159, 172, 174, 180, 189, 193, 197. Data are for persons with income aged 14 and over in earlier years, aged 15 and over in later years

Table 8.4   Female/male median annual income ratios, year-round full-time workers, by age, 1970–1996

	1970	1980	1990	1996	% change 1970–1996
15 years and over	0.59	0.60	0.71	0.75	20
15 to 24 years	–	0.82[a]	0.90	0.90	–
25 to 34 years	0.65	0.69	0.80	0.82	23
35 to 44 years	0.54	0.56	0.69	0.72	28
45 to 54 years	0.56	0.54	0.61	0.65	9
55 to 64 years	0.60	0.57	0.63	0.63	5
65 years and over	0.72	0.72	0.65	0.63	–10

[a] average of figures for 15–19 and 20–24 year olds.

Source: US Department of Commerce, *Current Population Reports* Series P-60 Nos. 80, 132, 174, 197.

These mixed results or outright losses among older employed women are due in large part to the decreased labour force participation rates among older men. Retirement rates have risen among all older men, but have risen more strikingly among lower-earning older men. Therefore, those men continuing to work into their late sixties tend to be higher-earning men.

Earnings are only part of the picture of how employment compensation differs by sex; unfortunately the other components of compensation are more difficult to quantify. It is clear from surveys that women generally have less fringe benefits such as health insurance, life insurance, and paid vacation time available to them in terms of total monetary value, partly because more women work part-time, and partly because the value of some fringe benefits is directly tied to earnings. The biggest monetary difference by sex is likely to be in pension benefits. On the one hand, women live longer — the life expectancy for a person born in 1994 is 72.4 years for men, but 79.0 years for women (US Department of Commerce, 1997b, p. 88). Many men do not even live until retirement age (although if they do, the life expectancy gap narrows: the average life expectancy in 1994 of a 65 year-old woman was 19.0 years; that of a 65 year-old man was 15.5 years) (US Department of Commerce, 1997b, p. 88). Women therefore can expect to collect pensions for a longer period of time. On the other hand, women's higher turnover rates and lower earnings reduce their benefits relative to men in defined benefit plans (plans where a certain percentage of earnings is guaranteed for each year of service). The net effect appears to be that women receive lower total benefits, so accounting for pensions would increase the gender earnings gap (and the effect is worse the higher the inflation rate, which leads to greater discounting of income received further in the future) (Pesando, Gunderson, and McLaren, 1991).

4.2 ADJUSTING THE GAP FOR DIFFERENCES IN PRODUCTIVITY AND TASTES

Possible causes of the gender earnings gap fall into three categories: (1) human capital differences between women and men, that is differences in education, experience, and training; (2) compensating differentials, that is differences in preferences for aspects of work other than pay; (3) discrimination, that is differences in pay caused by differences in persons' treatment by employers. Models of discrimination differ in whether they attribute prejudice to employers, employees, or customers; and in whether or not prejudice is assumed at all. In models where discrimination exists without prejudice, some form of labour market failure, such as the ability of individual employers or groups of employers to exploit workers (where it must also be assumed that female workers are easier to exploit than male workers), or imperfect information about worker ability, must be assumed.

Earnings ratios can be adjusted to account for differences between demographic groups in terms of education, age, geographical distribution, and other factors that are generally considered to reflect group differences in productivity and tastes; that is, categories (1) and (2) above. Accounting for differences in these variables narrows the gender earnings gap, but does not close it. For example, white women make 71 per cent as much as white men, but if men and women had similar characteristics, then white women would make 75 per cent as much as white men. The gap is 29 cents on the dollar (100 – 71), of which 4 cents, or 14 per cent of the gap, is explainable by differences in characteristics between white women and men. That leaves 25 cents, or 86 per cent of the gap, unexplained after the adjustment process. This portion of the gap is commonly attributed to discrimination, although the source of discrimination is not readily determinable.

4.3   RELATIONSHIP OF EARNINGS GAP TO SEGREGATION

Many commentators have noticed that female-dominated occupations appear to pay less to both men and women who work in them. Table 8.5 presents data on percentage female, female-male earnings ratios, and median weekly earnings for a variety of occupations. There appears to be a negative correlation between percentage female and median weekly earnings for this set of occupations. Also, the female-male earnings ratio is positively correlated with percentage female; that is, men still make more than women in every occupation, but the gap is narrower in the more female-dominated ones. The male-dominated occupations in the table include some of the most prestigious occupations: doctors; lawyers and judges; and college teachers. Female-dominated occupations include traditional service professions, such as nurses and elementary teachers.

Table 8.5   Percentage female, gender earnings ratio, and median weekly earnings for selected occupations, 1997

Occupation	Percentage female	Gender earnings ratio	Median weekly earnings
Engineers	9	0.84	977
Police and detectives	16	0.87	614
Computer programmers	30	0.85	840
Doctors	30	0.78	1120
Lawyers and judges	32	0.75	1163
Marketing managers	33	0.69	938
College teachers	36	0.89	888
Sales jobs	45	0.58	482
Editors and reporters	49	0.79	606
Waiters and waitresses	72	0.73	268
Elementary teachers	83	0.91	655
Nursing aides	89	0.87	296
Registered nurses	92	0.91	705
Secretarial jobs	98	1.00	411

Source: US Department of Labor, 1998, Table 39.

There is a strong correlation between lower pay and higher percentage female across most occupations. Also, women are more likely to be found on the lower rungs in any occupation. The question is why these patterns occur. Here the evidence is mixed. While some occupations show evidence of routinization and deskilling concurrent with women entering them, others, such as many of the professions, appear to be becoming more demanding. Also, while part of the gender pay gap may be attributable to differences in training and experience, women who have decided to enter the most demanding occupations in terms of training and yearly hours (that is, doctors and lawyers) face some of the largest gaps in earnings relative to men.

The crucial question is how much of this pattern is attributable to discriminatory behaviour on the part of employers and how much of this pattern is attributable to freely-made choices on the part of women. If women are systematically excluded from more desirable jobs and crowded into less desirable ones, this leads to an increased supply of female labour to the less desirable jobs and depresses wages in the less desirable jobs below what they would be if crowding were not occurring (Bergmann, 1974). Simultaneously, the wage is increased in the more desirable jobs due to the decreased amount of female labour. This model assumes that wage rates are ultimately determined by market forces, but that female labour supply is artificially reduced in the more desirable jobs. If this is the case, then policies are needed that attack the exclusion practices which limit entry into the more desirable jobs.

4.5 CONCLUSIONS ON CAUSES OF THE GENDER EARNINGS GAP

The US gender earnings gap has been reduced since its widest point in the mid-1960s, but the recent rise in female earnings relative to male earnings has still only brought female earnings to approximately 74 cents for every dollar men make for year-round full-time work.

SUMMARY

Why did women's relative earnings rise so much in the 1980s? Five explanations have been suggested by researchers: (1) a rise in the quality of female labour relative to male labour; (2) a decline in labour market discrimination; (3) the shift in the distribution of employment away from unionized, energy-intensive, foreign-trade-intensive industries has hurt men more than women; (4) union wage premiums and other male worker premiums in some sectors have declined; (5) the occupational distributions of men and women are converging. One researcher, looking at data from 1979 to 1984, decided that the most important factor during this period is (5) (Sorensen, 1991, pp. 16–18). She also found support for smaller impacts of (1) and (2), and an even smaller impact of (3). Also, while convergence in the industrial distribution of males and females has occurred, it does not appear to have had as big an effect as the occupational convergence. Interestingly, from 1979 to 1984, the returns to education rose for men, but hardly increased at all for women (Sorensen, 1991, p. 44). This implies that factor (1) may become even less important in the future, if education increases quality, but women receive a lower payback on quality.

5 HOW WELL-OFF ARE WOMEN RELATIVE TO MEN?

5.1 INCOME DIFFERENCES

While earnings are important measures of economic well-being, we might be less concerned about women's financial well-being if they have access to additional financial resources beyond their own earnings. Since men and women form family and household units together, access to monetary resources may best be measured at a household level. For instance, if high-earning men tend to be married to low-earning or non-working women, with the converse being true for high-earning women, then we would expect to see less variation in family income between the sexes than in individual earnings.

Table 8.6 demonstrates that this is in fact the case. The distribution of men and women by family income shows a relatively similar distribution, although women are more likely to be in low-income households, and men are more likely to be in high-income households. Still, the gender ratio of family median income is 0.87 and of mean income is 0.90, much higher values than the gender earnings ratios.

Table 8.6   Percentage distribution of household income, median, and mean household income, by sex, 1994

Income range	Men	Women
Below $5000	2.0	3.4
$5,000–9,999	4.5	9.2
$10,000–19,999	13.0	15.6
$20,000–29,999	14.5	14.3
$30,000–39,999	14.0	13.0
$40,000–49,999	12.1	10.8
$50,000–74,999	21.2	18.4
$75,000–99,999	9.6	8.4
$100,000–124,999	5.2	4.4
$125,000–149,999	2.2	1.8
Above $150,000	1.8	1.5
Median income	$40,957	$35,624
Mean income	$49,283	$44,261

Source: calculated by the author using data from the *Current Population Survey,* March 1995. The sample consists of persons aged 25 and over.

Men and women are just as likely to move up and down the household income scale, again illustrating that their fortunes are linked together through family structure. A survey conducted in 1987 and 1988 found that the incomes of 19.3 per cent of men and 19.1 per cent of women had declined one or more quintiles over the period, the incomes of 67.2 per cent of men and 68 per cent of women had stayed in the same income quintile, and the incomes of 13.5 per cent of men and 12.9 per cent of women had risen by one or more quintiles (US Department of Commerce, 1992, p. 5). Thus we can see that men are only slightly more likely to experience large shifts in household income than are women.

5.2   POVERTY RATES

In order to emphasize gender differences among people receiving the lowest incomes, it is useful to contrast poverty rates by sex. In 1996, women had a poverty rate of 15.4 per cent, while men had a rate of 12.0 per cent. Figure 8.4 plots the yearly poverty rates by sex, which shows their fluctuations over the business cycle as well as the systematic relationship between the rates over time. While the male and female rates move together, the gender gap remains fairly constant over time and shows no sign of closing.

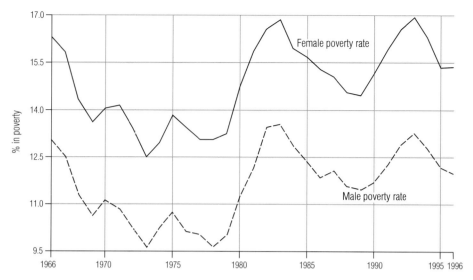

Figure 8.4 *Poverty rates by sex, 1966–1996*

Sources: 1959: Burkhauser and Duncan, 1991, p. 219; 1966–1995: US Bureau of the Census, *Current Population Reports* Series P-60 Nos. 95, 106, 133, 158, 181, 185, 188, 189, 194, 198.

For women of all ages, becoming separated, divorced, or widowed is associated with a heightened probability of entering poverty. Elderly women in particular are put at greater risk of suffering a drop in living standards through a change in marital status (Burkhauser and Duncan, 1991). For younger women, the rise in female-headed households, either through dissolution of marriage or through unmarried motherhood, is a critical factor in understanding the higher poverty rates for women. The poverty rate for members of female-headed families is 37 per cent, substantially higher than the rate of 7 per cent for other types of families (US Department of Commerce, 1997a, Table C-1).

5.3   INCORPORATION OF NON-MARKET INCOME

A more complete measure of resources available to women and men would take account of the value of non-market production as well. Since women spend more hours in non-market production than men, this type of measure will tend to make them look relatively better off than a measure that focuses solely on market income. Table 8.7 shows measures of total income, market and non-market, for women and men at two points in time (Fuchs, 1986). Non-market time was valued at hourly earnings rates, either the person's own earnings, or, if he or she did not do any market work, at the rate of comparable persons in terms of age and education.

Table 8.7   Total market and non-market income (for housework and child care) in 1983 dollars, ages 25–64, by sex, 1959 and 1983

| | 1959 | | 1983 | |
	Women	Men	Women	Men
Money	4139	18776	9026	22321
Imputed	8590	5137	9810	6600
Total	12729	23913	18862	28920
Women/men total income	0.53		0.65	

Source: Fuchs, 1986, p. 460.

Under this total income measure of economic well-being, women have improved their position relative to men over time, but are still at a disadvantage due to their lower wage rate. This measure yields a higher measure of economic well-being for women than market income alone: the median income ratio rose from 0.31 to 0.44 over this same period.

SUMMARY

While income dispersion is lower than earnings dispersion due to income pooling within families, women are still disproportionately represented among those persons in lower-income households, including those households falling below the poverty level. Even after accounting for the value of non-market production, rewards to women from both market and non-market work leave them with less total income than men.

6   WHAT CHANGES LIE AHEAD?

The continuing pace of technological change and sectoral shifts in employment, which affect both the USA and Western Europe, particularly as trade liberalization continues, appear to presage increasing rates of female labour force participation and a rising gender earnings ratio in all countries. However, the USA continues along a different path in many ways. Educationally, the USA continues to have higher college and graduate degree attendance rates, and a larger proportion of graduate students in the USA are female than in any other country. Demographically, the USA continues to have a higher divorce rate, as well as a larger number of female-headed households. These factors tend to imply that US women will continue to have high labour force participation rates, and will continue to be more likely to work full-time than Western European women.

The antidiscrimination legislation of the 1960s, while passed well ahead of similar initiatives in Australia and Western Europe (where such initiatives occurred in the mid-1970s), appear to have had much less effect on relative earnings in the USA than in other developed countries, perhaps because wage-setting in the USA is a less centralized procedure, given the lower level of unionism and government involvement in the process. While American women have nevertheless made progress towards parity with men, much ground remains to be covered. US policy initiatives in support of parity vary with the political climate. Under Presidents Reagan and Bush, few new initiatives were undertaken, even though the 1980s were the decade in which the gender earnings gap began to narrow. However, in 1992, with the arrival of a Democrat as President along with the continuation of a Democrat-controlled Congress, the political arena began to change. President Clinton's first legislative action was to sign into law a long-stalled national family leave bill, which provides twelve weeks of unpaid leave for employees of large firms (over 50 employees) to take care of personal matters such as caring for a sick relative or new baby without fear of losing employment. This action, however, merely begins to bring the USA into the same league as Western Europe, where lengthy paid family leaves are commonly found.

America lags behind European Community social service delivery in many other ways, such as in provision of universal health care and in development of coherent national educational policy. Improvement of the health care and child care systems are top priorities for Americans as the twenty-first century begins. These actions, while beneficial to a wide range of citizens, hold the promise of further equalizing economic outcomes for the sexes by reducing the burden of non-market responsibility that continues to fall disproportionately on women.

REFERENCES

Bergmann, B.R. (1974) 'Occupational segregation, wages and profits when employers discriminate by race or sex', *Eastern Economic Journal*, vol. 1, no. 2, pp.103–10.

Bianchi, S. M. and Spain, D. (1983) *American Women: Three Decades of Change*, Washington, D.C., US Government Printing Office.

Blau, F.D. and Grossberg, A.J. (1991) 'Real wage and employment uncertainty and the labor force participation decisions of married women', *Economic Inquiry*, vol. 29, no. 4, pp.678–95.

Burkhauser, R.V. and Duncan, G.J. (1991) 'United States public policy and the elderly: the disproportionate risk to the well-being of women', *Journal of Population Economics*, vol. 4, no. 3, pp.217–31.

Economic Report of the President (1998), Washington, D.C., US Government Printing Office.

Fuchs, V.R. (1986) 'Sex differences in economic well-being', *Science*, no. 232, pp.459–64.

Hamermesh, D.S. (1986) 'The demand for labor in the long run' in Ashenfelter, O. and Layard, R. (eds.) *Handbook of Labor Economics*, Vol. 1, Amsterdam, North-Holland, pp.429–71.

Howe, W.J. (1990) 'Labor market dynamics and trends in male and female unemployment', *Monthly Labor Review*, vol. 113, no. 11, pp.3–12.

Johnson, W.R. and Skinner, J. (1986) 'Labor supply and marital separation', *American Economic Review*, vol. 76, no. 3, pp.455–69.

Jonung, C. (1988) 'Patterns of occupational segregation by sex in the labor market' in Schmid, G. and Weitzel, R. (eds.) *Sex Discrimination and Equal Opportunity*, New York, St. Martin's Press, pp.44–68.

Lapidus, G.W. (1976) 'Occupational segregation and public policy: a comparative analysis of American and Soviet patterns' in Blaxall, M. and Reagan, B. (eds.) *Women and the Workplace*, Chicago, Illinois, University of Chicago Press, pp.119–36.

Michael, R.T. (1985) 'Consequences of the rise in female labor force participation rates: questions and probes', *Journal of Labor Economics*, vol. 3, no. 1, Supplement, pp.S117–46.

O'Neill, J. (1981) 'A time-series analysis of women's labor force participation', *American Economic Review*, vol. 71, no. 2, pp.76–80.

Oppenheimer, V.K. (1976) *The Female Labor Force in the United States: Demographic and Economic Factors Governing its Growth and Changing Composition*, Westport, Connecticut, Greenwood Press.

Parkman, A.M. (1992) 'Unilateral divorce and the labor-force participation rate of married women revisited', *American Economic Review*, vol. 82, no. 3, pp.671–78.

Parsons, D.O. (1991) 'Male retirement behavior in the United States', *Journal of Economic History*, vol. 51, no. 3, pp.657–74.

Pesando, J.E., Gunderson, M., and McLaren, J. (1991) 'Pension benefits and male-female wage differentials', *Canadian Journal of Economics*, vol. 24, no. 3, pp.536–50.

Peters, H.E. (1986) 'Marriage and divorce: informational constraints and private contracting', *American Economic Review*, vol. 76, no. 3, pp.437–54.

Robinson, J.P. (1988) 'Who's doing the housework?', *American Demographics*, vol. 10, no. 12, pp.24–8, 33.

Roos, P.A. (1985) *Gender and Work: A Comparative Analysis of Industrial Societies*, Albany, New York, State University of New York.

Saltzman, A. (1991) 'Trouble at the top', *US News & World Report*, 17 June, pp. 40–8.

Smith, J.P. and Ward, M. (1985) 'Time-series growth in the female labor force', *Journal of Labor Economics*, vol. 3, no. 1, Supplement, pp.S59–90.

Sorensen, E. (1991) *Explaining the Reasons Behind the Narrowing Gender Gap in Earnings*, Washington, D.C., Urban Institute.

US Department of Commerce, Bureau of the Census (1983) *Census of the Population, Subject Report 7C*, Washington, D.C., US Government Printing Office.

US Department of Commerce, Bureau of the Census (1992) 'Transitions in income and poverty status: 1987–88', *Current Population Reports*, Series P-70, no. 24.

US Department of Commerce, Bureau of the Census (1996) *Statistical Abstract of the United States*, Washington, D.C., US Government Printing Office.

US Department of Commerce, Bureau of the Census (1997a) 'Poverty status of persons and families', *Current Population Reports*, Series P–60, no. 194.

US Department of Commerce, Bureau of the Census (1997b) *Statistical Abstract of the United States*, Washington, D.C., US Government Printing Office.

US Department of Labor, Bureau of Labor Statistics (1991) *Working Women: A Chartbook*, Washington, D.C., US Government Printing Office.

US Department of Labor, Bureau of Labor Statistics (1998) *Employment and Earnings*, vol. 45, no. 1.

Vanek, J. (1978) 'Household technology and social status: rising living standards and status and residence differences in housework', *Technology and Culture*, vol. 19, no. 3, pp.351–75.

Waldman, E. and McEaddy, B.J. (1974) 'Where women work — an analysis by industry and occupation', *Monthly Labor Review*, vol. 97, no. 5, pp.3–13.

FURTHER READING

Bergmann, B. R. (1986) *The Economic Emergence of Women*, New York, Basic Books. A useful discussion of the trends and issues in the economics of gender, including an extended discussion of the ways discrimination can operate in the economy.

Bianchi, S. M. and Spain, D. (1996) *Balancing Act: Motherhood, Marriage, and Employment Among American Women*, New York, Russell Sage Foundation. Presents a demographic picture of the US economy up through approximately 1992 using a mixture of Census data and more frequently collected series; has sections addressing the major issues introduced in this chapter.

Blau, F. D. and Ferber, M.A. (1998) *The Economics of Women, Men, and Work, Third Edition*, Englewood Cliffs, New Jersey, Prentice-Hall. Textbook on the economics of gender, focusing on the post-Second World War American experience.

Fuchs, V. R. (1988) *Women's Quest for Economic Equality*, Cambridge, Massachusetts, Harvard University Press. Valuable discussion of US women, work, and family issues.

Goldin, C. (1990) *Understanding the Gender Gap: An Economic History of American Women*, Oxford, Oxford University Press. Thorough discussion of the pre-Second World War American experience, using modern economic techniques on historical data; also discusses post-Second World War experience.

Jacobsen, J. P. (1998) *The Economics of Gender, Second Edition*, Cambridge, Massachusetts, Blackwell. Textbook on the economics of gender, focusing on the post-Second World War American experience, but also containing sections on contemporary cross-cultural experience and American experience prior to the Second World War.

A NATION OF REGIONS: THE ECONOMIC GEOGRAPHY OF AMERICA

Richard Florida ★

1   INTRODUCTION

Picture America. What do you see? The hustle and bustle of New York with Wall Street, the theatre district and bohemian neighbourhoods. New England, the birthplace of the nation with its great universities of Harvard, Massachusetts Institute of Technology (MIT) and Yale. The sprawling, grey factory complexes of the Industrial Midwest. The high-technology industry and natural beauty of California. The old South with its tobacco and cotton plantations, or the new Sunbelt of modern skyscrapers and sprawling cities like Atlanta. The rugged terrain and snow-capped mountains of the Pacific Northwest.

America is a nation of regions. Thinking of America often causes one to think in terms of regions. Everything in America is regional — politics, culture and especially economics.

Writers and scholars who have attempted to describe the American experience have often looked to regions as a source of America's uniqueness. Writing one hundred years ago, the eminent American historian Frederick Jackson Turner proposed that the source of America's distinct social, cultural and economic nature — its difference from Europe — lay in the urge and ability of Americans to constantly open up new territory at 'the frontier'. For Turner, the American experience — 'like a huge page in the history of society' — could be read as a sequence of the opening up of new regions on the frontier. 'The role of frontier regions in the American experience,' he wrote:

> …begins with the Indian and the hunter; it goes on to tell of the disintegration of savagery by the entrance of the trader, the pathfinder of civilization; we read the annals of the pastoral stage in ranch life; the exploitation of the soil by the raising of unrotated crops of corn and wheat in sparsely settled farming communities; the intensive culture of the denser farm settlement; and finally the manufacturing organization with the city and factory systems.

(Turner, 1920)

Writing in the 1930s, Robert E. Park, whose influential studies of the development of the city pioneered much of modern sociology and urban studies, described America's social and economic evolution in terms of the development of increasingly complex urban and regional systems, defining regions as 'organic units':

> My conception of a region is one in which vegetation, animal and human life have acquired a character due to permanent association; to the fact that struggle for existence has brought about some sort of equilibrium among the competing and co-operating organisms.

> (Park quoted in Odum and Moore, 1938)

As we moved into the twenty-first century, those who wished to understand the American experience once again discovered the importance of regions. The 1990s saw an outpouring of popular and academic writing on the role of regions in contemporary social and economic life. Regions are once again seen as crucial organizing units of American society. Indeed, as the rise of the multinational corporation and the globalization of economic activity threaten to 'annihilate geography' and even endanger the viability of the nation-state, regions are seen as ever more important units of economic, political and social activities. America's foremost economic geographer, Richard Walker of the University of California at Berkeley, defines the role of regions in contemporary society as crucial sources of co-ordination and integration of complex forms of human and economic activities, writing that:

> Regions are systems of cities and towns in rural matrix, networks down whose channels flow deep and swift currents of goods, labor, information and money. Major transportation and communication arteries cement these linkages, but so do filaments of personal knowledge, institutional ties and cultural practices.

> (Sayer and Walker, 1992, p.143)

In an influential but controversial essay, Kenichi Ohmae, the Chairman of McKinsey and Company in Japan, pointed out that: 'The United States has never been a single nation'. It is a collection of regions or what he calls 'region states', such as: 'northern and southern California, the "power corridor" along the East Coast between Boston and Washington, the Northeast, the Midwest, the Sunbelt and so on'. Ohmae went on to suggest this new form of economic and social organization — the 'region state' — was coming to replace the nation-state as the centrepiece of economic and social life.

> The nation-state has become an unnatural, even dysfunctional unit for organizing human activity and managing economic endeavour in a borderless world. It represents no genuine, shared community of economic interests; it defines no meaningful flows of economic activity. On the global economic map the lines that now matter are those defining what may be called 'region states'. Region states are natural economic zones. They may or may not fall within the geographic limits of a particular nation — whether they do is an acci-

dent of history. Sometimes these distinct economic units are formed
by parts of states. At other times, they may be formed by economic
patterns that overlap existing national boundaries, such as those
between San Diego and Tijuana. In today's borderless world, these
are natural economic zones and what matters is that each possesses,
in one or another combination, the key ingredients for successful
participation in the global economy.

(Ohmae, 1993, pp.78–9)

The following pages provide a historical overview of the role of regions in
American society, focusing in particular on the regional bases of social and
economic organization in twentieth century America.

SUMMARY

America is and always has been as much a nation of regions as a single
national entity. Regions can be defined in a number of different ways:
as 'organic units'; as systems of networks; or as 'regional states' formed
by natural economic zones. The regional basis of economic activity in
America is increasing in importance.

2   REGIONALISM AND BIRTH OF THE NATION

America's regional identities were strongly shaped in the nation's first century. Born as an agricultural nation, the Industrial Revolution of the nineteenth century brought rapid change to the American economy, its politics
and its culture. During the early nineteenth century, New England emerged
as a centre for textile manufacturing. Many of the towns and communities
surrounding Boston became centres of modern factory production. Lowell,
Massachusetts emerged as an advanced centre for factory production In
these heady times, Lowell was seen as a technological utopia — a source of
unparalleled economic growth. By the mid-nineteenth century, industrialism
spread to New York, New Jersey and Pennsylvania as textile and other
types of factory production took root throughout the North.

Of course, industrialism was not without its problems. Rapid industrialization created a huge demand for land and labour, forcing many households
off the farm and into factories. Working conditions in many of these early
factories were horrifying and use of child labour common. The once heralded utopia of Lowell's textile mills came to be seen in a reverse light —
with reports of conditions in what came to be called Lowell's 'satanic mills'.

The rapid industrialization of the North led to serious political tensions, particularly with regard to the South which remained a centre of traditional
'plantation' agriculture. As is well known, these tensions are what ultimately
shaped the Civil War. The Civil War was at the heart of American 'excep-

tionalism' — its difference from Europe. Turner's ideas about the importance of the frontier and frontier regions continue to be a powerful force in American thinking and American life to this day.

SUMMARY

The early regional division within America was based upon the nineteenth century industrialization of the North as compared to the traditional 'plantation' agriculture of the South. This division was important in determining the reasons for the Civil War.

3   THE INDUSTRIAL REVOLUTION AND THE MIDWEST MANUFACTURING HEARTLAND

The Civil War unleashed a potent wave of industrial growth and economic expansion. Arms makers perfected new techniques of standardization and mass production. The nascent iron and steel industry was given an enormous boost. Former frontier outposts, like Pittsburgh, Pennsylvania were transformed into sprawling industrial centres. The Midwest stood poised for industrial expansion.

The industrial growth of the Midwest — stretching from Pittsburgh to Buffalo New York, west through Ohio, Indiana, St. Louis, Missouri, Chicago, Illinois and into parts of Wisconsin and Minnesota — was a new kind of industrialism. Earlier epochs of industrialization in the United States, in England, and on the European continent revolved around groups of craft workers and small-scale factory production. The new epoch of industrialization was premised upon a new system of large-scale factory production — which came to be called the 'American system of manufacture'. This new system combined two powerful economic rules — specialization of tasks and economies of scale and size. Frederick Taylor's ideas of 'scientific management' and 'time-and-motion study' brought increased specialization and greater efficiency to American manufacturing. Specialization broke down work tasks into their simplest and most basic elements. Now virtually any worker could perform these tasks. Specialization broke the power of skilled craft workers and their unions, and enabled American factories to 'import' large numbers of unskilled immigrant workers from Europe. Economies of size and scale were evident in the rise of giant factory complexes in Pittsburgh, Chicago and elsewhere employing tens of thousands of workers to produce steel and other industrial products.

At the turn of the century, a final element was added to this emergent industrial system — the moving assembly line. Pioneered by Henry Ford, for use in the automobile industry, the moving assembly line afforded management greater control over the pace of work. The automobile factories of

Detroit became the international exemplars of this new age of mass production or 'Fordist' manufacturing. Now industrial capitalists and their managements could effectively dictate the flow and pace of work. The combination of specialization, economies of scale and the moving assembly line produced tremendous efficiencies and the American industrial heartland eclipsed all other nations to emerge as the pre-eminent industrial region of the world. This new system of 'mass production', born and centred in the American Midwest, propelled the nation to economic greatness.

SUMMARY

The Civil War was a major stimulant to the industrial expansion of the 'frontier' Midwest region. It was here that the 'American system of manufacturing' was born, involving large-scale factory production. Later Henry Ford added the moving assembly line to create the industrial heartland of twentieth century America based upon the Midwest's mass-production system.

4 REGIONS WITHIN REGIONS: MASS PRODUCTION AND THE RISE OF SUBURBIA

The rise of this new system of mass production — or 'Fordism' as it came to be called — had powerful implications on the organization of American society. America became a 'Fordist society' consuming the mass products — the cars, appliances, and electrical devices that came off the assembly lines.

Originally, American cities were 'walking cities' — tight, compact, with land uses, factory production, merchants, and residential living, all jumbled together. As industrialism progressed, wealth expanded, and transportation technology became more advanced, cities expanded. The rise of the electric street-car system allowed for the first wave of suburban expansion, or what the historian Sam Bass Warner (1962) has referred to as the rise of the 'street-car suburbs'. As the street-car systems stretched out to formerly rural areas surrounding New York City, Boston, Philadelphia, and other cities new areas for residential development were forged. This created new avenues for profit and wealth for financiers and developers and new areas for consumption for the emerging American middle class.

After the hiatus during the Great Depression, mass suburbanization occurred with a vengeance in the 1950s and 1960s. With a massive amount of virgin land available at the periphery of the city, suburbia represented yet another 'new frontier' to be settled. The mass acceptance of the automobile, new housing policies and programmes which made cheap mortgages widely available, and massive public investment in roads, highways and other 'infrastructure' propelled the suburban boom of the 1950s and 1960s as millions of families left the cities for the suburbs. Factories followed people to the suburbs where land was both cheap and plentiful. Suburbanization by its very nature produced an even more massive consumer demand for cars, household appliances and other products of the assembly line. The end result was a powerful cycle of growth and expansion. This was perhaps best captured in the quintessential American slogan of the time — 'keeping up with the Joneses'.

Kenneth Jackson, the urban historian, captures the many dimensions of the suburban experience in his book, *Crabgrass Frontier*:

> In the United States, it is almost a truism to observe that the dominant residual pattern is suburban. The 1980 census revealed that more than 40 per cent of the national population, or more than 100 million people, lived in suburbs, a higher proportion than resided in either rural areas or in central cities. Suburbia has become the quintessential physical achievement of the United States; it is more representative of its culture than big cars, tall buildings, or professional football. Suburbia symbolizes the fullest, most unadulterated embodiment of contemporary culture; it is a manifestation of such fundamental characteristics as conspicuous consumption, a reliance upon the private automobile, upward mobility, the separation of family into nuclear units, the widening division between work and leisure, and a tendency toward racial and economic exclusiveness.
>
> (Jackson, 1985, p.4)

The effects of suburbanization on living standards and on American culture can perhaps best be seen in hit television programmes of the 1950s. The early fifties hit, 'The Honeymooners' starring Jackie Gleason, featured the hurly-burly working class life-style of two inner city families, both of whose breadwinners work in municipal jobs (as a bus-driver and sewer worker respectively) and live in small, rather squalid urban apartments lacking even any separation of kitchen and living room. Compare this to the ideal of suburban living in large houses with modern conveniences and sprawling yards (gardens) captured in late fifties hits like 'Leave it to Beaver' and the 'Donna Reed Show'. This was the 'golden-age' of mass-production Fordism — as a self-reinforcing cycle of mass production and mass consumption, which came to be known around the world as the 'American way of life', was reached.

Suburbanization was not without its problems. Perhaps the most visible of these was the 'strangling' of the inner city. Suburbanization created a particular pattern of organization within regions with relatively affluent suburbs surrounding increasingly impoverished inner cities. As the cities became the refuge of increasing numbers of minority group members moving from the South in search of economic opportunity, a distinct pattern of racial division came to overlay the city/suburb distinction. Increasingly white suburbs surrounded increasingly black cities. This combined with diminishing economic opportunities and racial abuses by city police forces and governmental agencies, which remained largely white, were the main factors which produced the racial unrest of the mid-to-late 1960s which swept cities from New York and Newark through Detroit and Chicago and all the way west to Los Angeles. Despite numerous government efforts to address these problems, including the massive Great Society programmes of the late 1960s and 1970s, these problems of racial and geographical division, if anything, grew deeper and more pervasive in the 1980s and 1990s.

SUMMARY

Mass production and mass consumption combined to stimulate the suburbanization of America, particularly during the Long-Boom of the 1950s and 1960s. Much production and consumption switched from the inner cities to the suburbs. With these developments, a distinctive suburban culture arose symbolizing the 'American way of life'. A kind of 'region within regions' developed, with clear divisions between decaying inner cities and outer affluent suburban rings. Often these also marked racial and ethnic divides.

5   THE RISE OF THE SUNBELT

Ever since the industrial revolution, the South was considered a 'backward' and at times a 'troubled' region. The failure of industrialization to take root in the South and the growing differential in growth rates between North and South was seen by some to be a primary cause of the Great Depression of the 1930s. President Franklin Roosevelt's New Deal provided federal funds for the modernization of the South, and developed programmes for the mechanization of Southern agriculture. The war mobilization effort for the Second World War also provided substantial government resources to build up Southern industry. And after the war, Southern politicians, bankers and industrialists launched successful 'booster' campaigns to attract industrial firms as well as government monies to the South. Their pitch was simple: warm weather, low wages, an absence of unions and politicians who would serve to further and enhance industry's needs.

This strategy obviously worked. Beginning in the late 1960s and continuing into the 1970s and early 1980s, the Sunbelt grew, in terms of both population and jobs at rates that far outpaced that of the traditional Northeast and Midwest regions. Cities like Atlanta, Georgia; Dallas and Houston, Texas; and Miami, Florida went from being small towns to becoming among the largest urban centres in the nation. Manufacturing companies relocated their northern factories in droves as they sought to capitalize on lower wages and avoid dealing with their unionized workforces. The expansion of the South also benefited from massive energy resources, particularly the huge oil reserves of Texas, Oklahoma and Louisiana. The Sunbelt's boom was also tied to generous outlays from the federal government, particularly increases in federal defence spending. Between 1950 and 1975, the Sunbelt gained nearly half a million defence workers, while the Northeast and Midwest lost more than 10,000 defence workers. By the mid-1970s, payrolls of the Sunbelt's 140 major military installations exceeded those of the rest of the US military posts combined. The Sunbelt also benefited from huge federal outlays for highways, road and bridge construction and other aspects of urban infrastructure.

In his best-selling book, *Power Shift*, Kirpatrick Sale brought the rise of the 'Sunbelt' to the attention of national and international audiences. According to Sale, the rise of the Sunbelt was tied to what he called 'six pillars': agribusiness, defence industry, federally-funded aerospace technology, oil, real estate development, and the leisure industry exemplified by Orlando, Florida's Disney World. In his words, the regional realities of America:

> …began to change with the advent of World War II and its new technologies and priorities. Slowly there grew up a rival nexus, based in the Southern and Western parts of the country that stand in geographical — and to a large degree cultural, economic and political — opposition to the Northeast, specifically in the **Southern Rim**, the broad band of America that stretches from Southern California through the Southwest and Texas, into the Deep South and down to Florida. Here, a truly competitive power base took shape, built upon the unsurpassed population migrations that began to draw millions and millions of people from the older and colder sections of the Northeast to the younger and senior sections of the South and Southwest; upon an authentic economic revolution that created the new postwar industries of defense, aerospace, technology, electronics, agribusiness and oil and gas extraction, all of which were based primarily in the Southern Rim and which grew to rival and in some cases surpass the older industries of the Northeast; upon the enormous growth of the federal government and its unprecedented accumulation of wealth, the great part of which went to develop and sustain the new areas and new government-dependent industries, the new ports and inland transportation systems, the new military and aerospace bases, and the new water and irrigation systems; upon the political development of the Southern Rim and its growing influence in almost all national party organizations of whatever stripe, its decisive role in the selection of candidates of both major parties, its control over the major committees and much of the inner workings of Congress. Over the last thirty years, this rival nexus, moving on to the national stage and mounting a head-on challenge to the traditional Establishment, has quite simply shifted the balance of power in America away from the Northeast and toward the Southern Rim.

The most obvious unity to the Southern Rim is climatic. In the area below this line are to be found all of the tropical and semitropical regions of the United States: the Florida beaches, the Deep South savannas, the Louisiana lowlands, the Texas and Oklahoma plains, the Southwestern deserts, the palmy California coast. Here is the zone in which the average annual temperature is above 60 degrees, the average maximum temperature is 74 degrees; there are between 250 and 350 days of sunshine a year, and frost, if it is to come, does not descend before November. This is, in short, America's sunbelt. There is a broadly metaphorical but rather apt way of describing these rival powerbases, the one of the Northeast and the other of the Southern Rim, as the yankees and the cowboys.

(Sale, 1975, pp.5–13)

Writing in the late 1970s, two of America's academic experts on the Sunbelt, David Perry and Alfred Watkins wrote in the introduction of their book, *The Rise of the Sunbelt Cities*, that there was a great:

> …level of surprise registered by both the national press and the academic world as the national economic order apparently shifted on its head with the 'rise of the Sunbelt'. That people and industries would leave New York, Chicago and Boston to live in the 'backwoods' of Georgia, with the 'cowboys' of Texas, or in the 'deserts' of Arizona was simply unthinkable. While these states were part of America they did not house our urban centres … However, it appears as if much of this past tradition has been profoundly altered. Now, academics, the press and politicians supply us with a new description of urban America. They cite a regional 'power shift', inaugurate Houston as the 'new diamond studded buckle' of America's economic empire, and claim that New York and other Northeastern cities may no longer just be 'decaying' — they may be actually dying.

(Perry and Watkins, 1977, pp.8–9)

The past twenty years have clearly seen a shift in economic power to the South and West, and this shift in economic power has brought with it a corresponding shift in political power. The Sunbelt has become a powerful political centre — in large measure because it has gone to great lengths to organize itself as such. Twentieth century American politics is marked by a long tradition of conservative Southern Democrats like Sam Rayburn and Lyndon Johnson which comprised and to some extent continue to be a powerful voting block in both legislative branches — the House of Representatives and the Senate. This political block was able to funnel large amounts of federal money into the Sunbelt — such as the major NASA centres in Florida and Texas, and huge defence and aerospace installations including major naval and air force bases across the South and West. During the 1970s, the Sunbelt states and their congressional delegations organized one of the nations' first and still most important regional political organizations, the Southern Growth Policies Board, to develop and implement political positions and public policy agendas that are important to the region. The last six elected American presidents — every elected President since 1964 — were from the South or West: two were former governors of California,

Richard Nixon and Ronald Reagan; two were from Texas, Lyndon Johnson and George Bush, a transplanted north-easterner from Connecticut; and two were governors of Sunbelt states, Jimmy Carter from Georgia and Bill Clinton from Arkansas. The only exception was Gerald Ford of Michigan who took office when Richard Nixon and his vice-president Spiro Agnew both resigned under the spectre of Watergate. And the presidential election of 1992 featured a three-way contest between southern politicians — Bill Clinton from Arkansas, Ross Perot from Texas, and George Bush. It is worth noting that the Democratic winning ticket featured two southerners, Bill Clinton of Arkansas and Al Gore, the former Senator from Tennessee.

The rise of the Sunbelt as a political force continues a long tradition of regional politics in American life. In *Regions*, Ann Markusen writes:

> In the United States, territorial politics have consistently displaced or pre-empted class politics as a national preoccupation. The Civil War pitted northerner against southerner. Populism attempted to organize southern and western farmers against eastern capital. In the recent postwar period, the Northeast clamoured against regional robbery in the guises of job loss, extortionary energy prices, biased federal aid flows toward the Sunbelt.

> (Markusen, 1987, p.1)

Long seen as a backward region of farms, deserts, cowboys and 'rebels', there can be no doubt that the Sunbelt has become a growing power centre of both the American economy and polity.

Indeed, the Southeast played a key role in launching the 1990's boom, as is testified by the report contained in Figure 9.1. This report indicates to the tentative start of the boom in the early 1990s, where different regions began their expansions hesitantly. But as the boom got underway all regions benefited. The early and strong start in the Southeast is attributed to its diverse economic base, and particularly to the role of inward foreign direct investment.

SUMMARY

Mobilization for the Second World War provided the initial impetus to modernize the 'backward' South. So began the rise of the Sunbelt — involving the growth of population, jobs, industry and commerce in the Southern states. These states benefited from huge Federal outlays on military and infrastructure projects. The notion of the Sunbelt gradually expanded, to encompass a broad sweep from Southern California, the Southwest and Texas, the Deep South and the 'new Southeast' of Florida, Georgia and the Carolinas, united above all by climate. With the relative increase in economic power of this 'Southern Rim' went a shift in the centre of gravity of American political power.

South-east leads US recovery

Barbara Harrison on the advantages of a diverse economic base

WHILE Washington frets about lagging job creation in the nation's glacially paced economic recovery, the South-east of the US is looking rosy on this score: the region is leading the country in job growth and its economy is rebounding faster than most others.

According to the Bureau of Labor Statistics, the region's eight states gained 30 per cent of all the 516,000 new jobs generated nationally during the first quarter, the latest period analysed. The region also accounted for 75 per cent of 28,000 new manufacturing jobs added nationally in the period.

The South-east's employment gains earlier this year were not just a fortuitous blip. The trend appeared to continue through the second quarter, according to Mr Donald Ratajczak, chief of the economic forecasting centre at Georgia State University. He said that, unlike the nation, which struggled at an overall economic growth rate of only 1.6 per cent during the second quarter, the South-east expanded at about 3 per cent.

The South-east's comparative prosperity is a feature of the unusually slow and very uneven national recovery, according to the Conference Board, the New York-based business think-tank. The organisation says that, unlike past, more robust recoveries, this one lacks a federal fiscal stimulus that helps the economy across the board. Consequently, "divergent regional trends are dominating the economic landscape."

The sharp differences in regional fortunes has led many to ask why some areas are prospering so disproportionately. Aside from the South-east, the Rocky Mountain states and the Mid-west have also fared relatively well since the recession of 1990-1991.

In the South-east, where job growth is strongest, analysts say that a diverse economic base is what has helped most. The region has a substantial amount of manufacturing in auto assembly, transportation equipment, building materials, home furnishings, textiles, chemicals, and food processing. It has also been less dependent on military contracting than

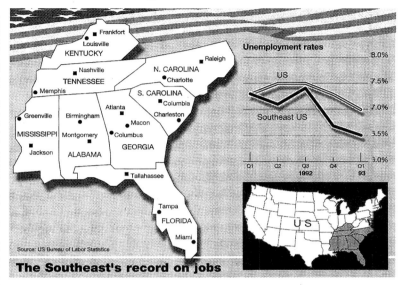

The Southeast's record on jobs

Source: US Bureau of Labor Statistics

other areas being hit with defence industry shrinkage.

The construction of BMW's new plant in western South Carolina is a boon in that state. Rising US car and truck sales are benefiting Japan's Nissan and GM's Saturn plants in Tennessee and Daimler Benz's truck assembly operation in North Carolina, which also appears poised to win the contest for Daimler Benz's new US car plant. The company, which is expected to make an announcement about its site selection by the end of this year, has been buying up land

options near its truck plant.

The region, especially the Carolinas, has been a magnet for foreign manufacturing investment because of relatively low production costs and wages. Service employment, up strongly, is also fairly well spread among banking, insurance, retail, communications, transportation, biotechnology and other sectors.

But the region's exceptional growth is in large measure being fuelled by construction. According to Mr Thomas Cunningham, chief regional economist at the Atlanta Federal

Reserve, it has a concentration of the industries that benefit most from the early stages of recovery. The region's building materials, textiles, furniture and white goods sectors have all been boosted by a nationwide recuperation of the housing market.

The South has in fact lead the surge in new home buying, thanks partly to migration from less prosperous regions. In addition, rebuilding after Hurricane Andrew last year in Florida has helped lift regional construction businesses.

Mr Cunningham also points out that, while the South-east is faring better than most other areas on job growth, the national figures on employment gains are being brought down by large job losses in just five big states, California, New Jersey, Connecticut, Massachusetts and New York.

Nonetheless, attitudes in the South-east also seems distinct from the rest of the nation. Consumer spending has been outpacing the nation as a whole. Even the political mindset appears to be a factor: "You don't have the yo-yo effect of consumers in other parts of the country," says Mr Ratajczak. "We were never that thrilled with Clinton's victory or chagrined with his policy."

Housing starts fall by 2.7%

THE US housing market is continuing to move sideways despite the lowest mortgage rates in two decades, figures indicated yesterday, writes Michael Prowse in Washington.

The Commerce Department said housing starts fell 2.7 per cent between June and July to a seasonally adjusted annual rate of 1.21m. In the first seven months of the year, starts were only 2.3 per cent higher than in the same period last year. The market's relative weakness may reflect consumers' reluctance to make

long-term financial commitments because of doubts about job security.

The weakness last month was concentrated in the Midwest, where building activity was adversely affected by flooding, and in California where economic recovery has been slow to take hold.

Starts rose modestly in the northeast and south. Building permits were more encouraging, rising 3 per cent last month and by 4 per cent in the first seven months relative to the same period last year.

Figure 9.1   Regional led recovery
Source: Financial Times, *18 August 1993*

6 THE NEW HIGH-TECHNOLOGY REGIONS — SILICON VALLEY AND ROUTE 128

The 1970s and 1980s also saw the rise of high-technology regions in America. The two that have received the most attention are Silicon Valley — a sunny, former agricultural area which is just a little bit south of San Francisco, California — and the Route 128 area around Boston and Cambridge, Massachusetts. It is often said that these two regions, Silicon Valley and Route 128, hold the key not only to the economic renewal of the United States, but could be used as 'models' for economic revitalization in Europe and even in the Third World nations as well. For most people, the main ingredient in the high-technology regions is a great university. It is frequently said that the impetus for Silicon Valley came from Stanford University in the 1950s and 1960s, especially its great engineering school, which was led at the time by a visionary dean, by the name of Frederick Terman. The Route 128 area is similarly seen by many to be an outgrowth of the two great universities of America's Cambridge — Harvard and especially MIT. The role of the universities in these two innovative regions is certainly important, but that is not the whole story. A number of other factors were and continue to be important as well.

America's high-technology regions are first and foremost regions of entrepreneurs. The entrepreneurs who provide much of the impetus for high-technology regions are a new breed of entrepreneurs and industrialists. They are entrepreneurs who have made their mark by introducing, marketing and selling advanced high-technology products to the world. In America, this new breed of high-technology entrepreneur and the companies they have founded has reached the exalted status of 'celebrity'. Perhaps the most famous of these new entrepreneur celebrities is Steven Jobs, the founder of Apple Computer. But there is also Bill Gates the founder of Microsoft, T.J. Rogers of Cypress Semiconductors and countless others. These high-technology entrepreneurs are not just inventors. They are true visionaries who have the foresight and the courage to be able to see new markets and develop new products for markets which do not yet exist. They are able to see that people will want to use a computer or word processing package, or that there will be a demand for a new kind of bio-genetic drug. And, they are able to devise a product people are attracted to and will want to buy. This new breed of entrepreneur is a team builder. They are able to put together the right mix of people to actually create, introduce and sell new technology. They are terrific motivators, who are able to motivate people to commit nearly all of their time to taking these new ideas from the idea stage and making them into an actual product. It is not uncommon for their employees to work 60, 70, 80 or more hours per week. A famous tee-shirt worn by Apple employees reads '80 hours a week and loving it'. And, this new breed of entrepreneur is able to generate the financing required to build these new businesses and develop new products. This financing comes from another major group of people who have created America's high-technology regions — the venture capitalists.

Venture capitalists who invest in high-technology are a particularly American creation. Venture capitalists are sophisticated high stakes gamblers — who gamble in high-technology business. These are people who devote their lives to identifying and investing in completely unproven and very high-risk technologies. America's leading venture capital funds include VenRock, Kleiner Perkins, the Mayfield Fund, Sequoia, Institutional Venture Partners, TA associates and many, many more. There are now between 600–800 venture capital firms in America — most of them located in these high-technology regions, though a considerable number are located in the financial centres of New York and Chicago as well — which control about $35 billion dollars in investment capital. Venture capitalists invest between $1.5 and $4 billion dollars a year in between 1,000 and 2,500 high-technology companies. Venture capitalists are the people which identify promising technologies and invest the capital required to get them off the ground. But they invest much more than their money. Venture capitalists are sometimes referred to as hands-on investors, who are involved alongside the entrepreneur in actually building a high-technology business. They are a unique breed — part capitalist and part entrepreneur. In fact, many of America's leading venture capitalists made their fortunes by being entrepreneurs. Venture capitalists assist entrepreneurs and high-technology companies, help develop their business plans, hire other top managers and researchers, even locate office space and factories, or set up joint ventures with larger companies. They are an important part of the supporting network of contacts and connections upon which entrepreneurial companies in America's premier high-technology regions depend.

America's leading high-technology regions have tremendous concentrations of leading high-technology companies and many of their suppliers. They are clearly the nation's dominant centres of high technology, home to thousands of high-technology companies and tens of thousands of their suppliers.

A tremendous supporting infrastructure of supplier companies, equipment companies, marketing firms, law firms, accountants, business consultants, employment agencies, and commercial real estate developers is another key element of America's high-technology regions. These regions have brought together a myriad of necessary support services which are required to support and nurture new entrepreneurial businesses. This includes lawyers who are experts in putting together business plans and other documents which new companies require; consultants who specialize in knowing high-technology market trends in the United States and world wide; real estate developers who can put together office space and factory sites for new companies; marketing gurus, like Regis McKenna, who can develop the image and advertising campaigns to sell new products like personal computers, notebook computers or the next wave in electronic products — the electronic personal organizer; and the list goes on and on.

America's high-technology regions are just that — regional concentrations of the resources, talent and institutions required to support, nurture and encourage high-technology industry. A good way to think of this support structure is as an integrated innovation system. This innovation system is made up of cutting-edge high-technology companies, a ready pool of talented engineers, managers and R&D scientists, an abundant supply of venture capital, and a concentration of business service firms like law firms, accountants and consultants. These formal and informal networks for information exchange and technology transfer make it easier to develop new innovations and turn them into products. Silicon Valley entrepreneurs and venture capitalists use the term 'virtual corporation' to describe the way the Silicon Valley technology network extends the boundary of the individual firm. The social structure of innovation is a major source of new ideas, market openings, and information on competitors' strategies and can even be the starting point for new companies. The power of high-technology innovation complexes like Silicon Valley and Route 128 can be seen in the 'pull' or magnetic effect they can exert on entrepreneurs and technology companies located in other parts of the country, even the rest of the world. One of the leading electronic design companies in the United States, for example, was founded in North Carolina. The company founders loved it there — it was their home. But, over time, the venture capitalists who invested in the company insisted that they move to Silicon Valley to take advantage of the innovation system that was already in place. They needed to hire more people to manage the business and market the product — and those people were mostly in Silicon Valley. They needed a good law firm to handle their growing legal business and contracts — and most of that capability was in Silicon Valley. So while the founders temporarily resisted, they eventually relented and moved to Silicon Valley, where incidentally they have been more successful than their wildest dreams.

Despite the tremendous success and innovation that have taken place in America's high-technology regions, these areas are not without their problems. And, these problems — which were once quite small and hard to even notice — grew worse and worse as we moved through the 1990s into the twenty-first century. The first problem is one that stems in part from the 'competitive edge' which motivates many entrepreneurs and high-technology companies. According to a growing number of high-technology executives and venture capitalists, America's high-technology regions are becoming 'hyper-competitive'. For example, entrepreneurs and venture capitalists may quickly switch their attention from one company to the next if a company is not making a sufficient amount of money. All the effort that went into creating the first company will have been wasted, and many people will lose their jobs and livelihood. In this hyper-competitive climate, employees learn to take care of themselves and not be particularly loyal to their company. Seeking 'big bucks' and dismayed by the absence of corporate loyalty, engineers and scientists are encouraged to switch jobs often. High-technology companies in Silicon Valley and Route 128 face employee turnover rates which are truly astounding — 25 to 35 per cent or even 50 per cent per year. This is rational because when employees switch companies they often get stock options in addition to their salary. So, if the company hits it big they can get very rich. Is is said that the day Apple's stock was issued on the stock market — more than one hundred Apple employees became millionaires. Employees who switch jobs are able to keep taking shots at hitting it big. In the words of one Silicon Valley executive: 'In Silicon Valley, if somebody wants to change jobs, all they have to do is turn into a different parking lot off a different freeway exit'.

This hyper-competitive climate is also reflected in a growing wave of law suits between and among companies for stealing each others' employees and the ideas those employees bring with them. Some experts have gone so far as to refer to the problems of high-technology regions as stemming from what they call 'chronic entrepreneurship' — too much entrepreneurship which leads to good companies and good ideas being abandoned in the quest for higher and higher profits. Others call it 'start-up mania'. Whatever it is called the results are the same — abandoned companies, disrupted research, wasted effort and burned-out workers. Venture capitalists can contribute to this problem by raiding established companies for good people to staff the new start-up companies. Venture capitalists have fallen victim to a herd mentality and funded similar or nearly identical companies which compete each other to death. An executive from one of Silicon Valley's leading companies compared the hyper-competitive environment of high-technology regions to the hyper-competitive nature of the theatre industry.

> Most [high-technology] companies are like so many Broadway plays. The venture capitalist is like the producer. An itinerant group of 'actors' get cast in the needed roles. The 'play' opens — has a 'run' (short or long) — then it closes. Time to put a new play together. Downstream of our 'play', a number of service organizations make their living supporting the successes then moving their efforts to the next 'play' after each completes its 'run'.

> (Intel Corp. quoted in Florida and Kenney, 1990, p.26)

Another weakness of America's high-technology regions is that they are centres of innovation but not manufacturing. They focus all their energy on inventing new things and introducing new products, but increasingly fail to produce them. That is increasingly left to Japan or other countries in Asia. Akio Morita, Sony's co-founder and chief executive calls this the 'hollowing out' of American high-technology industry:

> American companies have either shifted output to low-wage countries or come to buy parts and assembled products from countries like Japan that can make quality parts at low prices. The result is a hollowing-out of American industry. The US is abandoning its status as an industrial power.

> (Morita quoted in Geras, 1987, p.75)

A top executive of a leading American semiconductor company adds:

> The US is rapidly becoming a non-manufacturing nation. We sell our innovations and get a one shot infusion of capital not a continuous product stream. Manufacturing is the ability to make a lot of things, it is the engine which drives progress. If we lose this base, we don't have the economic engine to fuel innovation.

> (quoted in Florida and Kenney, 1990, p.134)

The end result can be tragic — rather than building up a core of companies that can manufacture products and remain competitive over the long haul, America's high-technology regions end up with one-shot 'breakthrough' companies — which create the new breakthrough product but fail to follow-through on it by turning it into a continuous stream of mass produced products that can sell on world markets. And, most of these companies are not only cut-off from one another, they are cut-off from the large manufacturing companies which could help them turn their ideas into commercial products. So, Silicon Valley, Route 128 and other high-technology regions remain centres of breakthrough innovation, but find themselves less and less able to follow-through on the innovations they make, and thus to generate the long-run economic growth, good jobs, and rising standard of living that American society needs. All of this was exacerbated by the very serious recession of the late 1980s which affected California and New England much worse than the rest of the American economy. In fact, the recession was a decidedly 'bi-coastal recession'.

As the twenty-first century approached, many Americans were beginning to question whether the high-technology regions, of which so much was expected just ten years earlier, could really create the wealth, economic growth, and good jobs upon which the society's long run future will be premised. And while there can be no doubt that these regions will remain important as centres of innovation and new technology for both America and the world, it is becoming apparent that they no longer provide the economic muscle that will be required to keep the American economy competitive in the twenty-first century.

SUMMARY

With the advent of 'high-technology' in the 1970s and 1980s new regional configurations developed in California (Silicon Valley) and in Massachusetts (Route 128). Driven by venture capital and individual entrepreneurs, they specialized in computer and electronic technologies. A wide and deep supportive infrastructure also emerged to service the leading companies and their suppliers. Despite their many positive contributions to the American economy, these regions and districts are characterized by 'start-up mania', a 'hyper-competitive' economic climate and 'chronic entrepreneurship'. The companies operating in these regions tend to be one-off innovators rather than continual manufacturers, unable to follow up an original breakthrough product with successive generations of new product developments. These inherent weaknesses could undermine the viability of the regions in the future.

7   THE BI-COASTAL ECONOMY

By the early 1980s, the regional realities of America began to shift once again. Growth during the Reagan years was concentrated mainly on the coasts. As the traditional centres of American industry declined, investment capital that previously would have supported the expansion of industrial plant and equipment poured into risky and in some cases highly speculative activities in the stock market, real estate development and venture capital financed high technology. The venture capital market grew rapidly, and the high-technology regions of Silicon Valley and Route 128 experienced a prolonged boom. The real estate frenzy and dynamic stock market of the period fuelled significant growth in major financial centres in New York, Chicago and San Francisco. This, in turn, sparked feverish real estate speculation in these cities, a rapid rebuilding and gentrification of inner city residential neighbourhoods, and significant speculation in new hotels, office complexes, inner city malls, and trendy festival markets such as New York City's South Street Seaport. At the same time that the Reagan administration preached fiscal conservatism and budget cutting, it set off one of the largest peacetime expansions in government spending in American history, through a rapid escalation in defence spending for high-tech equipment and weaponry. This conferred disproportionate benefits to the Coasts, and by the mid-1980s states like California and Massachusetts, which specialize in high-tech defence industries, were receiving in excess of $1,200 per person in federal defence spending, while the industrial Midwest, which was already feeling the effects of plant closures and downsizing, received an average of less than $450 per person in federal defence spending.

As a result, the regional realities of American economic life began to shift from a North-South to an East-West axis. In the summer of 1986, The Joint Economic Committee of the US Congress announced the emergence of yet another new era in American regionalism with the publication of a major study entitled *The Bi-Coastal Economy*. The report provided a wealth of evidence and data drawn from government and academic sources concluding that America had become a bi-coastal economy of thriving coasts and a lagging middle. According to the study, the bi-coastal economy was comprised of sixteen fast growth states — California, Arizona and Alaska in the west, plus thirteen East Coast states including New York, New Jersey, and Delaware, Massachusetts, Connecticut, Vermont, New Hampshire, and Maine in New England; and the Sunbelt states of Florida, Georgia, Virginia, Maryland and North Carolina. The report further noted that this group of 16 bi-coastal states:

> …accounted for nearly 70 per cent of real growth in wages and proprietorship income. Of the $234 billion dollars real growth in wage and proprietorship income that occurred nationally between the first quarter of 1981 and the end of 1985, less that $73 billion dollars went to the remaining 34 states which account for 58 per cent of the nation's population. On a per capita basis, real growth was one-third as much in the heartland grouping as it was in the 16 coastal states.

A more familiar measure of economic health is annual growth rates. The average growth rate for real GNP in the post-war era prior to Reagan was 3.4 per cent. The state-by-state numbers for growth in real GNP which occurred during the Reagan administration (1981–1986) would not have seemed slower to someone living either in California or on the East Coast. In fact, average annual growth in real wage and proprietorship income for the 16 states in the coastal grouping was 4 per cent, or considerably above average for the post-war period. The coast states (as of 1986 were), in fact, enjoying economic growth at about the level that the United States as a whole enjoyed during the 1960s. For the remainder of the country, however, the annual growth rate was only 1.4 per cent during this five-year period. During the post-war period, however, only once, from 1954 to 1958 did national growth average 1.4 per cent for a five year period and at no time was it below that level. Some of the regional disparity reflected by income figures was also reflected in employment data. Between the first quarter of 1981 and the end of 1985, slightly more than eight million new jobs were created in the United States. Fifty-eight per cent of those jobs were added in the 16-state coastal group, which computes to about 90 per cent more job growth per capita than in the remainder of the country.

(US Congress Joint Economic Committee, 1986)

Based on this, the report concluded that the available evidence from both statistical and anecdotal sources clearly indicates that 'the State of California and the East Coast of the United States have done quite well during the last five years (1981–1986), while progress has been limited in most other parts of the country'.

SUMMARY

As the 1980s progressed the main polarity of regional America began to 'shadow' the two predominant high-technology districts of California and Massachusetts with a more general shift from the North-South axis to an East-West one, centred along the entire Pacific and Atlantic coasts. This bi-coastal economy experienced significantly higher than average growth rates between 1981 and 1986.

8 FROM DE-INDUSTRIALIZATION TO REINDUSTRIALIZATION IN THE RUSTBELT

In stark contrast to America's high-technology regions with their glimmering industrial parks, entrepreneurs and venture capitalists and to the gleaming Sunbelt cities of Atlanta and Dallas stands the contrasting picture of the massive grey, steel-coloured industrial complexes of America's industrial heartland. Just a decade ago, most experts predicted the decline and de-industrialization of the American manufacturing belt. In fact, it came to be known as the Rustbelt. It was said that manufacturing plants and people would move south and west from the Rustbelt to the Sunbelt in search of lower costs and so-called 'better business climates' and away from unions and organized labour. Some of this was obviously true. During the 1960s, 1970s and early 1980s, large numbers of steel mills closed, as steel producers consolidated their operations or diversified into the energy sector or other businesses. The traditional steel making region around Pittsburgh was virtually abandoned — today a rusted mass of old buildings is all that remains; in one area a new amusement park rises from a decayed old steel site. Plant closings, business failures, and mass lay-offs hit the industrial Midwest harder than anywhere else during the late 1970s and early 1980s, pushing unemployment rates as high as 25 per cent. In scarcely more than a decade, the once-proud flagships of America's post-war industrial fleet were dismantled. And, people followed jobs to the new centres of opportunity, causing some cities like Pittsburgh, Buffalo, Cleveland and Detroit to lose hundreds of thousands of people.

By the early 1980s, a rather gloomy picture emerged. Nearly all the experts argued that the industrial Midwest — the once proud centre of American industry — would face long-run, secular, and chronic disinvestment and de-industrialization brought on by a shift of traditional industries to low-wage locations, the development of new high-technology complexes in California and New England, and a broader shift to a post-industrial service economy. The consensus view among business leaders, policy makers, and academics was that the Midwest would never again be a centre for competitive manufacturing — its costs were too high and its labour climate too conflictual. With heightened foreign competition and the emergence of the 'bi-coastal economy,' the industrial heartland seemed poised for continued decline. The manufacturing heartland, it was argued, would be left behind in a broad and fundamental shift to a post-industrial economy of high-technology, finance, and services.

But in what is perhaps the most remarkable regional turnaround in American history, the 1980s saw the industrial Midwest — the so-called Rustbelt — stage a remarkable economic turnaround — one that has the potential to match the economic miracles of post-war Germany and Japan. The industrial Midwest has not only started to grow again and attract new industries and factories, it has helped to bolster the American economy as a whole and to dampen the adverse effects of the early 1990s recession. Consider the following trends. The industrial Midwest region, stretching from western Pennsylvania and western New York through Ohio, Indiana, Illinois, Michigan, Wisconsin and Minnesota, remains the industrial centre of America, and currently accounts for 40 per cent of all manufacturing, 60 per cent of the nation's steel, 55 per cent of its automobiles, and 50 per cent of its machine tools. The region increased its share of durable goods manufacturing over this period. The Midwest produced more automobiles and steel in 1992 than a decade before, even with a significant number of plant closures by the Big

Three. The reason for this is a tremendous wave of Japanese and other foreign investment in state-of-the-art automotive and steel factories.

Although the manufacturing heartland is still feeling some effects of de-industrialization — too many manufacturers remain locked in the old mind-set of cost-cutting, downsizing, short-term management, disinvestment, and management-by-stress — regional economic revitalization is underway. Manufacturing employment has stabilized, capital expenditures are rising. The Midwest has become a new industrial frontier — a world-leader in the export of high value-added manufactured goods. This new industrial frontier is in the throes of a complex transformation and restructuring catalyzed by an emerging core of world-class companies from America, Europe and Japan — Xerox, Motorola, Corning, Steelcase, Honda, Sony, Matsushita, and Bosch to name just a few. This new industrial frontier has attracted a trans-plant automotive complex of more than 400 assembly, automotive parts, steel, and rubber and tyre manufacturers. Furthermore, the new industrial heartland is recreating its historic strength in consumer electronics with the location of state-of-the-art plants by Sony outside of Pittsburgh, Matsushita in Ohio, Toshiba in western New York, and acquisitions of US plants by major European producers, Thomson, Philips, and Siemens. The intersection of these two trends has produced pockets of growth alongside continued decline — a phenomenon of 'reindustrialization within de-industrialization'.

In contrast to predictions of de-industrialization, the Great Lakes has retained its status as the nation's premier manufacturing economy. During the height of de-industrialization, from 1977 to 1987, the Midwest's share of the nation's manufactured output declined from 44 to 36 per cent. Over the same period, manufacturing's share of the Great Lakes' economy fell from 29 to 23 per cent. But, since then such trends have abated. In 1989, the Midwest produced more than $345 billion in manufacturing output, 36 per cent of the national total. Overall, the Midwest produced $1.6 trillion in total output, roughly one-third of the national total. And, manufacturing continues to comprise a greater share of the Midwest economy (21.5 per cent) than for the nation as a whole (18.5 per cent). In fact, the Midwest produced 70 per cent more manufactured output in 1989 than it did in 1977.

The reindustrialization of the manufacturing heartland is vividly demon-strated by the impressive turnaround in the growth of its manufacturing output. In fact, from 1987 to 1988 the Midwest posed a remarkable 7.8 per cent growth rate in manufacturing output — surpassing the national rate of 7.4 per cent and eclipsing the manufacturing powerhouses of Japan (6.3 per cent) and Germany (5.2 per cent) as well. During de-industrialization, the Midwest suffered devastating losses in manufacturing employment. But, since then, employment losses related to manufacturing have subsided. From 1982 to 1986, the Midwest lost just 2 per cent of its manufacturing employment, and from 1986 to 1990, that loss was only 1 per cent. In 1990, the industrial Midwest, which is home to 30 per cent of the nation's population, accounted for 36 per cent of the nation's manufacturing employment.

The Midwest continues to provide high-wage manufacturing jobs. This stands in sharp contrast to the predictions of both the de-industrialization and post-industrial perspectives. And, while some sceptics might attribute the Midwest's reindustrialization to a shift from high-wage to low-wage, non-union manufacturing, the data clearly indicates that this is not the case. In 1990, the Midwest's average annual manufacturing wage was $30,671, roughly 6 per cent higher than the national average. As of 1988, more than half (57.1 per cent) of all national union membership in manufacturing remained concentrated in the Great Lakes region.

Midwestern industry has made enormous strides in productivity, registering productivity gains which, in some cases, surpassed those of the major industrialized countries of the world. From 1980 to 1988, manufacturing productivity in the Great Lakes increased by 36 per cent, which was less than Japan (52 per cent), but better than both Germany (15 per cent) and the USA as a whole (32 per cent). More significantly, between 1986 and 1988 productivity in the Midwest or heartland region increased by roughly 15 per cent — 6 per cent faster than Japan (9 per cent), and considerably better than the USA (–1 per cent) and Germany (–2 per cent).

Nevertheless, in terms of personal income changes the economic fortunes of the Mideast and Great Lakes regions did not figure so strongly in the later stages of the 1992–98 boom years. As Table 9.1 shows it was regions to the west of the Rocky Mountains and in the South that consistently returned a better than average performance.

Table 9.1 Regional personal income changes, 1995–97 (yearly percentage changes in current dollar terms)

	1995–96	1996–97
New England	4.9	6 0
Mideast	4.4	5 1
Great Lakes	5.0	5 1
Plains	7.3	4 7
Southeast*	5.6	5 7
Southwest*	6.2	7 5
Rocky Mountains*	6.4	6 6
Far West*	5.6	6 3
US average	5.4	5 7

* Those regions with a consistent equal to, or better than, average performance over the two years.

Source: 1995–96: *Survey of Current Business*, vol.77, no.5, May 1997, Table 1, p.96; 1996–97: *Survey of Current Business*, vol.78, no.5, May 1998, Table 1, p.12

SUMMARY

During the 1970s and 1980s it was the Midwest that seemed to suffer while other regions flourished. The term 'de-industrialization' signalled the dismantling of the industrial heartland in the face of domestic disinvestment and foreign competition. The Rustbelt was said to face long-run secular decline and with it the future of American large-scale manufacturing. But during the late 1980s the Midwest seemed poised on the threshold of a renaissance. It remains the American manufacturing heartland, bolstered by the inward foreign direct investment of world class companies. These are leading in a thoroughgoing restructuring of the entire region's economy. During the 1990s boom, however, this promise for the Midwest and Great Lakes region was only partially realized as strengthening economic ties with Mexico stimulated the South and West regional economies once again.

9   REINVENTING A REGION

A cornerstone of American history has been the ability of regions to reinvent themselves — the transformation from the old agrarian South to the new Sunbelt of industry and commerce, the rise of New England as an early centre for textile mills and boot and shoe manufacturing, its post-war decline, and revitalization around high-technology and Route 128, the transformation of the California economy into a centre of defence, aerospace and high-technology innovation. Today, America is in the throes of another regional transformation centred around the resurgence of manufacturing industry and the revitalization of the so-called Rustbelt.

Driving this transformation of the industrial heartland is a growing beach-head of world-class companies. These companies have acted as a powerful orienting force in regional transformation. They play the role of 'hubs' for modernization of the region's small and medium-sized manufacturing base. And, they are investing in workplace restructuring, total quality management and supplier modernization at levels that dwarf current or projected government outlays in these areas. These companies have also pioneered new models for investing in education, training, and the broader infrastructure required to support a high-performance economy.

I/N Tek, a joint venture between Inland Steel and Nippon Steel just outside South Bend, Indiana, provides a powerful example of this process at work. The factory itself is a paean to modern industrial architecture. Spanking white, with gleaming concrete floors and coloured rails, the machines and production equipment themselves sparkle. Workers, positioned in high-tech, climate-controlled operations booths, monitor the entire production process on advanced computerized equipment. I/N Tek has transformed the process of cold rolling steel into a continuous process that takes less than an hour from start to finish. This is a tremendous advance over the old way of producing cold-rolled steel in separate steps or 'batches' that could take as long as twelve working days to complete. The key to this transformation was unleashing the collective intelligence of the workforce. The company mobilized factory workers, engineers, and R & D scientists to combine the various batch processes one at a time. Workers, engineers and computer specialists recently worked together to connect the entire cold rolling process to another process, called electro-galvanizing, which coats steel, for corrosion-resistant automobile body parts. I/N Tek provides a powerful illustration of the new model of manufacturing — in the most basic of industries — steel. And for all those who still believe that such advances can only be made in the absence of a union — I/N Tek is a 'steel workers plant' — in fact, most of the workers were transplanted from Inland Steel's sprawling Indiana Harbor steel mill.

In this new factory, knowledge and intelligence replace physical labour as the fundamental source of value and profit. The factory is becoming more like a laboratory — the place where new ideas and concepts are generated, tested and implemented. It is no longer merely a place of dirty floors and smoking machines, grease, muscle and sweat, but is increasingly an environment of brain-power and technological innovation. Success in the new age of manufacturing requires linking the R & D laboratory and the factory in a seamless web of activity to unleash the intelligence of all workers. This is not the 'passive' involvement of the labour-management committees and American quality circle movement of the 1970s and 1980s. This is a new kind of direct involvement in which workers' intelligence and ideas are mobilized on a day-to-day basis as a source of new innovations and improvements in the manufacturing process. Ever since the transition from feudalism to capitalism, the basic source of productivity, value and economic growth has been physical labour and physical skill. The key to success in this new age of industry lies in workers' knowledge of production and the ideas and innovations that flow from it.

There is a phrase for this new age of manufacturing — 'high-performance manufacturing'. High-performance manufacturing means the ability to deliver high quality, high value-added products, tailored to customer needs on a just-in-time basis and at a competitive price. High-performance firms compete on quality in global markets, organize work in self-managing work teams, and are strongly committed to continuous improvement and organizational learning. High-performance production complexes rely upon just-in-time supplier and customer interactions to enhance innovation and produce the state-of-the-art products the world wants. At Honda's huge automotive assembly complex in central Ohio, engineers and managers are told that they must always listen to shop-floor workers who have the hands-on knowledge and the ideas required to improve the production process. In some cases, factory workers actually supervise engineers.

Powered by the shift to high-performance manufacturing, the industrial heartland is almost singlehandedly responsible for returning the United States to its status as the world's leading exporter. In 1991, the Midwest shipped over $100 billion dollars' worth of manufactured goods to more than 80 countries, including $9 billion to Japan and $5.6 billion to Germany. The Midwest's rate of increase in manufactured exports is double the national average. This increasingly outward focus is also reflected in a large and growing volume of foreign direct manufacturing investment. More than half of all Japanese foreign direct investment in automobiles, steel and tyres and rubber is concentrated in the four Great Lakes states — Ohio, Indiana, Michigan and Illinois. A key competitive advantage of this new manufacturing heartland lies in its ability to attract a growing constellation of the world's best companies.

Bolstered by exports and foreign direct investment, the Midwest is recreating its industrial base in traditional sectors like steel and automotive assembly and developing new high-technology sectors as well. The region is home to the world's newest and most advanced steel finishing and automotive assembly technology. It is a centre of world-class office furniture production, as companies like Steelcase pave the way to the electronic office of the future. It houses a state-of-the art image processing complex of Xerox, Eastman Kodak, and Bausch and Lomb. And, it is a budding centre of advanced television production anchored by Sony, Matsushita, major European television producers, and American suppliers of the flat glass used in picture tubes.

This combination of factors has fueled overall economic performance exceeding national averages. The Midwest was spared in the largely bicoastal recession of the early 1990s. During the downturn, twelve of the region's seventeen major industries outperformed their national counterparts. The unemployment rate for the Great Lakes states was below that of the nation in 1991. In the first quarter of 1992, over half the nation's housing starts occurred in the Great Lakes region. In addition, the region is less dependent upon Pentagon contracts than any other — with per capita defence outlays averaging less than half the national average. As a result, its manufacturers are more commercially focused and better positioned to weather defence cuts.

Battle Creek, Michigan, as much as anywhere else, is emblematic of the kind of turnaround that is occurring in the new heartland economy. During the 1970s and early 1980s, Battle Creek experienced one of the worst bouts of deindustrialization of any Rustbelt city. Its historic manufacturing base of food and cereal producers, agricultural equipment factories and automotive parts producers underwent significant decline and the city was rocked by plant closings. But, beginning in the late 1970s, Battle Creek developed a co-ordinated strategy to attract world-class, high-performance firms from around the world. The city began by turning a defunct army base, the old Fort Custer, into a new industrial park. It sent trade missions to Europe and Japan, and actually opened its own trade office in Japan. Battle Creek has now attracted more than a dozen Japanese automotive component parts manufacturers, including the giant Nippondenso and a number of its family of suppliers to the industrial park. Nippondenso is currently working with the local community college to restructure both its curriculum and administration along the lines of total quality, high-performance management. These firms have helped to bring economic stability and even growth to Battle Creek, providing a beach-head of high-performance firms which are a powerful example for local firms to follow.

Cleveland too is engaged in the transformation to the new economy. Under the leadership of Cleveland Tomorrow, an association of Cleveland's largest businesses and financial institutions, the city is repositioning itself for the new age of manufacturing. Cleveland Tomorrow has set up a variety of programmes and institutions devoted to transforming the manufacturing base, including programmes to assist manufacturing companies who seek to implement state-of-the-art technology and manufacturing-management techniques. Cleveland Tomorrow works closely with Cleveland universities to conduct focused research and to develop new strategies for regional manufacturing modernization and economic development. It is currently developing a regional strategy to help automotive component parts producers to tap the growing Japanese transplant market and move to high-performance manufacturing.

Perhaps the single most important regional reality of America in the twentieth century has been the rise, decline and rise again of the American manufacturing heartland. More than the rise of the Sunbelt and the high-technology complexes of Silicon Valley and Route 128, and in sharp contrast to so many predictions of impending disaster and decline, America's Midwest manufacturing heartland remains the centre of wealth, productivity and value creation for the American economy. In fact, during the late 1980s and early 1990s, many of the Sunbelt states, such as Texas, lapsed into prolonged recession, caused in large measure by cheaper international oil prices and the collapse of the domestic oil economy, which in turn resulted in a ripple effect of real estate and banking collapses. And as we move into the twenty-first century, the bi-coastal economy has been transformed into a 'bi-coastal economic crisis', as states like California, New York and Massachusetts continue to experience prolonged recession and teeter on the brink of budgetary crises. Today, it is the industrial heartland region that is escaping the iron grip of recession, and experiencing a modicum of economic growth. Once again, the economic position and fortunes of American regions have been reversed.

SUMMARY

The resurgence of manufacturing industry in the Midwest is leading to a modernization of American business and the potential emergence of a high-performance economy. Traditional labour and management practices are being recast, often at the behest of foreign techniques and know-how. This is happening as the high-technology industrial districts and Sunbelt regions lapse into a prolonged recession, stimulated in part by the collapse of defence spending.

10 CONCLUSION — REGIONS AND THE FUTURE OF AMERICA

America is a nation of regions. Regions are what give America much of its distinctive character. And America's regions themselves remain distinctive. Throughout American history regions have been divided across two classic divides — a North-South axis and an East-West axis. Today, those distinctions retain a great deal of meaning in American life. The American economy, American politics and American culture continue to be shaped by and respond to regional differences, regional identities and regional rivalries. One hundred years after they were first written, Frederick Jackson Turner's ideas of regionalism rather than class as a source of political identity and of the frontier experience as a source of America's unique character continue to remain relevant to the American experience. And, regions continue to play a fundamental role in American political life and in public policy. As we have seen, America fought its bloodiest war, the Civil War, over regional differences in government policy. Federal defence spending has had much to do with the rise of the Sunbelt and the West. In the late twentieth century, regions have organized along political lines — and created political bodies, such as the Southern Growth Policies Board, to advance their interests.

Regions continue to be a source of new ideas and new public policies. There is currently a national debate in the United States over the proper role of government in the economy, and the role which industrial and technology policy can play in economic renewal. States and regions are being increasingly recognized as the centres of new and innovative public policy efforts and some even refer to these state and local initiatives as comprising important 'laboratories of democracy' from which federal agendas may later be crafted. The Rustbelt states of Pennsylvania, Ohio and Michigan, which experienced so much economic hardship in the 1970s and early 1980s, have been lauded as leaders in economic development and technology policies. The Pacific states, which have long defined themselves in terms of their natural beauty and high quality of life, have become national innovators in the areas of environmental policy and health policy. California, with its diverse population, has taken the lead in the development of human and civil rights policies. Regions do not simply comprise powerful political forces, they are the sources of many of the most important ideas that inform American government and public policy.

Regions continue to play a powerful role in American life. While the economic experiences of American regions have converged — today, perhaps more than at any time in the past, America's regions are on a level economic playing field — there remains clear cultural and political identities among regions. In fact, regional realities of contemporary America may be more complex than at any time in the past. There is a Rustbelt, a Sunbelt, and now even a Gunbelt — those areas of the South and West where defence spending is concentrated. There are regions like the Northeast, particularly the New York City area, which specialize in finance, business headquarters and high-level administrative services and there are those which specialize in the incubation and growth of high-technology industries like Silicon Valley and the Route 128 area around Boston.

There are some reasons to believe that regions will become more important to the American economy — and to the world economy — in the current age of globalization. The Japanese analyst, Kenichi Ohmae, sees the United States at the cutting edge of the movement to 'region states'. In his view:

> The primary linkages of region states tend to be with the global economy, and not with host nations. Region states make such effective points of entry into the global economy because the very characteristics that define them are shaped by the demands of that economy. Region states tend to have between five million and 20 million people. A region state must be small enough for its citizens to share certain economic and consumer interests but of adequate size to justify the infrastructure — communications and transportation links and quality professional services — necessary to participate economically on a global scale. It must for example, have at least one international airport and, more than likely, one good harbour with international-class freight-handing facilities. A region state must also be large enough to provide an attractive market for the broad development of leading consumer products. In other words, region states are not defined by their economies of scale in production (which, after all, can be leveraged from a base of any size through exports to the rest of the world) but rather by having reached efficient economies of scale in their consumption, infrastructure and professional services.

> (Ohmae, 1993, p.80)

Region states, Ohmae points out, are fundamentally tied to the global economy through mechanisms such as trade, export, and both inward and outward foreign investment — the most competitive region states are home not only to domestic or indigenous companies, but are attractive to the best companies from around the world. In the United States, Ohmae argues, region states can be distinguished by the level and extent of their insertion in the international economy and by their willingness to participate in global trade. Ohmae writes:

> In the United States, for example, the Japanese have already established about 120 'transplant' auto factories throughout the Mississippi Valley. More are on the way. As their share of the US auto industry's production grows, people in that region who look to these plants for their livelihoods and for the tax revenues needed to support local communities will stop caring whether the plants belong to US or Japanese-based companies. All they will care about are the regional economic benefits of having them there. In effect, as members of the Mississippi Valley region state, they will have leveraged the contribution of the plants to help their region become an active participant in the global economy. Consider the fate of Silicon Valley, that great early engine of much of America's microelectronics

industry. In the beginning it was an extremely open and entrepreneurial environment. Of late, however, it has become notably protectionist — creating industry associations, establishing a polished lobbying presence in Washington, and turning to 'competitiveness' studies as a way to get more federal funding for research and development. It has begun to discourage and even to bar foreign investment, let alone takeovers. The result is that Boise and Denver now prosper in electronics; Japan is developing a Silicon Island on Kyushsu; Taiwan is trying to create a Silicon Island of its own; and Korea is nurturing a Silicon Peninsula. This is the worst of all possible worlds: no new money in California and a host of newly energized and well-funded competitors. Elsewhere in California, not far from Silicon Valley, the story is quite different. When Hollywood recognized that it faced a severe capital shortage, it did not throw up protectionist barriers against foreign money. Instead, it invited Rupert Murdoch into 20th Century Fox, C. Itoh and Toshiba into Time-Warner, Sony into Columbia, and Matsushita into MCA. The result: a $10 billion dollar infusion of new capital and, equally important, $10 billion less for Japan or anyone else to set up a new Hollywood of their own.

(Ohmae, 1993, pp.84–5)

Ohmae also foresees possible tensions between America's region states and its federal government, as regions become increasingly important players in the global economy. He continues:

For the Clinton administration, the irony is that Washington today finds itself in the same relation to those region states that lie entirely or partially within its borders as was London with its North American colonies centuries ago. Neither central power could genuinely understand the shape or magnitude of the new flows of information, people and economic activity in the regions nominally under its control. Nor could it understand how counterproductive it would be to try to attest to distort those flows in the service of nation-defined interests. Now as then, only relaxed central control can allow the flexibility needed to maintain the links to regions gripped by an inexorable drive for prosperity.

(ibid., p.37)

The future of America, like its past, will be shaped by its regions. There can be little doubt that regions will be increasingly seen as key economic units in the global economy. Creating a new balance between regional and national authority will be a central issue in coming years in the United States and throughout the advanced industrial nations. It used to be that regions and nations gained competitive advantage based upon their natural endowments such as being close to waterways or having large stores of raw materials. Advances in transportation and communications technology are 'shrinking the world', providing the ability to move resources around as needed and giving all of us the ability to share the same experiences and communicate directly with one another.

So, why will regions remain important? There is another even more important economic function that regions play. Regions organize and provide the human capabilities — the knowledge and the skill — required for technological and economic progress. Regions provide the human infrastructure of people, knowledge and skill, the manufacturing infrastructure made up of the combined capabilities of firms, and the technological infrastructure required for economic development. Some regions specialize in high-technology, others in manufacturing, still others in finance and banking. Even though companies and people can use advanced telecommunications and computer systems to communicate, regions will retain their crucial economic role. It is their regional infrastructure of people, knowledge and skill which forms the core of their advantage. Regions provide the capabilities and the infrastructure required to compete in the global economy

As we enter a twenty-first century age of accelerating technological innovation and sweeping globalization, one thing appears certain: regions will continue their role at the centre of American life — they may even turn out to be more important than before.

REFERENCES

Florida, R. and Kenney, M. (1990) *The Breakthrough Illusion: Corporate America's Failure to Move from Innovation to Mass Production,* New York, Basic Books.

Geras, N. (1987) 'The hollow corporation', *Business Week,* 3 March.

Jackson, K.T. (1985) *Crabgrass Frontier: The Suburbanization of the United States,* New York, Oxford University Press.

Markusen, A. (1987) *The Economics and Politics of Territory,* Totowa NJ, Rowman and Littlefield.

Odum, H. and Moore, H.E. (1938) *American Regionalism: A Cultural History of National Integration,* New York, Henry Holt.

Ohmae, K. (1993) 'The rise of the region state', *Foreign Affairs,* vol.72, no.2, Spring, pp.78–87.

Perry, D. and Watkins, A.J. (1977) *The Rise of the Sunbelt Cities,* Beverly Hills, Sage.

Sale, K. (1975) *Power Shift,* New York, Vintage Books.

Sayer, A. and Walker, R. (1992) *The New Social Economy: Reworking the Division of Labour,* Oxford, Blackwell Publishers.

Turner, F.J. (1920) *The Frontier of American History,* reprint, New York, Holt, Rinehart and Winston, 1962.

US Congress, Joint Economic Committee (1986) *The Bi-Coastal Economy: Regional Patterns of Economic Growth During the Reagan Administration,* Washington DC, Government Printing Office.

Warner Jr, S.B. (1962) *Streetcar Suburbs: The Process of the Growth in Boston, 1870–1900,* Cambridge, MA, Harvard University Press.

FURTHER READING

Gelfand, Mark (1975) *A Nation of Cities: The Federal Government and Urban America, 1933–1965*, New York, Oxford University Press.

Jackson, Kenneth T. (1985) *Crabgrass Frontier: The Suburbanization of the United States*, New York, Oxford University Press.

Markusen, Ann (1987) *Regions: The Economics and Politics of Territory*, Totowa, N.J., Rowan and Littlefield.

Ohmae, Kenichi (1993) 'The rise of the region state', *Foreign Affairs*, vol.72, no.2, Spring, pp.78–87.

Perry, David and Watkins, Alfred J. (1977) *The Rise of the Sunbelt Cities*, Beverly Hills, Sage.

Storper, Michael and Walker, Richard (1989) *The Capitalist Imperative*, Oxford, Basil Blackwell.

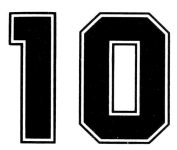

AMERICA IN TRANSITION: DOMESTIC CHANGE AND INTERNATIONAL COMPETITION

Stephen Burman ★

1 INTRODUCTION

The United States of America has exercised such a dominant role in international affairs since the Second World War that it comes as something of a shock to see its pre-eminence questioned. This is all the more true at a time when the collapse of communism has appeared to vindicate all the USA has stood for. But question it we must, for the end of the Cold War has left no aspect of international affairs unaffected. American leadership was based on the existence of an ordered system of international relations; as that order has collapsed so America's role as one of its main pillars must change The USA has sought a new role in the 1990s and it remains unclear whether it will be as dominant as before.

Whether American leadership continues will be determined less by international upheaval than by the capacity of its domestic economy to adapt to the pressures of globalization. Even during the Cold War many felt the USA was suffering from a creeping cancer that was undermining its vitality and power. Diagnoses of the crisis varied, some emphasizing a decline in moral standards and the loss of traditional disciplines, others stressing the growth of inequality and the loss of community, but most analyses agree that the basis of renewal has to be laid in a healthy economy.

The importance of the questions surrounding America's role in the world should not be underestimated. On the one hand, an enfeebled USA could leave a power vacuum at a time when the potential for conflict is still substantial and so make the achievement of a stable world order more difficult. On the other hand, a less dominant role for America might bring a more democratic and egalitarian tone to the governance of international affairs. Either way, the fate of many beyond America's shores will depend on a successful outcome of this transition. To explore these possibilities we must first review the implications of the end of the Cold War system and the debate on American decline it prompted. We shall see that the current state of flux presents the USA with opportunities for world leadership as well as great dangers to its position. Its diversity, and specifically its access to the supply of cheap labour, give it a potential competitive advantage over the other leading capitalist powers.

If it is to realize this advantage the USA will have to moderate the laissez-faire approach to the market that characterized the Reagan-Bush years. The 1980s saw the development of a more flexible labour market that was a harsh but perhaps necessary prelude to American economic renewal, but capitalizing on this will require going beyond free market orthodoxies that have marked its approach to globalization. Although market forces must be employed to avoid a reversion to the featherbedding of inefficiency in the name of community — enhanced competition from low-wage economies will require no less — the need to shape through collective action the global environment in which market forces operate must also be accepted.

It remains uncertain whether the Clinton administration has learned this lesson. The indications are that it has produced an economic revival that is restructuring the American economy around an optimum and uniquely American mix of cheap labour and hi-tech sectors (see Chapter 6). If these changes prove robust, they will provide the USA with a firm foundation for renewed leadership in world affairs. The stakes are high, for those who view America's influence on the world as malign will take no comfort from this conclusion; others may see it as the last best hope for humankind at the turn of the millennium.

2   THE END OF THE COLD WAR

2.1   A TIME OF UPHEAVAL

This is an era of massive change in international affairs, change on such a scale as to make commentary appear instantly dated and to bring all existing assumptions concerning international relations into question. A vision of what new order, if any, will emerge is clouded by current turbulence. The Cold War era has taken on a warm glow of nostalgia, seen retrospectively as having the benefits of relative stability associated with a balance of power. It may have felt much less safe at the time, but both the predictability and insecurity it generated were the consequence of nuclear competition between the superpowers. This provided a basis of competition that simultaneously guaranteed and threatened stability, and so determined the character of international affairs for more than a generation.

On the Soviet side of the superpower equation, change could not be more clear-cut. Not only has the Soviet state ceased to exist, its demise has also brought about the collapse of the socialist system it represented and defended. The change therefore involves more than the elimination of one player on the international stage; it also signals the elimination of the competing social system to capitalism. It was the struggle between socialism and capitalism which underlaid post-war world politics and which gave substance to the superpower rivalry, made manifest in a struggle between nation-states. The magnitude of the changes that have occurred can only be grasped by the realization that it is this fundamental struggle that has passed away with the triumph of capitalism, and that this accounts for everything now being brought into question.

2.2   AMERICA'S VULNERABILITY TO COMPETITION

The question of established roles in world affairs must therefore extend to the USA, despite the often-made claim that it was the victor in the Cold War. While carrying some plausibility, this claim should not lead to the conclusion that America can bask in its victory, relax and enjoy the prerogatives of its new status as sole superpower and undisputed world leader. On the contrary, much of America's hegemonic position during the Cold War stemmed from the protective role it played in the struggle between capitalism and socialism. The basis of this was the nuclear umbrella with which it gave shelter to its allies from the perceived military threat from the Soviet Union. It follows that if the military threat to the western socio-economic system has collapsed, then the need for this form of protection has disappeared. The demise of the Soviet Union has therefore made American nuclear capability effectively redundant in this context, and taken with it the greatest source of American power in world affairs. Victory in the Cold War then has proved to be pyrrhic, as much a threat to American hegemony as a platform for its extension.

The significance of this derives from the fact that its nuclear umbrella allowed the USA to exert discipline over its allies just as much as it inhibited adventurism by its enemies. America was able to exercise considerable influence over the shape and direction of post-war reconstruction of western Europe as much because of this protective role as because of its tangible material support. Similarly, the extension of US influence to other parts of the world, including the Middle East, Africa and South East Asia, was conditioned by the threat of the external enemy. The critical question therefore becomes, if the enemy has disappeared, where does this leave the USA in relation to its friends and allies? The answer is that it leaves America vulnerable to economic competition from them. This is true because the system which the USA managed is one in which economic competition is of the essence. The hallmark of America's hegemonic period was that the more extreme competitive characteristics of capitalism were moderated by the need for co-operation, within a framework of American domination, precisely because of the threat from outside the system. Without that constraint, the competitive imperative that results from the need to maximize profit is not necessarily a recipe for stability. Unchecked, it is more likely to produce chaos than a new world order.

SUMMARY

The world has moved on from the relative stability of the Cold War to a new era in which possibilities for chaos are as great as those for a new world order.

America's position in the Cold War depended on the perceived existence of the threat from socialism, spearheaded by the USSR.

The elimination of this threat has raised questions about America's vulnerability to economic competition from its capitalist allies.

3 A CHANGING ROLE FOR THE UNITED STATES

3.1 THE CASE FOR AMERICAN DECLINE

The irony then is that, having won the ultimate victory — beyond the wildest dreams of some of its most ardent cold warriors — the consequence has been to call into question the position of the USA in today's world. It is for this reason that discussions of recent international developments have been turned into a debate on American decline. More accurately, it has prompted the renewal of a debate which expressed the anxieties felt on this subject in America even during the Cold War. This debate was prompted by fears that America's leading role in world affairs was slowly but surely being undermined by longer-term trends, just as happened to all the other imperial powers in world history. The air of historical determinism implicit in such a view generated an atmosphere of fatalism and pessimism that is consonant with the *fin de siècle* but quite at odds with the optimism as to American capacities and potential expressed by its political leaders in the 1980s.

The debate on American decline gained intensity not only from the transformation in the world order but also as a result of the conflation of short- and long-term economic trends in the early 1990s. The prolonged recession experienced by the US economy after the rapid growth of the 1980s gave a sharp edge to the perception of decline. But it is important to separate problems associated with the vagaries of the economic cycle from underlying structural problems, if only because the two require different and perhaps inconsistent remedies. Cyclical recession, insofar as it is not self-correcting, is susceptible to a variety of stimulative measures, but these may exacerbate long-term problems if, for example, they focus on boosting consumption at the expense of the sort of investment needed to remedy deeper structural problems in the economy.

The argument that longer-term decline has been occurring beneath the cyclical variations has centred on the claim that there is a contradiction between the demands political and military leadership has placed on the USA and the strength of its domestic economy (Kennedy, 1988). The two are connected, in a phenomenon dubbed 'imperial overstretch', because the cost of servicing the strategic commitments generated by its world role has diverted economic resources away from civilian purposes and left the US economy weak. The argument carries an air of intractability because a hegemonic power cannot dispense with the costs of leadership if it is to retain its position. The domestic economic base should be the reservoir out of which the costs of leadership are borne; but failure here creates a vicious circle since a weak home economy makes the USA less able to meet its political commitments, with a consequent reduction in its status as a world power, which in turn further undermines its economic strength.

3.2   ALTERNATIVES TO DECLINE

The jeremiads in which these ideas are expounded can display an infatuation with the idea of decline that exaggerates the problems even as they are deplored. Other, less apocalyptic forms of relationship between political leadership and domestic economic strength are equally plausible: for example, insofar as these factors make competing demands on a finite level of resources, reducing the costs of leadership should permit a diversion of resources that enhances domestic economic strength and so recreates the basis for servicing leadership. Far from being a vicious circle, the relationship would be self-correcting.

The major alternative conceptualization of the relationship between economics and politics in this context is, however, the classic theory of imperialism. In this perspective they are seen to be mutually supporting (Burman, 1991), in the sense that political leadership is a euphemism for domination of other states, one of the fruits of which is the capacity for economic exploitation by the imperial power. Indeed the main reason for seeking political leadership is precisely the imperative to expand economic opportunities. The post-war era of American domination may be less dramatic than some earlier historical examples of imperial plunder, but few would doubt that benefits have accrued to US corporations from the relatively unfettered overseas investment and trade that US hegemony has entailed. And the complementarity is enhanced if the beneficial effects on the domestic rate of profit of arms production are included in the equation, for it is this which provided the main engine of post-war domestic growth in the US economy. Without it American society might have drifted into a permanent recession that would have threatened its social stability.

The truth lies somewhere in the middle. Just as military expenditure can boost demand when recession threatens, it can also promote inflation and under-investment in other parts of the economy when activity is high. If US hegemony aided overseas investment by American corporations, so too did it promote a regime of free trade which other countries, such as Germany and Japan, unburdened by the costs of military protection, were better able to take advantage of. There can be no hard and fast rule governing the relationship between domestic economic strength and international political leadership which holds across all historical circumstances; the possibilities are too numerous and cannot be reduced to a single dimension. It follows that any suggestion that American decline is inevitable due to the inexorable logic of its imperial position must be rejected. America's role in world affairs will change because its historical context will change. As it does, new expressions of the relationship between political leadership and economic strength will be found.

3.3   NEW OPPORTUNITIES FOR LEADERSHIP

The present period of upheaval, while undoubtedly presenting great challenges to the USA, can therefore be seen just as much as an era of opportunity as one in which it is doomed to decline. The basis for this is the fact that the newly emerging international order possesses the potential for great disorder. Centrifugal forces result firstly from the loss of rigid discipline on the behaviour of nation-states imposed by membership in one camp or the other of the Cold War, giving rein to the rediscovery of destructive nationalist tendencies; and secondly from the increased importance of economics in international affairs after the Cold War. The two aspects combine with the inherently competitive nature of the now global capitalist system to produce the threat of instability. The fact that this is most likely to manifest itself in new nationalist antagonisms helps to demonstrate the fallacy of the suggestion that the increased importance of economics in international affairs makes nation-states superfluous. It is widely argued that since the increased international mobility of capital and the power of transnational corporations have restricted the freedom of nation-states to make economic policy, their role in determining the flow of events has become marginal, and that even as powerful a country as the USA will become increasingly subject to these transnational forces. In fact almost exactly the opposite is the case.

The removal of artificial barriers to trade makes the home base more important rather than less for competitiveness. Competitive success derives from specialization in local networks of industries in allied fields which create a mutually enhancing pattern of skills and other resources (Porter, 1990). Silicon Valley in California is a classic example of a network upon which comparative advantage can be built and forays into the international marketplace can take place successfully. The size and location of these networks may vary, but they always arise under the jurisdiction of a single state which plays a critical part in determining whether they are economically competitive.

More generally, capitalism, as it has become global, has not so changed its nature that it can regulate itself. Even a market-oriented system requires a political framework in which to operate. That framework may range from *laissez-faire* at one extreme to substantial state control at the other, but the level of direct intervention does not alter the character of the framework as the product of political choice. The reason capitalist competition would manifest itself in struggles between nation-states is that firms — including multinationals, all of which retain a home base — which are uncompetitive will tend to enlist the support of their home states to try to redress the economic imbalance. State intervention would then transform the economic struggle into a political or even a military conflict. What is required therefore is a global political system which can prevent these tendencies from getting out of hand, pre-empting the escalation of competition turning into conflict.

One solution is to have a perfect balance of power between all the nation-states, in which discipline is exerted and stability achieved solely on the basis of fear. While fear of retaliation undoubtedly provides one element of international restraint, it is unlikely to be sufficient to create long-term stability because nation-states bring unequal resources to the competitive struggle. At the other extreme, stability could be provided by a single country acting as a benign autocrat, chastizing all who threaten the goal of stability. Again, this is an unlikely prospect. The temptation to turn absolute power to its own advantage would be too great for any nation-state that achieved such pre-eminence. In practice no state could become so powerful; the post-war experience of the USA, notably in Vietnam, demonstrates that the burdens of acting as global policeman are beyond the resources of even the most dominant state.

Far more sustainable than either of these alternatives is a system of co-operation based on the recognition of mutual interest in the free but stable conduct of international trade. Those who are optimistic about the role of America in the new world order claim it remains the country best able to guarantee this consensual order. This is a view reinforced by America's involvement in the Gulf War (1991) where its leading role was sanctioned by a broadly constructed, carefully crafted and assiduously maintained consensus in the United Nations. Since that conflict pessimistic views as to America's capacity have reasserted themselves as foreign policy has often appeared to lack direction and effectiveness, not least in the Gulf itself, reinforcing the perception that the Gulf excursion was no more than a hiccough in America's decline from its hegemonic pinnacle.

It is difficult to separate the surface noise created by everyday events from the longer-term problems, but to judge the hypothesis of decline we need to evaluate the core of the argument, the capacity of the American economy to respond to the challenge of gobalization. With America no longer enjoying the protection afforded by the Cold War and nuclear pre-eminence, it is this which will, in the long run, determine its ability to compete and thus its potential as a world leader. Even those optimistic about America's potential have to recognize the dangers inherent in the domestic structure of American society. To obtain a clear picture of America's potential for world leadership we must therefore analyse the domestic situation.

SUMMARY

Recent trends have intensified a pre-existing debate about whether America is in long term decline as a world power.

Arguments for American decline based on the idea of imperial over-stretch have been exaggerated. The transition to a new world order offers America opportunities for continuing to influence world affairs.

There will continue to be a need for world leadership. Whether the USA will be able to meet this need will depend crucially on the strength of its domestic economy and society.

4 DOMESTIC CHANGE IN AMERICA

4.1 A SICK SOCIETY?

The continuing buoyancy of its economy in the late 1990s has masked many of the problems of American society. These problems have three inter-related dimensions: social, cultural and economic. Socially, the threat of violence in everyday life, the decline of traditional family structures, the recreation of the idea of the undeserving poor that is guiding a new, tough approach to welfare, the persistence of poverty amidst plenty, the rise of the drug culture, the failure of the education system to teach the essentials needed for effectiveness in ordinary life, all testify to the continuing seriousness of the situation. Added to this, just beneath the surface lies the added strain of racial and ethnic tension. The black or Hispanic ghetto remains the clearest expression of this tangle of pathology and it is the abject condition of its minorities which symbolizes America's failure to live up to its aspirations and generates the fear that, when the economic boom is over, this failure will bring the social system crashing down in an orgy of bitterness, recrimination and violence. To some extent this might be tempered by the growth of a large black middle class over the last twenty years, but it is the heavily discriminated against underclass, probably 25 per cent of the black population, that represents the real political and economic problem.

There is a sense in which this crisis goes beyond party politics, since the description of so many of its elements is shared by both the right and the left. The political differences arise in the diagnosis of the causes of, and the prescription for, curing the problem. The right was ascendant for more than a decade, but with the election of President Clinton a left analysis gained ground. The influence of the New Right has not been lost entirely, however. While the dramatic victory of the Republicans in the 1994 congressional elections on a strongly right-wing platform has not produced the revolution in government it promised, this is in part because the administration moved to the right, adopting and implementing the Republican agenda on issues such as welfare. Although the Republicans have failed to capitalize on their victory politically, they have won the ideological battle by causing the Clinton administration to transcend traditional boundaries and take on many traits associated with a conservative approach.

President Clinton was elected because he was felt to have the best chance of reversing the generalized sense of malaise that prevailed at the start of the 1990s, the feeling of a society on the brink of collapse, dominated by fear, violence, antagonism and misery. One of the key elements of his approach was the belief that it was essential for America to focus on reversing its domestic decline before settling on the role it might play in the post-Cold War world. This renewed focus on domestic affairs drew urgency from the perceived sense of a culture in disintegration. It is impossible to separate social problems from the cultural ones because the cultural problem is rooted in the same loss of values that has permitted the social problems to develop. Values of thrift, hard work, self-discipline, family and loyalty are seen to have been replaced by a culture which celebrates greed, selfishness, hedonism, consumerism, narcissism, instant satisfaction and superficiality of all kinds. The crassness, slavish commercialism and dumbing down of mass culture, when combined with a high degree of political alienation (witness levels of voter turnout that jeopardize democracy), reinforces the message that the USA is no longer the vibrant exemplar for others to follow. Instead, the truth is dawning, at home and abroad, that, despite its buoyant economy, the conservative remedies of the 1990s have not restored America's position as the embodiment of world aspirations for freedom and justice. But whilst America may no longer be the promised land it once was, it still represents an enormous attraction for poorer immigrants from the South.

4.2   MORAL DECLINE AND FOREIGN POLICY

The American belief in the need to give absolute priority to putting its house in order holds its own dangers. There is a tradition of isolationism in American foreign policy that could easily be revived by this mentality. The problem is not that this would lead to a simple withdrawal from world affairs; the real problem is that isolationism is a misnomer in the modern context since its roots lie in resentment, anger and frustration, and it is these, rather than withdrawal, which would govern policy, to the detriment of all. This is a mentality whose invariable accompaniment is the belief that American foreign policy has helped others at the expense of its own well-being, allowing other countries to prosper while America has continued to carry the burdens of maintaining global stability. This applies not only to competitors like the EU and Japan, but also to Third World countries who are now benefiting from the export of American jobs, under the aegis of a system of free trade that the USA itself has done so much to sponsor.

The reaction to a sense that the USA has become a decadent society is therefore to create enemies abroad who are seen as culprits in America's decline. If it is informed by this sentiment, foreign policy could become an instrument of revenge. The USA would not simply withdraw from world affairs but use its power to gain a narrow advantage over other countries with the rationale that it was reversing past injustices. The recent revival of protectionism in the USA suggest this perspective is gaining ground. The dangers of adopting such an approach is that it would initiate a downward spiral of retaliation, with the potentially devastating consequences that the twentieth century has already demonstrated.

The perception of the moral decline of American society is also relevant to foreign policy because, as so many commentators have argued, one of America's greatest assets as a world leader has been its moral example. The Carter administration, for example, placed moral leadership at the heart of its foreign policy by stressing the importance of human rights from the outset. Its reason for doing so is understandable at a time when Vietnam and Watergate had undermined American moral authority, even though it was intended as much to restore America's faith in itself as to influence others. The contradictions in this policy became apparent in America's continued support of regimes throughout the world with abysmal human rights records. But the Carter administration learned *realpolitik* the hard way with the Iran hostages saga (1979–80) and the Soviet invasion of Afghanistan (1979). The resulting shifts in government policy towards a more realistic perspective only added to the confusion surrounding the principles that were governing policy. This experience suggests that while the moral dimension is not irrelevant to the exercise of American influence, it is rarely the primary factor. The lesson is that social and cultural issues speak to notions of example, whereas leadership speaks to power. The two are not mutually exclusive, but neither are they synonymous, and it is power which is the more relevant force.

Further, we must ask whether the current social and cultural problems of America are unique in their extent. When in recent years were inequality, consumerism, and violence absent from American society? When were African-Americans not badly treated in its history? All such traits were evident when America was at the height of its post-war power. Their existence did little to undermine its world role then, and this has remained true in the post-Cold War world. Social and cultural problems are relevant primarily as they pertain to the real source of potential weakness, one which is directly related to America's power in foreign affairs, that is the state of its economy.

4.3 ECONOMIC CHANGE AND THE PROBLEM OF COMPETITIVENESS

Despite an extended period of economic growth through most of the 1990s, it is only at the end of the decade that the benefits are percolating through to the living standards of ordinary families (see Chapter 6). The fact that it has taken a period of sustained economic growth that is almost without precedent to return living standards to earlier levels does not bode well for family incomes when the inevitable slowdown does occur. The underlying problem that this points to is a series of imbalances that continue to distort the US economy. The most general of these is a bias towards consumption at the expense of personal savings and longer-term investment activity. Taxpayers have responded to the tension between the ever-present inducement to consume and stagnation in disposable income by pressuring government to reduce taxes, so as to leave more income free for consumption. The constraint this has put on politicians of all parties is virtually absolute and it is a shibboleth for any aspiring American politicians to eschew rises in personal taxes. When even incomes protected from increased taxation have proven inadequate to finance desired levels of consumption, Americans have reduced their savings rate to below zero and taken on unprecedented levels of personal debt. Many have felt able to adopt what would appear to be an imprudent course because they have seen the value of the stock market triple under the Clinton administration. Share ownership is widespread in the USA and the rise in the market has given stockholders a feeling that the growing value of their capital assets means they can forego more traditional forms of saving. Again, the danger of this is obvious: the stock market cannot continue to rise at this rate indefinitely and whether the inevitable reverse takes the form of a crash or a soft landing, when it comes it will reveal starkly the unwisdom of an economy running without a cushion of savings to fall back on.

The federal government has found itself in a straitjacket in responding to these developments because, with the option of raising taxes ruled out, it has also found it difficult to cut expenditure. Most of the federal budget is earmarked for programmes such as social security, interest payments on the national debt, or military expenditure that each administration for their own reasons has treated as sacrosanct in recent years. Cuts have therefore been concentrated on a relatively few areas. One has been infrastructural expenditure, the inadequacy of which is apparent in dilapidated roads, bridges and public amenities. Another is welfare, cutbacks in which have contributed to the growth of inequality and the perpetuation of an underclass that is a visible indictment of the American dream. Economic growth has eliminated the chronic federal budget deficit but the resources this has made available to the federal government have not been employed to redress social problems. Instead the market has been relied upon to spread wealth via a trickle-down mechanism. In fact there has been little trickle down; profits have been distributed to shareholders bent on a quick return, used to pay vastly inflated remuneration to higher executives, or employed in either fending off or making take-over bids. The short-term, speculative orientation this gives rise to reinforces the concern that the US economic boom in the 1990s is built on shaky foundations.

Even a period of non-inflationary growth sustained beyond what most economists would have thought possible has its negative side. The rate of growth in the economy appears to have undergone a secular increase. One consequence is the transformation of the labour market. Stable career patterns and life-long jobs are becoming a thing of the past. Constant innovation, although it creates many new jobs, also engenders massive insecurity among workers. In a society where the social safety net in terms of welfare, health, pensions and education is not as comprehensive as in Europe, the effect of uncertainty in employment is doubly crippling. The job creation record of the American economy has been remarkable and many new jobs are highly paid and in technologically advanced sectors, but many are part-time, low paid and temporary and devoid of the accompanying social benefits that were until recently the norm. As traditional industries have declined the model of a single, usually male worker supporting a nuclear family has been supplanted by households in which both partners have to work, and even to moonlight, to maintain family income. As one saw has it — I know the economy is creating a lot of jobs; my wife and I have four of them!

In sum, the negative side of the US economic miracle of the 1990s consists of an undue reliance on unsustainable stock market appreciation, too little saving and a boom in employment whose price has been, until very recently, the proliferation of low paying, insecure work which, when combined with cutbacks on welfare and soaring income at the top of the scale, has produced growing inequality and prevented the benefits of growth from penetrating deeply into the society. Only since 1996, or thereabouts, have American average wages been rising, so any of the adverse trends have been masked by economic growth. When a downturn occurs, as it must, the new harshness of the economic climate will be exposed and, in the absence of remedial measures of which there seem no sign, many of the more vulnerable groups in society will suffer as they have not done for generations. The question that remains is what the implications of this pattern are for America's international competitiveness and hence for its ability to continue to play the leading role in international affairs.

SUMMARY

The social fabric of American society is threatened by problems in race relations, education, the family, drugs and the inner cities.

Underlying these problems is a perceived loss of moral values and standards in a debased culture.

But the relevance to foreign policy of these problems is not demonstrated.

More significant is the state of the American economy. Despite a long period of growth there remain significant weaknesses and this brings into question America's competitiveness and ability to maintain a leading role in international affairs.

5   AMERICA'S COMPETITIVE ADVANTAGE

5.1   THE RESILIENCE AND DIVERSITY OF THE AMERICAN ECONOMY

It is impossible to deny the weaknesses of the US economy and their impact on American competitiveness; equally, it is possible to exaggerate them. The flaw in the pessimistic view of American competitiveness lies in the assumption that there is a single model for economic effectiveness. Implicit in the argument is the desirability of a model of economic development based on manufacturing investment which permits specialization in high value added goods and the development of a well trained, skilled labour force and is underpinned by co-operation between government, business and labour that is single minded in its determination to raise economic output and develop overseas markets.

In a whole range of advanced economic activities, such as aerospace, pharmaceuticals, scientific equipment and computers, the USA is highly competitive with other countries; its low-wage sector is also competitive if compared with equivalent sectors elsewhere. The process of conflation disguises this and makes the USA seem weak by comparison with other advanced economies which do not contain a large low-wage sector to act as a drag on their macro-economic indicators. Most importantly, conflation disguises the advantages of the mixed American economic structure, in particular those resulting from the proximity of a Third World labour force. While it is the case that investment in the advanced sector is critical to economic success, equally vital is a plentiful supply of cheap labour. Despite technological advances which eliminate jobs or create a demand for highly skilled labour, unskilled labour remains essential to an effective economy. It is needed in the agricultural sector, in many service industries, and to provide a cheap manufacturing base. It is wrong to imagine that even an advanced economy can export all of its unskilled jobs, leaving only high skill, high-wage jobs at home. Both types of jobs are required in a balanced economy, and the USA has a labour force more appropriate to this balance than its competitors.

America has benefited from this balance historically through immigration, which has replenished the unskilled element of the labour force. While it has been a major source of its historic vitality, immigration has posed great challenges to America's social cohesion. In general the USA has shown the flexibility needed to cope with the adjustment problems inherent in massive movements of labour. Indeed by facilitating upward mobility for the existing labour force, immigration has reinforced notions of an American Dream of economic success for all-comers. Short-term problems of absorption have thereby been outweighed by a longer-term contribution to social cohesion and have resulted in a balance between dynamism and stability. The process has taken on a new lease of life since 1965 when changes in quotas permitted new waves of immigration into the USA from peoples of predominantly Hispanic and Asian origin, a supply of labour that has been complemented by a substantial, though unquantifiable, stream of illegal migration.

While the tension between whites and Hispanics in California demonstrates all too vividly the social problems that can arise from economically-driven migration, some of the new immigrant groups are providing a classic illustration of economic renewal within the context of global restructuring. Immigrants to New York from the Dominican Republic are combining labour that is cheap by American standards with entrepreneurship to generate ethnic success stories in areas such as the garment industry. They are overcoming the problem of capital generation by traditional, informal banking mechanisms based on a trust that is perhaps only possible in a tight-knit, marginal community. In the process they are creating dynamic enclaves within the American economy in much the same fashion as earlier waves of immigrants. This demonstrates that it is possible to make a significant contribution to American economic growth in a way that relies neither on outside support nor on the development of highly capital-intensive, technologically-advanced industry. Of equal significance in the contemporary world, the dynamism of this sector demonstrates the capacity of the American economic and social structure, unique among advanced societies, to remain competitive with low-cost Third World economies.

The North American Free Trade Agreement (NAFTA) will further this by securing for exploitation by American capital a massive supply of cheap labour in Mexico, with the added advantage of minimizing social problems since capital can without penalty move to where labour is rather than the other way around. This will complete a three-dimensional pattern of supply of cheap labour for the American economy; first, immigrant labour, both legal and illegal, available for work in agriculture, service industries and basic manufacturing within the USA; second, factories in the so-called maquilladora area specializing in the assembly of cheap manufactures which have developed rapidly around the USA-Mexican border; and third, with the advent of the NAFTA, access in principle to the whole of the Mexican labour force, the bulk of which will work for far less than typical US wages. The net effect of this is to increase the rate of return for American capital; although this involves substantial inequality, it is sustainable because it is based on common interests in the sense that even the low wages paid to this segment of the labour force are higher than any immediate alternative available to them.

5.2 CONSTRAINTS ON ECONOMIC GROWTH AMONG AMERICA'S COMPETITORS

Comparison with America's main competitors, the European Union and Japan, is instructive. Immigration is becoming an increasing problem within the EU and is likely to grow in significance. This is not due to an absence of cheap labour on its periphery; on the contrary, there is an abundant supply, for different reasons, both to the south and to the east. The problem lies in reconciling the economic imperative to capitalize on this with the social problems arising from the absorption of migrant labour. The history of EU countries demonstrates the difficulty they have in effecting such change harmoniously, particularly in times of economic recession where the racism of EU societies manifests itself in anti-immigrant sentiment. While it would be naïve to claim America is devoid of racism in this respect, the contrast with its tradition of openness when confronting these dilemmas remains striking. The rigidity of European societies seems likely to restrict the migration of cheap labour from outside the EU below the optimum level and therefore to act as an increasing break on its economic development.

Japan fares no better in this comparison. Foreigners constitute no more than 1 per cent of the workforce and half of this is the result of illegal migration.

It has been estimated that in 2000 Japan will have a labour shortage of 3.5 million workers. The problem is accentuated by the reduction in the size of the agricultural population which formerly acted as a reserve for the expanding urban labour force. Japan also suffers from a problem evident in the EU, an ageing population in which the ratio between the working age population and its dependant groups will worsen dramatically in the near future. A further mismatch arises from the fact that the need is for more unqualified labour whereas most immigrant labour is highly educated. Such tensions can be assuaged by a massive increase in immigration, but government, business and unions are all firm in their publicly-stated opposition to mass migration, for what are termed social reasons. The danger is that at least some of the gap will therefore be filled by a growth of illegal immigration, a solution which is no solution at all since in the long run it is likely to exacerbate the social problems that are a euphemism for a racist response by the native population.

The alternative solution is the export of jobs, taking capital to those areas which have reserves of cheap labour. The historical connotations of this are, however, problematic both for Japan and Europe since they raise the spectre of past imperial exploitation. This strategy is beset by a dilemma: if jobs are exported the capital employed requires a secure long-term environment free from the threat of expropriation in which to operate; but this is virtually impossible to guarantee. Either the receiving country's political independence is respected and the risk of a political challenge to the security of exported capital accepted; or security of investment is obtained in the short term by the creation of an imperial relationship with the receiving country, with all the long-term risks of repression, rebellion and destabilization history has shown this entails.

In Japan's case, the vast supply of cheap labour in the rest of south-east Asia provides an obvious reserve to tap as a way out of its economic problems. But, with memories of the former co-prosperity sphere in mind, other south-east Asian countries are unlikely to cede control of their needs to Japan. They are likely to adopt the strategy of using overseas capital drawn from global capital markets in combination with indigenous cheap labour as a platform for self-sustaining growth of their own economies. It seems likely that China in particular will follow in the footsteps of Singapore and Taiwan, welcoming overseas capital but only for these reasons, in its own interests and under its own continuing form of political control. Similarly, although the former communist states of eastern Europe provide a tempting source of cheap labour for Germany and other EU countries, and while these states are undoubtedly desperate to attract capital in the short term, their experience of oppression in the twentieth century and the political sophistication of their societies is unlikely to make them susceptible in the longer term to act as economic fodder for the enrichment of the EU.

Consequently, in the longer term a further danger arises: even if the export of jobs avoids the dangers associated with instability and lack of political control, it may well become self-defeating, benefiting the receiving countries more than those exporting capital, and succeeding only in creating new economic rivals. Were this to be the outcome, it would condemn Europe and Japan to repeat the experience of America, whose post-war investment in their devastated economies contributed to turning them into its leading competitors. In light of this array of problems it is difficult to see how either immigration or the export of jobs can fail to create a real constraint on the growth of both the EU and Japan.

SUMMARY

The American economy is more resilient and competitive than is often thought.

Its strength lies in its diversity, in particular in the availability of a substantial supply of cheap labour which acts as a complement to the advanced sectors of its economy.

America's leading competitors, Japan and the EU, will both have difficulty securing an adequate supply of cheap labour, either from immigration or the export of capital, and this will constrain their economic development.

6 THE RENEWAL OF AMERICAN LEADERSHIP

6.1 ECONOMIC RENEWAL AND THE MARKET

The relatively favourable position this places the USA in has made it possible to achieve a role in world affairs in the 1990s which is a good deal more promising than many scenarios of decline forecast at the beginning of the decade. Whether it can maintain this position is likely to depend on whether it can develop a strategy towards globalization that goes beyond the one that served it well in the Cold War era.

The basic assumption of the Reagan-Bush era was the classical one outlined in any introductory economics textbook, that is, a perfectly competitive market leads not only to full employment of the economy's resources but also to their optimal distribution. The implication for policy was taken to be that although perfect competition may never be achievable in practice, any movement towards it would improve social welfare. The goal therefore became to eliminate all market distortions, most notably those arising from the intervention of the state. This approach was applied very selectively; more attention was placed on distortions to the labour market produced by trade unions and welfare than on the consequences of the power of oligopolistic corporations; the employment of deficit financing for defence spending was Keynesian in all but name. Nonetheless, the crucial implication of the market philosophy of the Reagan-Bush years was the eschewing of any attempt at a government-sponsored industrial strategy on the grounds that market-based competition was a much better route to improved efficiency. During the 1980s the result was a decline in industrial competitiveness compared to countries such as Germany and Japan which recognized the effectiveness of a partnership between the state and business to create an environment in which market forces could produce their admitted but limited efficiency gains.

In the 1990s, despite the advent of an ostensibly more interventionist administration under President Clinton, in practice economic policy has changed little. There has certainly been more evidence in trade policy of a strategic partnership between American business and government (Garten, 1998) to the point where American economic nationalism has caused considerable friction with its competitors. There has also been a great deal more fiscal prudence as the federal budget deficit has been brought under control, with consequent beneficial effects on inflation and interest rates. But, for the bulk of economic growth the Clinton administration has continued to rely on market forces, notably a rapid rate of technological innovation, high consumer demand, growth in overseas markets as globalization has taken root, and the increasing employment of cheap labour both at home through immigration and abroad through capital export. The potential of the US economy has been realized because a transfer of resources into the advanced sector of the economy has been combined with the development of manufacturing based on the availability of cheap labour within the North American Free Trade Area. The key to economic competitiveness for the USA has been to achieve a balance between high- and low-tech sectors in its continental economy that takes advantage of its diversity and range. America has achieved an optimum mix of technologies on the basis of an appropriate distribution of both labour and capital within a single market. Despite the rhetoric of improving skills for all, this has proved a much more promising strategy for the USA than the pursuit of ever greater productivity from a more highly-skilled but static labour force.

6.2 LEADERSHIP AND THE INTERNATIONAL MARKET

Of equal importance is the need for continued American leadership on the international stage. If, as we have argued, America's competitors face constraints on their economic development because of the social consequences of immigration and because of their inability to secure the conditions of accumulation overseas, the fundamental condition for global economic stability is inter-state co-operation to fulfil the common interest in growth. This collective interest does not preclude competition but it must outweigh the destructive tendencies inherent in the capitalist mode of production. Achieving the appropriate balance between co-operation and competition as capitalism becomes global is not something that can be left to the market; it will require political leadership of a high order. To some extent this leadership must be collective and in this sense the era of unquestioned American hegemony has indeed passed. On the other hand, although concerted leadership will have to rest on consensus, the need for a single state to act as first among equals in managing the means by which the agreed goals are achieved remains compelling. The USA is the only country, for the foreseeable future, with the requisite combination of qualities for meeting this need and securing the conditions for the peaceful development of a global capitalist system. Hence we have come full circle, resuscitating and transforming the protective role on which American hegemony was based in the Cold War era.

6.3 THE SPECTRE OF PROTECTIONISM

At the other extreme from this benign and perhaps optimistic view of a harmoniously managed system of world capitalism is the spectre of each leading economic power attempting to create its own security through a protectionist regime. Domestic pressures to follow this path exist in the USA and are not difficult to understand. The gobalization of the capitalist economy involves massive shifts in production and not all sectors of its economy can benefit equally; some workers are bound to suffer substantially from the export of jobs, for example; equally, free trade in agricultural produce combined with the growth of world-wide surpluses must harm American farmers even if it reduces costs for the rest of the USA.

The resulting tensions are by no means trivial and the post-Cold War environment reinforces them. In its hegemonic phase the USA could afford to take a tolerant approach to, for example, Japanese trade practices because they did little to threaten its domestic economy and, by strengthening the Japanese economy, they provided the bulwark against communism that was the prime goal of American policy. In a world where the threat from communism has diminished such tolerance becomes anachronistic and US policy has become more narrowly self-serving in consequence (Trubowitz, 1998). But this trend reinforces the importance of managed change. If this is not done effectively such pressures will undermine American support for global restructuring and free trade which, if their excesses are curbed by collective co-operation, remain in the interest both of America and its competitors.

A more realistic alternative to a competitive descent into national protectionism is the attempt by the leading economic powers to obtain security and restrict competition by creating their own trading blocs. These blocs would be a USA-dominated Americas, a German-dominated Europe, and a Japanese-dominated south-east Asia. Should this come to pass the USA would remain well placed to compete. NAFTA may be seen as an insurance policy against this eventuality, although the slow progress on the plan for a Free Trade Area of the Americas (FTAA) by 2010 agreed at the Miami Summit in 1994 confirms that, although much touted, competitive regionalism seems unlikely to occur. It assumes too great a docility on the part of the junior partners within these blocs and, correspondingly, too much capacity and willingness to impose themselves on others in their sphere by the leading powers.

This is particularly true of Europe and Japan, neither of which is in the position to take the military and political responsibilities that would be necessary to assert control of a sphere of influence composed of reluctant client states. Each of these would have an interest in playing the leading powers off against the other, and would find other leading powers only too willing to co-operate in doing so. More than half of world trade already takes places between, rather than within, these regions, and it is difficult to envisage any one power being able to alter substantially this percentage in the face of the combined opposition of potential clients and rivals.

SUMMARY

The key to restoring American economic competitiveness is to restruc-ture its economy so as to create an optimum balance between advanced technology and cheap labour sectors.

This is best done by rejecting the doctrine of an unfettered market in favour of a strategy of government intervention to create the long-term environment in which American business can compete.

Maintaining the conditions for growth world wide will also require political leadership to manage the destructive tendencies of unregu-lated markets. Although this will be more collective than in the recent period of American hegemony, the USA retains the capacity to remain first among equals.

If co-operation is not achieved the alternative is a descent into protec-tionism. Although this would be destructive, the NAFTA would help the USA survive such competition more effectively than its rivals.

7   CONCLUSION

On balance then, what appears to be the most idealistic resolution to the current turbulence, the extension of free trade based on concerted leader-ship, and the predominance of co-operation over destructive competition between nation-states, is also the most probable outcome. It is an outcome which will continue to require a substantial leadership role for the USA. The domestic weaknesses in the United States' economy and society therefore need not act to undermine its international role. Politically, the stalemate created by the division between a Democratic administration and a Republican-controlled congress since 1994 has limited radical domestic action, but there has been a sufficiently widespread consensus on foreign affairs to prevent the checks and balances of pluralism from interfering with America's ability to act internationally. The fact that the Clinton administra-tion has not provided the answer to the social and cultural problems which beset the USA is, to a considerable extent, immaterial to its competitiveness because these problems are by their nature perennial and have over time had little impact on the USA's role in the world. American competitiveness remains primarily determined by the performance of its economy.

On this front comparisons have been misleading. In respect of at least one crucial factor which contributes to competitiveness, labour supply, the USA is better placed than the other leading world economic powers — the EU and Japan. The US economy is more diverse than those of its competitors and encompasses not only advanced sectors in manufacturing and services but also mass manufacturing, agriculture, and other services which depend on a supply of cheap labour for their effectiveness. The development of the North American Free Trade Agreement will only enhance the USA's advantage in this respect. Both aspects are critical to a balanced economy, but its competitors will have great difficulty in achieving the appropriate balance internally since they will be unable, for social reasons, to import the necessary labour. They will therefore have to secure access to it beyond their borders. They may attempt to solve this problem by creating trading blocks, but these have little prospect of success since all the leading economic powers have a greater interest in a global system of managed competition than in destructive regional competition. The inability of its competitors to secure access to cheap labour places them in a vulnerable position and their weakness will perpetuate dependence on the USA as the primary global guarantor of the conditions of economic growth and political stability. The USA, therefore, is well placed to maintain its economic competitiveness and on this basis continue its leading role in the modern world.

FURTHER READING

Burman, S. (1991) *America in the Modern World: The Transcendence of US Hegemony,* London, Harvester/Wheatsheaf.

Garten, Jeffrey, E. (1998) *The Big Ten: The Big Emerging Markets and How They Will Change Our Lives,* New York, Basic Books.

Kennedy, P. (1988) *The Rise and Fall of the Great Powers: Economic Change and Military Conflict from 1500 to 2000,* London, Unwin Hyman.

Porter, M. (1990) *The Competitive Advantage of Nations,* London, Macmillan.

Trubowitz, Peter (1998) *Defining the National Interest: Conflict and Change in American Foreign Policy,* Chicago, University of Chicago Press.

INDEX

ACKNOWLEDGEMENTS

Grateful acknowledgement is made to the following sources for permission to reproduce material in this book:

CHAPTER 2

Illustrations   p.9: reproduced with permission from the Archives of the Coca-Cola Company; pp.14, 21: courtesy Sears, Roebuck and Co; p.16: photograph by Adolphe Wittemann. Museum of the City of New York. The L.H. Bogart Collection; p.22: from the Collections of Henry Ford Museum & Greenfield Village; p.24: from the Caulfield and Shook Collection, Photographic Archives (Neg CS71790), Ekstrom Library, University of Louisville, Louisville, Kentucky; p.29: The Advertising Archives.

CHAPTER 3

Illustrations   p.43, p.44, p.46, p.50: from the Collections of Henry Ford Museum & Greenfield Village; p.62: George V. Klein/*Scientific American*.

Table   Table 3.1: courtesy of the Ford Motor Company.

CHAPTER 5

Figures   Figure 5.2: illustration by Ian Worpole from 'The mechanization of design and manufacturing' by Thomas G. Gunn, *Scientific American*, September 1982, domestic edition; Figures 5.3, 5.6a, 5.6b: OECD (1991) *Economic Studies*, No.17, Autumn 1991; Figure 5.4: Rivlin, A. (1992) *Reviving the American Dream*, The Brookings Institution; Figure 5.5: illustration by Andrew Christie from 'Toward a new industrial America' by Suzanne Berger, Michael L. Dertouzos, Richard K. Lester, Robert M. Solow and Lester C. Thurow, *Scientific American*, June 1989, domestic edition; Figure 5.8: Baily, M.M. and Gordon, R.J. (1988) 'The productivity slowdown, measurement issues and the explosion of computer power', *Brookings Papers on Economic Activity*, 2, pp.347–431, The Brookings Institution; Figure 5.9: adapted from 'Technology, employment and U.S. competitiveness' by Richard M. Cyert and David C. Mowery, *Scientific American*, May 1989, domestic edition.

Tables   Table 5.1: OECD (1992) *Historical Statistics*; Table 5.4: adapted from OECD (1992) *International Direct Investment: Policies and Trends in the 1980s*; Table 5.6: Baily, M.M. and Gordon, R.J. (1988) 'The production slowdown, measurement issues and the explosion of computer power', *Brookings Papers on Economic Activity*, 2, pp.347–431, The Brookings Institution; Table 5.7: adapted from Lawrence, R.Z. (1984) *Can America Compete?*, The Brookings

Institution; Tables 5.8, 5.9, 5.10: National Urban League (1992) *The State of Black America*.

Photograph   p.130: Ampex Systems Corporation.

CHAPTER 6

Figures   Figure 6.1: Waters, R., Labate, J. and Edgcliffe-Johnson, A. (1999) 'Dow Jones breaks 10,000 mark', *Financial Times*, 17 March 1999; Figure 6.3b: *OECD Economic Surveys: The United States 1997*, OECD; Figure 6.4: Borjas, G. J., Freeman, R. B. and Katz, L. F. (1997) 'How much do immigration and trade affect labor market outcomes?', *Brookings Papers on Economic Activity*, 1, The Brookings Institution; Figure 6.9: Farber, H.S. (1997) 'The changing face of job loss in the United States, 1981–1995', *Brookings Papers on Economic Activity: Microeconomics*, The Brookings Institution.

Table   Table 6.3: adapted from Krugman, P. (1998) 'America the boastful', *Foreign Affairs*, 77(3), © 1998 Council on Foreign Relations Inc.

CHAPTER 8

Table   Table 8.7: Fuchs, V.R. (1986) 'Sex differences in economic well being', *Science*, 232, pp.459–64, © American Association for the Advancement of Science.

Photographs   p.209: courtesy of AT & T Archives; p.220: courtesy of the MetLife Archives; p.222: Museum of American Textile Industry.

CHAPTER 9

Figures   Figure 9.1: Harrison, B. (1993) 'South-east leads US recovery', *Financial Times*, 18 August 1993.

Text   Ohmae, K. (1993) 'The rise of the region state', *Foreign Affairs*, Spring 1993, pp.78–87, © Kenichi Ohmae.

knead

expert breads
baguettes • pretzels
brioche • pastries
pizza • ravioli • pies

carol tennant

MQP
MQ Publications Ltd

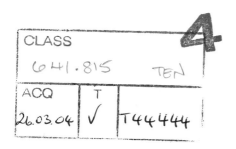
Copyright © 2001 MQ Publications Limited
Text copyright © 2001 Carol Tennant

Project editor: Kate John
Text editor: Coralie Dorman
Designer: Elizabeth Ayer
Photography: Janine Hosegood
Stylist: Vanessa Kellas

Published by MQ Publications Limited
12 The Ivories, 6–8 Northampton Street, London N1 2HY
Tel: 020 7359 2244 / Fax: 020 7359 1616
email: mail@mqpublications.com

ISBN: 1 84072 260 6

Printed and bound in England by Butler & Tanner Ltd

MQ 10 9 8 7 6 5 4 3 2 1

COOKERY NOTES:
All spoon measures are level, unless otherwise specified.
All eggs are large, unless otherwise specified. Seasoning is
sea salt, for preference, and freshly ground black pepper.
Vegetables are assumed to be prepared, e.g. onions,
potatoes and garlic are peeled.

contents

introduction

Making your own bread conjures up a cosy kitchen – and that glorious, unforgettable smell as it bakes. And bread is a lot easier to make in your own kitchen than you might think, as are pasta and pastry. Flour is the ingredient common to all three baking methods featured in this book, and you'll need to know a little about the difference between them before you start. Gluten is the vital ingredient in wheat flour that gives bread its 'spring', holds pasta together and gives pastry its flaky texture.

texture **Strong plain flour:** all the recipes calling for this have been tested using a high quality unbleached flour, now widely available everywhere. The recipes will work with bleached flour of course, but the flavour will not be as good. Bread flour has a high gluten content, typically, between 11.5% and 14%. Aside from bleaching, steel-grinding, the most common method of wheat grinding, also affects the gluten levels in the resulting flour. Heat from friction is generated during this type of fast grinding and this heat tends to damage the gluten level as well as the various vitamins and enzymes found naturally in the wheat germ. Consequently, these often have to be added back into the ground flour. Stonegrinding – a slower process producing far less heat and a better flour – is becoming more common and it is worth seeking out suppliers of stoneground flour.

Plain flour: this is the type of flour most commonly used in other types of baking and is also known as 'soft' flour. The gluten content is usually between 9% and 11%. Soft flours are mostly used with chemical raising agents in wet batters for making cakes or pastry.

Self-raising or cake flour: plain flour to which baking powder has been added. You can always mix your own using plain flour and baking powder.

'00' Italian flour: as a general rule, '00' flour is a hard flour with a high gluten content most commonly used for making pasta. If necessary, strong plain flour can be substituted.

kneading When you make bread, the dough is kneaded until the gluten 'sets up'. Gluten is formed by the combination of two proteins, gliadin and glutenin, that exist in high quantities in wheat flour. When these protein fragments are hydrated with water, or other liquid, they bond with each other creating a large protein aggregate – the gluten – which gives bread and pasta doughs their structure and strength. The longer the dough is kneaded (between 6-15 minutes is typical) the stronger the gluten becomes and the springier the dough feels. However, the friction of

kneading causes the temperature of the dough to rise. If you work a dough too long and too hard (for instance in a food processor or mixer) the heat begins to break the gluten apart and the dough will become unusable. This seldom happens when hand kneading. Where pastry making is concerned however, handling of the dough should remain light to ensure it stays as cool as possible. Overmixing will make a tough instead of flaky dough. If you knead bread dough in a food processor, it is best to do it in bursts of 30-45 seconds and then allow the dough to cool slightly before continuing, to prevent it overheating and spoiling.

equipment

ceramic baking beans
For baking pastry 'blind', the beans help to ensure an evenly baked pastry case.

nest of pastry cutters
Fluted style cutters are ideal for making pasta parcels.

brioche tin The steep sides assist the dough to rise during baking.

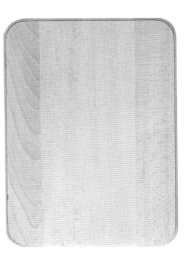

wooden chopping board
A sturdy board is best for slicing bread on.

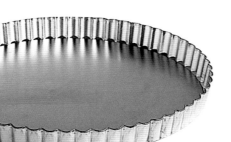

23cm fluted flan tin
A loose base makes it easier to serve a flan whole.

pizza stone
By maintaining an even heat during baking, the stone is ideal and can be used to serve the pizza.

baking tray
Ideal for baking rolls and round loaves.

1kg loaf tin
A staple piece of baking equipment.

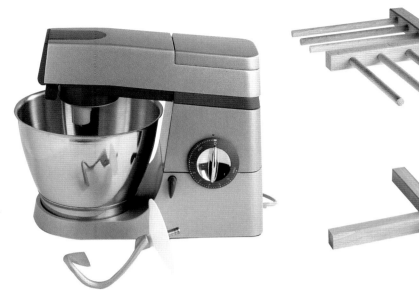

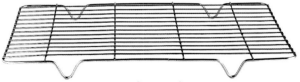

pasta drying rack
A simple and efficient way to dry pasta strands evenly.

mixer with dough hook
Useful for maximising the elasticity of a dough, but care is needed to avoid the dough from overheating.

pasta machine
It cuts the pasta-making time in half.

pasta machine with ravioli attachment
A simple way to prepare ravioli.

ravioli tray and rolling pin
This kit is a useful alternative to the pasta machine attachment.

wire rack
Prevents breads acquiring a soggy base during cooling.

bread knife A serrated blade cuts all types of bread.

small paring knife
A useful tool for trimming pastry and pasta.

scalpel
A handy implement for scoring across bread doughs before baking.

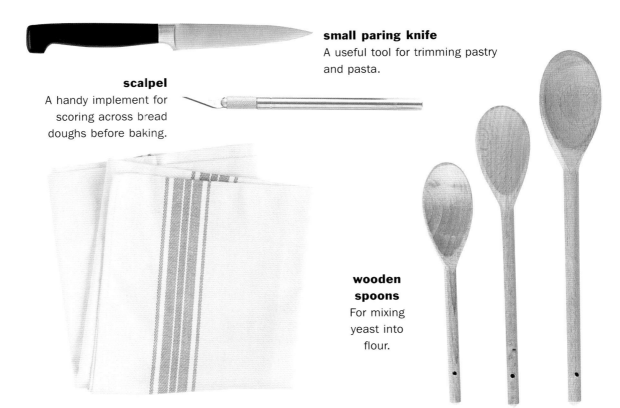

wooden spoons
For mixing yeast into flour.

tea towel
Use to cover doughs during rising.

measuring cup set
To use for US measuring.

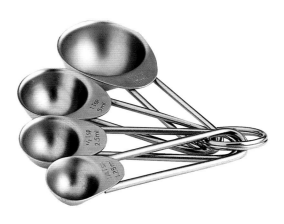

measuring spoon set
Level off ingredients in the spoons for accuracy.

sieve
Stainless steel
is best for
sifting all flours.

oil mister
For lightly spraying dough
before it rises.

measuring jug
Accurate measuring of liquids in
dough making is important.

weighing scales
Careful measuring will reap the
best dough results.

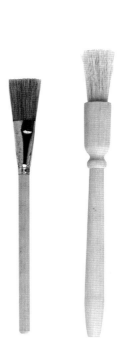

pastry brushes
Flat or round bristle –
used for applying
glaze finishes to
bread and pastry.

**rolling
pin**
Wooden
and
cylindrical
are best for
rolling out
pastry
evenly.

flour dredger
For flouring work surfaces.

pastry wheel
Ideal for sealing
filled pasta
shapes, and for
creating lattice
pastry tops.

**cheese
grater**
Handy for
grating fresh
Parmesan.

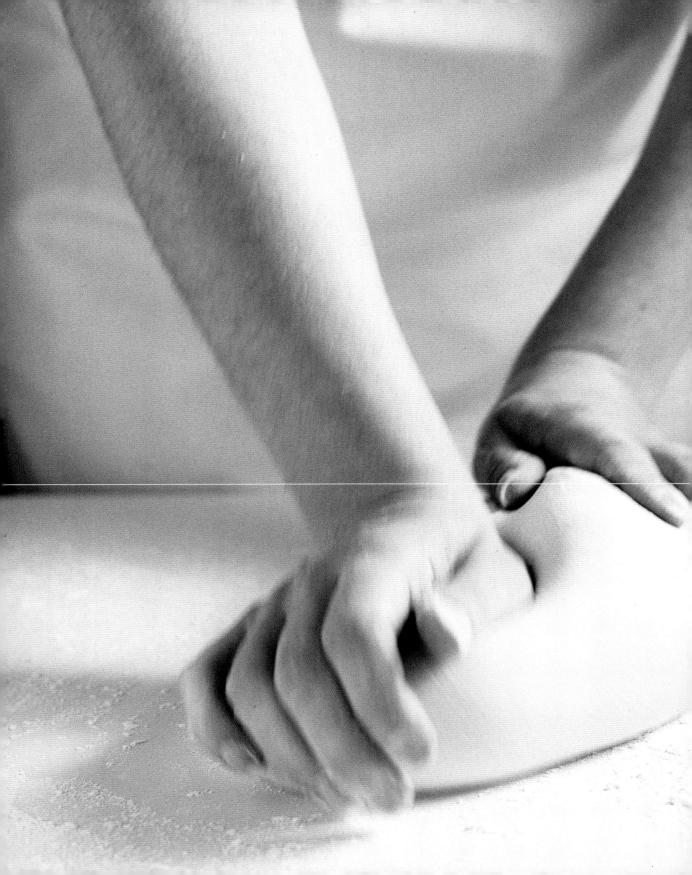

bread

bread introduction Is there anything more tantalising than the aroma of fresh bread, just out of the oven? Many people believe that bread-making is a long-lost traditional skill, surrounded by myth and mystique. The truth is, it couldn't be easier. Apart from flour, the other main ingredients in a loaf of bread are yeast, water, salt and sometimes sugar or honey. That's it. Yet the number of possible combinations appear to be endless and the different results you can achieve by varying one or the other of these constituents is astonishing. For example, when making bagels the dough is so firm that it can

burn the motor out on a mixer. A dough that is made with little water like bagels (see page 30) produces a bread with a close textured crumb. Other doughs, like the ciabatta (see page 36) or spiced potato bread (see page 29) recipes are so wet they can't be kneaded by hand and have a very open texture, almost glossy crumb with lots of large holes. To guide you, each recipe describes whether the dough should be soft, sticky, or firm.

Which yeast? **Fresh yeast:** this is the stuff that gives bread its

name for being difficult. Fresh yeast is available from health food shops and also from supermarkets with bakery departments but must be absolutely fresh or it will be unreliable. Commercial yeast is a by-product of the brewing industry. When fresh, it should be creamy coloured, moist and firm with a strong 'yeasty' smell. If it is crumbly or has discoloured dark patches, it is probably stale. Fresh yeast is usually dissolved in the liquid specified in the recipe, along with a little sugar and/or flour until it is frothy and active before being added to the flour. It only keeps for a few days, wrapped up in the fridge, but will freeze for up to three months in an airtight container.

Dried yeast: this is fresh yeast that has been dried into tiny balls and sold in cans. Use it in the same way as fresh yeast by dissolving it in the liquid then leaving it to froth before adding it to the flour.

Easy blend yeast: all the recipes in this book call for this type of dried yeast. It is highly reliable and so easy to use, as it is added directly to the flour. In a few of the recipes the yeast is mixed with some of the other ingredients and left to 'sponge' for up to several hours. This lets the yeast become very active but also allows the flavour of the mixture to develop, giving the finished bread a better taste. It's important to abide by the use-by date on the packet but the good news is that it will keep for up to six months in the freezer, and because it doesn't cake or stick together, can be used from frozen.

Bread the basic method

Once you've mastered the basic technique of kneading bread dough, the only limit is your imagination. Adding flavours, varying the texture, changing the shape are all variants on this basic method. See the recipe on page 18 for ingredients to prepare the basic bread dough.

The most critical stage in the bread-making process is the kneading, as it is during this process that the gluten in the flour is activated. The gluten develops further during rising, which is what gives the bread its finished texture.

step 1 Make a well in the centre of the flour mixture and pour in the water. Mix to a dough, starting off with a wooden spoon and bringing the dough together with your hands.

step 2 Turn the dough onto a lightly floured surface. The texture will be very rough and slightly sticky. Begin kneading by folding the dough over itself and giving the dough a quarter turn.

step 3 Carry on kneading the dough for about 8–10 minutes until it is very smooth and elastic and no longer sticky. Alternatively, knead the dough in a mixer fitted with a dough hook for 6–8 minutes.

step 4 Lightly oil a large bowl. Form the dough into a neat ball and drop the dough carefully into the bowl. Rub a little oil over the surface of the dough, or use an oil mister and spray lightly. Cover with clingfilm and leave to rise at room temperature for 1 hour or until doubled in bulk.

step 5 After about an hour, the dough will have risen nearly to the top of the bowl. Remove the clingfilm and tip the dough onto a lightly floured surface. This will knock the dough back. Knead for a further 2–3 minutes until smooth again.

step 6 To shape the dough, pat into a large oblong. Fold one end to the centre then fold the other end on top. Drop the dough into the prepared tin, seam side down.

Basic white loaf

675g strong plain flour, plus extra for dusting · 15g butter · 1 tbsp salt · 2 tsp easy
blend yeast · 425ml lukewarm water · oil for greasing (an oil mister is preferable)

MAKES 1 large or 2 small loaves

**This is a simple, basic white loaf recipe – the kind you
can whip up when you get home from work, if you feel so
inclined. The longer and slower the proving, however, as
with all breads, the better the flavour will be.**

1. Generously grease either one 1kg loaf tin or two 500g loaf tins.
Sift the flour into a large bowl. Rub the butter into the flour until
combined. Stir the salt and yeast into the flour.

2. Follow steps 1-6 in the basic method (see pages 16–17),
dividing the dough in two before shaping, if making two small
loaves.

3. Sprinkle the top of the dough with a dusting of flour then set the
tin or tins aside in an oiled plastic bag until the dough rises to the
top of the tin. This will take 30 minutes to 1 hour, depending on the
room temperature. Meanwhile, preheat the oven to
230°C/450°F/gas 8.

4. Just before baking, make a slash down the length of the dough
with a sharp knife or scalpel. Transfer the loaf or loaves to the
preheated oven and bake for 40–45 minutes for the large single
loaf and 35–40 minutes for the two smaller loaves. The bread is
cooked when it is a rich golden brown and sounds hollow when
tapped on the bottom. Remove from the tins and return to the oven
to crisp the sides and base, about 5 minutes. Let cool completely
before serving.

Basic wholemeal loaf

450g strong wholemeal bread flour, plus extra for dusting • 2 tsp salt • 1 tsp brown sugar • 2 tsp easy blend yeast • about 350ml lukewarm water • a little oil for greasing

MAKES 1 large or 2 small loaves

If you prefer, substitute half the wholemeal flour with granary flour or strong plain flour in this recipe.

1. Generously grease either one 1kg loaf tin or two 500g loaf tins. Mix together the flour, salt, sugar and yeast.

2. Follow step 1 in the basic method (see page 16), adding a little more or less water as necessary (wholewheat bread flour varies enormously in its absorption). Continue following steps 2 and 3, kneading only for 3–4 minutes until smooth. Then proceed to step 6 (see page 17). This bread does not require extensive kneading. Fit the dough into the tin or tins, pressing around the edges so that the top will be slightly rounded.

3. Dust the top of the loaf or loaves with extra flour then transfer to an oiled plastic bag. Leave to rise for about 30–45 minutes or until the dough reaches the top of the tin. Meanwhile, preheat the oven to 200°C/400°F/gas 6.

4. Bake for 20–25 minutes for the smaller breads or 30–35 minutes for the larger size.

5. Turn out of the tin and return to the oven, upside down until the sides and bottom are crisp, about 5–10 minutes. Check the loaf is cooked by tapping the bottom. It should sound hollow. Cool the bread on a wire rack before slicing.

Bread rolls

1 quantity of any of the following doughs • baguette (see page 26) • spiced potato bread (see page 29) • granary, hazelnut and raisin loaf (see page 22) • millet, cheese, and caraway loaf (see page 24) • rye bread (see page 47) • rosemary, walnut, and tomato bread (see page 49) • Toppings • sesame seeds • poppy seeds • pumpkin seeds • mixed seeds, e.g. caraway, fennel and poppy • finely sliced onion • grated cheese

NUMBER OF ROLLS will vary depending on the dough recipe used

These are fairly large crusty rolls, suitable for sandwiches, but also great with home-made soups.

1. Make your chosen dough up to the point at which it is shaped. Divide the dough into pieces weighing about 50g (the number of pieces will vary depending on the recipe). Cover the pieces you are not using with clingfilm or a clean damp tea towel.

2. To shape the dough, flour your hands and, working on a floured surface, form a piece of dough into an oval. Gently roll the dough using the palms of your hands making each end narrower than the middle. Twist each end into a point. Repeat to make all the rolls.

3. Transfer the formed rolls to a floured tea towel, cover with another tea towel and leave to rise until doubled in size, about 30 minutes to 1 hour.

4. Brush the tops of the rolls lightly with water and sprinkle over the topping of your choice. Transfer to a lightly oiled baking tray, spacing the rolls about 5cm apart.

5. Bake at the temperature recommended in the dough recipe, testing the rolls are cooked by tapping on the bottom, about 15–20 minutes. They are cooked when they sound hollow.

Granary, hazelnut and raisin loaf

450g granary flour, plus extra for dusting • 1 tsp salt • 25g butter, diced • 2 tbsp brown sugar • 1 tbsp easy blend yeast • 50g jumbo oats, plus extra for sprinkling • 300ml lukewarm water • 50g hazelnuts, roughly chopped • 50g raisins • vegetable oil, for greasing

MAKES 1 large loaf

This is a fabulous bread – full of flavour and texture – and there's no need bake it in a tin.

1. Mix the flour and salt in a large bowl. Rub the butter into the flour until combined. Stir the sugar, yeast and oats into the flour and stir well to mix.

2. Follow steps 1-5 in the basic method (see pages 16–17), leaving the dough to rise until doubled in size, 45 minutes. Turn the dough onto a clean surface. Follow step 1, (see right).

3. Lightly oil a large baking sheet and line with baking parchment. Shape the dough following step 2 (see right). Press any raisins on the surface into the dough or they'll burn. Cover with an oiled plastic bag and leave to rise until doubled in size, 20–30 minutes.

4. Meanwhile, preheat the oven to 220°C/425°F/gas 7. Remove the bag and brush the top of the bread with a little water. Sprinkle with a few extra oats. Using a sharp knife or scalpel, make several angled slashes across the top of the dough.

5. Transfer the baking sheet to the oven and bake until well-risen and dark golden and the loaf sounds hollow when tapped on the bottom, 35–40 minutes. Cool completely on a wire rack before serving.

step 1 Sprinkle the dough with nuts and raisins and knead well until incorporated.

step 2 Shape the dough into a neat oval and place on the prepared baking sheet.

Millet, cheese, and caraway loaf

225g strong plain flour · 225g strong wholemeal flour · 1 tbsp brown sugar ·
2 tsp easy blend yeast · 150ml lukewarm water · 50g whole millet · 150ml boiling
water · 2 tsp salt · 1 tsp caraway seeds · 100g grated strong Cheddar cheese ·
vegetable oil for greasing

MAKES 1 small loaf

**This bread involves making a starter 'sponge' – the extra
rising helps to add flavour to the bread. Buy millet from
health food shops.**

1. Lightly grease a 1kg loaf pan. Set aside. In a large bowl, mix
together 50g of both the white and brown flour, the sugar, yeast,
and water to make a smooth batter. Cover and set aside in a warm
place until doubled in bulk, about 40 minutes.

2. Cover the millet with boiling water. Leave to soak, 20 minutes.

3. Stir in the remaining flour, millet, and any water remaining, salt,
cumin, and cheese. Mix together well, with a little extra water if
necessary to form a stiff dough.

4. Follow steps 2–5 in the basic white loaf method (see page
16–17), leaving the dough to rise about 1–1 ½ hours or until
doubled.

5. Shape the dough following step 6 (see page 17). Cover the tin
with oiled clingfilm. Leave to rise until the dough reaches the top of
the tin, about 30–40 minutes.

6. Meanwhile, preheat the oven to 240ºC/475ºF/gas 9. Transfer
the tin to the oven and bake until risen and golden, 35–40
minutes. The bread should sound hollow when tapped on the
bottom. Let cool completely before serving.

Pesto bread

1 tbsp easy blend yeast • 600ml lukewarm water • 1kg strong plain flour, plus extra for dusting • 1 tbsp salt • 1 tsp sugar • 6 tbsp olive oil, plus extra for greasing • 2 garlic cloves, crushed • handful basil leaves, finely chopped

MAKES 1 loaf

1. Whisk the yeast and warm water together until the yeast has dissolved. Stir in half the flour until smooth. Cover and set aside in a warm place until the 'sponge' has risen by about one-third and is clearly active with lots of bubbles, about 1 hour.

2. Mix the remaining flour with the 'sponge,' salt, sugar and 2 tbsp of oil. Mix to a soft dough.

3. Follow steps 2–5 of the basic method (see pages 16–17), leaving the dough to rise until doubled in size, about 1–2½ hours.

4. Mix the remaining oil, garlic and basil. Season and set aside.

5. Line a baking sheet with baking parchment. Lightly grease the paper. Turn the dough onto a floured surface. Knead for 1–2 minutes then divide the dough in two. Shape into a large 23 x 40cm rectangle. Spread with the basil mixture.

6. Fold one long side of the dough over to fold in half. Cover with a clean tea towel and leave to rise, about 30 minutes.

7. Meanwhile, preheat the oven to 230ºC/450ºF/gas 8. Transfer the baking sheet to the oven and bake for 10 minutes. Reduce the oven temperature to 200ºC/400ºF/gas 6 and bake a further 15 minutes until well risen and golden. Remove from the oven and cover with a clean tea towel. Leave until cold.

Baguette

450g plain flour • 450g strong plain flour • 2 heaped tsp salt • 1 tsp soft brown sugar • 1 ½ tsp easy blend yeast • 600ml cool water • vegetable oil (an oil mister is preferable) • a little semolina for dusting • water in a mister

MAKES 3

1. Mix the flours, salt, sugar, and yeast together. Follow steps 1–5 in the basic method (see pages 16–17)), leaving the dough to rise for just 30 minutes.

2. Knead the dough 30 seconds then shape into a ball. Return to the bowl, cover and leave to rise until doubled in bulk, 1 ½ hours. Divide the dough into three pieces and shape into ovals. Cover with a damp tea towel or clingfilm and leave to rest, 10 minutes.

3. Shape the dough, one piece at a time. Place smooth side down on a lightly floured work surface. Flatten slightly with floured hands. Fold the top edge of the dough to the centre and fold the bottom edge up to meet it. Press down with your fingertips. Follow steps 1, 2 and 3 (see right). Cover with a damp tea towel. Leave until doubled in size, about 2 hours.

4. Preheat the oven to 240°C/475°F/gas 9. Put a pizza stone or heavy baking tray on a central rack. On another baking tray, scatter some semolina, and using the cloth to help you, roll the first loaf, top side down onto the tray. Using a sharp knife, slash the dough at an angle at regular intervals. Repeat with all three loaves.

5. Transfer the tray to the oven so that it sits on the pizza stone or heavy baking tray. Working quickly, spray the oven and the bread with water. Close the oven door. Spray again after 2–3 minutes, then lower the oven temperature to 230°C/450°F/gas 8.

6. Cook until the crust is golden and the loaves sound hollow when tapped, 20–25 minutes. Leave until just warm or completely cold.

step 1 (below left) Using the index finger of one hand, press down on the centre of the dough. Pinch the dough round your finger, using your other hand. Repeat 2 or 3 times until the dough is about 45-50cms long.

step 2 (middle) Gently roll the dough backwards and forwards until the sausage of dough is an even shape.

step 3 (below right) Lightly flour a clean tea towel and lay onto a baking sheet. Pull up at 5cm intervals to form long tunnels. Transfer the shaped dough to the tea towel, seam side up.

Soda bread

350g wholemeal flour · 100g plain flour · 1 tsp salt · 2 tsp bicarbonate of soda ·
25g butter · 300ml buttermilk

MAKES 1 loaf

**Soda bread makes an excellent accompaniment to hearty
soups and is very quick to make. It is best eaten on the
day it is made, but it toasts well on day two.**

1. Preheat the oven to 200°C/400°F/gas 6. Grease a baking sheet.

2. Sift together the flours, salt and bicarbonate of soda. Rub in the
butter then stir in most of the buttermilk – you may need more or
less depending on the flour. The dough will be quite lumpy.

3. Turn the dough onto a floured surface and knead until smooth
and slightly sticky, about 3 minutes. Shape into a lightly flattened
ball about 20cm in diameter. Transfer to the baking sheet.

4. Using a sharp knife, cut a deep cross in the top of the loaf,
without cutting all the way through. Transfer to the centre of
the oven.

5. Cook until the bread is deep golden and sounds hollow when
tapped on the bottom, 30–35 minutes. Cover with foil after about
20 minutes if the bread begins to overbrown. Eat warm or cold.

Spiced potato bread

125g plain flour • 275g strong plain flour • 100g cooked potato, mashed • 1 tsp salt • ½ tsp soft light brown sugar • ¾ tsp easy blend yeast • 1 tsp cumin seeds, lightly crushed • 300ml cool water • vegetable oil (an oil mister is preferable)

MAKES 1 loaf

This unusual dough looks quite rustic and has a lovely chewy crust. Excellent with soup or toasted with butter.

1. Mix together the flours, potato, salt, sugar, yeast and cumin seeds. Add the water and mix to a very soft and sticky dough.

2. Using a mixer fitted with a dough hook, knead the dough for about 6–7 minutes until very smooth and sticky. Scrape the dough into a clean bowl, cover and leave to rise until doubled, about 45 minutes to 1 hour.

3. Cover a baking sheet with baking parchment and generously flour the paper. Scrape the bread dough onto the paper, spray lightly with vegetable oil and cover loosely with clingfilm. Leave to rise until doubled, about 1 hour.

4. Meanwhile preheat the oven to 240°C/475°F/gas 9. Put a heavy baking sheet upside down on the centre shelf while the oven is preheating. Put an empty shallow roasting tray in the bottom of the oven. Transfer the bread to the baking sheet in the oven, paper and all. Quickly pour 500ml of water into the roasting tray and spray the oven walls and bread with water. Reduce the oven to 230°C/450°F/gas 8. Cook for 20 minutes until the bread is well coloured and sounds hollow when tapped on the bottom. Allow to cool on a wire rack.

Bagels

150ml lukewarm water • 2 tsp easy blend yeast • 675g strong
plain flour • 2 tsp salt • 1½ tbsp honey or 1 tbsp malt extract •
cornmeal for dusting

MAKES 8 bagels

**This makes quite a stiff dough, so if you are planning to
knead using a machine, be careful as stiff doughs can be
very hard on mixer motors. If your machine struggles,
you may have to knead by hand.**

1. Mix the water and yeast together and leave until the yeast has
dissolved, about 3 minutes.

2. Add 225g of the flour and stir well to make a thick batter. Set
aside in a warm place until doubled in bulk and obviously active with
lots of bubbles, about 1 hour.

3. Add the remaining flour, salt and honey or malt syrup and mix
to a stiff dough. Turn the dough onto a lightly floured surface and
knead until dense and dry, 12–15 minutes. If using a machine,
mix for 1 minute on a low speed until everything is combined then
knead on a medium speed (see introductory note above), 10–12
minutes. You may need to add a little more flour or water to achieve
the right texture.

4. Cut the dough into eight equal pieces and roll into balls. Cover
with clingfilm or a clean tea towel and leave to rest for 5 minutes.

5. Line a baking sheet with baking parchment and dust liberally with
cornmeal. Follow steps 1 and 2 (see right).

6. Put the formed bagels about 5cm apart on the prepared baking
sheet, enclose everything in an oiled plastic bag and leave to rise for

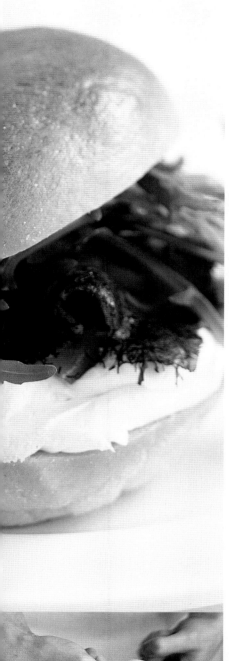

about 1½ hours until increased in size by about twenty-five per cent (this is a dense dough which will not rise as quickly as some lighter doughs).

7. The bagels can be cooked immediately, but they will improve if chilled at least 6 hours or overnight. Remove from the fridge 1 hour before cooking.

8. When ready to cook the bagels, preheat the oven to 240°C/475°F/gas 9. Fill a large pan with at least 10cm of water and bring to the boil. Reduce the heat to a gentle simmer. Working in batches, gently drop the bagels into the water. Do not crowd the pan.

9. After 1 minute, flip the bagels and poach for an additional 1 minute. Drain with a slotted spoon and place 5cm apart on a clean baking sheet, lined and dusted with cornmeal, as before.

10. Bake until golden brown, 10–12 minutes, rotating the pan halfway through the cooking time, to ensure they've baked evenly. Cool on a wire rack.

step 1 (far left) Poke a hole right through the centre of each piece of dough with your index finger. Repeat to make holes in all the balls of dough.

step 2 (left) Pick up a ball of dough and put your index fingers through the hole from each side. Turn the dough over and over to expand the hole to about 4cm.

English muffins

450g strong plain flour, plus a little extra for dusting • 2 tsp easy blend yeast •
1 tsp sugar • 1 ½ tsp salt • 225ml lukewarm milk • 4 tbsp hand hot water • a little
vegetable fat or oil

MAKES 12 muffins

**Unusually, these little buns are cooked on the stove. If
you don't have a griddle, use a heavy frying pan.**

1. Mix together the flour, yeast, sugar and salt. Follow steps 1–5 in
the basic method (see pages 16–17)), using the milk and water to
make the dough in step 1.

2. Tip the dough onto a lightly floured surface and roll it out to
about 1cm thick. Using a plain 10cm pastry cutter, cut out twelve
rounds, rerolling the dough as necessary.

3. Put the muffins on an ungreased, lightly floured baking sheet,
and sprinkle them with a little more flour. Cover loosely with a
plastic bag and leave to rise again in a warm place, about 25–35
minutes.

4. Lightly grease a griddle or heavy frying pan with a little vegetable
fat or oil. Put the pan over a medium heat and when hot, add 3 or
4 muffins (do not overcrowd the pan). Reduce the heat to low and
cook for about 7 minutes on each side until golden. Cook the
remaining muffins in the same way.

5. To serve, break the muffins open around the centre and toast.
Butter generously and serve.

Hazelnut and apricot dinner rolls

4 tsp easy blend yeast · 2 tbsp honey · 625ml lukewarm water · 500g strong plain flour, plus extra for dusting · 500g semolina flour, plus extra for dusting · 2 tsp salt · 50g blanched hazelnuts · 50g roughly chopped semi-dried apricots

MAKES 8 rolls

Although these rolls are reasonably substantial, they make an excellent accompaniment to salad at the beginning or middle of a meal.

1. Dissolve the yeast with the honey in the tepid water. Mix together the flours and salt in a large bowl. Make a well in the centre and add the yeast mixture. Mix together to form a soft dough.

2. Follow steps 2–5 in the basic white loaf (see pages 16–17).

3. Meanwhile, preheat the oven to 220°C/425°F/gas 7. Toast the hazelnuts, watching them carefully, until golden and aromatic, 3–5 minutes. Leave until cool enough to handle then roughly chop. Lightly grease a 23cm springform tin.

4. Turn the dough onto a clean surface and knead in the chopped hazelnuts and apricots. Break the dough into eight equal-sized pieces. Shape into balls and arrange in the tin, seven around the edge and one in the middle. Cover with oiled clingfilm and leave to rise until doubled in size, 40 minutes to 1 hour.

5. Transfer to the oven and cook until golden, 25–30 minutes. Tap the bottom to check if the bread is done. If it sounds hollow, it is cooked, otherwise return it to the oven for an additional 5–10 minutes.

6. Let the bread cool on a wire rack, then unmould and break into individual rolls.

Foccacia

1 tbsp easy blend yeast • 680ml lukewarm water • 1kg strong
plain flour, plus extra for dusting • 1 tbsp salt • 1 tsp sugar •
1 tbsp olive oil, plus extra for brushing • 2 large sprigs fresh
rosemary, leaves only, roughly chopped • 6 tbsp extra
virgin olive oil • 2 tsp coarse sea salt   MAKES 2 loaves

**Experiment with different toppings – finely sliced onions,
garlic, stoned olives, and chopped sundried tomatoes are
all excellent. This bread is made from a very sticky dough
which really must be kneaded by machine.**

1. Whisk together the yeast and the water until the yeast has
dissolved. Stir in half the flour until smooth. Cover and set aside in a
warm place until the 'sponge' has risen by about one third and is
clearly active with lots of bubbles, 1½–2 hours.

2. Put the remaining flour in the bowl of a mixer fitted with a dough
hook and add the 'sponge', salt, sugar and olive oil. Mix at the
lowest speed until firm but still sticking to the bowl, 7 minutes. Add
more flour or water as necessary.

3. Increase the speed to high and knead for 1 minute more until
the dough is elastic and springs back when pushed with a finger.

4. Follow steps 4 and 5 in the basic method (see page 17), and
leave the dough to rise until doubled in bulk, 1½–2 hours.

5. Turn the dough, which will be sticky, onto a well-floured surface.
Flour your hands and tap out into a rough rectangle. Fold in half,
then in three in the opposite direction. Divide the dough in two
and tap each piece into a rectangle again. Transfer to two floured
non-stick 23 x 33 x 2.5cm swiss roll tins, pushing the dough to fill
the tins evenly.

6. Cover both loaves with a tea towel and leave to rise, about 1 hour. Meanwhile, preheat the oven to 240°C/475°F/gas 9.

7. Using the tips of your fingers or the handle of a wooden spoon, poke holes in the dough all over. Sprinkle on the rosemary then drizzle with the extra-virgin olive oil. Scatter over the coarse salt.

8. Bake in the centre of the oven, 10 minutes. Reduce the heat to 200°C/400°F/gas 6 and cook until golden and risen, 15–20 minutes. Let cool in the tins before serving.

Ciabatta

500g strong plain flour, plus extra for dusting • ½ tsp easy blend yeast •
180ml lukewarm water • ½ tsp brown sugar • 1½ tsp salt • 2 tbsp extra
virgin olive oil • vegetable or olive oil, for greasing • semolina, for dusting •
water, in a mister

MAKES 2 loaves

**Ciabatta is another very wet, rustic style bread that
needs to be kneaded using a machine. Start making this
bread the day before you intend to bake it.**

1. To make the 'sponge', mix together half the flour with half the
yeast and the water. Whisk until smooth. Set aside until doubled in
bulk and very foamy, about 1–2 hours.

2. In the bowl of a mixer fitted with a dough hook, mix together the
remaining flour and yeast, olive oil, sugar, salt and 'sponge'. You
may need to scrape down the sides occasionally using a wet
spatula.

3. Mix on a medium speed, about 7 minutes. The dough will be
very wet and stretchy. If not, add a few drops of water.

4. Using a wet spatula, scrape the dough down into a rough mass.
Cover and leave to stand at room temperature about 3 hours. It will
rise very slowly. Transfer to the refrigerator and leave overnight.

5. Line two baking sheets with baking parchment. Brush lightly with
oil then sprinkle generously with semolina.

6. Dip your hands in some water and then transfer the dough to a
clean surface. Sprinkle the dough generously with flour. Dip a knife
in water and cut the dough in two equal pieces. Now flour your
hands and lift each of the pieces, stretching to about 30cm, and lay

each on its own sheet. The dough may shrink back but should remain oblong. Stretch the dough a little if necessary.

7. Enclose each baking sheet in an oiled plastic bag and leave to rise at room temperature until doubled in bulk, about 2 hours.

8. Meanwhile, preheat the oven 240°C/475°F/gas 9. Put a shallow roasting tray or ovenproof frying pan in the bottom of the oven. Put a pizza stone or heavy baking sheet on the centre shelf.

9. Slide the baking sheets out of their bags and burst any noticeable air pockets in the dough. Slide the dough, paper and all, onto the hot pizza stone or baking sheet. Spray the oven and breads with water and pour 500ml water into the roasting tray or frying pan. Shut the door quickly. Wait 2–3 minutes, then spray the oven again. Reduce the temperature to 230°C/450°F/gas 8 and bake until the crust is a deep brown, 20–25 minutes.

10. Turn the oven off and open the door slightly. Leave the bread in the oven for an additional 5–10 minutes, allowing it to finish cooking without burning. Remove the baking parchment and cool on a wire rack.

Pretzels

450g plain flour · 150g strong plain flour · 2½ tsp easy blend yeast · 2 tbsp soft light brown sugar · 1 heaped tsp salt · 875ml lukewarm water · 2 tbsp bicarbonate of soda · 2 tbsp kosher sea salt · vegetable oil (an oil mister is preferable)

MAKES 12 pretzels

These are large, soft pretzels. Sprinkle with sesame seeds or poppy seeds if you prefer. Eat them on the day they are baked.

1. Mix together the flours, yeast, sugar and salt in a large mixing bowl. Add 375ml of the water and mix to a soft dough. Knead for about 5 minutes until smooth and elastic. Shape into a neat ball and put into an oiled bowl. Lightly oil the surface of the dough and cover the bowl with clingfilm. Leave to rise 1 hour, or until doubled in bulk.

2. Cover 2 large baking sheets with baking parchment and set aside. Preheat the oven to 230°C/450°F/gas 8.

3. Cut the dough into 12 equal pieces. Take the first piece and roll it using the palms of your hands into a long thin rope, about as thin as a pencil and about 50–60cms long. Shape into a pretzel by crossing over the ends, twisting them, then folding them up over the loop. Set aside on a floured surface. Shape all the pretzels.

4. Mix the bicarbonate of soda with remaining lukewarm water until dissolved. Dip the pretzels, one at a time, into the solution then transfer to the prepared baking sheets, leaving them well-spaced. Sprinkle with the kosher salt. Leave to rise, 15–20 minutes until just puffed up. Bake 8–10 minutes until golden. Serve warm or cold.

Pooris

100g wholemeal flour • 100g plain flour • 2 tsp salt • 2 tbsp vegetable oil, plus more
for frying the pooris • 100ml water

MAKES 12 pooris

1. Mix the two flours with the salt. Drizzle over the oil and rub it in
with your fingertips until the mixture resembles coarse breadcrumbs.

2. Gradually add enough of the water to form a stiff dough. Turn the
dough onto a clean surface and knead until smooth, 10–12
minutes.

3. Form the dough into a ball and rub the surface with a little oil.
Put into a clean bowl and cover with clingfilm. Leave 30 minutes.

4. Knead the dough briefly and then divide into twelve equal balls.
Cover with a clean damp tea towel. Form the pooris by rolling each
ball into a 12.5cm circle. If possible, roll out all the pooris before
cooking and keep them covered with clingfilm. If space is at a
premium, you may need to work in batches.

5. When ready to cook, heat about 2.5cm of oil over a medium heat
in a deep frying pan large enough to hold one poori comfortably. Let
the oil get very hot. Meanwhile, line a plate with kitchen paper.

6. Lift one poori and lay it carefully in the hot oil. It'll sink, then rise
immediately and begin sizzling. Using the back of a large spoon or
tongs, push the poori into the oil. After a few seconds, when the
poori has puffed up, turn it over and cook an additional 10 seconds,
until golden and covered in puffed 'bubbles'. Drain on kitchen paper.
Cook all the pooris this way, layering them with paper towels, if
necessary. Serve hot.

Chapatis

**250g wholemeal or chapati flour, plus extra for dusting · 1 tsp salt ·
150ml lukewarm water · melted butter or ghee for brushing (optional)**

MAKES 8 chapatis

1. If using wholemeal flour, sift to remove the bran. Stir the salt into the flour. Gradually add the water and mix to form a soft dough.

2. Knead until smooth, 6–8 minutes adding a little flour if necessary. Form into a ball and put into a clean bowl. Cover with clingfilm and leave to rest, 30 minutes.

3. Knead the dough again briefly then divide into eight equal balls. Cover with a clean damp tea towel. With floured hands, take one ball of dough and, on a lightly floured surface, roll it into a 15cm circle, dusting often with flour to prevent sticking. Repeat to make all the chapatis.

4. Meanwhile, heat a heavy-based frying pan over a medium heat until very hot. Shake any excess flour off and put a chapati into the dry frying pan. Cook for about 30 seconds to 1 minute, until starting to colour. Turn and cook for an additional 30 seconds to 1 minute on the second side. If using, brush with melted butter or ghee and flip again to puff the chapati. Put on a plate lined with a clean dry tea towel. Repeat to make all the chapatis.

5. Eat straight away, or stack and wrap in foil then freeze. Reheat, wrapped in the foil, at 220°C/425°F/gas 7, 15–20 minutes.

Naan

250g self-raising flour • 1 tsp salt • 2 tbsp plain yogurt • 120ml lukewarm water • melted butter or ghee, for brushing (optional)

MAKES 4 naan breads

This bread is traditionally cooked on the walls of a tandoor, a large clay oven capable of very high temperatures. The only way to approximate this type of cooking at home is to use a very hot grill.

1. Sift the flour and salt into a bowl. Whisk the yogurt into the water. Make a well in the centre of the flour, pour in the liquid and mix to a soft dough. Turn onto a floured surface and knead until smooth, about 5 minutes.

2. Form into a ball and put into an oiled bowl. Cover with clingfilm and leave to rest, 30 minutes.

3. Preheat the grill to high. Divide dough into four and roll each piece into an oval about 20cm long. Grill each bread until puffed up and speckled brown, 1–2 minutes each side. Brush with the melted butter or ghee, if using. Serve warm.

Pita

450g strong plain flour · 1 tsp salt · 2 tsp easy blend yeast · 2 tbsp olive oil ·
350ml cool water

MAKES 8 pita breads

**You will get the best results from this dough if you use a
pizza stone to cook them on. Make sure you leave
enough headroom in the oven for the breads to puff up,
otherwise they may burn if they touch the top of the oven
or any of the oven shelves.**

1. Mix all the ingredients together until they form a ball. Tip onto a
lightly floured surface and knead, 12–15 minutes. Alternatively, mix
the ingredients in a mixer fitted with a dough hook and knead on
slow speed, about 10 minutes.

2. Put the dough into a lightly oiled bowl, oil the surface lightly, and
cover with clingfilm. Leave until doubled in bulk, 1½ hours.

3. Put a pizza stone or upturned heavy baking sheet in the top one
third of the oven and preheat to 240ºC/475ºF/gas 9. Divide the
dough into eight equal pieces. Roll each piece into a ball and flatten
into a disk. Cover with clingfilm and leave to rest, 20 minutes.

4. Roll the dough into rounds or oblongs about 6mm thick. Leave to
rest, uncovered, before cooking, 10 minutes.

5. Spray the pizza stone lightly with water and place as many pitas
on it as will fit without overlapping. Lower the oven temperature to
230ºC/450ºF/gas 8 and bake until they puff up, 3 minutes. Do not
wait for them to brown or they will be too crisp. Remove from the
oven and leave to cool on a wire rack. Repeat to cook all the pitas.

Pizza

225ml strong plain flour • ½ tsp salt • ½ tsp easy blend yeast • 125ml lukewarm water • 1 tbsp olive oil • 450g mixed fresh tomatoes, e.g. plum, beefsteak, red, yellow and orange cherry tomatoes, sliced • 200g mozzarella in brine, drained and broken into small pieces • handful basil leaves, roughly torn • extra-virgin olive oil for drizzling • semolina flour for dusting

MAKES two 23cm pizzas

1. Mix the flour, salt, and yeast. Stir in the water and olive oil and mix to a soft dough. Follow steps 2–5 of the basic method (see pages 16-17).

2. Lay the tomato slices onto a double thickness of kitchen paper and leave to drain. Do the same with the mozzarella, covering with more kitchen paper and pressing down well to soak up the excess moisture. Preheat the oven to 240°C/475°F/gas 9. Put a pizza stone or heavy baking sheet on the highest shelf.

3. Divide the dough in two and follow steps 1 and 2 (see below). Divide the tomatoes between pizza bases, leaving a rim of about 2cm. Sprinkle with cheese and basil. Season and drizzle with oil.

4. Carefully slide the pizzas from the baking sheet onto the hot baking sheet or pizza stone, and bake 12–15 minutes until golden and bubbling.

step 1 (below left) Using wet hands, stretch the dough into a rough circle about 23cm in diameter. Leave to rest for about 5 minutes.

step 2 (below right) Transfer the dough to a baking sheet dusted generously with semolina and continue shaping until about 25cm in diameter, with a slightly raised edge.

Quattro formaggi pizza with walnuts

2 garlic cloves, crushed · 4 tbsp olive oil · 1 quantity pizza dough, ready for topping
(see page 44) · 2 large tomatoes, thinly sliced · 2 tsp chopped fresh oregano ·
2 tbsp chopped walnuts · 150g mozzarella in brine, drained and broken into small
pieces · 50g dolcelatte, crumbled · 4 tbsp grated Parmesan · 150g fontina, sliced

MAKES two 23cm pizzas

1. Mix together the garlic and olive oil and set aside. Preheat the oven to 240°C/475°F/gas 9.
Put a pizza stone or heavy baking sheet on the highest shelf.

2. Brush the prepared pizza bases with the garlic and oil mixture. Top with the tomatoes,
oregano, walnuts, and then the cheeses. Season well and drizzle with any remaining garlic oil.

3. Transfer to the top of the oven and cook until the edges are browned, the cheese is melted
and bubbling, 10–12 minutes. Let cool for a few minutes before serving.

Roasted onion and goats' cheese pizza

1 quantity pizza dough, ready for topping (see page 44) · 4 red onions · 2 tbsp olive oil,
plus extra for drizzling · 4 tbsp tapenade or black olive paste · 100g thinly sliced
prosciutto, roughly torn · 100g sundried tomatoes · 1 tbsp fresh thyme leaves ·
225g rinded goats' cheese, thinly sliced

MAKES two 23cm pizzas

1. Preheat the grill to high. Peel the onions, trimming but leaving the root end intact. Cut
the onions into sixteen wedges through the root. Brush with olive oil and arrange in a grill
pan. Cook, turning once, until golden and tender, 6–8 minutes. Remove and set aside.

2. Preheat the oven to 240°C/475°F/gas 9. Put a pizza stone or heavy baking sheet on the
highest shelf.

3. Spread the pizzas with tapenade and divide the prosciutto between them. Scatter the
sundried tomatoes and onions on top. Sprinkle with the thyme, and top with the cheese
slices. Season well and drizzle with a little olive oil.

4. Transfer to the top of the oven and cook until the cheese is bubbling, 10–12 minutes.

Rye bread

For the 'sponge' • **125g strong plain flour** • **125g rye flour** • **1 tsp easy blend yeast** • **250ml cool water** • For the bread • **250g strong plain flour** • **1 tbsp soft light brown sugar** • **1 heaped tsp salt** • **½ tsp easy blend yeast** • **1½ tbsp caraway seeds** • **4 tbsp buttermilk** • **vegetable oil (an oil mister is preferable)**

MAKES 1 loaf

This is quite a pale rye bread. You could substitute strong wholemeal flour for the white flour, but you would need to increase the yeast to 2 tsp.

1. Combine all the 'sponge' ingredients in a mixing bowl. Stir well to form a smooth, thick paste. Cover the bowl with clingfilm and allow to rest at room temperature, until doubled in bulk, about 4 hours.

2. Combine all bread ingredients with the 'sponge' in the same bowl and stir until they form a ball. Follow steps 4, 5, and 6 in the basic method (see pages 16–17). Leave the dough to rise until doubled in bulk, 90 minutes. Meanwhile, flour a baking sheet.

3. Shape the dough into a neat oval and place on the prepared baking sheet. Rub or mist with vegetable oil and cover lightly with oiled clingfilm. Leave to rise until doubled in bulk, 1–1½ hours.

4. Meanwhile, preheat the oven to 220°C/425°F/gas 7. Put a heavy baking sheet upside down on the centre shelf. Put an empty shallow roasting tray in the bottom of the oven.

5. Transfer the bread to the baking sheet in the oven by sliding it off the well-floured tray. Quickly pour 300ml water into the roasting tray and spray the walls of the oven and bread lightly with water. Close the door, wait 2–3 minutes then spray again. Reduce the oven to 200°C/400°F/gas 6 and cook until well coloured and the bread sounds hollow when tapped on the bottom, 35–40 minutes. Let cool on a wire rack.

Rosemary, walnut, and tomato bread

350g strong wholemeal or whole grain flour • 1 ½ tsp easy blend yeast • 225ml cool water • 2 tsp salt • 2 tbsp honey • 1 tbsp finely chopped fresh rosemary • 50g walnut pieces, roughly chopped • 50g semi-dried (sunblush) tomatoes, drained and roughly chopped

MAKES 1 loaf

This is a beautifully coloured bread with a fine texture. It is delicious with soups, but also makes a fabulous and unusual sandwich bread.

1. Mix about one-third of the flour with 1 tsp of the yeast and the water. Mix to a thick paste, then cover the bowl with clingfilm and leave to rise, about 4 hours until well risen and very active.

2. Combine the remaining flour, yeast, salt, honey, rosemary, walnuts and tomatoes with the 'sponge' until the mixture forms a ball.

3. Follow step 3 from the basic method (see page 16), kneading the dough for about 15 minutes, then follow steps 4 and 5 (see page 17), leaving the dough to rise about 1 ½ hours until doubled in bulk.

4. Shape the dough into a neat round and transfer to a baking sheet lined with baking parchment. Cover loosely with a clean tea towel and let rise until doubled in bulk, 30–40 minutes.

5. Preheat the oven to 180°C/350°F/gas 4. Bake the bread in the lower third of the oven, 20 minutes. Turn the bread and bake until the loaf sounds hollow when tapped on the bottom, a further 30–40 minutes. Cover with foil if it starts to overbrown. Let cool on a wire rack.

Croissants

500g strong plain flour, plus extra for dredging · 1 tbsp easy blend yeast · 1 tsp salt ·
75g caster sugar · 100ml lukewarm water · 100ml cold milk · 250g unsalted butter ·
1 egg yolk mixed with 1 tbsp milk

MAKES 16 croissants

You need to start making these a day ahead of cooking them. It is well worth the effort, however, producing a crisp, flaky, buttery result. You may find using a mixer with a dough hook easier than kneading the rather sticky dough by hand. Leaving the dough to rest several times during rolling makes the job much easier.

1. Mix together the flour, yeast, salt and sugar, preferably in a mixer fitted with a dough hook. Add the water and milk and mix on low speed until combined. Increase the speed to medium and work until the dough is soft and sticky, but coming away from the sides of the bowl, about 6 minutes. Scrape the dough into a plastic bag and chill overnight in the refrigerator.

2. Take the butter out of the refrigerator so that it is neither hard nor softened either. Put a sheet of clingfilm on a clean surface and dredge with flour. Lay the butter on top. Sprinkle flour on the butter and then, using a rolling pin, knock it out into a rectangle about 1cm thick. Wrap with the clingfilm and return it to the refrigerator for a few minutes.

3. Take the dough out of the bag and put it on a floured surface. Scatter with more flour and roll out, turning frequently, into a rectangle about 1cm thick. Brush off excess flour then put the butter in the centre. Fold the edges of the dough over the butter so that they overlap slightly to enclose the butter completely.

4. Scatter more flour over. Rolling away from you, roll the dough out into a long rectangle about 40 x 67cm. Stop once or twice and leave the dough to rest for 5 minutes, then continue rolling. Fold one end in by a sixth and the other in by a sixth. Fold both ends over again by a sixth so that they meet in the centre. Fold the two together, as if closing a book. Turn the dough so the fold is to one side. Roll it out away from you into a long rectangle as before and fold one end in by a quarter. Repeat at the other end so that they meet in the middle. Fold again as if closing a book. Seal the edges with pressure from the rolling pin. Wrap and chill 30 minutes to 1 hour.

5. Roll the dough on a floured surface to as neat a rectangle as possible, about 30 x 75cm. Trim the edges straight, then cut in two lengthways. Cut out eight equal triangles from each piece.

6. Lay the triangles, one at a time, with the point away from you. Roll up away from you finishing with the point underneath. Transfer to a lined baking tray, cover with clingfilm and leave to rise until doubled in size, about 1–2 hours.

7. Meanwhile, preheat the oven to 200ºC/400ºF/gas 6. Brush the egg and milk mixture lightly onto the dough, brushing from the middle outwards. Bake in the centre of the oven, 10 minutes. Reduce the oven temperature to 170ºC/325ºF/gas 3 and bake until risen and golden, 20–25 minutes.

Caramel pecan loaf

450g strong plain flour • 15g butter • 2 tsp salt • 1½ tsp easy
blend yeast • 300ml lukewarm water • 175g unsalted butter •
175g light soft brown sugar • 100g pecans, roughly chopped •
2 tbsp double cream

MAKES 1 loaf

1. Generously grease a 23cm springform cake tin and set aside.
Sift the flour into a large bowl and add the butter. Rub the butter
into the flour until combined. Follow steps 1–5 of the basic method
(see pages 16–17).

2. Pat the dough out to a large 25 x 35cm rectangle. Cover and let
rest 10 minutes.

3. Meanwhile, cream together 100g of the butter with 100g of the
sugar until smooth. Stir in most of the pecans. Follow steps 1 and 2
(see right).

4. Cover the tin with a clean tea towel and leave until the dough
has risen to the top, about 30 minutes.

5. Preheat the oven to 200°C/400°F/gas 6. Transfer the tin to the
oven and bake until risen and golden, 30–40 minutes, covering the
top with foil if it begins to overbrown.

6. Meanwhile, put melt the remaining butter and sugar together
over a low heat. Add the cream and bring to the boil. Simmer
3–4 minutes, then add the remaining pecans and cook another 1
minute. Remove from the heat.

7. Remove the bread from the oven and immediately spread the
pecan mixture over the top. Let cool before serving.

step 1 (top) Spread the pecan mixture evenly over the dough, leaving a 2.5cm margin around the edges. Starting from a long side, roll the dough tightly into a sausage shape.

step 2 (above) Cut the dough into 5cm slices. Arrange the slices in the prepared tin, cut side up.

Danish pastries

1 quantity of croissant dough, prepared up to the end of step 4 (see page 50) • 1 egg, beaten lightly with 1 tbsp milk • 3 tbsp apricot jam • 75g icing sugar • 1-2 tbsp water or lemon juice • Cinnamon danish • 1 tsp ground cinnamon • 1 tbsp sugar • Pain aux raisins • 75g raisins • Fruit pinwheels • 100g marzipan • 6 canned apricot halves

MAKES 12–16 danish pastries

1. Roll the dough on a floured surface to a 25 x 75cm rectangle. Trim and cut into three equal squares.

Cinnamon danish: mix cinnamon and sugar and sprinkle evenly over one square. Press lightly into the dough. Cut into 2.5cm strips. Twist each strip then coil the lengths into circles.

Pain aux raisins: sprinkle raisins over a second rectangle. Roll up from one short end. Cut into 1cm thick slices.

Fruit pinwheels: cut the remaining rectangle into six squares. Divide marzipan into six and put in the centre of the squares. Top with an apricot half. Make four diagonal cuts from each corner of the pastry as far as the edge of the apricot. Fold alternate points down to the centre of the apricot.

2. When the pastries are shaped, lay well-spaced apart on a lined and greased baking sheet. Cover loosely with oiled clingfilm and leave in a warm place until well risen, about 2 hours.

3. Preheat the oven to 180°C/350°F/gas 4. Brush pastries with the egg and milk mixture and bake, 25–30 minutes. Melt and sieve apricot jam and brush over the warm pastries. When cold, mix together the icing sugar and water or lemon juice until you have a smooth, thick icing. Drizzle over the pastries.

Cinnamon raisin bread

675g strong plain flour, plus extra for dusting • 15g butter • 1 tbsp salt • 2 tsp easy blend yeast • 2 tsp sugar • 425ml lukewarm water • 1 tsp cinnamon • 50g light muscovado sugar • 75g raisins

MAKES 1 loaf

1. Generously grease a 1kg loaf tin. Sift the flour into a large bowl and add the butter. Rub the butter into the flour until combined.

2. Stir the salt, yeast, and sugar into the flour and stir well to mix.

3. Follow steps 1–5 in the basic method (see pages 16-17).

4. Tap the dough out into a large rectangle, cover, and leave to rest, 10 minutes.

5. Using a rolling pin, roll the dough into a rectangle measuring 25 x 35cm. Mix the cinnamon, sugar and raisins together and sprinkle evenly over the dough.

6. Starting from one short end, roll the dough, Swiss roll style, to enclose the filling. Tuck the ends under a little to fit the pan, then place the dough seam side down in the pan. Cover with oiled clingfilm and leave to rise to the top of the tin, about 30 minutes.

7. Meanwhile, preheat the oven to 220°C/425°F/gas 7. Transfer the tin to the oven and bake until risen and golden, 35–40 minutes, covering with foil after 15–20 minutes if necessary. The bread is cooked when it is a rich golden brown and sounds hollow when tapped on the bottom. Let cool on a wire rack.

Doughnuts

1 tbsp easy blend yeast • 175ml lukewarm milk • 175g plain flour • 280g strong plain flour, plus extra for kneading • 1 tsp salt • 75g unsalted butter, diced and softened • 2 medium eggs, beaten • 75g caster sugar, plus extra for coating • 2 tsp grated lemon zest • 1 tsp ground cinnamon • sunflower oil for brushing • oil for deep frying

MAKES about 20 doughnuts

1. Whisk yeast and milk to dissolve. Stir in the plain flour. Cover bowl with clingfilm. Leave until 'sponge' has risen, about 2 hours.

2. Put the strong flour in the bowl of a mixer fitted with a dough hook and add the 'sponge' and salt. Turn on the machine at the lowest speed and begin adding the butter, one cube at a time. Then add the eggs, one at a time, then the sugar and lemon zest. Knead 8 minutes. Turn the speed to high and knead 2 minutes.

3. Knead by hand on a floured surface, adding more flour, until elastic and smooth. Shape into a ball and put into a lightly oiled bowl. Lightly oil the top, cover, and leave until doubled in bulk, 2 hours.

4. Divide into twenty pieces and roll each into a neat ball. Make ring doughnuts by pressing your finger right the way through to make 2.5cm holes, or leave whole. Put the doughnuts onto a floured tray and cover with a clean tea towel. Leave to rise until doubled in bulk, 40–50 minutes.

5. Fill a large deep saucepan about one third with oil. Heat until the oil reaches 190°C/375°F/gas 5 or until a cube of bread browns in 50 seconds. Fry the doughnuts in small batches, taking care not to overcrowd the pan, turning them once until browned and puffed up, about 2–3 minutes. Drain on kitchen paper.

6. Mix extra sugar with the cinnamon on a plate and roll the doughnuts in the mixture while still warm. Serve as soon as possible.

Panettone

1 tbsp easy blend yeast • 150ml lukewarm milk • 450g plain flour • 1 medium egg •
4 medium egg yolks • 2 tsp salt • 75g caster sugar • 2 tsp. grated lemon zest •
2 tsp. grated orange zest • 175g unsalted butter, softened • 75g chopped mixed
candied orange and citron peel • 100g raisins

MAKES 1 large loaf

**This bread dough takes time to rise. Don't leave it in a
very warm place once the butter has been incorporated
or it will melt and the dough will be greasy.**

1. Line a 15cm round cake tin with a depth of 10cm with a double
layer of baking parchment that is 12cm higher than the rim of the
tin. Dissolve the yeast in 4 tbsp of the warm milk. Cover and leave
in a warm place until frothy, 10 minutes. Stir in 100g of the flour
and the remaining warm milk. Cover and leave to rise, 30 minutes.

2. Beat together the egg and egg yolks. Sift the remaining flour and
salt into the yeast mixture. Make a well in the centre and add the
sugar, eggs and lemon and orange zest. Knead until elastic, about
5 minutes. Work in the butter until evenly incorporated.

3. Form into a ball and place in a clean bowl. Cover and leave in a
cool place until doubled in size, 2–4 hours, the longer the better.

4. Preheat the oven to 200°C/400°F/gas 6. Turn the dough onto a
clean surface and knead in the candied peel and raisins. Form into
a neat ball and place in the prepared tin. Cut a cross in the top with
a sharp knife. Cover and leave to rise until the dough is 2.5cm
above the top of the tin.

5. Bake for 15 minutes, then lower the heat to 180°C/350°F/gas 4
and bake until well risen and golden, an additional 40 minutes.
Leave in the tin for 10 minutes, then transfer to a wire rack to cool.

Scones

450g plain flour · 1 tsp baking powder · ½ tsp bicarbonate soda · pinch of salt · 450g soft light brown sugar · 40g unsalted butter, soft · 125ml buttermilk · 1 tbsp milk · 1 egg, beaten · 3 tbsp demerara sugar

MAKES 6–8 scones

Although scone dough must be kneaded to bring it together, it is important not to overknead – this will make them tough, instead of light and flaky, as they should be.

1. Preheat the oven to 150°C/300°F/gas 2. Line a baking sheet with baking parchment. Sift the flour, baking powder and bicarbonate of soda into a large bowl. Stir in salt and sugar.

2. Add the butter and rub into the flour mixture until it resembles coarse breadcrumbs.

3. Stir in the buttermilk until the ingredients just form a ball, adding a little extra if needed.

4. Lightly flour a work surface and turn the dough onto it. Knead the dough briefly, then pat into a circle about 2.5cm thick and about 15cm in diameter. Cut the circle into six or eight wedges (you could use a pastry cutter, but you will have to reroll the trimmings, possibly resulting in overworked dough).

5. Transfer the wedges to the prepared baking sheet. Lightly brush the top with a little milk, then sprinkle with the demerara sugar.

6. Transfer to the oven and bake until risen and golden, about 20–25 minutes.

7. Cool the scones on a wire rack about 10 minutes before serving.

Brioche

500g strong plain flour, plus extra for dusting • 1 tbsp easy blend yeast • 2 tsp salt • 75g caster sugar • 4 tbsp lukewarm water • 5 eggs • 250g unsalted butter, softened, plus extra for the tins • 2 egg yolks • 2 tbsp milk

MAKES 2 brioche

This is another soft dough, similar to panettone dough, and is best made using a mixer. You need to start making this the day before you intend to bake it.

1. Mix the flour, yeast, salt, sugar, water and whole eggs using the paddle attachment of a mixer. Add the butter, one-third at at a time, then increase speed to medium. Mix until the dough is elastic, 15 minutes. Transfer to a large, clean bowl, cover and chill overnight.

2. Divide dough in two. Using floured hands, shape each piece into a ball, cover and set aside, 20 minutes.

3. Brush two fluted brioche tins liberally with butter and dust with a little flour. Put aside.

4. For each brioche, divide each ball in two, one about a quarter of the dough. Follow steps 1, 2 and 3 (see right).

5. Cover and leave to rise in a warm place until doubled in size, 1–2 hours.

6. Preheat the oven to 200°C/400°F/gas 6. For the glaze, beat the egg yolks with the milk and brush over the brioches. Transfer to the oven and bake 10–15 minutes, then reduce the oven temperature to 180°C/350°F/gas 4. Continue baking until risen and golden brown, 35–40 minutes. Allow to cool before serving in slices.

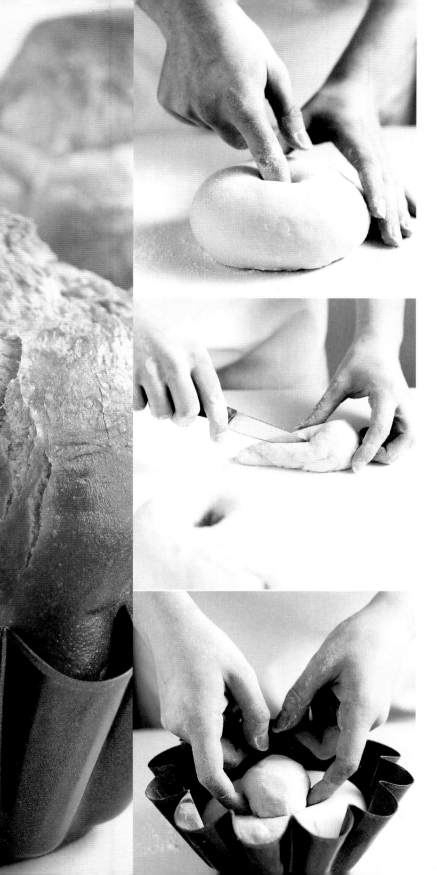

step 1 Shape the larger piece into a ball, then make a hole in the centre, pushing down with your finger until you break through the bottom.

step 2 Shape the second piece into a tapered cylinder. Cut through the tapered end halfway up. Put the cut end in the hole in the larger ball, pulling it through and tucking under the base. Drop into prepared tin.

step 3 Tuck the top edge of the large piece into the hole around the smaller piece – this will help keep the two pieces together as they rise. Repeat to make the second brioche.

Bread and butter pudding

75g unsalted butter, softened, plus extra for greasing • 300ml milk • 300ml double cream • 1 vanilla pod, split • about 6 slices from day-old white loaf, crusts removed • 2 tbsp apricot jam • 2 tbsp dried apricots, chopped • 1 tbsp raisins • 2 tbsp sultanas • 6 egg yolks • 4 tbsp sugar • single cream for serving

SERVES 8

This is a decadently rich dessert. Save it for special occasions and serve in small quantities. The better the quality of the bread, the better the pudding will taste.

1. Preheat the oven to 180°C/350°F/gas 4. Lightly butter a shallow 1.2 litre ovenproof dish.

2. Put the milk, cream, and vanilla pod into a saucepan and heat gently just to simmering point. Remove from the heat and allow to infuse, 15 minutes.

3. Butter the bread generously. Spread half the slices with the apricot jam. Cut all the bread slices diagonally into four triangles and use the bread spread with jam to line the bottom of the dish. Scatter the apricots, raisins, and sultanas over the bread in the dish. Arrange the remaining bread triangles attractively on top.

4. Meanwhile, whisk the egg yolks and sugar together until pale and creamy. Strain the milk and cream mixture onto the egg yolks and sugar, whisking all the time. Carefully pour the custard mixture over the bread as evenly as possible. Press the bread gently into the custard. Set aside 20–30 minutes.

5. Transfer the dish to the oven and bake until the custard is just set and the bread is golden and crisp on top, 30–35 minutes. Serve warm with cream.

For recipe illustration, see page 14.

Plaited fruit loaf

175g mixed candied and dried fruit, e.g. pineapple, raisins, sultanas, orange peel, glacé cherries, roughly chopped • 4 tbsp rum • 225g strong plain flour • ¼ tsp salt • 1 ½ tsp easy blend yeast • 2 tbsp light soft brown sugar • 100ml lukewarm milk • 1 egg, beaten • 50g marzipan, grated • 6 tbsp apricot jam • 15g unsalted butter • 1 tbsp sugar • 1 tbsp honey

SERVES 6–8

This is an unusual and beautiful loaf. Vary the fruit and alcohol according to taste – substitute all vine fruits, for example, or use brandy instead of rum.

1. Put the fruit in a bowl and add the rum. Cover and soak overnight.

2. Mix the flour, salt, yeast and sugar. Make a well in the centre and add the milk and egg. Mix to a soft dough. Knead until smooth, 10 minutes. Shape into a ball and put into a clean bowl. Cover and leave to rise, 1 hour until doubled.

3. Meanwhile, mix the soaked fruit, marzipan and jam together. Preheat the oven to 200°C/400°F/gas 6. Knead the dough again briefly for about 1 minute then on a lightly floured surface, roll out to a 30 x 35cm rectangle. Trim to a neat shape.

4. Spread the filling in a 7.5cm strip down the centre of the rectangle leaving a margin of 5cm at each end. Make diagonal cuts, each about 2cm wide in the dough down either side of the filling.

5. Fold the strips of dough up over the filling, overlapping alternate strips. Tuck in the two ends. Transfer to a greased baking sheet.

6. Cover with oiled clingfilm and leave to rise, 20 minutes. Melt the butter, sugar and honey and brush over the dough. Transfer to the oven and bake until golden, 20–25 minutes. Let cool before slicing.

pasta

pasta introduction Although a huge range of fresh pasta is readily available, often the commercially prepared variety is inferior to good quality dried pasta. Home-made fresh pasta however, using the best quality ingredients, is unbeatable.

mixing the dough Fresh pasta is not very difficult to make, being only a combination of flour, eggs and salt. The most difficult part of the process is getting the texture right so that it is neither sticky nor too dry and crumbly. As with pastry, this is best achieved through practice. The perfect pasta dough feels a little like very soft leather and is cool to the touch. When mixing the dough, add any water only a drop at a time and only if absolutely necessary to bring the dough together. Knead the dough, following the instructions in the recipe, until it is smooth. Fortunately, the dough gets extra kneading when it is passed through the pasta machine, so after the dough has rested you can let the machine do the work for you. A pasta machine, though not essential, is a worthwhile investment if you make pasta often. It is very difficult to roll the pasta dough thinly enough without one. Once the dough is rolled out, you should be able to see your hand through it. This is easily achieved with a machine, but is a lot of hard work with a rolling pin.

how long will it keep? Pasta dough is best made and used on the same day because if left overnight in the fridge the flour will begin to oxidise, giving the dough dark specks which although not harmful, are unappetising. However, fresh pasta dough can be frozen successfully for up to two months if wrapped well or in an airtight container. It is also possible to make the dough, cut it into the required shape then leave it to dry. Pasta left to dry this way can then be kept in an airtight container in the refrigerator for several days.

If you should find yourself with any leftover cooked pasta, keep it well covered in the refrigerator, either with or without sauce. The best way to reheat pasta without any loss of texture is in the microwave. Stir through the pasta well before serving to loosen the individual strands or filled pasta parcels.

how long does it take to cook? All pasta, whether fresh or dried, should be cooked until al dente – which means literally 'to the tooth' – or until still firm to the bite and not soft but without a hard uncooked centre. The time this takes will vary depending on the type of pasta, the shape and the thickness. The most important thing is that the pasta should be added to a large amount of salted water which has come to a rolling boil. Stir the pasta once or twice during cooking, though if it's in a big pan with plenty of water, it won't stick. There is no need to add oil to the water if you cook pasta this way.

Pasta the basic method

The best flour to use for making pasta is '00' pasta flour, readily available from Italian delis as well as many large supermarkets. Alternatively, substitute half plain flour and half strong plain flour. See the recipe on page 70 for ingredients to prepare the basic pasta dough.

A pasta machine is a worthwhile investment if you plan to make a lot of fresh pasta. Rolling dough by hand takes a lot of hard work to get it thin enough. A hand-cranked pasta machine will do the job very well and will last for many years.

step 1 Sift the flour and salt together into a bowl. Turn onto a clean surface and make a well in the centre. Add the eggs, egg yolk, and oil. Gradually work these into the flour, adding a little extra water if necessary to make a smooth dough that is not sticky.

step 2 Turn the dough onto a lightly floured surface and knead until the dough is smooth and soft, 6–8 minutes. It should feel like soft leather. Form the dough into a neat ball and wrap in clingfilm. Chill the dough at least 30 minutes before rolling.

step 3 Unwrap the dough and divide into eight equal pieces. Cover all but one of the pieces with clingfilm until needed. Flatten one piece so that it will pass through the pasta machine rollers. With the machine at its widest setting, pass the dough through.

step 4 Fold the dough in three, rotate the dough a quarter turn and pass through the machine again. Continue to pass the pasta sheet through the machine rollers, narrowing the gap by one setting each time, dusting with a little semolina flour if it begins to feel at all sticky.

step 5 If you are making noodles, it is best to stop at the second-to-last setting. For making filled pasta or if you need to use the sheets to make lasagne, carry on to the last, and finest, setting. For noodles, the dough sheets should be hung over a pasta hanger or draped over a clean wooden pole for about 5 minutes to dry slightly. If filling the pasta, t can be used straightaway, while still moist.

step 6 Fit the pasta cutter to the machine and pass each sheet of dough through the required cutters. Hang the noodles, again using a pasta hanger or drape over a pole until all the pasta is cut. Leave until dry but not stiff then coil the noodles into nests. Leave on a generously floured tea towel or in an airtight container until needed.

Basic pasta dough with fresh tomato sauce

225g '00' pasta flour • 1 tsp salt • 2 medium eggs plus 1 egg yolk • 1 tbsp extra-virgin olive oil • semolina flour, for dusting • For the sauce • 3–4 anchovy fillets in oil, drained • 2 tbsp milk • 2 tbsp olive oil • 2 garlic cloves, finely sliced • large pinch chilli flakes • 225g cherry tomatoes, halved • handful basil leaves, roughly torn • freshly grated Parmesan, to serve

SERVES 4

1. Follow steps 1–6 of the basic pasta method (see pages 68–69), cutting the dough into tagliatelle.

2. Put the anchovy fillets into a small bowl and cover with the milk. Leave to stand for about 10 minutes and drain, discarding the milk. Chop the anchovies finely.

3. Heat the oil in a large frying pan and add the anchovies, garlic and chilli flakes. Cook for 3–4 minutes over a medium heat until the anchovies have dissolved. Increase the heat and add the tomatoes. Toss and cook, about 2 minutes. Add the basil leaves and cook briefly.

4. Meanwhile, bring a large pan of salted water to a boil. Drop in the noodles and cook until al dente, about 2–3 minutes. Drain well. Toss the noodles with the tomato mixture. Season to taste and serve with grated Parmesan.

Ravioli with tiger prawns and roasted tomato sauce

450g ripe tomatoes, peeled and quartered · 1 tsp olive oil · 50g unsalted butter, softened · 1 tbsp lemon juice · 2 tbsp chopped fresh basil · 450g raw peeled tiger prawns · 1 tbsp chopped fresh parsley · 1 tbsp chopped fresh chives · 1 tsp grated lemon zest · 4 tbsp double cream · 1 quantity lemon pasta dough (see page 86), prepared to the end of step 2 in the basic method (see page 68)· semolina for dusting · sprigs of basil and lemon quarters to garnish

SERVES 4

1. Preheat the oven to 220°C/425°F/gas 7. Drizzle the tomato quarters with the olive oil and put into a roasting tin at the top of the oven. Roast until soft and a little charred, 15–20 minutes.

2. Remove from the oven and put into a food processor along with the butter, lemon juice, and half the basil. Process until smooth. Pass the sauce through a sieve to remove the seeds and season to taste.

3. Very finely chop the prawns and mix with the parsley, chives, remaining basil, lemon zest, and cream. Season well and set aside.

4. Continue to follow steps 3,4 and 5 of the basic pasta method (see pages 68-69), rolling the pasta for filling. You should have eight sheets.

5. Lay one sheet on a work surface, keeping the remaining sheets covered. Follow steps 1, 2 and 3 (see right). Generously dust a tray with semolina and lay the rounds on the tray. Sprinkle with more semolina. As the filling is very moist, do not leave for longer than 30 minutes.

6. Cook ravioli in a large pan of boiling salted water in batches until al dente, 2–3 minutes. Drain well and divide between serving dishes. Spoon over the sauce and garnish with sprigs of basil and lemon.

step 1 (below left) Dot teaspoons of the mixture at 5–7.5cm intervals. Brush around the filling with a little water.

step 2 (below middle) Take a second pasta sheet and carefully lay over the first sheet, pressing down around the filling to exclude any air pockets.

step 3 (below right) Using a 7.5cm fluted pastry cutter, cut around the filling.

Ravioli with pumpkin and crispy prosciutto

450g piece of pumpkin or butternut squash, seeds removed and peeled • 3 tbsp olive oil • 50g provolone or fontina cheese • 3 tbsp freshly grated Parmesan • 1 tbsp chopped fresh basil • 1 tbsp chopped fresh parsley • 1 tbsp toasted pine nuts, roughly chopped • 1 egg yolk • 2 tbsp double cream • 1 quantity basic pasta dough (see page 71), prepared to the end of step 2 (see page 68) • 4 slices prosciutto • 8 large sage leaves

SERVES 4

1. For the filling, preheat the oven to 190°C/375°F/gas 5. Cut the pumpkin into large chunks and brush 2 tbsp of the oil over them. Bake until tender, about 30–40 minutes. Allow the pumpkin to cool slightly, then put the flesh into a large bowl and mash until smooth. Add the cheeses, basil, parsley, pine nuts, egg yolk and cream. Season to taste and set aside.

2. Follow steps 3-5 of the basic pasta method (see pages 68-69), rolling the pasta for filling. You should have eight sheets of pasta. Cover.

3. Lay one sheet of pasta onto a lightly floured surface. Dot teaspoonfuls of the filling at 6cm intervals. Brush the edges and between the stuffing with a little water. Carefully lay a second sheet of pasta over the top and press along the edges and between the stuffing to seal. Cut between the stuffing and trim the edges using a pastry wheel to make little squares. Repeat using the remaining pasta and filling to make 20–24 ravioli.

4. Cook ravioli in a large pan of boiling salted water in batches until al dente, 3 minutes. Drain thoroughly and transfer to a serving dish. Fry prosciutto, one slice at a time, in remaining oil in a frying pan over a high heat until crisp, 30 seconds each side. Drain on kitchen paper. Reduce the heat and add the sage leaves. Cook gently until the leaves darken and turn crisp. Drain on kitchen paper. To serve, top the pasta with the crispy prosciutto and sage leaves. Drizzle with the oil from the pan. Serve with extra Parmesan.

Wide noodles with roasted wild mushrooms, garlic and parsley

450g mixed wild mushrooms, cleaned and sliced · 4 tbsp olive oil · 2 garlic cloves, sliced · 125ml vegetable stock · 125ml double cream · 2 tbsp chopped fresh parsley · 3 tbsp freshly grated Parmesan, plus extra to serve · 1 quantity chilli-flavoured pasta dough (see page 85)

SERVES 4

1. Preheat the oven to 200°C/400°F/gas 6. Clean the mushrooms by brushing or wiping with a damp cloth. Chop or slice into large pieces. Leave smaller mushrooms whole. Put the mushrooms into a shallow roasting tray and drizzle with 2 tbsp of the oil. Add the garlic and mix together. Transfer to the top of the oven and roast until the mushrooms are tender, but still firm.

2. Remove the mushrooms from the oven. Transfer to a large bowl. Put the roasting tray over a low flame and add the vegetable stock, stirring well to scrape up any sediment from cooking the mushrooms. bring to the boil and reduce by half. Stir in the cream, parsley and Parmesan. Add mushrooms and simmer briefly.

3. Follow instructions for making chilli pasta following the basic pasta method to the end of step 5 (see page 68) rolling the pasta for noodles. You should have eight sheets. Cut these into long, wide noodles.

4. Meanwhile, bring a large pan of salted water to a boil. Add the pasta and cook until al dente, 2–3 minutes. Drain well. Top the pasta with the mushroom sauce and grated Parmesan.

Cappelletti stuffed with prosciutto, mozzarella and sun-dried tomatoes

50g prosciutto, finely chopped • 100g buffalo mozzarella, drained and cut into fine dice • 50g sun-dried tomatoes in oil, drained and finely chopped • 50g stoned black olives, finely chopped • 1 tbsp each chopped fresh parsley and basil • 1 quantity of herb pasta dough (see page 86) • 4 tbsp extra-virgin olive oil • freshly grated Parmesan, to serve

SERVES 4

The filling ingredients need to be very finely diced or they tend to break through the thin pasta.

1. Mix the prosciutto, mozzarella, tomatoes, olives, parsley and basil together. Season and set aside. Follow the instructions for making herb pasta using your preferred method (see page 86) and the basic pasta method to the end of step 5 (see pages 68–69), rolling the pasta for filling. You should have eight sheets.

2. Follow steps 1–3 (see right). Repeat to make all the cappelletti, placing them on a clean floured tea towel as you go.

3. Bring a large pan of salted water to a rolling boil and add the pasta, in batches if necessary. Cook until al dente, 2–3 minutes.

4. Toss the hot pasta with the olive oil, season with plenty of black pepper and serve with freshly grated Parmesan.

step 1 (below left) Using a fluted 7.5cm pastry cutter, cut as many rounds from the pasta as you can. Cover and leave until slightly dry but still pliable.

step 2 (below middle) Put a teaspoonful of the prosciutto mixture in the centre of one circle. Brush all around with water, then fold over to enclose the filling and make a crescent shape. Press down all around to seal.

step 3 (below right) Hold the pasta shape with the fold pointing towards you. Bring the two corners across to meet, pinching the ends together to seal. Moisten with a little water.

Pappardelle with courgettes, sun-dried tomatoes, basil and pine nuts

1 quantity basic pasta dough (see page 71) • 3 tbsp extra-virgin olive oil • 1 tbsp pine nuts • 2 garlic cloves, sliced • 2 medium courgettes, thinly sliced • large pinch chilli flakes • 2 tsp grated lemon zest • 4 sun-dried tomatoes, chopped • handful basil leaves, roughly torn • freshly grated Parmesan, to serve

SERVES 4

1. Follow steps 1–5 in the basic pasta method (see pages 68–69), rolling the pasta for making noodles. Roll the pasta sheets from one narrow end into sausages. Using a sharp knife, cut the pasta crosswise into 2cm wide strips. Hang the strips on a pasta hanger or drape over a clean pole until needed.

2. Heat 1 tbsp of the oil in a large frying pan or wok. Add the pine nuts and garlic and cook gently until golden. Remove with a slotted spoon and drain on kitchen paper. Set aside.

3. Add an additional 1 tbsp of the oil and the courgettes. Increase the heat slightly and cook, stirring occasionally, until golden, about 5 minutes. Return the pine nuts and garlic to the pan with the lemon zest and sun-dried tomatoes. Cook until heated through, about 1 minute.

4. Meanwhile, bring a large pan of salted water to a rolling boil. Add the pasta and cook until al dente, 2–3 minutes. Drain, reserving a little of the water. Add the pasta to the pan with the courgettes along with the basil. Season well and mix together, adding a little of the reserved water if it seems a little dry. Divide between serving plates and top with freshly grated Parmesan. Serve immediately.

Mushroom tortelloni

15g dried ceps • 150ml boiling water • 50g pancetta or bacon, finely chopped • 40g butter • 1 tbsp olive oil • 225g flat mushrooms, finely chopped • 1 garlic clove, crushed • 2 tsp grated lemon zest • 125g ricotta • 2 tbsp freshly grated Parmesan, plus extra to serve • 1 small egg • 1 quantity basic pasta dough (see page 71)

SERVES 4

1. Put the dried mushrooms into a bowl and pour over the boiling water. Leave to soak, 20 minutes. Drain, reserving the soaking liquid. Finely chop the mushrooms.

2. Fry the pancetta in 15g butter and oil over a medium heat, 2–3 minutes. Add the chopped soaked mushrooms, flat mushrooms and garlic. Cook over high heat, stirring, until the mushrooms have softened and released their liquid. Add the reserved soaking liquid, straining it if necessary to remove any grit. Simmer until all the liquid has evaporated and the mushrooms have started frying again.

3. Remove from the heat and add the lemon zest. Stir well and let cool. Stir in the ricotta, Parmesan and egg. Season. Follow steps 1-5 of the basic pasta method (see pages 68–69), rolling the pasta for filling. You should have eight sheets of pasta. Keep covered.

4. Cut pasta into 7.5cm squares. Put a teaspoon of filling in the middle. Brush around the filling and up to the edges then fold in half diagonally to form a triangle. Press down well to seal. Place your index finger against the folded edge and bring the two corners around it to meet, pinching the ends together to seal, moistening with a little water if necessary. Repeat to make all the tortelloni.

5. Cook tortelloni in a large pan of boiling salted water in batches until al dente, 2–3 minutes. Drain and toss with remaining melted butter. Serve with some extra freshly grated Parmesan.

Two-tone ravioli with ricotta

1 tbsp olive oil • 400g can chopped tomatoes • 2 garlic cloves, crushed • 1 tbsp chopped fresh basil • pinch sugar • ½ quantity each plain and spinach pasta dough (see pages 71 and 85) • extra flour, for dusting • 225g fresh ricotta • 3 tbsp finely chopped mixed fresh herbs, e.g. basil, chives, parsley • 2 tsp grated lemon zest • 1 tbsp fresh lemon juice • 3 tbsp freshly grated Parmesan, plus extra for serving • 1 egg, lightly beaten

SERVES 4

1. Put the oil, tomatoes, 1 crushed garlic clove, basil, sugar and seasoning into a medium saucepan. bring to the boil and cover. Reduce the heat and simmer very gently, 30 minutes. Simmer, uncovered, until thickened, an additional 15 minutes.

2. For the filling, beat together the ricotta, herbs, lemon zest and juice, Parmesan, egg and seasoning. Chill until needed.

3. Follow the instructions for making spinach pasta (see page 85) and plain pasta using the basic pasta method to the end of step 5 (see pages 68–69) rolling the pasta for filling. You should have four sheets of plain pasta and four sheets of spinach pasta. Lay one sheet of plain pasta on a work surface. Dot with the filling about every 7.5cm. Brush around the filling with a little water. Take a sheet of spinach pasta and carefully lay over the first, pressing down around the filling to exclude any air pockets.

4. Using a sharp knife, trim the ends and long sides to leave an even margin around the filling. Cut between the filling to make squares. Set aside on a plate or baking tray dusted with semolina. Continue to make the remaining ravioli, between 20 and 24.

5. Bring a large pan of salted water to a rolling boil. Add the pasta, in batches if necessary and cook until al dente, 2–3 minutes. Drain.

6. Divide between serving plates and spoon the tomato sauce over. with extra freshly grated Parmesan.

Roast vegetable lasagne

1 large red pepper, deseeded and cut into chunks • 2 small courgettes, cut into chunks • 2 red onions, each cut into 8 wedges • 6 garlic cloves • 1 medium aubergine, cut into chunks • 2 tbsp olive oil • 2 large sprigs fresh thyme • 2 fresh bay leaves • 2 x 300g jars fresh tomato sauce • 300g jar artichokes in oil, drained and halved if large • 50g sun-dried tomatoes • 500g ricotta • 2 eggs, beaten • 4 tbsp freshly grated Parmesan, grated • ½ quantity basic pasta dough, prepared to the end of step 5 in the basic pasta method (see pages 68–69) **SERVES 4**

1. Preheat the oven to 200°C/400°F/gas 6. In a large bowl, toss the pepper, courgettes, onions, whole garlic cloves and aubergine with the olive oil. Tip everything onto a shallow roasting tray or heavy baking sheet. Tuck the thyme sprigs and bay leaves in among the vegetables. Cook near the top of the oven, turning once or twice, until tender and golden at the edges, 40 minutes. Reduce the oven temperature to 190°C/375°F/gas 5.

2. Remove the whole herbs. Mix the vegetables with the tomato sauce, artichokes and sun-dried tomatoes. Set aside.

3. Reserving about 3 tbsp of the Parmesan, in a large bowl, beat the ricotta until soft then mix in the eggs, remaining Parmesan, and plenty of seasoning. Set aside.

4. Spread a large spoonful of the vegetable mixture over the bottom of an ovenproof dish measuring about 20 x 25 x 6cm. Trimming the sheets to fit, top with a layer of pasta. Now add half the remaining vegetable mixture and top with half the remaining pasta. Add the last of the vegetable mixture and the final layer of pasta and top with the ricotta mixture. Sprinkle with the reserved Parmesan.

5. Bake in the centre of the oven until bubbling and golden, about 40–45 minutes.

Four-cheese sauce with spinach pasta

25g butter • 8 sage leaves • 125g dolcelatte, crumbled • 225g mascarpone •
125g taleggio or fontina cheese, chopped • 50g freshly grated Parmesan, plus
extra to serve • 1 quantity spinach pasta dough (see page 85)   **SERVES 4**

1. Follow the instructions for making spinach pasta (see page 85) following the basic pasta method to the end of step 6 (see pages 68–69), cutting the pasta into tagliatelle.

2. Melt the butter in a saucepan until foaming, then add the sage leaves. Cook gently until fragrant and the leaves are crisp, about 1 minute. Drain on kitchen paper and set aside.

3. Add the dolcelatte, mascarpone and taleggio or fontina to the same pan and allow to melt slowly over a gentle heat.

4. Stir in the Parmesan until melted and season to taste. Be careful adding salt, as Parmesan, dolcelatte and taleggio are all quite salty cheeses.

5. Meanwhile, bring a large pan of salted water to a rolling boil and add the pasta. Cook until al dente, 2–3 minutes. Drain well.

6. Put the pasta into a large serving bowl and toss with the sauce. Garnish with crispy sage leaves and serve immediately.

Flavoured pasta

Check out the basic pasta recipe on page 71, then
choose your favourite flavouring.

Mushroom

Soak 15g of dried wild mushrooms in 150ml boiling water until
softened, about 20 minutes. Drain well and squeeze any excess
liquid from the mushrooms. Chop very finely, using a food processor
if possible. Add to the basic pasta recipe along with the eggs.
Reduce the water to 2 tsp, adding more only if necessary.

Chilli

Deseed and very finely chop 1 or 2 hot red chillies. Add to the basic pasta recipe along with the eggs.

Spinach

Blanch 50g fresh spinach until wilted. Refresh under cold water and drain well. Squeeze out any excess water, then chop very finely or purée in a food processor. Add to the basic pasta recipe with the eggs.

Sun-dried tomato

Beat the eggs with 2 tbsp sun-dried tomato purée before adding to the flour in the basic pasta recipe.

Saffron

Soak a large pinch of saffron strands in 1 tbsp of hot water until the water cools, about 20 minutes. Replace whole egg in the basic pasta recipe with the saffron water.

Herb

There are two ways to make herb pasta.

Method 1. Add 3 tbsp of very finely chopped mixed herbs to the flour and salt in the basic recipe.

Method 2. Make the basic pasta recipe up to the end of step 4 (see pages 68–69). Pass the pasta sheets through the rollers until you have changed the setting three times. Lay the sheet on a floured surface and lay whole soft herb leaves, e.g. basil, parsley, coriander, dill, thyme or chives or a mixture, over half the dough to cover it. Fold over the other half to enclose and pass through the pasta machine again. Continue as in the main recipe. The herbs will stretch with the dough and create a speckled effect.

Black peppercorn

Coarsely crush 2 tsp black peppercorns using a pestle and mortar or spice grinder. Stir into the flour along with the salt in the basic pasta recipe.

Lemon

Finely grate the zest from 2 lemons and stir into the flour along with the salt in the basic pasta recipe.

Olive

Beat the eggs with 2 tbsp black olive paste or tapenade before adding to the flour in the basic pasta recipe.

Beetroot

Purée 2 cooked beetroots until very smooth, passing through a sieve if necessary. Leave out 1 egg from the basic pasta recipe.

Chocolate

Replace 50g of the flour in the basic recipe with an equal amount of sifted cocoa powder.

Squid ink

Add one sack of squid ink (available from fishmongers and large supermarkets) along with the whole eggs, leaving out the egg yolk.

Seared scallops in brown butter with saffron pasta

75g unsalted butter • 1 tbsp olive oil • 12 scallops, cleaned • 2 tsp grated lemon zest • 2 tbsp fresh lemon juice • 1 tbsp chopped fresh parsley • ½ quantity saffron pasta dough (see page 85), cut into tagliatelle • lemon quarters, to serve

SERVES 4 as a starter

1. Heat a third of the butter with the oil in a large, heavy non-stick frying pan until foaming and very hot. Add the scallops in two batches, and cook until golden, about 2 minutes on each side. Remove the scallops from the pan and set aside in a warmed dish.

2. Reduce the heat to a minimum and add the remaining butter to the frying pan. Swirl around until melted. Cook until the butter starts to brown and smells nutty, about 1–2 minutes. Add the lemon zest and juice and remove from the heat. Stir in the parsley and season to taste.

3. Meanwhile, bring a large pan of salted water to a rolling boil. Add the pasta and cook until al dente, 2–3 minutes. Drain well.

4. Divide the pasta between serving plates. Top each serving with three scallops. Drizzle over the butter sauce and serve immediately, with lemon quarters.

Pasta in brodo

1.8kg chicken • 1 carrot, cut into large chunks • 1 stick celery, cut into large chunks • 1 onion, halved • 2 whole peeled garlic cloves • 6 black peppercorns • 1 bay leaf • 1 sprig thyme • ½ quantity basic pasta dough (see page 71), prepared to the end of step 5 (see pages 68-69) • handful fresh herbs – basil, flat-leaf parsley, sage, mint, tarragon • 2 tbsp chopped fresh parsley

SERVES 6

1. Put the chicken into a large saucepan or stockpot along with the carrot, celery, onion, garlic, peppercorns, bay leaf and thyme. Cover with water and bring very slowly up to a boil. Skim the surface regularly to remove any scum that rises. Cover and simmer very gently, 1½ hours. Remove from the heat and let cool.

2. Carefully remove the chicken from the stock. Remove the skin and discard. Remove the flesh and set aside. Discard the carcass.

3. Strain the stock and chill overnight, if possible. The next day, remove any fat that has solidified from the top of the stock and discard. Put the stock into a large pan and bring to the boil. Boil until reduced to about 1.5 litres.

4. Continue to follow the basic pasta method to the end of step 5 (see pages 68–69), rolling the pasta for the filling. You should have four sheets. Follow steps 1, 2 and 3 (see right).

5. Return the stock to a large saucepan and bring up to a boil. Taste and season. Add the chopped cooked chicken flesh. Return to a boil and add the pasta squares. Cook until al dente, 2–3 minutes. Stir in the parsley and season to taste. Serve immediately.

step 1 Lay a sheet of pasta on a surface. Dampen lightly with water. Put individual leaves or small sprigs of herbs at regular intervals all along its length.

step 2 Top with a second sheet of pasta and press down. Using a rolling pin, gently roll over the top of the pasta to seal it.

step 3 Using a pastry wheel, trim the edges of the pasta and cut into squares, ensuring that the herbs are in the middle of the squares. Set aside on a floured tray until needed.

Rocket and hazelnut pesto

75g rocket leaves • 1 garlic clove, chopped • 25g roughly chopped toasted hazelnuts •
50g piece Parmesan • 6 tbsp extra-virgin olive oil • 1 tbsp capers, chopped • 1 quantity
basic pasta dough (see page 71), cut into noodles • freshly grated Parmesan, to serve

SERVES 4

1. Put the rocket, garlic and hazelnuts into the bowl of a food
processor and chop finely. Break or chop the Parmesan into smaller
pieces and add these to the rocket mixture. Process again until the
cheese is finely chopped but still recognizable.

2. Add 2 tbsp of the oil and process again briefly to mix.

3. Scrape the mixture into a bowl and add the remaining oil,
capers and seasoning.

4. Meanwhile, bring a large pan of salted water to a rolling boil.
Add the pasta and cook until al dente, 2–3 minutes. Drain well.

5. Return the pasta to the pan and add the pesto. Stir well until all
the pasta is well coated. Serve with extra freshly grated Parmesan.

Fresh crab, chilli and garlic with fine noodles

4 tbsp good quality extra-virgin olive oil · 2 garlic cloves, finely chopped · 1 red chilli, deseeded and finely chopped · 350g freshly picked crabmeat · 2 tsp. grated lemon zest· 2 tbsp fresh lemon juice · 2 tbsp chopped fresh parsley · 1 quantity basic pasta dough (see page 71), cut into fine noodles

SERVES 4

1. Heat 2 tbsp of the oil over a low heat in a large frying pan and add the garlic and chilli. Cook briefly stirring, 2 minutes.

2. Add the crabmeat, lemon zest and juice, and parsley, tossing everything together until well mixed. Cook until the crabmeat is heated through, about 1–2 minutes.

3. Meanwhile, bring a large pan of salted water to a rolling boil. Add the pasta and cook until al dente, 2–3 minutes. Drain well.

4. Add the drained pasta and remaining oil to the frying pan with the crab and stir well to mix. Season to taste and serve immediately.

Herb tagliatelle with lemon chicken

2 large boneless chicken breasts, skin on • 2 tbsp flour, well seasoned • 50g butter • 1 tbsp olive oil • ½ quantity herb pasta dough (see page 86), cut into tagliatelle • 2 tsp grated lemon zest • 2 tbsp fresh lemon juice • 1 tbsp drained capers, roughly chopped if large

SERVES 2

1. Wash then dry the chicken breasts. Put the seasoned flour onto a plate and coat both sides of each chicken breast. Shake to remove any excess flour. Set aside.

2. Melt half the butter with the oil in a frying pan until foaming. Add the chicken breasts, skin side down, and cook over a low heat until deep golden, about 10 minutes.

3. Turn the chicken breasts and cook on the second side for an additional 10 minutes.

4. Turn the chicken breasts again and cook until the chicken is cooked through, an additional 5–10 minutes.

5. Meanwhile, bring a large pan of salted water to a rolling boil. Add the pasta and cook until al dente, 2–3 minutes. Drain well.

6. Remove the cooked chicken breasts from the pan. Add the remaining butter and cook until foaming and beginning to brown. Add the lemon zest and juice and the capers. Scrape up any bits from the bottom of the pan. Remove from the heat and season.

7. Slice the chicken breasts thickly on the diagonal. Divide the pasta between serving dishes and top with the sliced chicken. Drizzle with the lemon butter sauce and serve immediately.

Tagliolini with spicy meatballs

450g boneless pork shoulder or turkey breast • 225g pancetta or bacon, chopped • 2 garlic cloves, chopped • 1 tsp salt • pinch ground cinnamon • pinch ground allspice • large pinch chilli flakes • 25g fresh breadcrumbs • 1 egg, lightly beaten • 4 tbsp olive oil • 1 onion, finely chopped • 1kg ripe tomatoes, skinned and roughly chopped • 150ml red wine • 1 tsp dried oregano • 2 tbsp chopped fresh basil • pinch of sugar • 1 quantity black peppercorn pasta dough (see page 86), cut into fine noodles • extra basil, to garnish • freshly grated Parmesan, to serve

SERVES 4

1. Cut the pork or turkey into chunks and put into the bowl of a food processor. Add the pancetta or bacon, garlic, salt, cinnamon, allspice, chilli flakes and freshly ground black pepper. Process until finely chopped. Transfer to a bowl, add the breadcrumbs and egg, and mix thoroughly. Using wet hands, shape tablespoonfuls of the mixture into even-sized balls. Chill at least 30 minutes.

2. Meanwhile, heat 2 tbsp of the olive oil then add the onion and fry until softened, 5 minutes. Add the tomatoes, red wine, oregano, half the basil and the sugar and bring to the boil. Cover and simmer gently, 30 minutes.

3. Heat the remaining olive oil in a frying pan over a medium heat. Add the meatballs in batches and cook, turning often, until golden, 5 minutes. As they brown, add them to the tomato sauce. Return the sauce to a boil and simmer until the meatballs are cooked and the sauce is thickened, 20–30 minutes. Stir in the remaining basil.

4. Meanwhile, bring a large pan of salted water to a rolling boil. Add the pasta and cook until al dente, 2–3 minutes. Drain well.

5. Divide the pasta between serving dishes and top with the meatball sauce. Garnish with more basil and serve with Parmesan.

Tomato pasta with Italian sausage and lentils

225g Puy or Umbrian lentils • 3 tbsp olive oil • 1 onion, finely chopped • 500g spicy Italian sausage • 2 garlic cloves, crushed • 400g can chopped tomatoes • 300ml chicken or vegetable stock • 1 quantity sun-dried tomato pasta dough (see page 85), cut into wide noodles • 1 tbsp chopped fresh parsley   **SERVES 4**

1. Pick over the lentils, looking for any grit. Rinse under running water and drain well.

2. Heat the oil in a large deep saucepan and add the onion. Cook over a low heat until soft and starting to brown, 5–7 minutes. Add the sausages and garlic, and cook until the sausages start to brown, 3–4 minutes. Add the drained lentils and continue cooking for an additional 1 minute.

3. Add the tomatoes and stock. Season lightly and bring to the boil. Cover, lower the heat and simmer gently until the sausages and lentils are tender, 40–45 minutes. Check seasoning.

4. Meanwhile, bring a large pan of salted water to a rolling boil. Add the pasta and cook until al dente, 2–3 minutes. Drain well.

5. Divide the pasta between serving dishes and spoon over the sausages and lentils. Sprinkle with the chopped parsley and serve.

Ragu bolognese

2 tbsp olive oil · 1 onion, finely chopped · 1 carrot, finely chopped · 1 stick celery,
finely chopped · 75g bacon or pancetta, finely diced · 225g minced pork · 225g minced
beef · 300ml red wine · 2 tbsp tomato purée · 300ml beef stock · 4 tbsp double
cream · 1 quantity basic pasta dough (see page 71), cut into fine noodles ·
1 tbsp chopped fresh parsley

SERVES 4

1. Heat the oil in a large saucepan. Add the onion, carrot, and celery and cook gently for 10–12 minutes until softened.

2. Add the pancetta or bacon and cook an additional 3–4 minutes before adding the pork and beef. Increase the heat and cook until the meat is no longer pink, about 8–10 minutes. You may want to drain off any excess fat at this stage.

3. Add the wine and simmer until nearly evaporated, about 10 minutes. Add the tomato purée and about half the beef stock. bring to the boil and reduce the heat to a simmer.

4. Simmer gently about 1½ hours, adding more stock as necessary. Most of it will evaporate.

5. Bring a large pan of salted water to a rolling boil and add the pasta. Cook until al dente, about 1–2 minutes. Drain well.

6. Add the cream to the meat sauce and stir well. Simmer an additional 1 minute before adding the parsley. Season to taste. Toss the sauce with the drained pasta and serve immediately.

Pasta calabrese

6 tbsp olive oil · 50g fresh white breadcrumbs · 450g broccoli florets · 3 anchovy fillets in oil (optional), drained and chopped · 2 garlic cloves, finely sliced · large pinch chilli flakes · 2 tsp grated lemon zest · 1 quantity of basic pasta dough (see page 71), cut into tagliatelle · freshly grated Parmesan, to serve

SERVES 4

1. Heat 2 tbsp of the olive oil in a large frying pan and add the breadcrumbs. Cook, stirring often, until golden. Drain on kitchen paper.

2. Bring a large pan of salted water to a rolling boil and add the broccoli florets. Blanch for 3 minutes then remove with a slotted spoon to a colander. Reserve the cooking water to boil the pasta. Refresh the broccoli under cold running water and drain again. Dry on kitchen paper.

3. Heat an additional 2 tbsp of the oil in a large frying pan or wok. Add the anchovy fillets, garlic and chilli flakes and cook over a medium heat until the anchovies have broken down and the garlic is starting to colour, 2 minutes.

4. Add the broccoli florets and cook, stirring often, until the broccoli is heated through, about 4 minutes.

5. Meanwhile, return the pan of water in which you blanched the broccoli to a rolling boil. Add the pasta and cook until al dente, 2–3 minutes. Drain well.

6. Add the lemon zest, and remaining olive oil to the broccoli mixture and season well. Add the pasta to the pan and stir well to mix. Serve immediately, sprinkled with the breadcrumbs, and plenty of freshly grated Parmesan.

pastry

pastry introduction

Successful pastry-making relies on a light touch, careful handling and accurate measuring. The golden rule is to keep everything cool – the dough, the work surface, any utensils and your hands. All the recipes for pastry are made with butter as it gives the best flavour and crispest texture. The texture of the flour, however, will also determine the crispness of the finished pastry. If you like wholemeal pastry, substitute half the plain flour with wholemeal flour, as using it alone can produce a very soggy result.

Another important element in the making of pastry is water. Too much and the pastry will be tough and will shrink back excessively in the pan. Too little, and the dough will be difficult to handle and will fall apart easily when cooked. The only real way to judge the amount of water needed is to practise, to get a feel for it. Although some kneading is required when making all the pastries, the idea is to bring the dough together so that it is smooth but without the gluten 'setting up', and keeping the butter in little pieces as they are rubbed in. This is what makes the pastry flaky – if overworked, it will end up tough and greasy.

Make shortcrust pastry either by hand or in a food processor. If you have naturally warm hands, opt for the food processor method. Or, the butter can be cut into the flour using two knives, but this is more time-consuming. The recipe for rough puff is very easy and makes a fabulously light, flaky pastry. If you are

worried about making puff pastry, or haven't the time, try this method instead. Puff pastry is, without question, the most difficult and time-consuming type of pastry to master and it does take some practise. But all-butter puff pastry is difficult to buy, so if full-flavour is what you're after, this is the pastry to make.

Baking blind

Once shortcrust pastry has been rolled and used to line a pan, it is often pre-cooked or 'baked blind' before being filled. The reason for this is to ensure that the pastry base is cooked through and to stop the filling soaking through. After lining the tin, put it into the fridge to rest, about 20–30 minutes. Alternatively, put in the freezer where it can stay for up to one month. You can bake blind from frozen. Remove the lined tin from the fridge or freezer and line with foil or baking parchment. Now add either specially made ceramic baking beans or use dried pulses or rice. These baking beans conduct the heat and help to cook the pastry as well as keeping it from puffing up in the oven. If you use dried pulses or rice, let them cool then keep in a sealed jar especially for this purpose.

Shortcrust pastry **the basic method** There is

a great deal of mystique surrounding the making of shortcrust pastry. In fact, the method is very straightforward and just takes a little practise. If you're worried that your hands are too warm to rub the butter in as described below, try using two knives to cut the butter into small pieces. Rest the dough before rolling or it may shrink on cooking, producing an uneven result. See the recipe on page 109 for ingredients to prepare the basic shortcrust pastry dough.

step 1 Sift the flour into a mixing bowl with the salt. Add the butter and using your fingertips, rub or cut the butter into the flour until the mixture resembles coarse breadcrumbs.

step 2 Add 2 tbsp of the water and using your hands, start to bring the dough together, adding a little more water if necessary. Do not use too much water or the resulting pastry will be tough.

step 3 Turn the dough onto a lightly floured surface and knead briefly, just until the dough is smooth. Form into a neat ball, flatten into a disk, and wrap in clingfilm. Chill at least 30 minutes.

step 4 Remove the pastry from the fridge. Unwrap and put onto a lightly floured surface. Lightly flour the top of the dough and a rolling pin. Begin rolling the dough by exerting pressure on the rolling pin while rolling it back and forth. Try not to stretch the dough by pulling – allow the weight and pressure of the pin to roll the dough.

step 5 Roll the pastry into a rough circle at least 5cm in diameter larger than a loose-bottomed 23cm fluted flan tin. Gently roll the pastry onto the rolling pin, then unroll it over the tin to cover. Carefully press the pastry into the edge of the tin, removing any overhanging pastry with a knife.

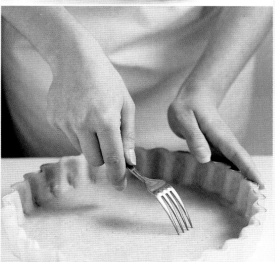

step 6 Prick the base all over with a fork, being careful not to make holes right through the dough. This helps to keep the dough from rising in the middle during blind baking. Chill 20 minutes.

Honey and mixed nut tart

175g plain flour • pinch salt • 85g cold butter, diced • 2-3 tbsp cold water •
For the filling • 75g butter • 250ml honey • double cream, to serve •
350g mixed nuts, e.g. pecans, walnuts, hazelnuts, almonds

SERVES 8

Shortcrust pastry is really versatile, and here encases a delicious honey and nut filling.

1. Follow the basic shortcrust pastry method (see pages 106–7) to the end of step 6.

2. Preheat the oven to 200°C/400°F/gas 6. Remove the tin from the fridge and line with foil or baking parchment. Fill with baking beans and transfer to the oven. Bake 12 minutes then carefully remove the paper and beans. Return the pastry to the oven until pale golden, an additional 10 minutes. Cool on a wire rack.

3. Reduce the oven temperature to 190°C/375°F/gas 5.

4. For the filling, put the butter and honey into a medium saucepan over a low heat. When the butter and honey have both melted together, increase the heat and allow to bubble until starting to darken, 1–2 minutes. Stir in the nuts and return the mixture to simmering point. Remove from the heat and allow to cool slightly.

5. Transfer the mixture to the prepared pastry shell. Return to the oven and bake until the nuts are golden and fragrant and the pastry is nicely browned, 5–7 minutes. Serve warm with cream.

Rough puff pastry the basic method This is an

unusual method for making rough puff pastry, as the dough includes baking powder and is bound with buttermilk. This helps to give the pastry a good rise as well as an excellent flavour. It produces a dough that is softer than butter puff pastry and so is best suited to savoury rather than sweet recipes. This dough can be frozen, well wrapped, for up to 2 months. Allow to thaw completely before using. See the recipe on page 112 for ingredients to prepare the basic rough puff pastry dough.

1. Sift the flour, salt, baking powder and bicarbonate of soda into a mixing bowl. Cut the butter into dice, add to the flour, and rub together, using your fingertips until the mixture resembles very coarse breadcrumbs. The pieces of butter should still be discernible, but all coated in flour.

2. Follow steps 1, 2 and 3 (see right).

3. Transfer the dough to a baking sheet or tray lined with baking parchment. Cover with clingfilm and chill, about 20 minutes.

4. Remove from the refrigerator and repeat the rolling and folding twice more. Prepare to this point if using to top a pie or for use in the recipe that follows.

step 1 Stir in about half the buttermilk and begin mixing the dough together, adding just enough of the remaining buttermilk to make a soft dough.

step 2 Turn the dough onto a floured surface and dust with flour as well. Roll the dough out to 2cm thick. Lift the dough from the surface and fold it, like a letter, in thirds.

step 3 Give the dough a quarter turn. Flour the surface and dough again and reroll the dough into a rectangle, of the same thickness. Repeat the folding and turning.

Butter biscuits

225g plain flour · ½ tsp salt · 1 tsp baking powder · pinch of bicarbonate of soda · 175g unsalted butter · 6 tbsp cold buttermilk · 1 tbsp melted butter, for brushing

MAKES 10-12 biscuits

Although this recipe for rough puff pastry is ideal for topping savoury meat pies, it also makes fabulous biscuits. The dough can be made ahead and refrigerated or frozen and then baked fresh to eat with soup, or for breakfast or with roast meat and gravy.

1. To make the rough puff pastry, follow the method on the previous pages up to the end of step 4.

2. Roll a final time to a 2cm thick rectangle. Now either cut the dough into triangles or use a pastry cutter to cut the dough into rounds.

3. Put the cut dough about 2.5cm apart on a paper-lined baking sheet. Cover with clingfilm and chill for at least 20 minutes.

4. Preheat the oven to 240°C/475°F/gas 9. Brush the tops of the biscuits with melted butter. Transfer the baking sheet to the oven and reduce the temperature to 190°C/375°F/gas 5.

5. Bake until golden all over, 12–15 minutes. Let cool 5 minutes, then eat while still warm.

Puff pastry the basic method

Well-made, all butter puff pastry is a real indulgence. Making your own is time-consuming, but well worth the effort. As it isn't worth making a small amount of puff pastry, this recipe makes about 675g. This dough freezes beautifully, however, so although some of the puff pastry recipes that follow only require half the recipe, the remaining half can be set aside and used for a quick recipe another day. See the recipe on page 116 for ingredients to prepare the basic puff pastry dough.

1. Put one quarter of the flour into a bowl with the butter. Using an electric mixer, combine the butter and flour thoroughly. Scrape the butter paste onto a sheet of clingfilm, shape into a 12.5 x 15cm rectangle, and leave in a cool place (but not the refrigerator).

2. Put the remaining flour, egg yolks, water and salt into a bowl and mix to a dough. If necessary, add a little more water, but the dough will soften on resting. Turn the dough onto a floured surface and knead until very smooth and elastic, about 10 minutes.
Alternatively, put all the ingredients into the bowl of an electric mixer fitted with a dough hook and mix to a dough. Knead on a low speed, between 6–8 minutes.

3. Form the dough into a neat ball and wrap in clingfilm. Rest in the refrigerator for at least 1 hour or overnight if possible.

4. Follow steps 1, 2 and 3 (see right). Place on a clingfilm-lined tray and cover with more clingfilm. Chill 1 hour.

5. Put the dough on a floured surface so the fold is to one side. Roll again as before and give the dough a single turn (see step 3, right), followed immediately by another. Wrap in clingfilm and chill overnight before using.

step 1 Lightly flour a work surface and roll out the dough to an 28cm square. Place the rectangle of butter paste in the centre and fold the corners of the dough over to completely enclose. Wrap in clingfilm and chill for 30 minutes.

step 2 Place the dough on a lightly floured surface. Roll the dough out into a 40 x 70 cm rectangle. Fold one end in by a sixth, then the other end in by a sixth. Fold both ends until they meet in the centre. Now fold the two together, as if closing a book.

step 3 Turn the dough so that the fold is to one side. Roll dough as before and fold one end in by a third, repeat at the other end to cover the first fold. Fold in half from left to right again as if closing a book. Brush off excess flour. This step is a single turn.

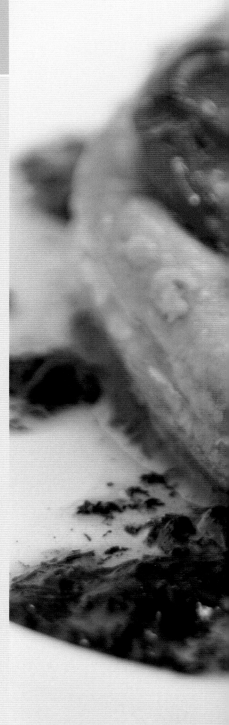

Tomato and basil tartlets

350g plain flour • 175g unsalted butter, softened • 2 egg yolks •
6 tbsp cold water • 1 tsp salt • For the tart filling • 24-28 ripe
cherry or baby plum tomatoes, halved • 1 tsp finely chopped fresh
rosemary or thyme • 6 tbsp extra-virgin olive oil • handful basil
leaves, roughly torn   MAKES 8

**You will end up with about 675g of puff pastry and you
need only half to make 8 of these delightful tartlets.
Freeze the remaining pastry, well-wrapped, for use in
another recipe.**

1. To make the puff pastry, follow the basic method up to the end
of step 5 (see pages 114–115).

2. Next day, preheat the oven to 200ºC/400ºF/gas 6. Roll out half
the pastry to a 20 x 42cm rectangle and using a plain 10cm pastry
cutter, cut out eight rounds. Put onto a lightly greased baking sheet.

3. Divide the tomatoes between the rounds leaving a 1cm border.
Sprinkle with the rosemary and drizzle with 2 tbsp of the olive oil.
Season well and bake until the pastry is risen and golden, 12–15
minutes. Meanwhile, put remaining oil and basil in a blender or
small food processor and blend until smooth. When the tartlets are
cooked, drizzle with the basil mixture and garnish with roughly torn
basil leaves. Serve hot.

Chicken and spring vegetable pie

1.5kg chicken • 1 large carrot, cut into chunks • 1 onion, halved • 1 celery stick, cut into chunks • 1 bay leaf • 1 sprig thyme • 6 black peppercorns • 450g mixed spring vegetables, e.g. baby carrots, peas, asparagus, green beans, baby leeks, small courgettes or pattypan squashes, baby fennel • 50g butter • 2 tsp. fresh thyme leaves • 50g plain flour • 150ml double cream • 1 quantity rough puff pastry (see page 112), prepared to the end of step 4 (see page 114)• 1 egg, beaten   **SERVES 4-6**

1. Gently simmer the chicken with carrot, onion, celery, bay leaf, thyme, peppercorns and water to cover, in a covered saucepan, 1 hour. Skim off scum that rises to the surface. Leave to cool. Remove the chicken from the stock and set aside. Strain the stock into a clean saucepan and bring to the boil. Simmer rapidly until reduced to 600ml. Season. Skin chicken and cut flesh into chunks.

2. Scrub, trim and slice until all the spring vegetables are the same size. Drop them into the boiling stock and return to the boil. Blanch for 3 minutes until tender. Remove with a slotted spoon and set aside, reserving the stock. Melt the butter in a saucepan, add the thyme and flour and stir well. Gradually add the reserved stock, stirring well after each addition, until smooth. Increase the heat, bring to the boil, stirring constantly, and simmer gently 2 minutes. Remove from the heat and stir in the cream and reserved chicken, vegetables and parsley. Season to taste.

3. Preheat the oven to 200ºC/400ºF/gas 6. Roll out the prepared pastry and cut a strip just larger than the rim of your pie dish. Brush the rim of the dish with water and attach the strip. Cut another piece for the lid. Spoon the filling into the pie dish. Dampen the pastry strip, add a pastry funnel, then top with the pastry lid. Crimp the edges to seal. Use pastry trimmings to decorate the top of the pie then brush with beaten egg. Transfer to the centre of the oven and bake until the pastry is risen and golden and the filling is bubbling, 25–30 minutes. Cool slightly before serving.

Potato, bacon, and egg pie

175g butter, diced • 275g plain flour • pinch salt • 1 tsp fresh thyme leaves •
1 tsp cumin seeds • 1 egg yolk • 1–2 tbsp cold water • 450g potatoes, diced •
1 tbsp olive oil • 1 onion, finely chopped • 225g bacon, chopped • 2 tbsp chopped
fresh parsley • 5 eggs

SERVES 4

1. For the pastry, rub the butter into the flour with the salt until the mixture resembles coarse breadcrumbs. Stir in thyme and cumin.

2. Mix the egg yolk and 1 tbsp of the water together and add to flour mixture. Start to bring the dough together, adding a little more water if necessary. Follow step 3 of the basic shortcrust pastry method (see page 106).

3. Meanwhile, cook the potatoes in boiling salted water until just tender, 5 minutes. Drain well and set aside. Heat the oil in a frying pan and add the onion. Cook over a medium heat until softened and starting to brown, 5–7 minutes. Add the bacon and cook an additional 5 minutes until the onion is brown and the bacon crisp. Leave to cool slightly. Preheat the oven to 200°C/400°F/gas 6.

4. Follow step 4 in the shortcrust pastry method (see page 107), rolling out two-thirds of the pastry to fit a 23cm pie plate. Use the pastry to line the pie plate, saving the trimmings to decorate the pie. Spoon in the cooked potato, onion and bacon mixture and sprinkle with the chopped parsley. Season.

5. Make four little wells in the potato mixture and break an egg into each one. Roll out the remaining pastry to just larger than the pie plate. Brush a little water onto the rim of the dish and top with the lid. Press down well to seal. Make a decorative edge, if desired and decorate with trimmings. Beat the remaining egg and brush over the top of the pie. Bake until golden, 30 minutes. Serve in wedges.

Beef and caramelised onion pies

4 tbsp vegetable oil • 2 large onions, sliced • 1 tsp brown sugar • 675g lean rump steak, cubed • 2 tbsp plain flour • 1 carrot, finely chopped • 2 garlic cloves, finely chopped • 225g baby button or baby chestnut mushrooms • 150ml beef stock • 150ml stout • 1 tbsp tomato purée • 1 tbsp Worcestershire sauce • 1 tbsp fresh thyme leaves • 1 bay leaf • 350g potatoes, cubed • half quantity puff pastry (see page 116), prepared to the end of step 6 (see pages 114–15) • 1 egg, beaten

SERVES 4

1. Heat half the oil in a large frying pan. Add the onions and cook over a medium heat until lightly golden, 5–7 minutes. Add the sugar, stir well and cook until caramelised, 4–5 minutes. Set aside.

2. Preheat the oven to 140°C/275°F/gas 1. Toss the meat cubes in the flour, shaking off and reserving any excess. Heat the remaining oil over a medium heat in a large flameproof casserole and add the meat. Cook until browned all over, 5–7 minutes. Add the carrot, garlic and mushrooms and cook until softened, further 3–4 minutes. Stir in the rest of the flour. Gradually add the stock and stout.

3. Add tomato purée, Worcestershire sauce, thyme and bay leaf. bring to the boil, cover and cook in oven, 1 hour. Add the potatoes, return to the oven and cook until tender, 20 minutes. Increase oven temperature to 200°C/400°F/gas 6. Spoon the steak mixture into four 300ml individual ovenproof pie dishes. Top with the onions.

4. Roll the pastry out thinly and cut four ovals or rounds about 5cm wider than the pie dishes. From these, trim a 2.5cm wide strip. Wet the rims of the dishes and attach the pastry strips. Wet the pastry strips and attach the pastry lids. Seal and make a decorative edge. Decorate with trimmings.

5. Brush the pastry with beaten egg. Bake until the pastry is risen and golden, 25 minutes. Let cool slightly before serving.

Mushroom tart with walnut pastry

50g walnuts • 175g plain flour • pinch salt • 85g butter, diced • 2–3 tbsp cold water •
25g butter • 1 tbsp vegetable oil • 1 small onion, finely chopped • 350g mixed fresh
wild or cultivated mushrooms • 2 garlic cloves, finely chopped • pinch freshly grated
nutmeg • 2 egg yolks • 200ml double cream • 1 tbsp chopped fresh parsley

SERVES 6

1. Grind the walnuts in a food processor or spice grinder until fine,
but not pasty – if you overgrind them, they will become very oily and
sticky which will make the pastry very difficult to handle. Follow the
basic shortcrust pastry method (see pages 106–7) to the end of
step 6, adding the ground nuts to the rubbed in mixture. Preheat
the oven to 200°C/400°F/gas 6.

2. Line the pastry with foil or baking parchment and fill with baking
beans. Transfer to the oven and bake for 12 minutes. Remove the
baking beans and foil or baking parchment and cook for a further
10 minutes until golden. Remove from the oven and set aside to
cool. Reduce the oven temperature to 180°C/350°F/gas 4.

3. Melt the 25g butter and vegetable oil in a large frying pan. Add
the onion and cook until softened, about 5 minutes. Increase the
heat and add the mushrooms. Cook until softened, an additional
4–5 minutes. Add the garlic, nutmeg, and seasoning. Stir briefly
and remove from the heat.

4. Spoon the mushroom mixture evenly over the pastry case.
Whisk the egg yolks, cream, parsley and seasoning together. Pour
evenly over the mushrooms. Bake for 30–35 minutes. Let cool 15
minutes before serving.

Caponata and feta cheese tart

175g plain flour • pinch salt • 85g butter, diced • 2 tsp finely chopped fresh rosemary •
2–3 tbsp cold water • 3 tbsp olive oil • 1 medium aubergine, cut into 1cm cubes •
3 celery sticks, thinly sliced • 400g can chopped tomatoes • 2 tbsp capers, drained and
rinsed • 75g stoned black olives • 2 tbsp red wine vinegar • 1 tbsp sugar • 1 egg yolk,
beaten • 225g feta cheese, crumbled • 1 tbsp fresh thyme leaves

SERVES 6

1. To make the pastry, follow steps 1–6 of the basic shortcrust pastry method (see pages 106–7), stirring the rosemary into the rubbed in mixture. Preheat the oven to 200°C/400°F/gas 6. Line the pastry case with foil or baking parchment and fill with baking beans. Transfer to the oven and bake for 12 minutes. Remove the baking beans and foil or baking parchment and cook for a further 10 minutes until golden. Remove from the oven and set aside to cool. Reduce the oven temperature to 180°/350°F/gas 4.

2. Heat the olive oil in a large frying pan over a medium heat and add the aubergine. Fry until golden but not overcooked, about 10 minutes. Remove the aubergine from the pan using a slotted spoon and drain on kitchen paper. Set aside.

3. Add the celery and tomatoes to the pan and simmer 10 minutes. Add the capers, olives, vinegar, sugar and seasoning. Cook until fairly thick, an additional 5 minutes. Stir in the aubergine and cook for a further 5 minutes until tender, but still holding its shape.

4. Remove from the heat and let cool.

5. Fold the egg yolk and feta cheese into the aubergine mixture and spoon it into the prepared pastry case. Sprinkle with the thyme leaves. Bake until the filling is bubbling, 12–15 minutes. Serve hot or warm with a green salad.

Duck tart with shallot chutney

150g whole walnuts or pecans • 225g plain flour • ½ tsp salt •
100g cold butter • 3–4 tbsp cold water • 350g skinned duck
breast, thinly sliced • 2 tbsp olive oil • 90g wild rice • 3 spring
onions, finely chopped • 1 tbsp chopped mixed thyme, marjoram,
oregano • 4 tbsp dry sherry • 3 eggs, beaten • 200ml double
cream • For the chutney • 225g shallots, peeled and halved if
large • pinch sugar • 1 garlic clove, finely chopped • 1 tbsp
chopped fresh thyme • 2 tbsp balsamic vinegar • 150ml red wine

SERVES 4

1. To make the pastry, grind the walnuts or pecans in a food
processor or spice grinder until fine, but not pasty – if you overgrind
them, they will become very oily and sticky which will make the
pastry very difficult to handle. Follow the basic shortcrust method to
the end of step 6 (see pages 106–7), adding the ground nuts to the
rubbed in mixture. Preheat the oven to 200ºC/400ºF/gas 6. Line the
pastry case with foil or baking parchment and fill with baking beans.
Transfer to the oven and bake for 12 minutes. Remove the baking
beans and foil or baking parchment and cook for a further 10
minutes until golden. Remove from the oven and set aside to cool.
Reduce the oven temperature to 190ºC/375ºF/gas 5.

2. Bring a large pan of water to a boil and add the wild rice. Lower
the heat and simmer until the rice is split and tender, about 35–45
minutes. Drain and set aside.

3. Heat the oil in a large frying pan and add the duck. Stir-fry until
browned and nearly cooked through, 3–4 minutes. Add the spring
onions. Cook until softened, 1 minute. Add the herbs and wild rice
and cook an additional 2 minutes. Add the dry sherry and simmer
until reduced and syrupy. Remove from the heat and season well.
Let cool slightly. Spread evenly over the pastry case.

4. Whisk eggs, cream and seasoning. Pour over duck mixture then
bake, 25 minutes. Leave to cool about 15 minutes before serving.

5. Meanwhile, to make the shallot chutney, heat the remaining olive oil in a medium saucepan and add the shallots. Cook over a low heat until softened, about 10 minutes. Add the pinch of sugar and stir well. Cover and cook very gently until the shallots are golden and tender, a further 20 minutes.

6. Add the garlic and thyme and cook briefly before adding the balsamic vinegar. Swirl around the pan to deglaze, then reduce until syrupy. Add the wine and cook until reduced to about 2 tbsp, about 5 minutes. Remove from the heat, season, and let the mixture cool before serving with the tart.

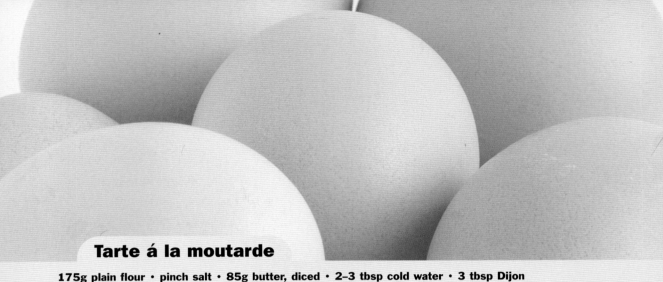

Tarte á la moutarde

175g plain flour · pinch salt · 85g butter, diced · 2–3 tbsp cold water · 3 tbsp Dijon
mustard · 125g Gruyère cheese, grated · 200g can chopped tomatoes, drained ·
3 egg yolks · 200ml double cream

SERVES 4

1. To make the pastry, follow the steps in the basic shortcrust
pastry method (see pages 106–7) to the end of step 6.

2. Preheat the oven to 200°C/400°F/gas 6. Remove the pastry-
lined ring from the fridge and line with foil or baking parchment. Fill
with baking beans and transfer to the oven. Bake 12 minutes, then
carefully remove the paper or foil and beans. Return to the oven an
additional 5 minutes. Remove from the oven and let cool. Reduce
the oven temperature to 170°C/325°F/gas 3.

3. Spread the mustard evenly over the base of the pastry. Sprinkle
over the cheese, then spread the tomatoes over the cheese. Whisk
the egg yolks and cream together with some seasoning. Pour over
the cheese and tomatoes.

4. Transfer to the oven and bake until just set and the pastry is
golden, about 1 hour. Allow to cool slightly before serving with a
crisp green salad and some crusty bread.

Potato and goat cheese tart

175g plain flour · pinch salt · 85g butter, diced · 2–3 tbsp cold water · 2 large potatoes, sliced · 2 tbsp olive oil · 3 leeks, thinly sliced · 1 garlic clove, finely chopped · 1 tbsp fresh thyme leaves · 2 tbsp pine nuts, toasted · 100g firm goat's cheese, sliced thinly · 3 egg yolks · 200ml double cream

SERVES 4

1. For the pastry, follow the basic shortcrust pastry method to the end of step 6 (see pages 106–7). Preheat the oven to 200°C/400°F/gas 6. Line the pastry case with foil or baking parchment and fill with baking beans. Bake for 12 minutes. Remove the baking beans and foil and cook for a further 10 minutes until golden. Remove from the oven leave to cool. Reduce the oven temperature to 190°C/375°F/gas 5.

2. Bring a saucepan of salted water to a boil. Add the potato slices and cook until just tender, 4–5 minutes. Drain well and set aside.

3. Heat the olive oil in a frying pan and add the leeks, garlic and thyme. Cook gently until softened, but not browned, 10 minutes. Remove from the heat and let cool slightly.

4. To assemble the tart, spread the leek mixture over the pastry base. Lay the potato slices on top. Arrange the goats' cheese slices on top of the potatoes. Whisk the egg yolks and cream together with some seasoning until smooth, then pour into the pastry case. Scatter with pine nuts and bake until set and golden, 25–30 minutes. Let cool 15 minutes before serving.

Crumble topped blueberry pie with cinnamon pastry

For the pastry• **225g plain flour** • **pinch salt** • **1 tsp ground cinnamon** • **115g butter, diced** • **3–4 tbsp cold water** • For the filling • **675g blueberries** • **75g sugar** • For the crumble topping • **175g plain flour** • **pinch salt** • **115g butter, diced** • **75g light soft brown sugar** • **75g flaked almonds**

SERVES 6–8

1. Prepare the pastry following steps 1–3 in the basic shortcrust pastry method (see pages 106–7), adding the cinnamon to the flour and salt and mixing well. Roll the pastry into a rough circle at least 5cm larger than a 5cm deep, loose-bottomed 23cm fluted flan tin. Gently roll the pastry onto the rolling pin, then unroll it over the tin to cover. Carefully press the pastry into the edges. Prick the base all over with a fork. Chill for 20 minutes.

2. Preheat the oven to 200°C/400°F/gas 6. Line the pastry case with foil or baking parchment and fill with baking beans. Transfer to the oven and bake for 12 minutes. Remove the baking beans and foil and cook for a further 10 minutes until golden. Remove from the oven and set aside to cool.

3. Mix the blueberries and sugar. Set aside.

4. For the crumble topping, put the flour and salt into a large bowl. Add the butter and rub into the flour until coarsely combined, with largish lumps of butter still showing. Stir in the sugar. Spoon the blueberries into the pastry case and top evenly with the crumb mixture. Sprinkle over the flaked almonds.

5. Transfer to the oven and bake until golden and bubbling, 20–25 minutes. Let cool and serve warm or cold with whipped cream.

Spiced palmiers with apples and raisins

For the palmiers • 1 quantity puff pastry (see page 116), prepared to the end of step 5 (see page 114) • 4 tbsp sugar • 2 tbsp icing sugar • 1 tsp ground cinnamon • ½ tsp ground ginger • ½ tsp grated nutmeg • 150ml double cream, lightly whipped, to serve • **For the apple and raisin compote** • 450g Bramley apples, roughly chopped • 4 tbsp sugar • 1 tbsp raisins • 1 tbsp dried cherries or cranberries • 2 tsp grated orange zest

MAKES about 36 cookies

These little cookies are delightfully tasty served with a tangy apple compote and fresh cream.

1. Prepare the puff pastry (see page 114). Roll it out thinly and trim to a 25 x 40cm rectangle. Cut the pastry dough in two to make two smaller rectangles. Sift the sugar, icing sugar, cinnamon, ginger and nutmeg together. Dust both sides of both pastry sheets with about a quarter of the spiced sugar.

2. Working one rectangle at a time, lay the pastry in front of you with one long edge nearest you. Fold the pastry in half, away from you then unfold to give a crease down the middle. Fold the edge of the pastry nearest you halfway to the crease and repeat with the edge of the pastry furthest from you. Dust liberally with more of the spiced sugar.

3. Repeat the fold so that the edge nearest you meets the edge furthest from you in the middle where you creased the pastry originally. Dust again with sugar. Reserve any sugar that you have leftover for later.

4. Finally, fold again down the crease to give a long thin rectangle. This will give you six layers in all. Repeat with the second rectangle. Wrap each in clingfilm and put into the freezer to rest, 1 hour.

5. Preheat the oven to 180°C/350°F/gas 4. Remove the pastry from the freezer and dust with any remaining spiced sugar. Cut each crosswise into eighteen slices. Lay slices well spaced apart on a baking sheet and transfer to the oven. Bake 10 minutes, then turn and bake until golden, 5–10 minutes. Cool on a wire rack.

6. Meanwhile, put all the apple compote ingredients into a saucepan. Cover and cook over a gentle heat until the apple is soft, about 15 minutes. Stir well and set aside to cool.

7. To serve, put the apple compote into a serving bowl, put the whipped cream into a second bowl, and arrange the palmiers on a dish.

Coffee and walnut pie

175g plain flour • pinch salt • 85g butter, diced • 2–3 tbsp cold water • 175ml maple syrup • 1 tbsp instant coffee granules • 1 tbsp boiling water • 2 tbsp butter, softened • 175g soft light brown sugar • 3 eggs, beaten • 1 tsp vanilla extract • 115g walnut halves • whipped cream or ice cream to serve

SERVES 4–6

If you like pecan pie, you'll love this coffee-maple-walnut alternative.

1. Make the pastry following steps 1–6 in the basic shortcrust pastry method (pages 106–7). Preheat the oven to 200°C/400°F/gas 6. Line the pastry case with foil or baking parchment and fill with baking beans. Transfer to the oven and bake for 12 minutes. Remove the baking beans and foil and cook for a further 10 minutes until golden. Remove from the oven and leave to cool. Reduce the oven temperature to 180°C/350°F/gas 4.

2. Put the maple syrup into a saucepan and heat until almost boiling. Mix the coffee granules with the boiling water, stirring until they have completely dissolved. Stir this mixture into the maple syrup. Leave until just warm.

3. Mix the butter with the sugar until combined, then gradually beat in the eggs. Add the cooled maple syrup mixture along with the vanilla extract and stir well.

4. Arrange the walnut halves in the bottom of the pastry case, then carefully pour in the filling. Transfer to the oven and bake until browned and firm, 30–35 minutes. Let cool about 10 minutes. Serve with cream or ice cream.

Old-fashioned peach and raspberry pies

For the pastry • **225g plain flour** • **pinch salt** • **115g butter, diced** • **3–4 tbsp cold water** •
For the filling • **4 large ripe peaches, stoned and roughly chopped** • **115g raspberries** •
75g caster sugar, plus extra for sprinkling • **juice ½ lemon** • **1 tbsp milk** • **crème fraîche
or soured cream, to serve**

SERVES 4

1. Make the pastry following steps 1–3 in the basic shortcrust
pastry method (see pages 106–7).

2. Mix together the peaches, raspberries, sugar and lemon juice
and set aside.

3. Preheat the oven to 200°C/400°F/gas 6. Divide the pastry into
four equal portions. Working with one portion at a time, divide into
one-third and two-thirds. Roll out the larger piece to fit a 10cm
round pie tin. Add a quarter of the peach mixture. Wet the edges of
the pastry and roll out the smaller portion of pastry. Use to top the
pie, trimming off the excess and crimping the edges to seal. Snip a
cross or hole in the top of the pie to allow steam to escape.

4. Brush the pastry with a little milk and sprinkle with sugar.
Repeat to make four pies. Transfer the pies to the oven and bake
until the pastry is golden, about 20–25 minutes.

5. Let cool about 10 minutes, then carefully turn the pies out of
their tins. Serve with soured cream.

Linzertorte with a lattice top

225g plain flour • pinch salt • 50g ground almonds • 115g unsalted butter, diced • 4 tbsp light soft brown sugar • 2 eggs, separated • 3–4 tsp cold water • 450g fresh raspberries • 100g sugar • 2 tsp cornflour mixed with 2 tsp cold water • 1 tbsp fresh lemon juice • icing sugar, to decorate • double cream, to serve

SERVES 8

1. For the pastry, mix the flour, salt and almonds. Add the butter and rub in until the mixture resembles fine breadcrumbs. Stir in the brown sugar. Mix the egg yolks with the cold water. Add to the pastry and bring the dough together. Knead briefly until smooth. Wrap in clingfilm and chill, 30 minutes.

2. Put the raspberries and sugar into a saucepan over a low heat. bring to the boil, stir in the cornflour mixture and cook 2 minutes. Remove from the heat, stir in the lemon juice and leave until cold.

3. Preheat the oven to 200°C/400°F/gas 6. Put a heavy baking sheet on the centre shelf to preheat with the oven. Roll out about two-thirds of the pastry and use to line a loose-bottomed 20cm deep fluted flan tin, following steps 4, 5, and 6 in the basic shortcrust pastry method (see pages 106–107). Remove trimmings and reroll with the remaining pastry. Cut into ten long strips, each 2cm wide using a pastry wheel.

4. Spoon the raspberry mixture into the pastry case. Dampen the edges of the pastry using the egg white, then lay the pastry strips over the top of the filling to make a lattice pattern. Lightly press the edges of the pastry together and trim off excess pastry.

5. Put the tart on the preheated baking sheet and bake, 20–25 minutes until the pastry is golden. Let cool 5 minutes. Remove from the tin and leave an additional 10–15 minutes. Dust with icing sugar. Serve warm cut into wedges with cream.

Freeform strawberry rhubarb pie

For the pastry • 175g plain flour • pinch salt • 85g butter, diced • 50g ground almonds • 50g caster sugar • 3–4 tbsp cold water • **For the filling** • 450g rhubarb, cut into chunks • 75–100g caster sugar, to taste • 1 vanilla pod • 2 strips lemon zest • 2 tsp cornflour or arrowroot • 350g strawberries, hulled and halved if large • 2 tsp demerara sugar

SERVES 4–6

1. Make the pastry following steps 1–3 in the basic shortcrust pastry method (see pages 106–107), adding the ground almonds and sugar to the rubbed in mixture. You may need a little extra water to bind this pastry.

2. Put the rhubarb, 75g of the sugar, vanilla pod and lemon zest into a saucepan over a gentle heat. Cook, stirring often, until the rhubarb is tender and quite juicy but still holds its shape, about 8–10 minutes. Taste for sweetness and add remaining sugar if necessary.

3. Mix the cornflour with a little water until smooth. Stir into the rhubarb, return the mixture to a gentle simmer. Cook until thickened, about 1–2 minutes.

4. Remove from the heat and stir in the strawberries and set aside until cold. Remove the vanilla pod and lemon zest.

5. Preheat the oven to 200°C/400°F/gas 6. Roll out the pastry to a large circle about 37cm in diameter. Transfer the pastry to a large, non-stick baking sheet. Spoon the cold strawberry-rhubarb mixture into the middle of the pastry and gather the pastry around the filling, leaving an open top. Brush the pastry with a little cold water and sprinkle with the demerara sugar.

6. Transfer the baking sheet to the centre of the oven and bake until the pastry is golden, about 20–25 minutes. When cold, serve cut into wedges.

Lemon chiffon pie

For the pastry • 175g plain flour • pinch salt • 85g butter, diced • 50g caster sugar • 2 tsp. grated lemon zest • 2 tbsp cold water • 1 egg yolk • For the filling • 200g caster sugar • 3 eggs and 2 egg whites • 3 large lemons, grated zest and juice • 75g butter

SERVES 6–8

1. For the pastry, follow step 1 in the basic shortcrust pastry method (see page 106). Stir the sugar and lemon zest into the rubbed in mixture. Mix together the cold water and egg yolk and add to the dough. Bring the dough together – add a little more water if necessary.

2. Follow steps 3–6 in the basic shortcrust pastry recipe (see pages 106–7). Reduce oven temperature to 150°C/300°F/gas 2.

3. For the filling, in a large heatproof bowl, whisk together half of the sugar, the whole eggs, the lemon zest and juice and butter. Put the bowl over a pan of simmering water and continue whisking until thick, about 15 minutes. Remove the bowl from the heat and put the base of the bowl into cold water – either in the sink or in a larger bowl. Continue whisking until the mixture has cooled.

4. Beat the egg whites until stiff then gradually beat in the remaining sugar until thick and shiny. Fold one large spoonful of this mixture into the lemon mixture to slacken it, then fold in the remaining egg whites. Pour into the pastry case.

5. Bake in the centre of the oven until just set, 25–30 minutes. Cool on a wire rack before serving.

Upside-down pear tart with cardamom

125g sugar • 3–4 tbsp cold water • about 10 green cardamom pods • 4–6 ripe but firm pears, depending on size, cored and quartered lengthways • 50g unsalted butter, diced • half quantity puff pastry (see page 116), prepared to the end of step 5 • crème fraîche or soured cream to serve

SERVES 4–6

This is really a Tarte Tatin made with pears. Cardamom is a surprisingly effective flavour with pears.

1. Put the sugar and water into a 25cm ovenproof frying pan. Stir over a low heat until the sugar has dissolved completely. Increase the heat and bring the mixture to a rapid simmer.

2. Remove seeds from cardamom and finely crush. As soon as the sugar begins to colour, sprinkle over the cardamom. Do not stir. Carefully add the pear quarters in concentric circles. The sugar will slow down, but you must watch it now as you want it to colour evenly. Tilt and turn the pan often until the sugar bubbling up between the pears is deep brown and smells nutty. Immediately remove from the heat and add butter wherever there are spaces between the fruit. Let cool about 20 minutes.

3. Preheat the oven to 200°C/400°F/gas 6. Roll out the prepared puff pastry thinly, then cut a circle about 2.5cm larger than the diameter of the frying pan. Carefully put the pastry over the pears, tucking it down the sides of the pan to enclose the fruit.

4. Transfer the frying pan to the oven and bake until the pastry is risen and golden, 25 minutes.

5. Remove from the oven and leave to stand about 10 minutes before turning out. Serve warm, cut into wedges, with cream.

Banana toffee cheesecake

For the pastry • 225g plain flour • pinch salt • 115g butter, diced • 50g sugar • 3–4 tbsp cold water • For the filling • 115g plain chocolate, broken into pieces, plus extra for decoration • 400g can sweetened condensed milk • 250g mascarpone cheese • 150ml double cream, lightly whipped • 3 large ripe but firm bananas • juice of ½ lemon   SERVES 10–12

1. Follow steps 1, 2 and 3 in the basic shortcrust pastry method (see pages 106–107), stirring the sugar into the rubbed in mixture.

2. Follow step 4 of the basic method, rolling the pastry into a large circle about 5cm larger than a 23cm plain pastry ring set on a baking tray. Ease the pastry into the ring following steps 5 and 6 of the basic method. Preheat the oven to 200°C/400° F/gas 6. Line the pastry case with foil or baking parchment and fill with baking beans. Transfer to the oven and bake for 12 minutes. Remove the baking beans and foil and cook for a further 10–12 minutes until golden. Remove from the oven and set aside to cool. Carefully brush off any crumbs from inside the pastry case.

3. Melt the chocolate in a bowl set over a pan of simmering water. Using a pastry brush, paint the chocolate onto the pastry case to cover completely. Chill until set.

4. Meanwhile, for the toffee put the can of condensed milk into a deep pan and cover with water by at least 5cm. bring to the boil and simmer for 4 hours, topping up with water as necessary. Keep the can completely submerged at all times. Remove the pan from the heat and leave the can until it is completely cold before opening.

5. To assemble the cheesecake, thickly slice the bananas and drizzle with the lemon juice. Beat the mascarpone cheese until softened then stir in the cream. Carefully fold the cream mixture and toffee together but don't overmix – leave them marbled. Fold in the bananas, then spoon into the pastry case. Grate remaining chocolate over the top.

Tarte fine aux pommes

½ quantity puff pastry (see page 116), prepared to the end of step 5 (see pages 114-15) • 2 dessert apples • 1½ tbsp icing sugar • 2 tbsp apricot jam • cream, to serve

SERVES 4

1. Prepare the puff pastry (see pages 114-15). Roll the pasty out thinly and cut out a 23cm circle. Transfer to a lightly greased baking sheet.

2. Preheat the oven to 190°C/375°F/gas 5. Halve the apples and thinly slice lengthways. Lay on the pastry in concentric circles, overlapping slightly and leaving a 1cm margin around the edge. Dust generously with the icing sugar.

3. Transfer the baking sheet to the oven and bake until the pastry is risen and golden and the apples are tender and golden at the edges, 20–25 minutes.

4. Gently heat the apricot jam in a small saucepan then press through a sieve to remove any large pieces. While the jam and tart are both hot, brush the jam generously over the apple slices to glaze. Leave to cool slightly and serve warm with cold cream.

index

Suppliers

Kitchen equipment kindly supplied by
Gill Wing Cookshop,
190 Upper Street, London N1 1RQ
Tel: 020 7226 5392

Kenwood Chef mixer kindly supplied by
Kenwood Electronics UK Ltd
Kenwood House, Dwight Road, Watford,
Herts, WD18 9EB
Tel: 01923 816444
email: enquiries@kenwood-electronics.co.uk